M.

I

Philosophical Issues in Education

JOHN KLEINIG

p.p. 1-9

CROOM HELM
London & Canberra

ST. MARTIN'S PRESS
New York

© 1982 John Kleinig
Croom Helm Ltd, 2-10 St John's Road, London SW11

British Library Cataloguing in Publication Data

Kleinig, John
    Philosophical issues in education.
    1. Education—Philosophy
    I. Title
    370'.1   LB17
    ISBN 0-7099-1517-9
    ISBN 0-7099-1518-7 (pbk)

First published in the United States of America in 1982
All rights reserved. For information write:
St. Martin's Press, Inc., 175 Fifth Avenue, New York, N.Y. 10010

ISBN 0-312-60524-2
Library of Congress Catalog Card Number: 82-50084

Printed and bound in Great Britain by
Biddles Ltd, Guildford and King's Lynn

CONTENTS

Preface
Introduction
1. Philosophy of Education   1
2. Education   11
3. Teaching and Learning   23
4. Teaching and Related Concepts   41
5. Indoctrination   54
6. Autonomy, Community and Education   69
7. The Justification of Education   81
8. The Institutionalisation of Education   91
9. Neutrality in Education   102
10. Equality, Schooling and Education   117
11. Intelligence   132
12. Curriculum Choice   146
13. Competition   162
14. Assessment and Grading   175
15. Children and Rights   195
16. Education and Authority   210
17. Schooling, Education and Discipline   220
18. Education and Punishment   231
19. Moral Education   243
20. Religious Education   257
Further Reading   269
Indexes   295

To Bill Andersen –
in appreciation

*A school is a place through which you have to pass
before entering life, but where the teaching proper
does not prepare you for life.*

Ernst Dimnet

*Nothing in education is so astonishing as the amount
of ignorance it accumulates in the form of inert
facts.*

Henry Adams

Education consists mainly in what we have unlearned.

Mark Twain

*We are faced with the paradoxical fact that education
has become one of the chief obstacles to intelligence
and freedom of thought.*

Bertrand Russell

*My schooling not only failed to teach me what it professed
to be teaching, but prevented me from being educated to
an extent which infuriates me when I think of all I might
have learnt at home by myself.*

George Bernard Shaw

In 1971 I was invited to take part in a postgraduate course in philosophy of education at the University of Sydney. It kindled my interest in an expanding range of issues whose progress and scope have been somewhat contracted and artificially frozen in this volume. In 1974 I had the opportunity to mount my own undergraduate course in philosophy of education at Macquarie University, and it is from this later development that the book has evolved. I say 'evolved', since my thinking on both general and specific philosophical issues has undergone a number of mutations since then, and I do not anticipate that what is now presented represents my 'final thoughts' on the matters discussed. We see through a glass darkly, and it is to be hoped that those who make use of this book will see its intentions as provocative rather than definitive.

Apart from my students, several people have been good enough to comment on the material as it has emerged in draft form. Kevin Harris and Robert Young were indefatigable in their attentions to a complete draft of the work, and Richard Archer, Mike Bailey, the late Helen Freeman, John Kilcullen, Bruce Langtry, Richard Peters and Jim Walker offered helpful criticisms of portions of the material. From each I have learned a great deal, though each would no doubt complain that I have not learned enough. Ultimately, I have had to exercise my own judgment as to what I would say and how I would say it. To Barbara Young I am grateful for typing and retyping early drafts with unflagging good humour. And to Elizabeth Sinkovits and Hazel Gittins I am indebted for help in preparing the script for publication.

Only two chapters have previously appeared in a significantly similar form, though in each case there are quite substantial differences. Earlier versions of Chapters 9 and 15 appeared as 'Principles of Neutrality in Education' and 'Mill, Children and Rights' in *Educational Philosophy and Theory*, VIII, 2 (October, 1976), 1-16, and VIII, 1 (April, 1976), 1-16, respectively. I am grateful to the editor for permission to make use of that material here.

John Kleinig

This volume is being written at a time when philosophy of education, even more than most other fields of inquiry, is experiencing the effects of rapid social and intellectual change. The technological advances of the past half-century, particularly the post-war years, have demanded and reflected an increasingly specialised division of labour, including intellectual labour. Philosophy of education, as a specialist field of inquiry, is to some extent a product of this professionalised narrowing of focus. In the United Kingdom, the first Chair in philosophy of education was created only after the Second World War. Somewhat earlier in United States' universities, John Dewey did much to carve out philosophy of education as an identifiable field of inquiry, but here, too, most of the pressure for its professionalisation has belonged to the post-war period.

Unlike most other branches of philosophy, philosophy of education has not generally been taught in philosophy departments, but only as an adjunct to programmes in education, in particular teacher training programmes. This has contributed to the peculiar difficulties it has experienced. For one thing, it has been part of the somewhat chaotic post-war burgeoning of studies in education. The rapidly increasing demand for a skilled, adaptable and compliant workforce has made education a field of almost phrenetic activity, and this has not been conducive to the establishment of a clear identity for philosophy of education. Moreover, the isolation of philosophy of education from general philosophy has often resulted in a philosophically inferior product. Many of those who were drafted into teaching philosophy of education had little or no philosophical training.

However, in the late fifties and early sixties . there was an observable shift as a number of philosophers – notably Israel Scheffler in the United States and

R.S. Peters in the United Kingdom – moved into academic education, bringing with them skills that had to that point been all too rare in the crescendo of expansion. Strategically placed (Scheffler at the Harvard Graduate School of Education, and Peters at the University of London Institute of Education), they decisively influenced the philosophy of education at a critical time in its development. Of the two, Peters has probably been the more influential, yet it would probably be true to say that the United States was better prepared for the turmoil of the late sixties and the radical critiques which emerged in the seventies. To some extent this has come about because the American philosophical tradition is less insular and more diverse than the British. Dewey's progressivist views had already forged a link between philosophy of education and political philosophy, and though the upheavals of the sixties brought them and their latter-day successors under scrutiny of a fundamental kind, they did not attract the same unqualified denunciation that was to befall analytic philosophy of education in the United Kingdom and Australia. Twentieth century British philosophy fell under the spell of Moore and Wittgenstein, and it was the methodological tradition of Moore and Wittgenstein that Peters introduced into British philosophy of education. However, when it was introduced, its ascendancy was just beginning to wane, and, for reasons for which Peters cannot be held wholly responsible, his work served to perpetuate its dominance in British philosophy of education well after the climate in academic philosophy had changed. The seventies have seen a strong reaction against the aseptic and piecemeal analyses of the fifties and sixties, and a return to philosophy on the more ambitious scale of earlier centuries.

Peters' own work has been subject to two general criticisms. One is methodological – his apparently narrow conception of the proper task of philosophy. The other is political – what is seen as his moderate reformist stance with regard to the practice of education. There is a tendency for radical critics to see the two as closely connected. Viewed sociologically, there probably has been an indirect causal connection between an analytic approach to philosophy and non-radical politics, but too many other conditions are necessary for it to be plausibly argued that conceptual analysis is inherently conservative. Taken as a whole, Peters' work does in fact amount to a substantial undertaking in social philosophy, a point that may be overlooked if some of his methodological statements are taken at face value. Although he insists that it is not for philosophers to make psychological and sociological pronouncements, he is not averse to importing into his work what he believes sociological and psychological investigation to have established.

The foregoing notes on the current tensions in philosophy of education provide some background to the present volume. It is intended as a text in philosophy of education courses, and I make no apologies for the fact that in some ways it manifests the schizoid nature of contemporary philosophy of education. The tradition of Moore and Wittgenstein no longer seems adequate; on the other hand, the radical alternatives appear doctrinaire and utopian. Nevertheless, the conceptual sensitivity that analytic philosophy encouraged ought not to be despised; nor, for that matter, should the historical consciousness which characterises the radical critique. In the chapters that follow, I have endeavoured to move in the direction of a *via media* which recognises both the value and limitations of conceptual analysis on the one hand, and the concrete historical forces which inform and colour the philosophical task on the other.

The form in which the material is presented requires some explanation, as does the selection of topics. It is sometimes argued that a topical approach obscures the relations which exist between 'problems', deflecting attention from the underlying and more fundamental social determinants of which these 'problems' are in important respects an expression. As a warning, the point is well taken, and I have endeavoured to indicate where necessary that these are not discrete and isolated issues. The reader will have to judge whether or not I have been successful. On the other hand, the topical approach possesses some pedagogical value, since it begins, even if it does not end, at the level at which people express their puzzlement. If the reader is then led to see the wider ramifications of the topic, there is little to which the critic could object. On the choice of topics, my case is less defensible. Put baldly, it simply indicates where I've got to. As my interests in philosophy of education have developed, the range of topics has grown from the standard fare of contemporary British philosophy of education (education, teaching, indoctrination, etc.) to topics which are less commonly covered (competition, assessment and grading, intelligence, etc.), but which are of no less importance if philosophy of education is to be the critical and constructive enterprise it ought to be.

In each chapter, I have endeavoured to introduce a range of philosophically significant issues relating to a particular topic. No more than an introduction is intended. It has been my purpose to write to length, and not to attempt an exhaustive exploration of any topic. The chapter notes and bibliographies at the end of the book are intended to supplement that material. If what I have written stimulates further and critical inquiry, I shall be well pleased. If that inquiry has as its context the struggle to make of schooling an educative experience, I shall be delighted.

Chapter 1

PHILOSOPHY OF EDUCATION

As with other forms of inquiry, it is impossible to provide a timelessly true account of the nature and scope of philosophy of education. Philosophy of education does not exist in a vacuum but within a particular socio-historical context, and what is regarded as its legitimate practice is conditioned by that context. This does not make the task of delimitation impossible, so much as provisional. There are continuities and discontinuities. We must make critical and creative use of what is presented to us in order that we may identify and engage in it; at the same time we must avoid being bound by it, lest what is historically given be taken as eternally settled. It is the peculiar temptation of philosophers and politicians to see themselves as gods.

Delimitation is doubly difficult in philosophy of education, for we need to be sensitive to the socio-historical dimensions not only of philosophy but also of its focus, education. In this chapter we will attempt to provide an account of philosophy of education which is not only clear but also at the same time flexible enough to allow for development.

What is philosophy?

Among the continuities that constitute philosophy a practice of considerable antiquity is its claim to be a reflective or critical activity. Whether our interest is in Plato, Aquinas, Marx or Wittgenstein, there is evident in what they are doing a professed unwillingness to pontificate or take things for granted; there is a preoccupation with the question, 'For what reason?' They engage in a serious and systematic attempt to subject the taken-for-granted of human life and experience to questioning. True, there may be serious doubts as to whether the particular philosophical methodologies they employ serve to further the critical function constitutive of their profession, but this does not negate the continuity of critical purpose. To what end is such critical questioning? For some philosophers, it has had no purpose beyond the satisfaction of intellectual curiosity; for others it has been generated by the psychological need for identity - for location within the universe; for most it has served other, more limited, practical ends. For philosophical reflection is an activity of active, productive beings, who are guided not by instinct but by thought, albeit thought conditioned by a particular socio-historical context.

The question, 'For what reason?' is deliberately ambiguous. Much recent philosophy has drawn attention to a distinction between explanatory and justificatory reasons, relegating concern with the former to the physical and social sciences, etc., and restricting the scope of philosophy to the latter and its preconditions (clarification, canons of validity, etc.). But earlier philosophers were not so tight-reined about the enterprise in which they were engaged. The gradual discrimination of philosophical, scientific, sociological and historical questions is largely a post-Renaissance phenomenon, a concomitant of the vast social and technological changes which have occurred during the past four centuries. The Enlightenment philosophy of progress made increasingly specialised demands on human intellectual and physical labour to the point where, for many, the differing forms of human inquiry now appear as autonomous, self-contained (and, in some cases, all-embracing) disciplines. Our contemporary tendency to understand philosophy as an autonomous enterprise with a distinctive and discrete focus does not therefore provide an historically unconditioned essence, but instead reveals a diversification of intellectual endeavour existing in mutual interplay with social and technological change. This is no reason for avoiding the attempt to construct a critically useful account of philosophical inquiry. But it does require that any such attempt acknowledge and respond to its historical parameters.

There is little doubt that intellectual, no less than vocational, diversification has gone too far. The search for certainty characteristic of western rationalism has in recent decades imprisoned much philosophy within the supposedly impervious cocoon of 'conceptual analysis'. In itself, the search for clarity and certainty through conceptual analysis is harmless enough - Plato's Forms are striking testimony to its longevity - but coupled with the view that there is *no more* to philosophy than conceptual analysis, it presages intellectually neuter and socially conservative offspring. However, the social and political upheavals of the sixties, the revival of interest in Marx, and the growing rapprochement of Anglo-Saxon and Continental philosophy, have begun to overtake such tendencies. The social and normative character of conceptualisation, and consequently of the subject matter and tools of conceptual

2

analysis, has led to a reappraisal of the distinctness and distinctiveness of philosophical endeavour. The philosopher king no longer sits in splendid isolation on the seat of pure reason.

Philosophical reflection is frequently characterised as theoretical, rather than practical. This is innocuous if intended only to draw attention to the fact that in their work philosophers are not generally concerned to perform scientific experiments, conduct surveys, etc. Philosophical reflection may generate or be generated by such activities, it may be integral to them, but it is not identified in terms of them. The view of philosophy as theoretical becomes dangerous when it is taken to mean that the results of philosophical reflection can or do have no practical implications. No doubt some philosophical reflection is at such remove from other human activities that it would be futile to look for its practical application apart from the contribution it makes to the activity of philosophising – though this is hardly a contribution of no consequence: badly designed tools may defeat the purposes for which they were constructed. Sometimes, however, philosophers have been tempted to see their activity as 'leaving everything as it is', as having no normative or practical implications. But this view, generally associated with certain writers in the logical positivist and analytic traditions, relies on an unsupportable asocial and ahistorical understanding of conceptualisation, and has in fact aligned philosophy with conservative practice rather than the neutral function these writers have often claimed for it.

Conceptual analysis

We can come at the preceding points more directly by considering in greater detail the perennial interest of philosophers in what has become known as 'conceptual analysis'. Though this is sometimes represented as a revolutionary innovation in philosophy, its roots are as deeply embedded in Plato and the western philosophical tradition as in contemporary circumstances.

The term 'conceptual analysis' is in some respects a felicitous one, for it focuses our attention not on words, the standard medium of conceptual representation, but on the ideas, concepts or practices, etc. represented by or conveyed through the medium of those words. Thus, when Socrates considers questions of the form 'What is x?', where x is piety, justice, virtue, knowledge or love, the question is more complex than the sort that can be settled by an appeal to the dictionary, though dictionaries are not necessarily useless. The question is not parallel to 'What is zymurgy?', where the term 'zymurgy' is likely to be unfamiliar to us. The terms 'piety', 'justice' etc. are in common employment, and what is sought in the Socratic

3

question is some clearer delineation of the kind of activity, state of affairs, object, process, or relation represented in the use of the particular term. This will involve some consideration of its relations to other kinds of activity, etc., the presuppositions underlying its differentiation from those other kinds of activity, etc., and the implications of this conceptual differentiation for the questions which initially generated interest in it.

The formation and acquisition of the conceptual structures embedded in our language cannot be represented as an individualistic mirroring of 'reality'. Whatever philosophical stories we might like to tell about 'the beginnings', the only legitimate context within which we can speak of such formation and acquisition is a social one. We are not born with a language, nor do we acquire one as a simple product of maturation. It is as initiates into and participants in an historical community that we learn to conceptualise the reality in which we are placed. We are of course not passive in this process. We have our own 'natures', but how those natures are developed and come to express themselves in the conceptual structuring of reality cannot be explained independently of a particular socio-historical context. The language we acquire is not a simple expression of private experience.

We can take this a bit further by switching our attention from the issue of individualism to that of mirroring. It is a common belief that our concepts represent reality somewhat as a mirror image or (slightly less misleadingly) a photograph. This seriously distorts the matter. When we come to reality we come with a set of needs and interests which influence the way in which it is perceived. Human beings are not cameras, though they may use them. The commonplace activities of description or identification, even when engaged in with unquestionable objectivity, involve a selection of features from the total available, in accordance with a range of interests. Where the objects of description are human activities, the role played by interests in selecting relevant features becomes very explicit.[1] Structuring reality by reference to human interests is a condition of its intelligibility for us. In itself, it does not distort reality. Distortion occurs when those interests have been conditioned by a theoretical framework in which the role played by them is no longer perspicuous.

Because conceptual structures are socially constituted in relation to interests, changes in those interests can be expected to manifest themselves in conceptual shifts. Changes in interests are most likely to occur in the wake of substantial changes in material and social circumstances. This is something Plato failed to acknowledge in his Theory of Forms. Forms - what we would most conveniently refer to as concepts - were for Plato timeless and changeless, able

4

to be perceived by those who, through the exercise of reason, had succeeded in seeing beyond the mirage of sensed particulars to the reality which in some measure they reflected. Plato failed to recognise that 'reason' itself belongs to history and cannot be divorced from it. There is no such thing as 'reason' in the abstract: there is the human activity of thinking, an activity conducted in accordance or at variance with certain canons of rationality. As the history of philosophy amply illustrates, these canons have been the occasion of continuing controversy.[2]

In contemporary Anglo–Saxon philosophy, Plato's mistake has been repeated in the view that philosophy, or more specifically conceptual analysis, is neutral. It has sometimes been held that conceptual analysis involves no normative commitments, and that once completed, philosophical puzzles will be resolved (or dissolved). Philosophy, Wittgenstein argued, 'is a battle against the bewitchment of our intelligence by means of language'.[3] Such bewitchment occurs 'when language is like an engine idling, not when it is doing work'.[4] Conceptual analysis for Wittgenstein took the form of mapping language at work. However, he believed that such philosophising should 'in no way interfere with the actual use of language; it can in the end only describe it'.[5] There was good point to these claims; but when they are made (as they were by his disciples) to delimit the proper scope of philosophical reflection, and this is insulated from the wider socio-historical context which informs not merely the content of such analyses, but also the very programme of philosophical inquiry which generates them, a quite misleading impression is given. Rather than constituting a neutral technique for the resolution of philosophical problems, this 'Wittgensteinian' prescription manifested the fragmentation of intellectual activity which has characterised twentieth century industrial society.[6] In the course of this, it misrepresented philosophical problems as merely semantic, thus deflecting philosophers from their traditional normative role. In this sense, conceptual analysis tended to play a conservative social function. Since the sixties, however, we have begun to realise that the fragmentation of intellectual inquiry has had severe distorting effects, whatever redress it may have brought with it.

Philosophical puzzles are not simply the product of idling language, though no doubt such abstraction has sometimes exacerbated those problems. Conceptual analysis is best seen as one of a number of activities in which a philosopher might properly engage, a technique whereby the conceptual *status quo* may be clarified, a means whereby conceptual shifts may be identified, in order that the critical activity in which philosophy has traditionally engaged can proceed with some degree of precision. This does not mean that conceptual analysis is the foundation on which later philosophical reflection is built, for the identification of issues in relation to which the techniques of conceptual analysis are employed involves questions of considerable philosophical importance. Why, it might be asked, spend one's time analysing the concept of discipline as a preliminary to discussing the place of discipline in the classroom, when the important issue is the justifiability of schooling (as presently structured)? Philosophy, if it is to constitute a genuinely critical activity, must be able to reflect on and make use of what is now investigated separately and seen as belonging to 'independent' disciplines. The suggestion by some analytic philosophers, that empirical research has no bearing on philosophical questions, disclosed only how fragmented intellectual labour had become, a complete failure to appreciate the social structuring of philosophical inquiry. Equally, the exclusion from philosophical respectability of the construction of theoretical models and integrating schemata that earlier generations of philosophers had engaged in was self-deceptive, to say the least, for it presupposed its own unexamined theoretical model according to which the production of knowledge was structured by autonomous forms of inquiry.

Philosophy of education

In philosophy of education, the critical reflection which characterises philosophy generally is brought to bear on that range of experience titled 'education'. The development of such a specific field of inquiry is a product of contemporary specialisation, and until recently has displayed the same fragmented approach to intellectual activity that has been evident elsewhere. In the classical philosophers, what we would call specifically educational issues were not considered separately from moral and political questions, and problems in epistemology and philosophical psychology. It is important that these links not be severed, just as it is important that philosophical inquiry generally not be abstracted from the matrix of social practices of which it is a part.

Disputes about what constitutes philosophy of education have generally been disputes about the nature of philosophical inquiry. Perhaps they should equally have been disputes about the nature of education. However, so deeply entrenched has the identification of education and schooling become, that for many people the school and its teaching function have bounded the inquiry. Of course schools cannot be ignored, just because they claim to educate, but we should not be surprised if our investigation suggests that the major *educative* influences are more likely to be located elsewhere. It may be that in restricting the teaching of philosophy of education to teacher education programmes we are perpetuating a myth about the purpose of schooling.

The increased specialisation of social life generally has reflected itself in the progress of philosophy of education during this century. Early works written under the name of 'philosophy of education' often relied on a broader understanding of philosophy than has been customary in academic philosophy. These early works were little more than fairly systematic distillations of 'educational wisdom'. Generalisations about the nature, purpose and achievement of education were put forward, related, and supported in a vague way by reference to certain general ideals. The effort in such treatises was concentrated on the conclusions and not on the argument or methodology which might have been invoked on their behalf. This was their great drawback. Their great merit however, lay in the integrated epistemology which informed their pages and gave them a profundity and insight often lacking in later work. Works of this genre were not wholly absent from the 'academic' sphere, and some of them showed a much greater concern for argument and methodology, implicitly if not explicitly. John Dewey, Bertrand Russell, A.N. Whitehead and W.H. Kilpatrick all left work of continuing philosophical interest. It is only recently, with the advent of radical critiques of the fragmented state of learning, that there has been something of a return to a style of philosophising which is not continually fearful of involvement in academic demarcation disputes.

If the earlier phase of twentieth century philosophy of education was marked by a holistic approach, its teaching, in the United States at least, was also strongly relativistic. American pluralism expressed itself in an approach to philosophy of education which resembled a smorgasbord of '-isms' or an eclectic *melange*. Typical of this approach were the survey (in which the thoughts of famous writers on education were extracted and systematised), and the guided tour through realism, rationalism, idealism, personalism, existentialism *ad infinitum* in order that the student might pick that position which most suited him/her. In such works, chronology and catalogue replaced history and controversy. Such criticism as there was tended to be second-hand and ahistorical. Ideas were detached from their original settings and transplanted into the present. Commenting on this approach, R.S. Peters has noted somewhat sceptically that

> valiant attempts are made to relate these
> works to modern problems and to extract
> guidance from them. Plato's thought, for

7

instance, is used as a launching pad for
discussions about élites, indoctrination and
the use of fables; Rousseau's for
animadversions about child-centred education
and learning by experience. [7]

There is an appearance, here, of philosophical engagement
with genuine issues, but because of their narrative
character, most attempts at this style of philosophising
about education have lacked rigour and a critical
appreciation of socio-historical context.

In the United Kingdom, the professionalisation of
philosophy of education brought with it something of a
rapprochement between philosophy of education and academic
philosophy. This occurred at a time when logical
positivism, though still influential, was beginning to give
way to the less rigid approach of the later Wittgenstein.
An influential early venture in this area was D.J.
O'Connor's *Introduction to the Philosophy of Education*. [8]
This volume purported to provide no more than a neutral
analysis of some key concepts common to both philosophy and
educational theory. There was nothing of Dewey's explicit
concern with rational construction, social prescription and
justification. O'Connor's interest in education did little
more than draw attention to some conceptual overlaps between
current academic philosophy and educational theory. There
was little to link it more with philosophy of education than
with any other branch of philosophy. American students were
rather better served by Israel Scheffler's anthology,
Philosophy and Education, [9] in which the overlap between
philosophy and education is much more apparent, even though
most of the contributions were not originally written as
'philosophy of education'.

Far more enterprising than O'Connor have been those
writers who have allowed what they have understood to be the
practice of education to guide the direction of
philosophical inquiry. Peters put it thus:

The philosophy of education is a family of
philosophical inquiries linked together by
their philosophical character and by their
relevance to educational issues. This
relevance to education provides the point of
entry which determines their selection from
the general corpus of philosophical inquiry.
The inquirer may be led, of course, by the
logic of his probing into the most general
problems of metaphysics and logic. but if he
is, his route will be marked by a thread
leading back to the centre. [10]

It is slightly misleading to say that education provides the point of entry which determines the selection of issues 'from the general corpus of philosophical inquiry', since some of the issues treated at length in recent philosophy of education could not have been previously found in that corpus. In Peters' case, it also links philosophy of education a bit too closely with problems that arise in the context of schooling, since for Peters the institution of schooling is defined by reference to its educative role. We shall later have reason to question this connection. Nevertheless, there is a genuine effort to engage in a philosophical examination of educational issues. Here again, American philosophy of education had a less restricted understanding of philosophy of education. Adrian Dupuis' anthology, *Nature, Aims and Policy*, [11] which grew out of the Illinois Philosophy of Education Project in the mid-sixties, works with a broader conception of the scope of philosophy of education than has until recently been characteristic of its British counterpart.

The approach to philosophy of education taken by Peters had its recent origins in C.D. Hardie's *Truth and Fallacy in Educational Theory*. [12] In that book, Hardie took a number of influential educational theories (those of Spencer, Herbart and Dewey), and subjected them to critical analysis in the spirit of Moore, Broad and Wittgenstein. It was another eighteen years before Scheffler's *The Language of Education* appeared, [13] some six years before Peters' major work, *Ethics and Education*. [14] However, following the social upheavals of the late sixties the methodology used to implement this approach to philosophy of education has come under increasing fire. Most importantly, it has been charged with representing itself as other than it is, that is, with obscuring its own socio-historical origins and claiming to provide analysis and argument which could function as independent, non-partisan constituents in debates about the justifiability of particular educational practices. By representing itself as it did, post-war analytic philosophy of education functioned to endorse the dominant cultural tradition. Though critics of analytic philosophy of education have frequently over-reacted to its conservative possibilities, [15] the general thrust of their critique cannot be ignored. Philosophy of education is a social practice, and in evaluating it account needs to be taken not only of what might be thought to follow 'strictly' from the arguments used by its practitioners, but also the causal effects of those arguments within the social context of which they are a part. This is particularly true if philosophy of education is seen as accounting or having implications for educational practice. What we call 'education' is generally believed to take place not in a laboratory in which the only variables are known and controlled, but for the most part in institutions such as schools, universities, etc. which are tied in various ways

9

to political and economic structures, and whose functions cannot be exhausted without reference to those structures. Arguments about what education is, what methods of teaching are justifiable, what flexibility there ought to be in the curriculum, what capacities children have, and how schools ought to be administered, all take place within a context in which schools are designed to fulfil certain social and economic functions, and in which certain things tend to be taken for granted - compulsory and age-related schooling, a competitive learning situation, mass teaching, the social standing associated with various subjects, and so on. These issues are not mere appendages or impediments but constitute the concrete situation with which philosophical discussions about education must presently grapple.

NOTES

1. See the discussion in J. Kovesi, *Moral Notions*, London: Routledge & Kegan Paul, 1967, Chs. 1,2.
2. For some additional comments, see *infra*, Ch. 20.
3. L. Wittgenstein, *Philosophical Investigations*[2], trans. G.E.M.Anscombe, Oxford: Blackwell, 1958, §109e.
4. ibid., §132e.
5. ibid., §124e.
6. However as Wittgenstein's posthumously published *On Certainty* (Oxford: Blackwell, 1974) shows, he himself was not unmindful of these problems.
7. R.S. Peters, 'The Philosophy of Education', in J.W. Tibble (ed.), *The Study of Education*, London: Routledge & Kegan Paul, 1966, p. 64.
8. London: Routledge & Kegan Paul, 1957.
9. Boston: Allyn & Bacon, 1958. A second edition was published in 1966.
10. Peters, p. 68.
11. Urbana: University of Illinois Press, 1970.
12. Cambridge University Press, 1942; re-issued by Teachers College Press, Columbia University, 1962.
13. Springfield, Ill.: C.C. Thomas, 1960.
14. London: Allen & Unwin, 1966.
15. See A. Wertheimer's balanced discussion, 'Is Ordinary Language Analysis Conservative?' *Political Theory*, IV, 4 (November, 1976), 405-22.

Chapter 2

EDUCATION

Each society is faced with the problem of its own persistence. In a slowly evolving society, this will tend to present itself as the problem of the *coming* generation - newcomers unfamiliar with its ways, but vital to its continuation, culturally as well as biologically. In a rapidly changing society, however, the problem is posed no less for its *current* adult membership. Practices, skills, values, expectations, etc. acquired in childhood, become redundant or unsuited to the changing conditions, and need to be revised, replaced, upgraded or restructured. The range of activities, both formal and informal, whereby people are initiated into or realigned with the evolving traditions, structures and social relations is taken to constitute their education.

There are two general problems with this unsophisticated but familiar account. The first concerns an apparent dichotomy between individuals and the evolving traditions, and the priority that is given to the latter: the education of individuals takes the form of co-ordinating their development with changes going on in society. As we shall later suggest, this relates the individual much too passively to the changes occurring in society. Education should enable the individual to transform and not simply to conform. The second problem with the account is that it is too bland: it does not pick out sufficiently explicitly the critical function which the concept is often given. Plato, for example, was concerned to distinguish being educated from being merely trained - or more fashionably, socialised.[1] Only the latter is indicated by the unsophisticated account. But not any and everything that is passed on or acquired is accorded educational status - or even everything that keeps the wheels turning. In so far as education is socialisation at all, it is socialisation of a selective and normative kind. It is the problem posed by this selectivity which has occupied much of the attention of philosophers of education.

11

In the course of this chapter, we will attempt to construct a critically valuable concept of education – that is, a concept which will enable practices and their outcomes to be judged in terms of their educational value. I will make frequent reference to the work of R.S. Peters. There are two reasons for this. First, no contemporary philosopher has given more detailed attention to the matter, and in many circles Peters' earlier views have acquired the status of orthodoxy. Secondly, the evolution of Peters' views over the past twenty years is interesting and instructive. [2]

Preliminaries

At the outset we should not be too distracted by three distinctions that have gained some currency in the discussion. The first has to do with a supposed contrast between content- and child-centred approaches to education. According to the content-centred approach, traceable to the Latin *educare* (to train, or mould according to some specification), education is to be characterised in terms of social or other goals external to the educand. According to the child-centred approach, traceable to the Latin *educere* (to lead out), education is to be characterised by reference to the nature of the educand. [3] The contrast tends to be more apparent than real, since the nature that is to be 'realised' or 'actualised' in education is inevitably characterised in ways deeply ingrained with social values. Thus the common claim of those who trade on the distinction, that the former approach leads to totalitarian theories of education whereas the latter recognises the value of the individual, relies on a limited appreciation of the possible sources of oppression. A social formation theoretically dedicated to the value of self-realisation will tend to characterise the 'self' to be realised in a way which secures the preservation and reproduction of the dominant *status quo*.

The second distinction is between instrumentalist and non-instrumentalist accounts of education. In his earlier writings, R.S. Peters reacted against the tendency of many educationists and educational administrators to see in education a means to certain – particularly social – ends, such as vocational training, socialisation and mental health. This 'instrumentalist' approach, as he called it, failed to grasp the specific character of the concept of education, and to it he opposed his own 'non-instrumentalist' account. A number of the points which Peters made in this connection – for example, that instrumentalism provided a sociological rather than a discriminatory account of education, [4] that the means-end model was not appropriate to all educationally valuable learning, [5] that the ends to which education was said to be

12

instrumental were too broad to account for the distinctiveness of the educational enterprise,[6] and that it overlooked the normativeness of the concept of education,[7] were, in a limited way, well-taken. But as arguments against an 'instrumentalist' approach to education they will not do. At best they point to difficulties in certain kinds of 'instrumentalist' understandings of education. Moreover, the distinction, when pressed, is both vague and ambiguous, and in his recent writing Peters has abandoned this general way of talking.[8]

The third distinction is between educational processes and the state of being educated. The origins of this distinction lie in the fairly obvious point that education is the result of deliberate effort. It is not an impersonal process like maturation. Feral children do not come to acquire the valued qualities that we might want to associate with being educated. But in the course of discussion, some writers suggested that a person might just *possibly* come to possess those qualities without going through the processes associated with education. Since refusal to regard such a person as educated would smack of arbitrariness, two senses of 'education' were postulated – a 'task'-sense and an 'achievement'-sense – terms borrowed from Gilbert Ryle.[9] The problems inherent in this distinction will be considered elsewhere.[10] Here it is sufficient to note its artificiality. To the extent that *A* is being or becoming educated, to that extent *A* is educated. To separate the state from the process is to force apart what belong to a conceptual unity. The point about stories of ready-made educated people popping into existence is that they are not true, and conceptualisation occurs in response to what is believed to be true. Should it be discovered that some apparently educated people have not been involved in any deliberate process of education (whether or not it is called 'education'), then obviously some conceptual re-thinking will be in order, but until that happens we should not artificially separate education into process and product.

There is one further distinction, however, which does have some importance for the debate – the distinction between non-normative and normative concepts of education, or as I would prefer to express it, between sociological and discriminatory concepts of education. When Peters first advocated his normative or discriminatory concept of education, it was criticised as unduly narrow or stipulative. What this criticism often amounted to was the claim that 'education' could be used in contexts in which the value he attributed to it was not implied. Peters' response was to distinguish two senses of 'education' – an 'older' use, in which it could be interchanged with 'training' or 'schooling', and a 'more recent' normative use.[11] He allowed that the older use would render intelligible the opposition to education that is sometimes encountered. Further, it would also account for the currency given to 'instrumentalist' views of education, since it made good sense to ask for the purpose and justification of education conceived as training or schooling. But this was not the sense that interested him and which he believed should be of interest to educators. Of much greater importance is the normative or discriminatory use. In this regard Peters is surely on the right track, though his suggestion that it has its origins in the nineteenth century ideal of 'the educated person' is more appropriate to the content with which he invests his discriminatory concept. The distinction between discriminatory and non-discriminatory concepts goes back as far as Plato and Aristotle.[12] A critically valuable concept of education has always existed to differentiate a 'better kind of learning'. The key problem has been to develop a set of justifiable and workable criteria whereby such 'better' learning can be identified.

In its discriminatory sense, education marks out some change for what is presumed to be the better. The value of education is not accidental or contingent, but is enshrined in the purposes for which we have developed the concept. It is thus able to fulfil a critical function. As Peters puts it, it 'is not a concept that marks out any particular type of process such as training, or activity such as lecturing; rather it suggests criteria to which processes such as training must conform.'[13] At the same time, however, this normative aspect of education also makes it ideologically vulnerable, since it can be (and indeed is) used to characterise and endorse practices without it being made clear whose interests are being served by such endorsement.[14] For example, where, as is commonly the case, education is conceived of as something that *A* gives to *B*, there is a strong tendency to see it in terms of *A*, the teacher, and *A*'s interests, rather than *B*, the learner, and *B*'s interests. The schooling model is so pervasive that even the critical concept is influenced by it. Of course, this tendency will not be as obtrusive if the view that education is something that *A* gives to *B* is combined with a horticultural model of education, as Froebel and other educational romanticists have suggested. However, the view that personal growth is like the growth of a plant, in which innate and structured potentialities are brought to fruition under the careful hand of a gardener, overlooks the predominantly social construction of personality, and the susceptibility of such a construction to alien and oppressive interests. In an important sense we *learn* to be persons. What is really needed is a break with the model of education in which its 'natural' association is believed to be with teaching rather than learning, something very difficult to do given the close alliance between philosophy of education and teacher training programmes. At times

14

Peters acknowledges this point, though he does not fully appreciate the tension it causes within his own theory. Referring to the horticultural model, he notes that despite its defects it has the merit of drawing attention to the importance of the *manner* in which education is achieved – the importance, as he puts it, 'of letting individuals choose for themselves, learn by experience and direct their own lives'.[15] How this is reconciled with the present structure of schooling is not made clear.[16]

Education as a critical concept

In attempting to construct a critically valuable concept of education, it will be useful to work through the account presented by Peters in *Ethics and Education*. The deficiencies of this account, acknowledged to some extent in Peters' most recent work on the subject,[17] are instructive for the way they alert us to matters which a critically valuable account will need to accommodate.

Central to this earlier account was the engagement in what were called 'worthwhile activities'. Three criteria for worthwhileness were offered. The first was that the activities involved 'a broad cognitive perspective', that is, they depended on knowledge having broad implications. In this respect, education was to be differentiated from training, for the latter 'suggests the acquisition of appropriate appraisals and habits of response in limited conventional situations'.[18] Thus physical education, as distinct from physical training, implies an approach to and understanding of physical development which sets it into a larger framework of knowledge. Further, it suggests why certain activities (Peters suggests golf and bingo) have only a limited educational value. They bear no strong epistemological links with other things in our lives.

The second criterion is linked to the first. The person's broad cognitive perspective must not be inert; it must affect his/her way of looking at things. To be educated, a person cannot be merely learned or erudite. Merely inert knowledge that fills someone's head has no more value than an encyclopedia which sits on the shelf. It must be related to life.

There is much to be said for these first two criteria, but in *Ethics and Education* their discussion did little to challenge the ideological character of what passes for education. Peters' specification of activities which might fulfil the condition of worthwhileness left unexamined the form in which they manifest themselves within 'the education system'. 'Science, mathematics, history, art, cooking and carpentry feature on the curriculum, not bingo, bridge and billiards'.[19] But, we must ask, are they conceived and taught in a way which reveals their cognitive scope, or rather, and more likely, in a fashion which serves narrowly

15

conceived classificatory and vocational ends? By failing to consider such questions, Peters left the impression that curricula comprising scientific, literary and historical studies would be educationally acceptable, whereas those comprising bingo, bridge and billiards would not. He thus overlooked what, given the context of his discussion, was surely crucial, namely, the form taken by such studies in schools and other 'educational' institutions.

Similar comments might be made about Peters' handling of the second criterion. His abstracted reference to the traditional curriculum subjects leaves the impression that these meet the condition of relating knowledge to life. But a good deal of what is taught is quite remote from the interests and concerns of those who learn, serving as a basis for little more than the examination and certification functions of traditional schooling. And in so far as it does relate to life, this is frequently unrelated to its content. It enables people to be classified and stratified, not in order that they may better transform the world around them, but that they may be shaped to the purposes of others.

The third criterion of worthwhileness was that the knowledge possessed by the educated person 'must involve the kind of commitment that comes from being on the inside of a form of thought and awareness.'[20] Here Peters endeavoured to exclude an 'external' or 'instrumental' engagement in otherwise worthwhile activities. Peters' point was not altogether clear, and generated some criticism. W.H. Dray, for example, claimed that the commitment requirement would have the 'paradoxical consequence' of denying the appellation 'educated' to a person who, having thought through it, rejected his/her culture.[21] Peters' response was to claim that he did not understand 'commitment' to mean an acceptance of the substantive beliefs of a culture, or products of 'a form of thought and awareness', but rather a care for the standards and procedures implicit in those forms of thought and awareness.[22] But it is not obvious that procedures and content can be so easily separated, nor that the former are less open to revision and rejection than the latter. The progress of thought has been marked as significantly by revisions of the 'standards and procedures' implicit in current 'forms of thought and awareness', and indeed in the conception of those 'forms of thought and awareness', as it has by the aggregation of knowledge by means of those standards and procedures. Peters' response promised greater flexibility than it provided.

What is meant by a care for the standards and procedures implicit in 'a form of thought and awareness'? In *Ethics and Education* Peters appears to have meant the engagement in a particular form of cognitive enterprise for its own sake rather than simply as a means to 'external' ends. If one's sole commitment to the scientific enterprise is to advance one's status and salary, then, though one may

16

use the procedures which are implicit in scientific investigation, one does not display an educated commitment to them. This form of involvement is likely to be both distorting and stultifying - distorting, in that it encourages 'cut corners', and stultifying in that it distracts from the kind of self-criticism to which particular 'forms of thought' ought to be continually subjected. It is clear that much schooling fails in this regard. The competitive framework in which it is cast, the carrots of status and material success, and the sticks of shame and failure, encourage an involvement alien to a proper appreciation of the cognitive engagement. Understood negatively, the third criterion is eminently acceptable. But in *Ethics and Education* Peters also interpreted it positively to enjoin 'the pursuit of knowledge for its own sake'. This possesses ideological potentialities which Peters failed to guard against. The human engagement with reality in the production of knowledge is social in form and structured by socially influenced interests. The divisions of accumulated knowledge, the so-called forms of thought and awareness, are irreducibly linked to certain social ends, ends which may come up for criticism. 'The pursuit of knowledge for its own sake' may thus constitute a piece of mystification, since it can disguise an essentially conservative and unquestioning engagement in research behind a recognition of the defects of a 'merely instrumental' approach.

We may pursue what I have referred to as the ideological potential of the *Ethics and Education* account of education by considering one further aspect of Peters' position - his characterisation of education as a form of initiation.[23] Education, he wrote, 'consists in initiating others into activities, modes of conduct and thought which have standards written into them by reference to which it is possible to act, think, and feel with varying degrees of skill, relevance and taste'.[24] The special relevance of the figure of 'initiation' was that it drew attention to 'the enormous importance of the impersonal content and procedures which are enshrined in the public traditions'. This content, he allowed, was revisable; however, 'the critical procedures by means of which established content is assessed, revised, and adapted to new discoveries, have public criteria written into them that stand as impersonal standards to which both teacher and learner must give their allegiance'.

Now, we have already noted the somewhat tendentious character of this separation of content and procedures - a tendentiousness axiomised in the claim that the questions one asks determine the answers one gets. But further than this, there is a heavy weight placed upon the impersonality of the public traditions into which the educated person must be initiated. On one side, this involves a salutary

17

recognition that individual development is social and not individualistic. The development of mind is not a generalisation from solipsistic experience but takes shape in response to social as much as individual experience. But on the other side, these public traditions are idealised. They, or at least their procedures, are given a status which masks the variety of sectional interests which they may and frequently do serve. The alternative to idiosyncrasy is not necessarily objectivity. Not only may the public traditions perpetuate cultural distortions, but in hierarchically organised societies these traditions will tend to be identified with the traditions of the dominant group. To determine whether initiation into these public modes of thought is educational, therefore, we need to *evaluate* them and not merely ascertain whether they have been properly assimilated.

Peters has not remained wholly unreceptive to criticisms of the kind we have been making, and since 1974 his views have undergone a noticeable change. Gone is some of the earlier emphasis on conceptual questions, and the assurance that went with it. There is a greater recognition of the ways in which schools tend to inhibit the kind of development implicit in education.[25] Yet he is still reluctant to see this as endemic to most schooling. Authoritarian headmasters, rigid and fragmented curricula, reliance on punishment and reward for motivation, competition, the selective function of schools, and so on, seem to be regarded as unhappy if prevalent and continuing contingencies, whose significant melioration might be effected without major structural changes to society. This apparent persistence of liberal optimism underestimates the deep confluence which exists between the institution of schooling and what is in many ways an illiberal *status quo*.[26]

A central feature of Peters' earlier account of education was its stress on the development of knowledge and understanding. Education was conceived of as a state of mind in which reason found its articulation in a variety of public forms. There was little to suggest that strength of will, emotional maturity, and agency were part of this account – though they might have been there as its precondition or consequence – and there was a deliberate steering away from views which emphasised 'total development' or 'development of the self as agent' or 'humanisation' as the point of education. In the intervening years, partly, one suspects, as a result of his work on the ideas of moral development and autonomy, and partly in response to criticism, Peters has moved toward a more holistic view of education. For the tradition which radically distinguishes reason, will and feeling, cannot survive scrutiny. They are but abstractions from a single centre of activity, each of which (in the experience of

18

persons) presupposes the other. This shift is to be welcomed. Apart from its importance in answering questions about the value of cognitive development, the earlier emphasis on cognitive development left the value of education unclear. There is greater recognition that any plausible understanding of education must include some conception or vision of personhood.

Because personhood is learned, the development of cognitive capacities will be of great importance. But persons are not simply knowing subjects, and there is no necessity that their learning should take the intellectualistic form suggested by most school curricula. As far as the education of *persons* is concerned, cognitive development must not only transform the knower and the knower's understanding of the world, but also enable the knower to transform the world around him/her. This involves an active engagement with the world in which cognitive development and practice mutually interact. In this respect, much schooling divorces children from the world, or at least restricts them to an artificial world, in which cognitive development of a kind which enables transformational interaction with the world is inhibited rather than promoted.

Even in his later work, with its greater feeling for the development of persons in education, Peters' preoccupation with the priority of cognitive development leads him in the direction of the balanced soul rather than the transforming agent. By stressing development in the different forms of understanding enshrined in the public tradition, rather than the development of rational agency through an engagement with the world as it presents itself - an approach in which young children delight until it becomes too much trouble to their parents - Peters fails to guard against the development of a form of understanding in which the realities of the lived world are obscured by a critical tradition which is oriented toward a heteronomy-producing *status quo*. Instead of being an effective agent in the world, the individual learns to move within an artificial given, with only the illusion of control over his/her present and future.

My suggestion, then, is that the development of a critical concept of education presupposes a conception of distinctively human living and being which one learns to actualise in society with others. Included in this conception is one's development as a rational/feeling willing agent, able to participate in and change one's world, with a realistic understanding of its possibilities. In essence, this is the development of autonomy. The failure of contemporary schooling is in large measure its failure to develop in children the ability to participate effectively in the world. What is called their education is simply their initiation into an ongoing tradition of

19

practice and theory which presents itself as a given and whose critical tools provide no means whereby their own credentials can be assessed.

NOTES

1. Plato, *Laws*, 643b et seq.
2. Peters' views were first articulated in a B.B.C. talk given in the late 1950s, and republished as a chapter entitled 'Must an Educator have an Aim? in *Authority, Responsibility and Education*, first edn. London: Allen & Unwin, 1959. In 1963 a more detailed and considerably expanded account was given as the Inaugural Lecture when he was appointed to the Chair in Philosophy of Education at the University of London Institute of Education. Entitled *Education as Initiation* (London: Evans Bros., 1964), a version was published in R.D. Archambault (ed.), *Philosophical Analysis and Education*, London: Routledge & Kegan Paul, 1965, pp.87-111. An expanded version of this was published as two chapters in his *Ethics and Education*, London: Allen & Unwin, 1966, pp.23-62. In the meantime he gave, in 1965, a public lecture in London, entitled 'What is an Educational Process?, some of which found its way into *Ethics and Education*, and the whole of which was eventually printed in R.S. Peters (ed.), *The Concept of Education*, London: Routledge & Kegan Paul, 1967, pp.1-23. A further slight development came with a symposium paper (with responses from J. Woods & W.H. Dray), entitled 'Aims of Education – A Conceptual Inquiry', at an International Seminar on Philosophy and Education, held in 1966 at the Ontario Institute for Studies in Education. The symposium papers were printed in B.S. Crittenden (ed.), *Philosophy and Education*, Toronto: Ontario Institute for Studies in Education, 1967, pp.1-32, but are more easily accessible in R.S. Peters (ed.), *The Philosophy of Education*, London: O.U.P., 1973, pp.11-49. In the face of criticism, Peters offered modifications and defence of his views in 'Education and Human Development' in R.J.W. Selleck (ed.), *Melbourne Studies in Education*, Melbourne U.P. 1970, pp.83-103, and in a paper entitled 'Education and the Educated Man', delivered at the 1970 Annual Conference of the Philosophy of Education Society of Great Britain (in *Proceedings*, IV, 1 (January, 1970), 5-20), versions of which are reprinted in a number of places. The collection *Philosophy of Education*, edited by Peters in 1973, probably contains the best of the 'early' Peters. From 1974 the picture becomes less clear as modifications become more substantial. On the

one hand, there is the assimilation of work done in the area of moral development into his model of education. This work is collected in R.S. Peters (ed.), *Psychology and Ethical Development*, London: Allen & Unwin, 1974, especially Pts. 2 & 3; and R.S. Peters, *Reason and Compassion*, London: Routledge & Kegan Paul, 1973. On the other hand, there is a chipping away at the foundations of some of his early work. This is best represented in 'Ambiguities in Liberal Education and the Problem of its Content' and 'Dilemmas in Liberal Education', both written in 1977 and collected in R.S. Peters (ed.), *Education and the Education of Teachers*, London: Routledge & Kegan Paul, 1977, Chs. 3, 4. Even more recent and radical is 'Democratic Values and Educational Aims', *Teachers College Record*, LXXX, 3 (February, 1979), 463–82.

3. *Authority, Responsibility and Education*, p.90.
4. Archambault, p.89. For some expansion of this distinction, see my 'Neutrality in Moral Education', *Discourse*, III, 1 (Autumn, 1982).
5. P.H. Hirst & R.S. Peters, *The Logic of Education*, London: Routledge & Kegan Paul, 1970, p.68.
6. Archambault, p.90.
7. ibid., p.92.
8. See, e.g. 'Ambiguities in Liberal Education and the Problem of its Content', esp. pp.48–54.
9. See G. Ryle, *The Concept of Mind*, London: Hutchinson, 1949, esp. pp.149–53.
10. See *infra*, Ch. 3. For a critique of Peters' use of this distinction, see K. Robinson, 'The Task-Achievement Analysis of Education', *Educational Philosophy and Theory*, IV, 2 (October 1972), 17–24.
11. See 'Education and the Educated Man'.
12. Plato, *Laws*, 643b et. seq.; Aristotle, *Politics*, Bk. VIII, Ch. 2.
13. Archambault, p.92.
14. Here and elsewhere I use the term 'ideology' and its cognates in their pejorative sense, to mean, roughly, a set of practices and ideas which serve to misrepresent social reality.
15. Archambault, p.96; cf. *Ethics and Education*, pp.45, 54.
16. In a number of places Peters leans heavily on a Piagetian model of child-development to reconcile this criterion with schooling.
17. See, e.g. 'Moral Development and Moral Learning' and 'Subjectivity and Standards', both reprinted in *Psychology and Ethical Development*, Ch. 17, esp. pp.375–76, and Ch. 19; 'Introduction: the Contemporary Problem', in R.S. Peters (ed.), *The Role of the Head*, London: Routledge & Kegan Paul, 1976, pp.1–8; 'Dilemmas in Liberal Education'; and

'Democratic Values and Educational Aims'.

18. *Ethics and Education*, p.33.
19. ibid., p.144.
20. ibid., p.31.
21. Dray, 'Aims of Education – A Conceptual Inquiry', in Peters, (ed.), *The Philosophy of Education*, p.37.
22. On caring, see further, D. Cave, '"Care" in Educational Debate', in D. Cave (ed.), *Problems in Education: A Philosophical Approach*, Victoria: Cassell Australia, 1976, pp.116–26; R.E. Hult, Jr., 'On Pedagogical Caring', *Educational Theory*, XXIX, 3 (Summer, 1979), 237–43; J. Passmore, *The Philosophy of Teaching*, London: Duckworth, 1980, Ch. 10.
23. Peters' model of initiation is criticised in K. Robinson, 'Education and Initiation', *Educational Philosophy and Theory*, II, 2 (October, 1970), 33–46.
24. This quote and those which follow are from Archambault, pp.102–07, but do not present a position which differs from that taken in *Ethics and Education*, Ch. 2.
25. See *supra*, fn. 16.
26. See *infra*, Ch. 8.

Chapter 3

TEACHING AND LEARNING

Education is a social product, in which a person's
capacities for realistic and effective intervention in the
world are developed. Were we to ask how this development
comes about, an expected response would be: through
teaching. Yet this is not wholly unproblematic. Education
is a matter of learning, and whether, and if so to what
extent, learning requires teaching is disputable. Moreover,
the authoritarian, repressive and indoctrinatory activity we
frequently identify as teaching seems far removed from
education. And no doubt that is so. Nevertheless, apart
from the rare Stirnerite, support for the view that
education could or should be accomplished without any form
of teaching would be difficult to find. Even radical
libertarians such as the early Spencer acknowledged the
importance of advice and guidance, albeit without the
coercion so often associated with teaching. Still, the
somewhat problematic relation which frequently appears to
exist between teaching and education makes it important that
we consider more closely the teaching relationship. Apart
from helping us to understand its apparently anomalous
character, such an investigation will also enable us to
challenge the necessity of those attitudes and practices so
often identified with teaching.

Teaching as polymorphous

Closer attention to the sheer variety of behaviour which
might be classified as teaching strongly suggests that it is
polymorphous. Unlike shooting or walking or changing gears,
teaching may take many forms. It is more like killing or
locomotion, both of which can be accomplished in a great
variety of ways. Indeed, there seem to be very few *a priori*
restrictions on the forms which teaching may take. A person
may teach not only by the familiar classroom techniques of
instruction, demonstration and drilling, but also (given a
suitable story) by doing head-stands, showing films,

23

discussion, excursions, giving dinners, and so on. The polymorphous character of teaching is ignored, impossible to implement or even rejected in the rigidified structures of some schools, where teaching that is not authoritarian and conventional (i.e., having the form of lecturing, drilling, demonstrating) is thought to be something other than teaching. Alternatives are viewed as entertainment or play - as though teaching couldn't be entertaining or playful. A narrow view such as this overlooks the teaching of a hidden curriculum which so often accompanies such conventional teaching methods, and the unquestioning acceptance of authority, passivity, inarticulateness, etc. to which it leads. The problem is not all on one side. Those who urge the abandonment of teaching in favour of more student-based and co-operative methods of learning have also tended to identify it with the conventional institutionalised techniques of lecturing, etc. This close identification of teaching with a certain limited range of institutionalised activities evokes some sympathy for attempts to detach education from teaching. However, provided that we are careful not to encourage such misleading identifications, this is not really necessary. We shall, therefore, endeavour to provide an analysis of teaching which will account not only for a defensible connection with education, but also for its frequent association with practices whose educational value is less obvious.

Activity and intention

A central preoccupation of those who have sought to clarify the nature of the teaching relationship has been the connection between teaching and learning. This has generated discussion as to whether teaching is an activity, whether there are different senses of the verb 'to teach', and the nature of learning.

We might start with the generalised remarks of P.H. Hirst regarding the way in which we go about differentiating activities:

> How ... are we going to characterise specific teaching activities...? I think the answer to this is that they can only be characterised in the way in which we fundamentally characterise all human activities, by looking at their point or purpose. It is by clarifying the aim, the intention of what is going on, that we can see when standing on one's head to demonstrate something or any other activity is in fact teaching and not, say, simply entertaining. [1]

24

There is a surface plausibility to this position. If we think of an activity (as distinct from a single act or action) as an organised set of related actions, it is reasonable to expect that the intention(s) of the person(s) engaging in that activity will be relevant to its characterisation. Intentions, either explicit or ascribed, will give point to the linking together of diverse actions. Whether a statement of intention is sufficient to characterise an activity is a question we can leave aside for the moment. It is enough for Hirst's position that we recognise the importance of intentions, and that in the case of teaching the relevant intention is an intention to bring about learning.

Whatever plausibility Hirst's account may appear to have, it represents only one side of what has been a protracted and frequently pointless debate. Most of those who have discussed the issue are agreed that there is a close relation between teaching and learning.[2] But there is substantial support for the view that teaching requires not merely (if at all) the *intention* to bring about learning, but learning as its *outcome*. Here we might comment on three matters. First, the assumption that teaching is an activity. Secondly, the relation between teaching and learning. And thirdly, the point (if any) of the debate. I shall comment on the last of these matters in the course of discussing the other two.

Our first difficulty here relates to the assumption that teaching is or must be an activity. As soon as we turn our attention from those conventional, institutionalised occasions and techniques of teaching, most of which would not occur without those engaging in and employing them intending to bring about learning, it becomes clear that we may and often do teach others without intending to do so. Think of how much we can be taught by someone's example – in cases where if teaching was intended it might not have been the example it was: a kindness done in response to someone's need, and without a thought for what it might teach; hypocritical acts, which speak louder than the words that were intended to teach; and so on. It may be the case that, if the point of teaching is to bring about learning, this is more likely to come about if it is intended than if it is not, since one has (at least *prima facie*) greater control over the learning situation. It may also be the case that, if the bringing about of learning is what we have a stake in, then that which does so is likely to be characterised by deliberateness. But this need not be the case, and the purposes of conceptual differentiation are better served if it is not. What I mean is this: why should it be of any interest to us to differentiate teaching by reference to the intentions of those engaged in it? To say, as Hirst seems to, 'Well, teaching is an activity, and the point of activities can be located only by reference to the intentions of those engaged in them', amounts to little more than an uninteresting conceptual observation, unless we can see what purpose is served by cutting up the world in this way rather than some other. Hirst's conceptual observations aren't in any obvious way tied to human interests and concerns.

An alternative approach, with rather different conclusions, can be sketched briefly as follows. Conceptualisation, as we have already observed, does not occur in a vacuum, but against a background of interests.[3] If we take Hirst's observation that activities are differentiated by reference to the intentions of those engaged in them, we can link this with the more general theoretical point about conceptualisation by noting its background in our conception of ourselves as agents, who conceptualise much of what we do by reference to criteria which express agency. What we intend is thus likely to be of great importance in the characterisation of what we do. However, and this Hirst appears to have overlooked (perhaps because he did not ask why intentions should be thought important as a basis for differentiation), the ascription of agency is not limited to what is intended. Not all acts (to be distinguished from the more specific category of activities) need characterisation in terms of the intentions of those who perform them. And some in fact exclude such characterisation - e.g. acts of negligence. Now teaching, I believe, falls into the class of doings which express agency but do not require characterisation by reference to intentions. To teach is to do something for which (importantly) responsibility can be ascribed. It is an agent-based concept. This is obscured and distorted if we limit what is taught to what is intended: it ignores the great number of things which others learn from us and for which we can be held responsible, even though we did not intend that they learn them. Were we to speak simply of what others learn from us when that learning comes about without our intending it, we would fail to distinguish cases where some responsibility for what they learn can be sheeted home to us from those where it cannot.[4] When we consider what is taught in schools (and therefore what learning schools/teachers can be held at least partially responsible for), we need to look beyond statements of intention to those practices, structures etc. which lie within our power to affect, and from which those in the schools have learned.

To return to Hirst: it may well be that activities are to be characterised by reference to the intentions of those engaged in them. If that is so, and if what a person does can be characterised as teaching independently of his/her intentions, teaching is not an activity. This need not be thought eccentric. We are not denying that teaching is something which people do. Nor are we denying that when they teach they may be engaged in certain

26

activities – giving a demonstration, showing a film, etc. All we are saying is that the teaching in which these activities (and other things that we do) result is not itself an activity.

The second problem is related to the first. If we allow that for teaching to take place the *intention* to bring about learning is not required, the temptation to leave the connection between teaching and learning at the level of intentions is reduced. If X is taught without its learning being intended, it is nevertheless implied that it was learned. However, an invariant connection between teaching and learning cannot be established quite so easily. Those who wish to insist that teaching implies no more than the intention to bring about learning point to the intelligibility of claims such as 'Although I taught the class for six months they didn't learn anything'. I wish to argue, however, that cases of 'unsuccessful teaching' do not force us to adopt the 'intentional' view. Like many other terms relating to human action, 'teaching' has been extended from its central use and been given an institutionalised identity, whereby people can be identified as 'teachers' and what they do as 'teaching', not by reference to what they bring about but simply by locating them and it within a particular institutional structure: what they are employed as, their saying these things at this particular time in this place to these people, etc. This institutionalised sense of 'teach' is not primary, but secondary, and lends some plausibility to the view that the intention to bring about learning is central. Because even institutionalised teaching (i.e. teaching which does not imply that something was learned) is something for which those who engage in it can be held responsible, the extended use does not involve any radical violation of the point of the concept. However, there is a difference, like the difference between rape and attempted rape, which is obscured by running them together. Those who teach others, where teaching implies learning, do something to them (and not merely attempt or risk doing something to them), and for that reason the responsibility of the teacher is a heavy one.

Task or achievement?

Nevertheless, the case for 'unsuccessful teaching' (and the 'intentional' view) is often thought stronger than I've so far presented it. The 'undeniable fact that teaching, even good teaching can take place without the occurrence of learning'[5] seems too recalcitrant to be given the institutionalised shrift that I've suggested. I am not wholly persuaded that there is this recalcitrance. However, the belief that there is, coupled with those uses which strongly suggest that learning is implied, has prompted the view that 'teach' is used in at least two senses. The form

27

in which this distinction is expressed varies, but the most popular medium has been a utilisation of Gilbert Ryle's distinction between 'task' and 'achievement' words. 'Teach', in the task-sense, is explicated simply as the attempt to bring about learning; in the achievement- or outcome-sense it indicates that something has been successfully learned. Statements such as 'Mary Smith teaches philosophy' and 'Joe Brown taught me English' are said to imply no more than the task-sense, since it cannot be directly inferred whether anything was learned; [6] whereas statements such as 'Mary Smith teaches students to analyse arguments' and 'Joe Brown taught me to understand Chaucer' do imply that what is taught is learned. This position is further 'buttressed' by the argument that since activities are identified by reference to their intentions, the task- and not the achievement-sense is primary. We have already had a fair bit to say about this latter position, and will not pursue it further, except incidentally. Instead we will focus on two other issues. The first concerns the supposed primacy of the task-sense. The second, which is in the form of an excursus, concerns the utilisation of Ryle's task-achievement distinction in this and other contexts.

We have already seen reason to doubt the primacy of the task-sense. That is, we have questioned whether teaching is an activity. Further, we have raised doubts whether, even as an activity, the necessary reference to intentions would be sufficient to preclude a necessary reference to some outcome. We can expand on these doubts. In 'The Concept of Teaching', Helen Freeman argues strongly that where a word is said to possess task- and achievement-/outcome-senses, 'the outcome is logically prior to any possible conception of a related task, and therefore to any 'task' sense. A task is only understood by an agent in terms of what would count as a successful upshot for him'.[7] Applied to teaching, we can understand what it is to engage in the task of teaching only if we know what would count as 'successful teaching' (bringing about learning). Moreover, 'I logically can't *intend* to teach unless I already know what teaching is. For if I am trying to teach it is my attempts which can be successful or unsuccessful, not my teaching.'[8] Where only the intention to bring about learning is implied, it is preferable to speak of attempting or trying or intending to teach. The point of these remarks is not simply to argue the primacy of the outcome-sense, but to suggest that the alleged task-sense be dropped altogether.

However, the main thrust of Freeman's paper is to argue that teaching is not an activity after all. She produces a varied range of examples where we would say that people had taught others even though they had not intended to bring about learning. She then argues that if we assume (with Hirst) that activities are partially or wholly characterised and differentiated by the intentions of those who engage in

28

them, teaching could not be an activity. Instead she speaks of it as a perfience. [9] Perfiences are differentiated as follows:

> 'By doing P, A was x-ing B' where B is a person, x is the perficient verb (as distinguished from an activity verb) and some condition in B is the perficient outcome. The criterion for judging the truth or falsity of a perfience claim is whether or not the outcome implied in B has been brought about *through A's actions*. Thus, unlike actions, activities and performances, perfiences may be intentional or unintentional. [10]

In calling teaching a perfience, Freeman does not wish to suggest that it has some unique status. The class of perficient verbs is large, and among them she enumerates 'hurt', 'offend', 'interrupt', 'upset', 'dominate', 'embarrass', 'cure', 'interest', 'humiliate', 'satisfy', 'convince', 'frighten', 'kill', 'bore', 'entertain', 'comfort', 'help', 'hinder', 'inspire', 'insist', 'alarm', 'reform', and 'antagonise'. I would want to add 'educate' and 'indoctrinate' to the list.

In distinguishing this category of perficient verbs, Freeman has, I believe, cut through the Gordian knot into which the discussion has become tied. I offer just one minor modification of her thesis. Her schematic representation of a perfience runs together perfiences in general, and a sub-class of perfiences which can be termed perficienary transactions. Not all perficient outcomes fit the schematic representation, 'By doing P, A was x-ing B', in which some transaction between two persons, A and B, is implied. Thunderstorms can frighten me, a landslide can kill me, and an evening at home can bore me. Freeman's schema should be taken to represent a perficienary transaction. Teaching would appear to be almost exclusively a perficienary transaction - unless of course, one wishes to argue that not only is there no teaching without learning but also no learning without teaching. And this, though it would not imply an equivalence of teaching and learning (the relation would be a causal one), would involve us in stretching 'teach' beyond the point of conceptual usefulness. For, even though teaching may not be intentional, we have argued that an important point of being able to say that B was taught X by A is to locate responsibility for B's learning X. To say, 'No one taught X to B', is either to deny that anyone is to be held responsible for B's learning X, or perhaps to suggest that B taught him/herself and is the only one to be held responsible. Of course we can - and no doubt we sometimes do - use 'teach' more broadly than this, but such usage is parasitic on the responsibility-bearing transaction that gives the term its point.

Before taking up the second issue, we should note two additional constraints which Hirst places on the teaching relation. First, in order for A to be said to be teaching X to B, A's behaviour must be in some sense 'indicative' of X:

> The activity must, either implicitly or explicitly, express or embody the X to be learnt, so that this X is clearly indicated to the pupil as what he is to learn ... It must be so available in some sense that the pupil's learning activity can be directed to this as its object. [11]

Hirst's purposes in adding this condition appear to be twofold. First, there are numerous activities which might be performed with the intention of bringing about learning, but which are only remotely connected with the X to be learned (e.g. opening the windows to improve the learning conditions). Secondly, there are some things which we learn from others for which there was no basis in what they were doing. Indicativeness, however, is not up to the purpose Hirst gives it. It seems *ad hoc* to exclude from the description of the teaching situation those elements which do not 'express or embody the X to be learnt'. Opening the windows, like many other elements in the teaching situation, might be causally important to the teaching of X while not embodying X, and it is arbitrary to require some tighter connection. Should Hirst reply that all he means by indicativeness is that the act/activity be such that it could contribute to the teaching of X, then the criterion becomes circular, and insufficient to distinguish teaching from merely incidental learning.

Hirst's resort to something like indicativeness can be more easily explained. If, as we have suggested, part of the function of teaching claims is to locate responsibility for learning that takes place, then the indicativeness criterion can be seen as an inadequate way of expressing a limitation on A's responsibility for B's learning of X. To say that what A did was 'indicative' of X is a somewhat misleading way of pointing out that A could have anticipated in doing what he/she did (where this covers a range of related acts) that B would have learned X. To say that what A did was not 'indicative' of X is thus an equally misleading way of denying that B's learning of X from A could have been anticipated, thus absolving A from responsibility for it.

Hirst's second constraint, that the teaching activity 'must be indicatively expressed so that it is possible for this particular pupil B to learn X' [12] may appear to fare better. The point is clear enough. Reading the relevant sections of *Philosophical Investigations* to six-year-old B is not (normally) to teach him/her Wittgenstein's objections to private languages. Here it could be argued that unless what is done is at a level roughly appropriate to B's present state of knowledge, skill, etc., A could hardly be said to intend that B learn *X*. This would preserve a connection with intentions and avoid the charge of *ad hoc* qualifications. However, the argument fails. A may have hopelessly misjudged the capacities of B – the intention was there all right, though not much sensitivity. And it is difficult to see the condition as more than a way of saving a position from obvious counter-examples. The problem does not arise if teaching is seen as a perficienary transaction. A's reading the relevant sections of *Philosophical Investigations* to B constitutes an attempt (like attempting to knock someone unconscious with a feather duster) to teach B Wittgenstein's objections to private languages. As an attempt it bears the *prima facie* marks of responsibility, though in a case such as this, where there is so little likelihood that learning will take place, we may think the person crazy.

Excursus on Ryle's task-achievement distinction

Consideration of the second issue, Ryle's task-achievement distinction, may now appear otiose. In a way it is. Yet so much of the discussion, not only of teaching, but also other education-related concepts (e.g. learning, education), has been permeated by appeals to that distinction, that some consideration of its appropriateness may be called for. Here we are well-served by an article of J.D. Marshall, and what follows is a brief resume and application of Marshall's discussion.[13] Its purpose is not to claim that talk of task and achievement has no place in the philosophy of education. 'But Ryle's distinction is not our ordinary language distinction between a task and an achievement. It is a technical distinction partially defined in terms of logical distinctions between tensed propositions.'[14]

In *The Concept of Mind*, Ryle drew attention to a distinction between what he called task- and achievement-verbs.[15] Within the former category he included 'kick', 'treat', 'hunt', 'clutch', 'listen', 'look', 'travel', 'run', and 'tie'. Within the latter category were included 'score', 'heal', 'find', 'hold fast', 'hear', 'see', 'arrive', 'win', 'unearth', 'cure', 'convince', 'prove', 'cheat', 'unlock', 'safeguard', and 'conceal'. It is to be noted that Ryle sees task- and achievement-verbs as distinct, and not, as philosophers of education usually apply his distinction, as two distinct senses of the same verb. Moreover,

31

> one big difference between the logical force
> of a task verb and that of a corresponding
> achievement verb is that in applying an
> achievement verb we are asserting that some
> state of affairs obtains over and above that
> which consists in the performance, if any, of
> the subservient task activity.[16]

Here Ryle claims (contrary to Hirst and others) that the tasks are subservient to the achievements – in such a way, Marshall adds, that it is more appropriate to refer to the task in other terms. Thus while we may sometimes speak of a person's 'winning the race from the start', it is better to speak of his/her 'leading the race from the start'.

Marshall distinguishes between the two classes of verbs in these terms: if 'John wins the race' is true now, then the simple past proposition 'John won the race' will be true tomorrow. However, if 'John is running the race' is true now, it is not necessarily the case that the simple past tense proposition 'John ran the race' will be true tomorrow. Further, 'John is running the race' is true only if the perfect tense proposition 'John has run the race' is false. In the case of achievement-verbs the opposite is true.

However, Marshall believes that Ryle's two-fold classification is oversimplified. Various distinctions may and should be drawn within and to some extent across his distinctions. *First*, within the general class of active verbs there is a distinction to be drawn between what he terms *action verbs* and *static verbs*. Action verbs possess, and static verbs do not, a continuous present tense. On this basis, 'run', 'write', 'swim', 'hop', 'paddle', 'laugh', 'dig', 'kill', 'punish', 'wash', 'repair', 'recover' and 'recuperate' may be classed as action verbs; and 'know', 'love', 'recognise', 'hate', 'win', and 'cure' are to be classified as static verbs. *Secondly*, within the class of action verbs a further distinction is to be made between *task-completion verbs* and *performance verbs*. With regard to task-completion verbs, propositions of the form 'A is x-ing ' imply propositions of the form 'A has not x-ed'; whereas in the case of performance verbs it does not seem very appropriate to say either that propositions of the form 'A is x-ing' do or that they do not imply propositions of the form 'A has not x-ed'. On this basis 'kill', 'punish', 'wash', 'repair', 'recover', and 'recuperate' may be classed as task-completion verbs; and 'swim', 'paddle', 'hop', 'laugh' and 'dig' as performance verbs. *Thirdly*, static verbs may also be subdivided into what may be termed *state verbs* and *accomplishment verbs*. In the case of state verbs, propositions of the form 'A has x-ed' imply propositions of the form 'A x-s'; whereas propositions containing accomplishment verbs do not carry this implication. On this basis, 'hate', 'know', and 'love' are to be classified as state verbs, and 'recognise', 'win' and 'find' as accomplishment verbs.

Given this expanded classification, it can be seen that what Ryle refers to as achievement verbs fall into both the accomplishment and performance categories; and that what he calls task verbs also fall into the performance category. Does this then mean that his distinction collapses? Marshall thinks not. Following a suggestion of Aristotle, he draws a further distinction in terms of the *completeness* or *incompleteness* of the performance. Given a performance covering the time-span $t_1 - t_n$, the performance can be described as complete if, when asserted at t_1, a continuous present proposition of the form 'A is x-ing' implies a perfect tense proposition of the form 'A has x-ed'. Otherwise it is incomplete. On this basis, 'keep' shows itself as a complete performance verb, and 'show' and 'dance' as incomplete.

To simplify the foregoing, we may represent it diagrammatically as follows:

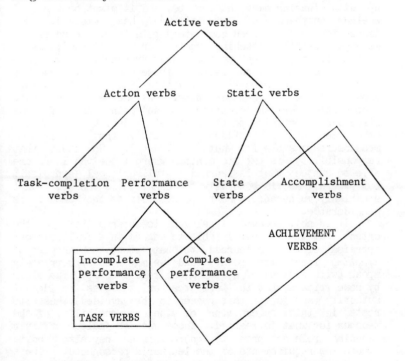

Where does this leave us with respect to 'teach'? Taking as our example a non-elliptical teaching assertion, we can see (with Marshall) that it functions as an action verb; i.e. it has a continuous present use:

33

'I am teaching algebra to John.'

It is, moreover, a performance verb; that is, it is *not* the case that

'I am teaching algebra to John'

implies

'I have taught algebra to John.'

Thus 'teach' is, within the Rylean classification, a task verb. This, however, carries no implications for our previous discussion of the relation between teaching and learning, for the achievement or outcome spoken of there was of a different kind altogether. On the Rylean classification, not only 'teach', but also 'learn', is a task verb.

In these two sections, much of our time has been taken up with clearing away the cobwebs, and it might be wondered whether anything of significance has emerged.[17] Our discussion has not been completely pointless. In so far as we have shown that teaching, whether or not intended, is a responsibility-bearing perficiency transaction, we have established that an onus falls on those who teach. Whether they engage in specific activities such as lecturing, showing films or demonstrating, or whether they are responsible for the setting up and maintenance of those structures from which people learn attitudes, values and the other contents of 'hidden curricula', they are in some measure responsible for what is learned. No doubt that responsibility is at its minimum where those who learn are able to subject what is learned to full critical appraisal; but where, as is generally the case, those who are taught are highly vulnerable, the responsibility of the teacher is considerable.

It is not, perhaps, irrelevant to observe that to the extent that the learner is able to engage in a full critical appraisal of what is learned, to that extent the language of *teaching* loses its point, and we may more appropriately speak (with Freire) of a dialogical relationship. The claim by some writers that the term 'teacher' embodies the idea of authority (and is for that reason to be avoided) has its roots in this recognition of the responsibility of the teacher for what is learned. Those who are jealous of their teaching role are prone to ignore this as they also tend to ignore the requirements of the learner's personhood. There is a sense in which a teacher should seek to make him/herself redundant. Failure to do so carries with it a heavy responsibility.

Given the close relations between teaching and learning, any discussion of one without some consideration of the other is bound to be incomplete. Yet curiously, the flood of books and papers on the concept of teaching has been accompanied by a mere trickle on learning. We are better served by books and papers on the psychology of learning and cognitive development, though much of that reeks of behaviourism.[18] Here, as elsewhere, our preoccupation with *technique* (in Jacques Ellul's sense[19]) shows through. In the case of teaching and learning, it frequently amounts to little more than not-so-well disguised manipulation.[20]

The variety of things that may be taught is matched (not surprisingly) by a similar variety in what may be learned. To use a standard classification, teaching and learning may be propositional, performative or dispositional – a classification sometimes roughly marked as teaching/learning *that*, teaching/learning *how to* and teaching/learning *to*. Here we need not exercise ourselves over the adequacy of this classification, though it is of some importance to note that these different dimensions of learning are closely interrelated. There are not three (or more) senses of 'learn' that need to be explicated; the same point is being made, even if the objects are different.

A much-debated issue concerns the relation between learning and knowing, an issue which has implications for teaching no less than learning. If, as some argue, learning implies knowing, and knowing presupposes the correctness of what is known, then teaching involves the passing on of what is correct. This connection is not lost on Israel Scheffler:

> Any teaching is geared to what the teacher takes to be true .... In so far as the teacher is teaching, he is, in any event, risking his own particular truth judgments.[21]

Yet, as Scheffler himself recognises, making the connection too tight overlooks the 'obvious fact' that many of the things we learn (and are taught) turn out to be false. His solution is to distinguish two senses of 'learn', a 'pedagogical' sense ('In school I learned that X'), in which the correctness of what is learned is not implied, and a 'discovery' sense ('Following extensive inquiries it was learned that X'), in which the correctness of what is learned is implied. If Scheffler is right, then the sense of 'learn' which is associated with 'teach' does not imply the truth of what is learned, even if, as he argues, teaching is 'geared to what the teacher takes to be true'.

35

Scheffler has a point here, but I do not think he has managed to appreciate it fully. The problem , I believe, is this. 'Learn' looks in two directions. On the one side, it looks towards the teaching transaction, where it indicates that as a result of A's responsible doing, B came by X. Inasmuch as 'learn' is used in the context of teaching, it indicates that A has brought about an understanding in B for which A must take some responsibility. But 'learn' is not restricted to such contexts. Not all learning requires teaching. And here a major focus is on the correctness of what is learned. Were this not the case, the concept's point would vanish. Learning is an agent-based concept which, among other things, reflects an interest in acting effectively in the world, an interest likely to be satisfied only if our ways of understanding the world are realistic. On our part, therefore, there is a presumption that what we have learned is correct. When I say 'I learned ____X'[22] I do not imply any likelihood that I may be wrong (although of course I may be wrong). In avowing that one has learned something, one is staking one's reputation, putting one's credibility on the line.[23] One is taking responsibility for what one says. The complication in the case of teacher-based learning is that the correctness and effectiveness criteria may become separated. Although teaching (to retain its point) must be 'geared to the truth', not everything that is taught is correct and that of course implies that not everything that is learned is correct. We try to accommodate this by using distinctive locutions: 'What I learned from A was wrong' makes better sense than 'What I have learned from A was wrong.' And sometimes we try to take refuge by switching our talk from what we learned to what we were taught. We are locating responsibility for what we previously believed and indicating that we are no longer willing to back it. The point, then, is that in so far as there are two senses of 'learn', this is because of a breakdown in our transactions such that the point of teaching, viz. someone's learning (what is correct), is not fully realised.

Understanding and behaviourism

The statement form 'I have learned ____X' implies more than (belief in) the correctness of X. It implies: 'I know ____X'. The significance of this implication is that it indicates on my part an *understanding* of X. I have not acquired X by mere rote.[24] The correctness of X is not fortuitous on my part. This is implicit in Scheffler's account of teaching:

> To teach, in the standard sense, is at some points at least to submit oneself to the understanding and independent judgment of the

pupil, to his demand for reasons, to his sense of what constitutes an adequate explanation.[25]

If teaching implies learning, then it also implies on the part of the learner some understanding or appreciation of X. That understanding may not be as great as we would like, and it may be deeply infected by ideological factors, and to that extent represent a misunderstanding of X. But misunderstanding is a form of understanding nevertheless.

This linking of learning with understanding shows up the crucial weakness in behaviourist accounts of teaching and learning. Typically, behaviourist accounts analyse learning in terms of some stable behavioural change brought about in response to some situation encountered by the organism. Teaching is directed to some determinate behavioural outcome, and the achievement of that outcome is seen not simply as evidence of learning but as its substance.[26] The virtue of such accounts is supposed to lie in their amenability to 'scientific measurement'. Such accounts fail completely. The behavioural changes (if they occur) do not constitute but rather express or exhibit what is learned. The learning is characterised by understanding, and for this there may be no behavioural equivalents, except, perhaps, in the most attenuated sense (e.g. 'corresponding' neural processes).[27] Even in cases where the learning does imply some performance (learning to drive a car, and not merely learning how to), there is implied not only an understanding of what is being done but also certain standards of performance: not *any* way of driving the car counts as having learned to drive it. Behavioural changes, more often than not, are simply evidence that one has learned; maybe one would doubt the claim if no behavioural change was forthcoming when it was appropriate for it to do so, but this is still a long way from translating learning into behavioural changes. Indeed, to attempt such translation is to obscure the distinction between 'stable behavioural changes' that are learned from those that are not. Drugs, disease and electric shock treatment may all occasion 'stable behavioural changes', but they do not thereby bring about learning.

Conclusion

If teachers are serious about their task, they will be serious not only about producing 'the right responses' in those they 'teach'; they will also be concerned to encourage that kind of understanding which is appropriate to knowledge; and that will involve an encouragement of critical appraisal, experimentation, etc. It must be a form of understanding which allows for overcoming not simply the failure to understand but also misunderstanding. However, it is very clear from the way in which most 'educational' institutions are structured, and the methods which they employ in 'teaching', that this kind of understanding is given minimal encouragement, or, if encouraged, is deeply ideological in that the tools of criticism are placed beyond criticism. For example, teaching by means of discrete and separate subjects, with little attempt to indicate and explore connections, teaching which keeps what is learned at the level of academic knowledge because no ability to apply what is learned has been taught, teaching which takes subjects and syllabus for granted and recognises criticism only at the level of internal detail, teaching via methods which sacrifice understanding to performance on the basis that alternatives are 'time-wasting' - all these features of present-day schooling mask the world rather than reveal it, and in so doing remove control over their lives from those who learn. Of course, teachers alone are not responsible for this, for their behaviour has been partly structured by the institution whose servants they now are. Responsibility belongs also to those whose interests have been embedded in the 'educational' edifice, and, to a lesser extent, those outside who might but fail to do anything about it.

NOTES

1. P.H. Hirst, 'What is Teaching?' in R.S. Peters (ed.), *The Philosophy of Education*, London: O.U.P., 1973, pp.166-67.
2. There are a few mavericks - e.g. B.P.Komisar - but their arguments have not carried conviction. See P. Dietl, 'Teaching, Learning and Knowing', *Educational Philosophy and Theory*, V, 2 (October, 1973), 3-4; W.F. Hare, 'Unsuccessful Teaching', *Educational Philosophy and Theory*, I, 2 (October, 1969), 56.
3. See *supra*, Ch. 1.
4. To restrict teaching to what is intended confers conceptual status on the individualistic ethic which pervades so many of our social relations. What we do in a responsibility-bearing way is not limited by what we intend.
5. Dietl, 3.
6. Though no doubt it might in a particular context.
7. H. Freeman, 'The Concept of Teaching', *Proceedings of the Philosophy of Education Society of Great Britain*, VII, 1 (January, 1973), 9.
8. ibid.
9. A term inspired by J.L. Austin's language of perlocutions in *How to do things with words*.
10. Freeman, 18. Freeman is wrong to suggest that actions cannot be unintentional.
11. Hirst, p.173. Dietl puts it somewhat more acceptably when he says that what is done must be the 'proximate

cause' of learning (Dietl, 3).

12. Hirst, p.173. Hirst seems to waver on this point, for on p.174 he goes on to allow that 'we are strongly inclined to think there could be teaching even when the present state of the pupils is grossly misjudged.'

13. J.D. Marshall, 'The Concept of Teaching', *Proceedings of the Philosophy of Education Society of Great Britain*, IX (July, 1975), 105–18.

14. ibid., 116.

15. G. Ryle, *The Concept of Mind*, London: Hutchinson, 1949, pp.150–53.

16. ibid., p.150.

17. The usefulness of such an enterprise has been questioned by C.K. Harris, 'Conceptual Analysis and the Concept of "Teaching"', *Forum of Education*, XXXIII, 1 (March, 1974), 65–79.

18. A useful introduction to theories of cognitive development is J. Langer, *Theories of Development*, New York: Holt, Rinehart & Winston, 1969. A philosophical critique of a number of such theories can be found in D.W. Hamlyn, *Experience and the Growth of Understanding*, London: Routledge & Kegan Paul, 1978.

19. Stated by R.K. Merton as referring to 'any complex of standardised means for attaining a pre-determined result' (in his foreword to Ellul's *The Technological Society*, New York: Vintage, 1964, p.vi). Ellul explains it as 'the totality of methods rationally arrived at and having absolute efficiency (for a given state of development) in every field of human activity' (p.xxv).

20. This also lies behind John Holt's rejection of 'education'. See his *Instead of Education : Ways to Help People do Things Better*, New York: E.P. Dutton, 1976.

21. I.Scheffler, *Conditions of Knowledge*, Chicago: Scott, Foresman & Co., 1966, p.13.

22. This schematic representation is intended to be neutral with regard to learning that/how to and /to.

23. A point derived from J.L. Austin's discussion of 'know' (in 'Other Minds'), and impressively argued for 'learn' by Dietl (9ff).

24. So called 'rote-learning', I shall argue in Ch.4, is better thought of as 'rote-memorisation'.

25. I. Scheffler, *The Language of Education*, Springfield, Ill.: C.C. Thomas, 1960, p.57.

26. The influence of behaviourism on curriculum theory can be seen in the writings of Ralph Tyler and Hilda Taba. See *infra*, Ch.12.

27. On understanding, see J.R. Martin, *Explaining, Understanding and Teaching*, New York: McGraw-Hill, 1970; H.G. Petrie, 'Learning With Understanding', in J.R. Martin (ed.), *Readings in the Philosophy of*

Education, Boston: Allyn & Bacon, 1970, pp.106–21; R.G.Woods, 'Understanding and Education', *Educational Philosophy and Theory*, IV, 2 (October, 1972), 1–16.

Chapter 4
TEACHING AND RELATED CONCEPTS

Human learning takes place in a social context, facilitated
and to a large extent structured by the activities and
practices of others. Some of the things we learn are picked
up as a result of our own initiatives, but a good deal of
our early life is spent learning from the initiatives of
others. The contexts for this vary from fairly informal
peer group and family relationships to the formal and highly
structured environment of most secondary schools. Within
such contexts, what is learned is generally thought of as
being taught - whether intentionally or otherwise. The
means whereby this teaching occurs are various: example,
dialogue, instruction, demonstration, practical involvement,
and so on. The enormous technological advances and growth
of industrialisation which have characterised the past
century have led to increasing institutionalisation of the
learning process. Preoccupation with learning theory in
psychology has been matched by a preoccupation with teaching
techniques in education. The virtues and/or vices of
instruction, discovery techniques, training, drilling,
conditioning and indoctrination are perennial topics in
handbooks and conferences on teaching. It is probably true
to say that our vocabulary of teaching is (still) dominated
by the schooling context, and that this is (still) heavily
committed to certain routinised forms and procedures. These
usually ascribe a dominant role to the teacher. Techniques
of teaching are seen very largely in terms of *doing
something to others* rather than in terms of *getting others to
do something for themselves*. Even though teaching
implies learning, and 'successful' techniques will involve
a certain active understanding on the part of those who
learn, the level of activity, and its capacity for
self-motivated elaboration, is often not very high.

But there has also been a long tradition of opposition
to teacher dominance, and this has endeavoured to give
greater weight to what is taken to be the child's natural
curiosity. Especially in the post-war period, rapid social

change has made some of the traditional rigidified techniques of teaching less appropriate to social demands, and in primary schools at least there has been increasing resort to so-called discovery methods of learning (teaching). This shift away from traditional techniques has not gone unchallenged. In this chapter, we will look at some of the most commonly discussed forms and techniques of institutionalised teaching, particularly in relation to their educative value. To the extent that these forms and techniques predominate in schools and are educationally problematic, we will be able to make some judgment on the educational rationale normally advanced on behalf of these institutions.

Instruction

The terms 'instructor' and 'teacher' are frequently used interchangeably, and it is probably reasonable to say that the most characteristic technique and image of teaching is instruction. Yet if the arguments of the previous chapter are broadly acceptable, instruction and teaching are not to be identified. For one thing, instruction is only one teaching technique. Besides instruction, a person may teach by means of gesture, demonstration, showing slides, hints, discussion, encouraging self-help, puzzles, taking people on excursions, and so on. More importantly, while teaching actually results in learning, instruction may not necessarily do so. Instruction is at best a technique whereby learning *may* be brought about. Someone who is trying unsuccessfully to instruct others is not someone who is failing to bring about learning so much as someone whose efforts fail to express the criteria for instructing - e.g. because continually interrupted or shouted down.

As a technique, instruction would seem to possess at least two distinctive features:

(1) It is difficult to conceive of instruction without *verbalisation* of some sort. One instructs by means of language. It may be spoken - as in a lecture - or written - as in an instruction manual. This being the case, it presupposes a certain minimum of intellectual development on the part of the instructee. One trains rather than gives instruction to an animal or very young child. Unless it is supposed that the instructee can *understand* a language, the verbal form in which instruction is cast can function only as a stimulus to some conditioned response.

(2) Clearly, verbalisation is not sufficient to pick out instruction as a teaching technique or form of presentation. Discussion also involves verbalisation, but does not constitute instruction. In instruction there is a *directness* with which information is presented which is not

shared by other verbal techniques. The person learns by following what the instructor says. He/she does not *have to* engage in independent thinking of his/her own. The form in which the material is presented by the instructor is the form in which it is intended to be learned by the instructee. This of course does not rule out all thinking or understanding. However, unlike teaching through questioning, discussion, discovery methods, written assignments, and so on, teaching through instruction does not generally require a high level of mental application on the part of the learner.

Instruction is frequently criticised for the minimal demands it makes on instructees. This need not be the case, but generally is, since the instructor does not usually see what is being conveyed as requiring anything more than absorption by the instructee. Were more thought necessary, it is unlikely that instruction would constitute the mode of presentation. At least it would not constitute the predominant mode of presentation. Instruction easily encourages a form of intellectual passivity on the part of the learner. This of course is well suited to the labour market's demand for 'informed', obedient workers. It is not as obviously suited to the development of those capacities which enable people to take the initiative as responsible actors.

This points to what is probably the most significant problem concerning instruction: the status presumed for what is conveyed by it. Because of its formal limitations as a technique, instruction is generally geared to the imparting of information. In that form, there is implied a certain finality about what is presented. It is put forward as material which is stable, objective, and valuable, requiring only to be accepted. If there is any doubt about what is conveyed, it is not for the instructee to express that doubt, except at second-hand. The instructee is placed in rigid subservience to 'the expert'. Because of its tendency to discourage questions about what is conveyed, the instructional technique obscures the extent to which knowledge/information, and the importance given to pieces of it, is a social product - a reflection of the interaction of human beings with their environment and not a simple mirroring of reality. The 'giveness' and ranking of facts are at best provisional, in so far as they come to be represented in a communicable form. The growth/revision of knowledge is not simply a function of more and more sophisticated techniques of detection, but of the theoretical and practical concerns which direct attention and which structure and evaluate what is found by means of such techniques. Instruction, therefore, tends to possess a conservative function as far as the growth and dissemination of knowledge is concerned. It tends to represent as given what is inherently contestable. This is not to deny it a place - even a proper place - in the repertoire of teaching techniques, but it is meant to suggest that as far as growth and discernment in knowledge is concerned, it should play a supplementary rather than a dominant role. Taken in conjunction with techniques which stress the activity and autonomy of the learner, it may perform a valuable function.

There are some situations, however, in which instruction would seem to be eminently suitable and highly desirable as a significant part of teaching procedure. These are situations which focus on the teaching of a limited range of routines and skills - as in the use of a particular piece of machinery or in using the resources of a library. *Taken in conjunction with* demonstration and practical involvement, instruction can be an economical and effective means of conveying an understanding of the rationale and employment of such procedures. It is, perhaps, mostly in such contexts that we speak of instructors (driving instructors, army instructors, etc.). At the same time, it needs to be recognised that only a small (even if important) portion of learning which is constitutive of education can be accomplished by instructional techniques. Unless the skills learned - e.g. the use of library resources - are able to be effectively utilised, little of educational worth will be achieved. It is much to the discredit of schooling as an educational device that so much of the teaching activity is instructional in form. [1]

Learning by discovery

As a technique of teaching, instruction is frequently contrasted with 'learning by discovery'. Taken at face value, there is of course a conceptual asymmetry between them. While instruction *may* result in learning, 'learning by discovery' *necessarily* does. One may instruct in what is believed to be false, but one can discover only what is believed to be true. However, it is clear that the proponents of discovery methods do not intend this asymmetry. As a technique, 'discovery methods' operate in the hope or expectation of discovery. For present purposes we shall assume that they are symmetrical as teaching techniques.

The supposed contrast between instruction and discovery methods is variously stated. The former is said to be characteristic of traditional schooling, the latter of progressive. The former is said to be content-centred, the latter child-centred. The former is said to be direct, the latter indirect. The former is said to be dogmatic, the latter open-ended. At best, these express tendencies, but they may be roughly represented in terms of the rationale behind them. This is that teaching ought to engage the active involvement of learners as much as possible. It is for this reason that discovery methods are not as direct as instructional techniques. For the same reason, it is not possible to delineate discovery methods with the same degree of exactness that is possible with instruction. The relevant discoveries may be accomplished through library research, discussion, questioning, direct observation of the world around one, and so on. However, in so far as discovery methods are seen as methods of teaching, they differ from research, which, though it may be supervised, does not presuppose a teacher.

The use of discovery methods has been thought advantageous to the teaching-learning situation in a number of ways. First, both the quality and quantity of learning is thought to be improved where learners are not passive recipients of information, but are actively involved in following out ideas, constructing hypotheses, looking for connections, etc. Secondly, it is argued that discovery carries its own satisfaction, and becomes a strong motivation to learning, thus diminishing the need for extrinsic motivations of the reward/punishment kind. Thirdly, it is suggested that the problem-solving techniques developed through discovery learning permit of extension to other areas of inquiry/practice. And finally, it is claimed that what is learned through the kind of participation involved in discovery methods is retained better than what is learned through instruction. For the success of discovery methods depends on connections perceived by the learner, whereas this is not required of material learned through instruction.

However, these advantages may be less real than is supposed. First of all, there is a great deal of variation in so-called discovery methods. At one extreme, there is an almost completely unstructured situation in which people are more or less left to find out things for themselves. Neither problems nor methodology nor data is provided, except, perhaps, in response to a specific request from the learner. At the other extreme, the problems, methodology and data are provided and it is left to the learner only to apply the methodology to the data in a stereotyped fashion for the problems to be solved. In general, discovery methods tend toward the latter end of the spectrum. Teachers usually have a firm view of the 'right' answers and of how to obtain them, but wish their students to 'find them out for themselves'. And, on reflection, it would appear that the 'effectiveness' of discovery methods depends largely on the prior setting-up of the learning situation by the teacher. In Jerome Bruner's words, 'discovery, like surprise, favours the well prepared mind'.[2] Unless this occurs, the situation is, at least in the case of younger people, likely to remain intractably ambiguous. However, as soon as we admit this, we can see that discovery methods, despite the suggestion of freedom they contain, tend to be circumscribed by the initial conditions. Thus, while they

45

may be psychologically beneficial to learning, they *may* not escape the charge of conservatism which is so easily levelled at instruction. Indeed, in so far as the constraints in discovery methods are less visible, giving, perhaps, only an illusion of freedom, they may in this respect be less desirable than instruction.

This possible conservatism in so-called discovery methods (as distinct from the discovery which may emerge from research), can be brought out by a consideration of their effectiveness. If their effectiveness is thought of in terms of certain practical benefits - such as the learner's self-confidence, his/her ability to engage in effective action, etc., then we have a reasonably clear and acceptable basis for evaluating them. However, if their effectiveness is thought of in terms of their informational value, that is, in terms of their ability to impart a specific content, we are put in the position where this will be judged by the correspondence of what is 'discovered' with the views of the teacher or observer. This may be relatively benign in mathematics, but beyond that judgments of effectiveness in terms of informational value become increasingly tendentious. It may be more difficult to reassess what one has learned via discovery methods than what one has learned via instruction.

When looked at in actual classroom contexts, additional problems may emerge. It is sometimes argued that discovery methods are most effective in a mass teaching situation, whereas their effectiveness in a one-to-one situation is less obvious. Sometimes this is put down to the competitive nature of the classroom situation, with students vying for the 'honour of discovery'. In so far as this is the case, the argument from intrinsic motivation loses much of its initial plausibility. Further, within such situations it has been observed that even when thought most successful, discovery methods inspire the participation of only a limited number of those in the class. Poor competitors or those not competitively oriented may withdraw from the contest. Where this occurs, the stratifying and alienating effect of institutionalised schooling is reinforced. What is inspiring for some, positively disadvantages others.

There is no *need* for discovery methods to have this kind of effect. More than instructional techniques, they offer much greater opportunities for co-operative or 'dialogical' learning. Such learning, apart from being more effective,[3] gives a more realistic picture of the growth of knowledge than the image of the individual entrepreneur so often presented as the norm. Even exceptional talent usually flourishes in co-operative ventures with others, rather than in isolation. Unfortunately, most schools are not geared to co-operative learning. Especially after primary school, when the institution becomes more obviously shaped to the certification and stratification requirements of a competitive technologically orientated society, co-operative effort, except of a minimal kind, tends to be actively discouraged. There is a curious paradox in this. For even in a learning situation oriented to individual rather than co-operative effort, those who do well are frequently those whose work is most reliant on others (their teachers, textbooks, references, etc.). Academically, there is something bizarre about excluding from what is finally produced for assessment the insights and work of one's peers.

A final point, of a quasi-empirical kind, relates to the retention value of discovery methods. Whether what is learned by discovery techniques is more likely to be retained would seem to depend, not simply on the technique, but on the assimilation of what is learned into the broader cognitive perspective of the learner. As Friedlander observes, 'the student's pleasure at going beyond the evidence to perceive a truth is likely to be little more than a passing fancy if the experience is not followed by a process of synthesising in which the new idea or fact is incorporated into a systematic context'.[4]

In other words, no blanket case can be made for discovery methods independently of some particular specification of the input involved and background against which they are being employed. The apparent advantages in increasing involvement in learning, acknowledging and encouraging autonomy, the provision of co-operative opportunities, etc. may be nullified by the stratifying effect of a classroom, their use in relation to content which is not connected with people's interests and broader perspectives, and a hidden conservatism which can creep into the initial conditions.[5]

Drilling

A less commonly but by no means rarely used classroom technique, particularly at younger levels, is drilling.[6] Involved in drilling is the repetition of stereotyped exercises. These exercises may, but need not, be verbal: certain kinds of physical exercise are referred to as drill. Unlike instruction, drill does not require (at least in every instance) verbalisation on the part of the 'teacher': drilling may be done to music or signals as well as in response to verbal cues. Also unlike instruction, drilling does involve some form of active participation on the part of those drilled. However, this does not necessarily indicate a greater degree of intellectual or cognitive involvement.

If there is a tenuous relationship between instructing and educating because of the quality of learning which instruction often tends to encourage, that between drilling and education is even more tenuous. As with instruction, drilling is agnostic with respect to the value of what is drilled. However drilling, even more than instruction, tends to overlook the need for rational appreciation and understanding. The mastery that it provides is very limited. But then, for the most part, so is its employment. It is more naturally associated with training and simple skills than with knowledge and creative autonomy. It becomes pernicious if this is not realised. Drilling which is not supplemented with explanation is likely to result only in parrotting or mindless routines. For this reason it is often associated with conditioning (when the object is behaviour) and indoctrination (when the object is belief).

It might be protested that these comments on drilling charge it with being what it is not intended to be. The point of drilling as a technique, it may be argued, is as an aid to memory (in the case of beliefs) and facility (in the case of behaviour). Thus, when we 'drill something into someone', the emphasis is on impressing something on someone's mind (i.e. the retention of knowledge or the facilitating of skill) rather than on bringing that person to new knowledge, understanding or skill.

There is some point to this protest. Yet it is not irrelevant to ask why drilling has had such an important role in the schooling of the young. To defend the possible usefulness of drilling is not to defend the actual use of drilling. Do repetitious drill performances constitute the only means by which information is retained or practice is encouraged? Or does the resort to such techniques reflect the irrelevance of what is taught - its lack of connection with the perceived needs and interests of those who are subjected to it? Practice, indeed, makes perfect, but drill is merely the husk of practice, since the latter, unlike the former, requires a focusing of attention on what is being done, a concentration of effort coupled with critical appraisal. There is some reason to think that the need for drilling is, for the most part, a judgment on what is being drilled - not necessarily in itself, but at least in the form and circumstances in which it is being presented.

The resort to drilling may also reflect structural defects in the 'education system'. Where class sizes are large, and the atmosphere unconducive to co-operative and constructive interaction, drilling provides an easy way out. As every army officer knows, regimentation is the key to control. In the context of a hierarchical structure such as a school, regimentation thus provides for ease of control. At the same time it helps to develop those habits of submission to authority which will later be so vital to the maintenance of the dominant social *status quo.*

Training

Teaching and training are often run together. They are both

48

perficiences: both imply some result in the one taught or trained. Nevertheless, the focus of training tends to be narrower than that of teaching. The objects of training are habits, skills, responses, routines, and the like. Training thus tends to be more *directly* connected with behaviour or performances than with independent mastery, the acquisition of knowledge and understanding. We train seals and dogs. Perhaps we can teach them too, though it is less speculative to speak of training them, since the intellectual component in the learning which their training requires tends to be very limited. It is more a learning of responses than an acquisition of a knowledgeable understanding of what they are doing. This limited reference to an intellectual component is reflected in our willingness to talk of training plants, such as roses or creepers. We speak of training them since they adapt in a fairly permanent way to our manipulations of them. We cannot teach them, however, since they cannot learn. Some training of course does presuppose understanding - training in skills, for example - since its object requires discrimination and judgment on the part of its possessor.

People are trained in or to do certain fairly narrowly prescribed things. Thus drilling may sometimes be an effective vehicle of training. This narrowness helps to distinguish training from education. The move from 'teacher training' to 'teacher education', even if it is little more than a change of nomenclature and papering over of the cracks, is intended to convey a change in understanding and competence. The teacher, so the rhetoric goes, is to be seen less as a skilled operator, and more as an autonomous, innovative and understanding catalyst for the development of young selves. Alas, the greater flexibility and resourcefulness is often little more than an expression of the workplace's need for a more malleable product.

The direct emphasis on performance may seem to be belied by talk of training the mind or character training. But even in these cases the emphasis is on the development of skills, albeit mental, or consistency in behaviour of a certain kind. A trained mind may well be indoctrinated and the trained character is all too often mechanical.

The foregoing observations are not intended to suggest an incompatibility between training and education. There is of course a sense of 'education' in which it is used synonymously with 'training'. But even in its primary critical use an educated person may also be trained - indeed, in certain areas, is quite likely to be so. However, education is a richer notion, embodying a wider range of development and a greater capacity for independent action than is accommodated by training, and embodying a standard of selection which does not attach to training. A person can be trained as a thug, but not, I take it, educated as one. [7]

This last example warns us against assuming that, because some training may be compatible with and even contributory to education, all training is. In the schooling context anti-educative training is naturally more subtle. Pupils are trained in habits of uncritical obedience, conformity, and in mental skills which encourage little intellectual integration (the separation of disciplines), limited critical ability (teacher, at least, is right), and a divorce of life from thought (the externally organised syllabus needing to be covered for examination purposes). It is not, therefore, enough to say that there is more to education than training, for some training may inhibit education.

Conditioning

The term 'conditioning' has come into popular use through the technical vocabulary of psychology. Generally two kinds of conditioning are distinguished. Classical (or respondent) conditioning, generally associated with Pavlov, refers to an association which is formed between a stimulus and a particular response as a result of its repeated presentation contiguous with another stimulus (putatively unconditioned) which produces that response. Conditioning has taken place when the response can be elicited simply on presentation of the 'artificial' stimulus. It is generally agreed that classical conditioning, if it occurs at all, does so only in a limited number of cases.

In cases where classical conditioning might be involved, no recourse to ideas of rationality or understanding is required. Conditioning, like training, is connected with what might be broadly called behaviour; but whereas training may have regard to skills, techniques, etc., classical conditioning is limited to responses or reflexes. The learning and exercise of skills and the utilisation of techniques exhibit a degree of understanding on the part of their possessor; conditioning bypasses rationality and understanding altogether. It does not manifest agency. This means of course that classical conditioning can hardly be considered a method of teaching, since teaching implies learning, and even learning of a minimal sort requires some wittingness on the part of the learner. There is an active participation in learning which is absent in the formation of conditioned responses – though of course one could learn that one had been conditioned to respond to a particular stimulus. If we wish to speak of a conditioned response as a learned response, we need to recognise that not much more is meant than 'not innate'.

The second kind of conditioning, much favoured in educational circles, is known as operant (or instrumental) conditioning. It has its origins in the work of B.F. Skinner. Here, desired behaviour is reinforced by a stimulus which it produces. For this to occur the stimulus must be seen as in some sense desirable. Here the subject does not merely respond to a stimulus, but acts to reproduce it by repeating the behaviour.

It may be wondered why operant conditioning is so called. Hamlyn argues that whereas there is an essentially mechanical connection between stimulus and response in the case of classical conditioning, in the case of operant conditioning the subject must recognise 'that a certain state of affairs is desirable to it and that this state of affairs will be brought about by what it does'.[8] For this reason, the terminology of 'conditioning' is misleading. A.J. Watson, in reply, allows that there are substantial differences between the two, but claims that this may be accounted for as a difference in the complexity of the mechanisms involved. Thus, with regard to the subjective conditions postulated by Hamlyn, these may be essential to our *identification* of the learner's actions, but not to their *explanation*.[9] However, the identification of what is learned cannot be separated from its explanation in this way. In so far as the explanation is an explanation of the agent's actions and not just some unidentified movements, we need to see the way in which the agent sees what he/she is doing. By retaining the language of conditioning within learning theory we thus invite confusion.

But it has even more unfortunate effects. If learning is viewed as conditioning – even operant conditioning – it encourages 'teaching' which is manipulative rather than rational. Emphasis on the reinforcement of desired behaviour deflects attention from the rationality both of the behaviour and of the subject's engagement in it. Operant conditioning presupposes a teaching context in which what the teacher presents is true, to be assimilated by the learner in a non-critical manner. 'Wrong' responses get no or negative re-inforcement; 'right' responses are positively reinforced. Furthermore, this positive reinforcement need not take the form of confirmation (the accumulation of additional evidence), but may consist simply of approval and other question-begging devices. That these manipulative, elitist and non-rational tendencies underlie the theory of operant conditioning is well-illustrated by Skinner's own application of the idea in *Beyond Freedom and Dignity*.[10] There, autonomy is devalued in favour of a none-too-clear (human?) happiness (determined by whom?), to be realised with the aid of the carrot of operant conditioning.

Conclusion

Our purpose in this chapter has been largely negative. We have looked briefly at a variety of techniques and practices commonly found in the context of schooling, and have

51

endeavoured to bring out the ways in which they might be anti-educative. They do not by any means exhaust the range of techniques and practices which might be associated with teaching, and in the case of discovery methods at least, our discussion has only hinted at the vast range of activities which might come under that head, some of which are of central importance to educationally valuable learning. Dialogue, experimentation, questioning, criticism and training in the use of resources should all have an important place in the teacher's vocabulary, and though the structure of schooling is such that severe limitations are necessarily placed on these activities and perficiences, their utilisation at least offers some hope that the constraints of schooling will not be permanently binding or damaging.

NOTES

1. Before passing on, we should, perhaps, note an ambiguity in 'instruction' - or perhaps an extension of meaning. 'Instruction' is sometimes used in contexts in which there is no intention to teach. If Alice Jones instructs Bill Smith to do something, she is giving orders, not attempting to foster learning. 'Instruction' in this sense presupposes a position of authority or superiority, but in this case one of status rather than knowledge. It is only when Alice Jones instructs Bill Smith *in* something that there is an intention to bring about learning. Sometimes 'instruction' is used in a sense mid-way between the two we have outlined. The 'instructions' which accompany an appliance are generally framed in an imperative mood, but at the same time are intended to teach us how to use the appliance.

2. J.S. Bruner, 'The Act of Discovery' in R.C. Anderson & D.P. Ausubel (eds.), *Readings in the Psychology of Cognition*, New York: Holt, Rinehart & Winston, 1965, p.607.

3. See D.H. Russell, *Children Learn to Read*[2], Waltham, Mass.: Blaisdell, 1961; W.J. McHugh, 'Teams Learning in Skill Subjects in Intermediate Grades', *Journal of Education*, CXLII (December, 1959), 22-51.

4. B.Z. Friedlander, 'A Psychologist's Second Thoughts on Concepts, Curiosity, and Discovery in Teaching and Learning', *Harvard Educational Review*, XXXV, *1* (Winter, 1965), 28.

5. This last point is frequently made in radical critiques of 'free' or 'progressive' schooling. See R. Sharp & A. Green, *Education and Social Control : A Study in Progressive Primary Education*, London: Routledge & Kegan Paul, 1975.

6. 'The scriptural method of educating children is teaching

by rote, memorising and learning from the examples of history, especially Bible history which was written for our admonition' (Rona Joyner, in *STOP Press*, IV, 1, p.6; quoted in J. Freeland, 'STOP! CARE to COME and PROBE the Right—Wing', *Radical Education Dossier*, No. 8 (Autumn, 1979), 5).

7. The reasons for this should become clearer in *infra*, Ch.6.
8. D.W. Hamlyn, 'Conditioning and Behaviour', in R. Borger & F. Cioffi (eds.), *Explanation in the Behavioural Sciences*, Cambridge U.P., 1970, p.147.
9. A.J. Watson, 'Comment', in Borger & Cioffi, p.160.
10. New York: Knopf, 1971; see *infra*, Ch.7.

Chapter 5

INDOCTRINATION

Much of what purports to be education is charged with being indoctrination. It is implied that the two are incompatible. Though both involve (but are not simply reducible to) the acquisition of beliefs and attitudes (a feature which generally serves to distinguish indoctrination from classical conditioning), indoctrination, unlike education, is given a negative evaluation. Just how this evaluation is to be seen in relation to the concept of indoctrination is a point about which there is some dispute. Is indoctrination something like killing – generally regarded as a bad thing – but in no way so by definition? Or is it more like murder, which picks out killing of a particularly despicable kind, and which cannot be defined without reference to normative considerations? The issue is somewhat confused by etymological and historical factors. There is no doubt a use of 'indoctrination' in which it means little more than the inculcation of attitudes, beliefs, doctrines or teachings (cf. the *Oxford English Dictionary*), a use which still has some currency in certain military contexts (an indoctrination programme may be seen as a desirable part of a soldier's training). Where so used, the goodness or badness of indoctrination awaits additional information. But that is not the use which has figured in contemporary educational discussion, and which we shall be considering here. As used in contemporary discussion, the disvalue of indoctrination is built into the very concept.

This latter point has not always been recognised, even by those who see indoctrination as uniformly bad. According to a particular variety of analytic philosophy, analyses of concepts must be neutral with respect to normative considerations. But this is to overlook the fact that normative considerations generate many of our concepts in the first place, determining their 'logical geography'. They are not a subsequent 'overlay'. The analysis of indoctrination, then, reveals not only its boundaries, but also those considerations which constitute it the undesirable practice that it is.

However, we should note that the normativeness of indoctrination does not show all indoctrination to be wrong, any more than the normativeness of lying shows that all lying is wrong. It does, however, place an onus on the indoctrinator or liar to show why his/her behaviour should not be condemned.[1] Some have claimed that in certain cases this challenge can be met. Thus J.S. Brubacher, summarising what he calls the 'scholastic realist' position in education, reports:

> The immutability of truth and goodness lays yet a further imperative upon the teacher. If he is imparting what is unmistakable and eternal truth or what are well-known essentials, it will be legitimate for him to indoctrinate. He will even be inclined to this procedure where there is uncertainty as to the final form of truth or goodness, for then his duty will be to pass on the most approved view to date. To let a youth arrive at his own conclusions independently may result in an extravagant waste of time, to say nothing of his running the risk of failing to put in at the proper port at the end. If this method of instruction seems to disregard minority or contrary opinions, suffice it to say that the truth, if it really is *the* truth, must be intolerant of error.[2]

Here it is not being suggested that indoctrination is normatively neutral, but that when it comes to essential truths, it is more important that they be held than that they be held rationally. Whether this is so is something we shall come back to later.

If, as we have suggested, the concept of indoctrination is partially constituted by those characteristics which make it undesirable, the task of analysing the concept takes on greater significance than is acknowledged in some of the now extensive literature on the subject. Within that literature, four (not necessarily exclusive) ways of isolating the concept have been suggested: reference to the (1) content, (2) methods, (3) intentions, or (4) outcome of what is communicated to others. It will be my contention that the last of these is conceptually central, and that the other three are related only by virtue of their causal significance.

(1) *Content*

The content-criterion of indoctrination gains apparent plausibility from etymological considerations. Thus

R.S. Peters argues that 'whatever else "indoctrination" may mean it obviously has something to do with doctrines, which are a species of beliefs',[3] and J. Gribble notes that 'there is a degree of logical oddity in claiming that something is a case of "indoctrination" if it does not involve the passing on of a doctrine'.[4] A further consideration which may be urged in favour of this view is the fact that the charge of indoctrination arises most frequently in relation to those areas in which we are most willing to speak of 'doctrines' - religion, politics and morals.

The etymological argument, however, is rather weak, not simply because it is always risky to determine the meaning of a term by inspecting its etymology (cf. lunatic, from *luna* = moon), but because 'doctrine' at the time at which the term 'indoctrination' came into currency did not have the specialised meaning it now has. It referred simply to what was taught. Doctrines were scientific as well as religious. Even in our more specialised sense of 'doctrine' (as, roughly, a set of interconnected normative beliefs), it is questionable whether indoctrination can be understood simply as the teaching of doctrines. On the one hand, it is dubious whether we would want to call every passing on of doctrines indoctrination. If a group of students, as a result of extended, open discussion with their teacher, come to believe that a socialist system would be preferable to the capitalist one in which they are presently located, have they been indoctrinated? They *may* have been, though I think it just as likely that they have not. On the other hand, it would seem possible (even if slightly pointless) to indoctrinate people with beliefs that would not usually be called doctrines - a belief that the earth is flat, that all modern music is bad, that they are insignificant, and so on. Even commonly accepted moral beliefs concerning, say, the evil of rape, are not generally thought of as doctrinal in character. This is not to deny that a case could be made out for another look at these beliefs and at the term 'doctrine', to see whether a deeper connection can be traced, but it points to the need for such a case.

This deeper connection has in fact been sought by a number of writers. Thus Gribble refines the notion to characterise 'a body or set of beliefs which rest on assumptions which are either false or for which no publicly acceptable evidence is or can be provided.'[5] This suggests (contrary to the drift of Gribble's argument) that the beliefs themselves may be true even if the assumptions on which they are based are false or not known to be true (by the person who promulgates them? by anybody?). But whether or not Gribble wishes to allow this, there would seem to be substantial problems with this way of stating the connection. On the one hand, it would seem possible to indoctrinate true beliefs (or, given the difficulties with that, beliefs agreed to be true by both the indoctrinator and the person who is levelling the charge of indoctrination). Sheehan, for example, offers the following:

> Consider a case in which some American pilots are captured over North Vietnam, and are subjected by the North Vietnamese to an intensive programme of 'instruction' about the origin and development of the war, and about past U.S. policies towards Vietnam and the origin of present policies, and so on. Let us further suppose that they use the full battery of 'indoctrination' techniques – presentation of highly simplified and slanted evidence, alternating isolation and group pressure, a certain amount of physical torture, glaring lights, etc., in an attempt to get the reluctant U.S. pilots to believe their propositions. Now it is surely clear that what we have described here is a case of indoctrination, and that this judgment is not affected by the truth or falsity of what is taught.[6]

Sheehan uses this illustration not merely to counter Gribble, but also to impress his own position – the centrality of the method of teaching – and to that extent I have reservations about his example. Nevertheless, if the pilots do come to believe what is told them, it does seem clear that they will have been indoctrinated irrespective of its truth. (Whether we can say simply that they have come to *believe* what is told them, or whether we need to add that they must also have acquired new *attitudes*, is something we shall touch on later.)

On the other hand, there is some reason for thinking that the passing on of false beliefs, or at least sets of beliefs based on assumptions which are false, is not necessarily indoctrination. Were that so, then much of the science teaching of our youth should be characterised as indoctrination, since many of the assumptions we worked with were either known to be false by our teachers (who wished not to confuse us with the niceties of relativity, etc.), or have been subsequently found to be false. Even the passing on of beliefs for which no publicly acceptable evidence is or can be given (say, that quarks are the fundamental particle, that pornography is not harmful, that democratic structures are to be preferred to alternatives), is not necessarily indoctrination. In Gribble's sense of the phrase, no 'publicly acceptable evidence' is or can be given for these beliefs, since it is not true that 'anyone who tests the evidence will come to the same conclusion'.[7]

Indeed, it is difficult to think of any beliefs which would pass this test. The point to note, however, is not simply the deficiencies of Gribble's account, but the problematic character of any account which uses some 'verifiability' criterion. Not only is the specification of such criteria (however stated) inherently controversial, but adherence to a particular criterion may itself manifest indoctrination. One of the more illuminating aspects of the indoctrination controversy is the tendency to see indoctrination as something which 'they' and not 'we' do.

(2) *Methods*

As noted, Sheehan's example was designed partly to add plausibility to his view that indoctrination is to be distinguished by its methods. An immediate question raised by that example concerns how, if at all, on this view, indoctrination is to be distinguished from brainwashing. Brainwashing, it is usually claimed, is a set of techniques for altering a person's outlook or beliefs. On the methods-criterion, brainwashing is probably to be seen as a rather severe form of indoctrination, tending towards harshness and brutality (anxiety, fear, drugs, group 'analyses', enforced isolation, and so on), and more 'appropriate' to the established beliefs of adults than the more malleable minds of children. Other methods, which may not be as easily characterisable as brainwashing, are also frequently said to be indoctrinatory — e.g. propagandising, drilling, censoring, authoritarian teaching.
     The important and problematic question to ask is: What is it about particular methods which makes them indoctrinatory? A mere enumeration of methods will not do, partly because of its apparent arbitrariness, and partly because a particular method may sometimes be indoctrinatory and at other times not — e.g. drilling, sleep-teaching. Sheehan proposes the following account: Indoctrination is constituted by

> those methods which induce beliefs in a way
> which by-passes the reasoning process of the
> person to which they are applied, or coerce
> his will and are systematically applied over a
> prolonged period.[8]

But the problem here is that not all indoctrination by-passes a person's reasoning processes. Indeed, those who are most indoctrinated can generally produce an impressive defence of their position. Where they are indoctrinated with whole systems of belief it is most likely that their rational processes will be considerably exploited. Sheehan could of course reply by specifying some precise sense in which 'reasoning processes' is to be understood; but then

58

we need to notice the shift which has occurred in his account from methods to the outcome of certain methods. Sheehan's criterion allows for no simple enumeration of indoctrinatory methods since a particular method sometimes may, and sometimes may not, by-pass the person's reasoning processes. It is true that some methods are much more likely to do that than others, but this amounts only to a causal connection between indoctrination and the criterion he settles for.

Similar difficulties confront David Cooper's account, though his approach is different. Cooper terms indoctrination a 'perlocutionary-type' act (what Freeman speaks of as a perfience), but, unlike Freeman, he believes that there is still room for a 'task' and 'achievement' distinction within such acts. Using 'persuade' as an example, he claims that 'we could describe a person as persuading even if no one is persuaded.' This is possible because, as with other 'perlocutionary-type' acts, what the person is doing 'is designed to, or is likely to, result in someone's being persuaded'.[9] The same applies to 'indoctrinate'. Now, says Cooper, the only way to tell whether acts have this tendency is by taking notice of their method and manner. Thus,

> indoctrination will be identified as such by the tendency of the activities involved to produce certain effects, e.*g*., to result in non-evidentially held beliefs. And the criterion for judging that the activities have this tendency must concern the manner and method of these activities.[10]

However, I think Freeman's account is to be preferred. It is less misleading (i.e. more to the point of such terms) if we say that the person was *attempting* to persuade when he/she failed to persuade. That certain methods are more likely to result in someone's being indoctrinated is of course as much reason to condemn them as it would be if they succeeded - just as we might condemn negligent or reckless driving even though no accident occurs. But this does not require that the methods be more than causally related to the bad effects. Cooper attempts to strengthen the distinction by claiming further that

> the fact that certain results do take place does not always establish that the relevant act was performed. It may be, for example, that I say something and you are persuaded by this to join the Foreign Legion. But it would be peculiar to say that I had persuaded you, unless what I said was the sort of thing likely to persuade people.[11]

This, however, does nothing for Cooper's case. If anything, it strengthens the view that 'perlocutionary-type' acts are distinguished as embodying outcomes. What it does show, however, is the way in which we mark or negate responsibility when referring to such acts. Notice how Cooper switches from the passive 'you are persuaded' to the active 'I had persuaded you'. We could of course have just as reasonably said, 'you are persuaded *by what I said*'. This would have indicated the cause of persuasion, but without locating responsibility for it. The same no doubt may be true of indoctrination, provided that we switch to the passive voice. A person may be indoctrinated as a result of his/her contact with another, even though there was no way in which the other could have anticipated the result. The passive use is manifestly secondary. As with Sheehan's argument, Cooper's also slides towards an outcomes-criterion.

(3) *Intentions*

By far the most popular criterion of indoctrination in recent writing is that in terms of intentions. Its formulation differs from writer to writer, but the most plausible version goes somewhat as follows: a person indoctrinates if and only if he/she intends the beliefs he/she teaches to be held regardless of the evidence. It needs noting that the intentions-criterion is a somewhat unusual one – after all, not any intentions will do: only the intention to bring about certain kinds of outcomes.

Does a person have to intend to indoctrinate in order to indoctrinate? It would appear not. If, as it is frequently asserted, Western schooling often constitutes indoctrination with capitalist values, it is not very plausible to claim that this is deliberate. Teachers take such values for granted rather than deliberately endeavour to impart them. They form the context of their teaching rather than the intention. Competition, rivalry, certain kinds of material rewards, class and school organisation, the arrangement of syllabi: all manifest values which maintain the dominant capitalist *status quo*. They are (for the most part) imparted unthinkingly and absorbed uncritically.

In response, some supporters of the intentions-criterion have employed an expanded understanding of 'intention'. Snook, for example, argues that 'in the context of moral responsibility, "intention" can connote (i) what is desired, and (ii) what is foreseen as likely'.[12] This is an implausible account. For, first of all, I may intend to do something which I have no desire to do. More importantly, the extension of 'intention' to cover 'what is foreseen as likely' is illegitimate. What we foresee and what we intend are quite different, as is suggested by their objects: we foresee consequences but intend results. The latter but not the former are internal to our acts. Cooper illustrates the difference as follows:

> Suppose I try to escape from a P.O.W. camp, knowing that my capture and torture to death is a likely consequence. Still, I prefer to risk that than to rot to death as a prisoner. If Snook is right, there is a perfectly good sense of 'intend' in which I intend to be captured and tortured to death. But, of course, there is not.[13]

This does not mean that we cannot be held responsible for consequences as well as results, only that they are differently related to what we do. One source of Snook's trouble, and a reason why he thinks it plausible to stretch the meaning of 'intention', is to be found in his confusion of a technical philosophical use of the term 'intentional' (not 'intentionally') with his broader sense of the term.[14] In the technical sense, 'intentional' means, roughly, 'goal-directed' or 'rule-governed', which is both narrower and wider than the use implicit in the intentions-criterion. Another, slightly more plausible, source of Snook's confusion lies in his resort to a technical legal use of 'intention' to justify the conflation of 'intend' and 'foresee'.[15] But a technical legal use is just that, and, as H.L.A. Hart notes, is to be sharply differentiated from our ordinary use of 'intention'.[16]

Even so, may we not reformulate the intentions-criterion to avoid the objections we have raised? Take the following: a person indoctrinates if and only if he/she intends the beliefs communicated to be held regardless of the evidence, or foresees that they will be so held.

Three problems arise here:
(a) Parallel to the methods account, we need to know what makes the disjunction 'intends ... or foresees' plausible, and why further disjuncts are not allowable. In other words, we need a rationale which will show unity in duality. Such rationale as there is relates, I suspect, to the pejorative character of indoctrination. The extension is allowable only because one can be held responsible for what one foresees as the consequences of one's actions as well as for what one intends. But this rationale will permit further extensions to the one suggested since, presumably, one might negligently and hence blameworthily indoctrinate a person. Negligence requires neither intention nor foresight.
(b) It is difficult to see what is odd about speaking of unintentional (or unforeseen) indoctrination. Indeed, it would appear to be very common. Even those who have tried

to avoid it may have caused it to occur: a religious indoctrinator may see his/her activity as a *clearing away* of the mental blocks caused by sin - a freeing of the mind from indoctrinated beliefs, not their inculcation. The only thing in favour of the cruciality of intentions is the potential control they give over what is done: it is, presumably, more likely that we will succeed in indoctrinating if we intend it.

(c) A person may intend but fail to indoctrinate - if, for example, he/she has a thoroughly inadequate grasp of the psychology of his/her hearers. Despite the intention to do so, this person doesn't indoctrinate. He/she merely attempts to indoctrinate. However, it is to be noticed that this does not remove culpability, as the intentions proponent might fear. Attempts, no less than successes, may be blameworthy.

My suggestion, then, is that in so far as content, methods and intentions are related to indoctrination, and I have not wanted to deny that relation, it is because of a causal connection. The communication of certain kinds of beliefs, attitudes, etc., the use of certain methods of communication, and the possession of certain intentions all render it more likely - perhaps very likely - that indoctrination will occur. But they themselves are not constitutive of indoctrination.

(4) *Outcomes*

The outcomes-criterion is rarely espoused, yet it seems to be the most plausible one. Simply stated, it is that indoctrination is teaching in which the beliefs, attitudes, values, etc. taught are held in such a way that they are no longer open to full rational assessment. As a sub-class of teaching, indoctrination is, to use Freeman's terminology, a perficienary transaction. [17] It implies some doing on the part of A in which there is a certain outcome in B. What is learned in indoctrination is held in a manner which no longer makes it readily available for rational assessment. This is not the same as saying that it is held without reasons. No doubt many of our beliefs, attitudes, values, etc. are held without reasons. We have acquired them unreflectively and have had no occasion to examine them. But there is no barrier to our doing so. Equally, an indoctrinated person may give reasons for what he/she believes, values, etc. Indeed, many indoctrinated people can offer an impressive-sounding rationale for these things. The point of saying that they are no longer open to full rational assessment is to indicate that they form a closed and impervious set of beliefs, attitudes, values, etc. The indoctrinated person falls back on implausible claims to self-evidence, continually engages in distortion, resorts to question-begging devices, professes to find reasonably clear objections unintelligible, or becomes chronically unable to feel their weight against his/her position. All of these might come to the surface only after a good deal of reason-giving has been engaged in.

Although it is usually *beliefs* which are said to be indoctrinated, it is almost more appropriate to speak of *persons* being indoctrinated. Attitudes and values can be learned and be no more or less rational than simple beliefs. Indeed beliefs are unlikely to be indoctrinated unless attitudes and values are. It is the setting in which particular beliefs are placed which determines whether or not there is indoctrination. Where, for example, particular beliefs become closely identified with a person's feelings of security, or take on strong moral associations such that questioning them would induce guilt-feelings, we could expect them to be indoctrinated. With regard to the indoctrinated person we could anticipate that any newly acquired belief, attitude, value, etc. which is linked or believed to be linked with indoctrinated beliefs, attitudes, or values, will also be indoctrinated, even if it is acquired through reading a book.

In *Indoctrination and Education*, Snook raises three explicit, and one implicit, objections to the outcomes-criterion:

(a) The outcomes could be produced in other ways: low intelligence, temperament, etc. If 'we have reason to believe that the person is like he is because of a motor accident, we do not call him indoctrinated'.[18] This latter case, however, fails because it does not pick out an instance of teaching, and indoctrination is a species of teaching. But suppose that the accident, like 'low intelligence' and 'temperament', simply predisposes a person to hold beliefs in such a way that they are no longer open to full rational assessment? We can answer this in two ways, depending on how we understand the particular 'deficiencies'. If we see them as structural - most plausible in the accident case where we can posit brain damage - we are confronted with people who are, because of this, very easily indoctrinated. This, then, will lay certain duties of care on the teacher, lest these tendencies be improperly exploited. If, however, we see the 'deficiencies' as environmental - for example, as the product of poor socialisation (most plausible in the case of temperament) - then indoctrination is to be seen as having already occurred. In neither case do we have anything like an objection to the outcomes-criterion.

(b) 'Indoctrination' is a task-achievement term, in which the task-sense is primary: 'we would not call a man indoctrinated unless we had reason to believe that he had been subjected to some process which we call indoctrination.'[19] Leave aside for the moment Snook's assumption of a task-achievement sense, and of the former's primacy. We may then note that it is no part of the outcomes-criterion to reject the suggestion that the indoctrinated person 'had been subjected to some process which we call indoctrination'. After all, it is implicit in the idea of an outcome that it is the outcome *of* some 'process'. This is the point of insisting that indoctrination is a species of teaching. Snook's assumption of a primary task-sense of 'indoctrinate' lies behind his third objection.

(c) Because indoctrination is a process 'it can occur without anyone being indoctrinated'.[20] Here the primacy of the task-sense is presupposed. And exactly the same objections as were raised against Hirst's account of teaching are again appropriate.[21] It is only in terms of the outcome that the task is intelligible. The person who attempts but fails to indoctrinate does just that – *fails* to indoctrinate. Does this mean that we can't speak of 'a completely unsuccessful indoctrinator'? In a sense, yes. However, like 'teacher', 'indoctrinator' may come to refer to an institutionalised role, participation in which does not necessitate, in each particular case, at least, its successful performance.

(d) The fourth, implicit objection to the outcomes-criterion may be put roughly as follows: 'Indoctrination is evil, and the indoctrinator is morally reprehensible. The outcomes-criterion, unlike the intentions-criterion, fails to account for this, and it therefore fails as a criterion of indoctrination.' Like an earlier argument, this too trades on the failure to recognise that B's indoctrination is the outcome *of* A's actions. Responsibility can therefore be sheeted home to A – whether or not A intends the outcome. However, we should remember that A's responsibility for B's indoctrination does not *strictly* entail A's blameworthiness – though the onus of justification lies heavily on A. For A *may* be able to adduce additional factors – e.g. the consequences of A's not indoctrinating B, the situation in which A had to operate, etc. – which diminish A's blameworthiness or remove it altogether.

The foregoing analysis has in no way claimed to be a morally neutral exercise, for it has been grounded in the assumption that indoctrination is inherently undesirable, and has sought to explicate it in such a way that the grounds for its undesirability will be revealed. Nevertheless, although it makes no pretence to moral neutrality, it offers an analysis which does not need to involve an appeal to values other than those which might be shared by proponents of the criteria we have rejected. For, by noting the causal connection between instances of the other criteria and a certain outcome (the holding of beliefs, attitudes, values, etc. in such a way that they are no longer open to full rational assessment), we have provided an account which gives *some* reason for condemning them *as* indoctrinatory. That reason remains, even if their instantiation is not accompanied by the outcome which we have claimed to be the conceptual core of indoctrination. Creating risks, no less than causing harm, warrants our condemnation.

What is wrong with indoctrination?

What has our analysis revealed to us about the undesirability of indoctrination? Centrally, indoctrination constitutes one form of assault on the person. If we see people as responsible agents – as beings who can be held accountable for what they believe and do – in other words, as autonomous productive beings, then indoctrination constitutes a partial frustration of their realisation. It involves a violation of people's personalities such that the beliefs, attitudes, values, etc. which they hold, either in themselves or because of their association with certain other beliefs, attitudes, values, etc. are not available for appraisal. To the extent that this is so, they lack independence and control over their lives. The indoctrinated person is not likely to hold every belief, etc. in an indoctrinated fashion. Usually indoctrination is restricted to areas of normative pre-eminence: those areas of a person's life on which great significance is placed, generally because of their practical implications (hence the frequent association of indoctrination with 'doctrines'). For this reason indoctrination tends to be almost symmetrically opposed to education. In both, there is a focus on beliefs, attitudes and values which are central to a person's agent status, but in the case of indoctrination they are corrupted by being cemented in. Agency, the power to take responsible control of one's life, is in important respects diminished rather than enhanced.

Of course the ideal of autonomous agency is not sacrosanct. Adherents of the 'scholastic realist' position outlined earlier will wish to give it considerably less importance, and to accord greater importance to having the *right* belief. We should not diminish the importance of having right belief. However, following Mill,[22] we might ask whether any of us is in such a strong position with regard to the identification of right belief as to justify our indoctrinating others with it. And even if we can identify such belief, it is questionable whether holding it is of any real value when it is held in an indoctrinated fashion. Indoctrinated belief, whatever its truth-value, is little better than superstition. Its possession lacks those qualities which should render those who hold it commendable, praiseworthy, or at least accountable.

By evidencing a lack of respect for persons, indoctrination constitutes a debasement of the teaching relationship, which divorces it from educationally valuable ends. It generally expresses a fixation with truth that divorces truth from claims to truth, thus failing to recognise that knowledge is a social product. Truth, in so far as it is apprehended, is shaped by the social/personal interests of the apprehender, and to impart truth to others as though it were a fixed and unquestionable 'given', is to distort its character for us. There is reason to think that much, if not most, traditional state-controlled schooling is indoctrinatory, and that one of its indoctrinated illusions is that indoctrination is exemplified in, say, Communism and Catholicism, but not in its own case. To some extent this piece of ideology is safeguarded by the content, methods and intentions criteria. For, given the functioning of the hidden curriculum, the examples of indoctrination which most readily come to mind as exemplifying these criteria are of teachings, methods and intentions alien to one's own. In the fight against indoctrination we are victims of our own. One might suspect that the ideology goes even deeper: Do Communists and Catholics really teach their children differently? Do Communists and Catholics really have different intentions to the rest of us when they teach? Does Communist and Catholic belief differ all that radically in its justificatory structure from the beliefs that pervade and structure *our* schooling system? The belief in the teacher's authority which so permeates our 'education system' is in fact one of its most insidious indoctrinatory devices: not because epistemic authority does not exist, but because it has become so closely identified with the hierarchical relations of institutionalised schooling.

Fortunately, it is not true that 'once indoctrinated, always indoctrinated.' People who are indoctrinated still have to live their lives, and the gradual accumulation of experience may eventually force upon them, albeit unexpectedly, a perspective which casts their beliefs, attitudes, values, etc. in a new light. Once this has occurred, it is difficult for things to be the same again. Nagging doubts have a habit of snowballing, and, if the psychological needs to which the indoctrinated beliefs are usually bound can be satisfied in some alternative way, the doubts may gain sufficient momentum to collapse the structure in which the beliefs have been bound. It is to be noted, however, that the overcoming of indoctrination is not, in the first instance, in response to the initiative of the indoctrinated person. Rather, something happens to him/her, which sets in train the sometimes agonising reassessment which is the overcoming of indoctrination.

Equally, however, it is not true that once exorcised always exorcised, and those who struggle to be rid of one form of indoctrination cannot presume that the devil exorcised will not be replaced by seven worse than the first. In so far as deep-level theoretical and practical change is most likely to occur in the presence of a

66

comprehensive alternative structure, with its own internally validated procedures, there is a permanent risk that one form of indoctrination will be replaced by another.

NOTES

1. This 'room for justification' may not be available in respect of every normative concept. See Julius Kovesi's discussion of 'complete' and 'incomplete' moral notions in *Moral Notions*, London: Routledge & Kegan Paul, 1967, p.109.
2. J.S. Brubacher, *Modern Philosophies of Education*⁴, New York: McGraw-Hill, 1969, pp.356-57.
3. R.S. Peters, *Ethics and Education*, London: Allen & Unwin, 1966, p.41.
4. J. Gribble, 'Education or Indoctrination?' *Dialogue*, III, 2 (August, 1969), 36.
5. ibid.
6. P. Sheehan, 'Education and Indoctrination: Some Notes', *Dialogue*, IV, 1 (March, 1970), 60.
7. Gribble, 38.
8. Sheehan, 66.
9. D.E. Cooper, 'Intentions and Indoctrination', *Educational Philosophy and Theory*, V, 1 (March, 1973), 53. See further T.L. Benson, 'The Forms of Indoctrinatory Method', in I.S. Steinberg (ed.), *Philosophy of Education 1977*, Proceedings of the Thirty-third Annual Meeting of the Philosophy of Education Society, Urbana, Ill.: University of Illinois, 1977, 333-44; reply by K. Price, 345-53.
10. Cooper, 53.
11. ibid. We might compare this with Hirst's 'indicativeness' criterion, discussed in Ch.3, *supra*.
12. I.A. Snook, *Indoctrination and Education*, London: Routledge & Kegan Paul, 1972, p.50.
13. Cooper, 47.
14. See Snook's example on p.50.
15. In 'The Concept of Indoctrination', *Studies in Philosophy and Education*, VII, 2 (Fall, 1970), 65-108, esp. Sect. III.
16. H.L.A. Hart, *Punishment and Responsibility*, London: O.U.P., 1968, p.120.
17. For a discussion of perficiences and perficienary transactions see *supra*, Ch.3, and references.
18. Snook, *Indoctrination and Education*, p.40.
19. ibid., pp.40-41.
20. ibid., p.41. We shall ignore the problems attaching to Snook's use of 'process'. However, see, J.E. McClellan, *Philosophy of Education*, Englewood Cliffs, N.J.: Prentice-Hall, 1976, pp.14-17.

21. See *supra*, Ch.3.
22. J.S. Mill, *On Liberty*, ed. D. Spitz, New York:
    W.W. Norton, 1975, Ch.2.

Chapter 6

AUTONOMY, COMMUNITY AND EDUCATION

We have suggested that education involves the development of people whose position in the world is that of agents. Although agency presupposes cognitive development, it involves more than this, and such cognitive development as there is, is hardly to be identified with the traditional school curriculum/syllabus, whatever overlaps there may be. An agent must be able to act with realistic effect in the world. For this to be the case, what is learned must enable intervention which reflects an accurate and reliable understanding of the context of action. The general failure of schools lies in their inculcation of an understanding of and responsiveness to the world which is divorced from practical realities. So often those who pass through the system find that much of what they have learned is irrelevant to the practical demands of living, or, alternatively and more critically, they fail to realise that the understanding they have of their subsequent actions is defective. It may be defective either because what they *believe* they are doing is only a part, perhaps the least important part, of what they *are* doing, or because what they believe they are achieving or can achieve in what they are doing is seriously astray. Where theory is divorced from practice these failures are almost inevitable.

In much recent philosophy of education, education has been closely linked with the development of personal autonomy. In part, this is to be seen as an extension of the liberalism which has been so influential during the last two or three centuries of our culture. Liberalism, however, is not all of a piece, and consequently no single account of autonomy has emerged. Kant, Spencer and Mill all work with substantially different understandings of autonomy, and the traditions that have developed from them, though somewhat eclectic, have continued to display significant differences in emphasis. An ideal of autonomous personhood, however, has not been confined to liberalism. Certain traditions of Marxist thought have also seen in autonomy a personal and

69

social goal appropriate to humankind. Mill's portrayal of individuality found considerable sympathy with Marx, whose criticisms related mainly to the destructive economic theory and practice in which he believed it to be embedded.

There is much to commend in the emphasis on personal autonomy as an educational ideal. For one thing, it draws attention to a link between educational and personal control which is overlooked in many traditional accounts of education. Furthermore, it draws attention to a quality of control which goes beyond mere responsibility (though of course responsibility is presupposed). The autonomous person is not just a chooser, for a chooser may simply choose to go along with whatever is put to him/her. Initiating agency, as well as choice, is involved. And where the autonomous person is responsive to others, as he/she must often be, it is in a way that reflects independence and not mere acquiescence. On the negative side, however, the idea of autonomy is none too clear, and a number of attempts to articulate it are open to serious objection, particularly in regard to their underlying individualism. In what follows, we will attempt, partly by way of criticism, to develop an account of autonomy which is clear and defensible as an educational ideal. We shall not claim that it is the only educational ideal, though ways in which it is compatible with other educational ideals will be briefly indicated.

The liberal tradition

As most writers within the liberal tradition have recognised, the possession of autonomy is not like the possession of scientific knowledge. It does not pick out an area of belief. Nor is it to be identified as a specific practical skill or attitude, though it may be manifested in these, as in the sphere of belief. It is a quality of being and doing which may suffuse all our activities. Just how this quality is to be articulated has been the dividing point. For some it is predetermination by rational deliberation or choice which is central, for others it is a more vaguely conceived independence or self-determination, for yet others it is a self-origination. We shall briefly consider some of the strengths and weaknesses of these accounts.

Prominent among those who see rational determination as the key to autonomous belief and behaviour is R.F. Dearden. Drawing on the Kantian tradition, he characterises autonomy as follows:

A person is autonomous to the degree ... that what he thinks and does, at least in important areas of his life, are determined by himself. That is to say, it cannot be

explained why these are his beliefs and
actions without referring to his own activity
of mind. This determination of what one is
to think and do is made possible by the
bringing to bear of relevant considerations
in such activities of mind as those of
choosing, deciding, deliberating, reflecting,
planning and judging.[1]

To the extent that we see autonomy and ratiocination as
distinctively human possibilities, there is a good deal of
attractiveness about this account. We would have little
hesitation in refusing to ascribe autonomy to someone who
was unable to bring relevant considerations to bear on
his/her choices, decisions, deliberations, etc. But this
does not imply Dearden's account, for, by restricting the
sphere of autonomy to 'activities of the mind' like
'choosing, deciding, deliberating, reflecting, planning and
judging', he has mistaken the part for the whole. It is not
only choices, decisions and deliberations, etc. which may
be judged autonomous, but also emotions, needs, attitudes,
preferences, feelings and desires. Indeed, unless there is
autonomy with respect to these, there will not be autonomy
of choice, decision and deliberation. Autonomy of 'mind',
as Dearden understands it, is not properly isolable from
autonomy of need, feeling and desire.
    But this is not the only problem with Dearden's
account. The crucial notion of self-determination is left
practically unexplained. The reference to explanations
which connect with one's 'own activity of mind' is too vague
to discriminate between autonomous and heteronomous
behaviour. And the explication in terms of 'determination
... by the bringing to bear of relevant considerations in
such activities of mind as those of choosing ...' overlooks
the possibilities for heteronomy which this phraseology
masks. Criteria of relevance are not immune to ideological
structuring, and those who bring to bear on their choices,
etc. what are believed to be relevant considerations may
show only their heteronomy in doing so. What is more, even
if the considerations *are* relevant, they might be
heteronomously applied. There is a tendency for writers in
the liberal tradition to see 'reason' as a virginal given,
waiting to be appealed to. There is, however, no such
thing.[2] There are simply human beings who number among
their accomplishments the ability to think about what they
do, and who have acquired and developed standards for
assessing that thinking. For us, those standards are in the
first instance learned from others, and they may function
not to enhance but instead to frustrate autonomy. Thus, it
is not naively by virtue of its character as 'rational' that
a person's activity is autonomous, for this is to obscure
its vulnerability to ideological reconstruction. The

standards of rationality tend to be the standards of the dominant culture, and those who do not internalise them tend to be regarded disparagingly as deviants.

The Millian account of autonomy, in contradistinction to Dearden's, correctly sees that autonomy attaches primarily to persons, and not simply to a form of ratiocination, but it, too, runs into difficulties. In an eloquent portrayal of the autonomous person, Mill writes that

> The human faculties of perception, judgment, discriminative feeling, mental activity, and even moral preference, are exercised only in making a choice. He who does anything because it is the custom, makes no choice. He gains no practice either in discerning or in desiring what is best. The faculties are called into no exercise by doing a thing merely because others do it, no more than by believing a thing only because others believe it.... He who lets the world, or his own portion of it, choose his plan of life for him, has no need of any other faculty than the ape-like one of imitation. He who chooses his plan for himself, employs all his faculties. He must use observation to see, reasoning and judgment to foresee, activity to gather materials for decision, discrimination to decide, and when he has decided, firmness and self-control to hold to his deliberate decision. And these qualities he requires and exercises exactly in proportion as the part of his conduct which he determines according to his own judgment and feelings is a large one. It is possible that he might be guided in some good path, and kept out of harm's way, without any of these things. But what will be his comparative worth as a human being? It really is of importance, not only what men do, but also what manner of men they are that do it. Among the works of man, which human life is rightly employed in perfecting and beautifying, the first in importance is surely man himself.... Human nature is not a machine to be built after a model, and set to do exactly the work prescribed for it, but a tree, which requires to grow and develop itself on all sides, according to the tendency of the inward forces which make it a living thing.[3]

By making choice the exclusive possession of an autonomous person, Mill tends to overstate his case. The heteronomous person, who acts in a particular way just because it is the custom, chooses to do so, in that sense of 'choice' which implies accountability. Even though such a person's reasons do not reflect that independence which is generally associated with autonomy, he/she is in a very different position to the person who is compelled to act in that way. Choices can be heteronomous as well as autonomous. On the plus side, however, Mill does not narrowly confine the sphere of autonomy to reasoning. Judgments of autonomy take into account all of a person's 'faculties'. Intellect, emotion and will must all be considered. Though he does not explicitly say so, Mill's account acknowledges that the traditional division of the human psyche into intellect, emotion and will involves a gross oversimplification and reification of the multi-aspectual character of the human personality. Such divisions represent at best conceptual simplifications with some hermeneutical value. They do not pick out separate or separable pieces of mental apparatus.

What vitiates Mill's account of autonomy is its strand of romantic individualism. The Froebel-like metaphor of the tree, needing only room to allow the 'inward forces' to develop it on all sides, overlooks - to continue the metaphor - the need for water, good soil and climatic conditions if those inward forces are to manifest themselves in a manner which makes autonomy the valuable thing it is. But in the case of human beings - and here the metaphor breaks down - nurture does not function analogously to water, good soil and climatic conditions. Trees are inwardly structured to be what they become, whereas the 'inward forces' of human beings await a determinate structure. It is in the manner of that internal structuring, learned over a period of years, that autonomy is developed or denied. Mill sometimes acknowledges the power inherent in social structures, but fails to integrate it into his general argument.[4]

An attempt to break the nexus between social structuring and autonomy has been made by Ross Poole. Although his account is intended as an alternative to liberalism, it is really an extension in which the power of social structures to inhibit the development of autonomy is more realistically accommodated. Poole's solution is to characterise autonomy in terms of

> some explanatory gap between ... external
> factors (e.g. social pressures,
> environmental factors, influence of friends,
> etc.) and the formation of the relevant
> principles, beliefs, attitudes and emotions,
> and the action consequent upon these ...
> which must be filled by the person himself

73

bringing his own prior set of principles, beliefs, attitudes and emotions to bear on what is externally provided.[5]

This, he recognises, is regressive, but, he believes, not unhelpfully so:

I am autonomous just to the extent that I have played a part (one must add: been allowed to play a part) in the development of my present conative, cognitive, and emotional structure. Where aspects of this, and as a result, patterns of my present behaviour, were fixed in some very early experiences (say, early socialisation) in which I had no power of participation or intervention, then to that extent I am not my own person, i.e. I am not autonomous. Under these circumstances I can work towards autonomy and, through a process of self-examination, perhaps discover the extent to which what I now am merely expresses what has been external to me. In order to do this, I must be able to distance myself, and treat it as if it were external. Only by thus identifying myself independently of that aspect which is under examination will I be able to assess it as answering or not answering to my present wants, beliefs, principles, and so on. That the I who undertakes such an examination is, pro tem, an unexamined I is inevitable, but it need not remain unexamined. That we must, to adapt Neurath's metaphor, reconstruct our personal boat while sailing on it, does not mean that there is some part of it which must remain forever unreconstructed.[6]

Thus, whereas Dearden resolves autonomy into a question of the role of rationality in a person's life, Poole follows Mill in resolving it into a question of the source of a person's rational standards, attitudes, emotions, etc. To the extent that they have originated with him/her, to that extent they are autonomous. Poole seems to be suggesting that we can progressively work towards a primitive 'I' which can then be credited with being the source of our 'conative, cognitive and emotional structure', and hence autonomous. This at least is the position implied by his opposition of internal and external sources. But the primitive 'I', unstructured by external sources, is as mythical as the pot of gold at the end of the rainbow. Not only is the end of the rainbow always just over the next hill, there isn't a pot of gold there anyway. The metaphor of the tree, explicit in Mill, seems to be implicit in Poole. Human beings are seen as possessing inbuilt structures which social existence either nourishes or frustrates. Where Mill and Poole differ is in the kind of social existence which they believe will benefit or impede personal (i.e. autonomous) development. But, as we have already noted, human beings are not like trees. Though their biological needs must obviously be met, and though these needs ground some minimal internal structure, the situation of feral children should make it clear that what we are willing to acknowledge as distinctively human existence requires more than this.[7] Beyond their obvious biological contours, human beings are constituted by a range of capacities for development (learning) which depend for their structuring as well as nurture on social existence. Thus it is only through social existence that there can be an 'I' of recognisably human proportions.[8] This is obscured by Poole's search for an internal rather than an external source of 'conative, cognitive and emotional structure'. It is true that engagement in the kind of self-examination Poole discusses is crucial to autonomous personhood, but this needs to be supplemented with an account (equally examinable) of a form of desirable social existence within which it can go on. Structure and content cannot be divorced in this context. It is only in a context in which the tools for self-examination allow for a development of the individual's capacities in ways which do not serve to produce or sanctify the manipulation of one person by another that the notion of an autonomous existence can be fleshed out.

The capacity for self-examination, or, as Harry Frankfurt expresses it, 'reflective self-evaluation' appears to be distinctively human. In contrast to the lower animals, human beings can acquire the ability to form not only desires to do this or that (first order desires), but also desires that their desires (preferences, choices, willings) be or be other than what they are (second and higher order desires).[9] However, this structure of first and later order desires constitutes only a *formal* component of autonomy. It is a condition of its manifestation, but not sufficient to characterise it. Until we say something more substantive about the concrete details of this structure, the self in which this structure is embedded, and the social context of its operation, we will not be in a position to distinguish the heteronomous from the autonomous person. To be autonomous, a person must possess a high degree of internal integration and coherence. This will involve emotional maturity and stability, self-awareness, and the ability to persevere at a task. There needs also to be a willingness to take the initiative in interpersonal transactions and an ability to enter into constructive relations with others. And in addition, a person must have access to information relating to his/her situation, and the skills which will enable its processing and evaluation. Autonomy has 'outer' and 'inner' dimensions, for people are persisting beings, and there is something odd about a characterisation of personal autonomy which leaves this out of account. Our picture of an autonomous person, then, is of a self-aware and reflective being, developing in a coherent and co-operative way, able to act realistically and effectively in the world.

Autonomy and community

I have endeavoured to indicate that personal autonomy is not an empty structure, a bare self-reflectiveness. It presupposes the existence of a person with quite specific character traits, and existing in reasonably determinate relations with others. It is aspects of this latter which I now want to discuss in slightly greater detail. I do so, beause many accounts of autonomy tend to construe the ability to form second and higher order desires as an *overcoming* of social influences. But this seems to be a mistake. Although authenticity - reasoning, responding and acting out of, and not merely with, conviction - presupposes the formation of a person who can differentiate him/herself from 'the world', and is an important ingredient in personal autonomy, it does not require that a person be radically separated from the world.[10] It is important to the characterisation, development and maintenance of personal autonomy that a separation does not occur. Autonomy, after all, is not a natural endowment with which socialisation (in a broad sense) necessarily interferes. It is a social product, intelligible only within a social framework, and dependent upon it. It is not society as such which constitutes a threat to autonomy, but only social relationships of a particular kind.

Social interdependence is manifested at a number of levels. In our early years, for example, we are almost totally dependent on the care of others, and the passage from an organic bundle of potentialities to autonomous personhood is crucially dependent on the quality of that care. Proper food, emotional warmth and sensitivity, consistency of treatment, and opportunities for cognitive growth are causally important to the development of a structure of reflective self-evaluation which is autonomously directed. This infantile dependence is not so much abandoned as transformed in later development. As adults, whether autonomous or heteronomous, we remain significantly dependent on the support and productive labour of others for the wherewithal to form, make, and express our attitudes, decisions and desires. This book, for example, is not the product of isolated effort. Its appearance in this form at this time is the result of a vast network of social interactions: my academic background and present employment situation, students and colleagues who have commented on the material, the psychological support of family and friends, the food industry, typing and library facilities, a publisher, and so on. To the extent that this work manifests a degree of autonomy, it is because of these social factors, and not in spite of them. The point, of course, is not to endorse the social *status quo*, for what may contribute to one person's autonomy may detract from the autonomy of many others. If autonomy is to be a general educational ideal, and not the preserve of an élite, we must obviously look at the total effects of particular social arrangements, and not simply to their value for a narrow caste.

But the interdependence which characterises personal autonomy goes even deeper than I have indicated. Some of our most important desires - desires which, if frustrated, put our autonomy at risk - are intersubjective and conceptually dependent on the autonomous responsiveness of others. Desire for the love, friendship or co-operation of others presupposes on the part of those others a certain degree of autonomy. Certain kinds of social formation will tend to be inimical to the satisfaction of such desires. Such is the common complaint of both radical and liberal writers - the former arguing that capitalism generates a class antagonism which is antipathetic to the development and maintenance of autonomy on the part of a large section of the population, the latter arguing that totalitarianism or collectivism, by requiring the individual's surrender to the group, enforces a commitment on all which is incompatible with personal autonomy at the level of basic orientation.

There is a problem here which is not easy to solve. Large and complex social arrangements have productive possibilities not available in smaller groupings. Some of those possibilities may be highly beneficial to members of that arrangement, but to translate them into practice may require a co-ordination of effort which does not allow individual members to pursue some of the ends which will enhance or express their autonomy. Small groupings can more easily afford to direct their efforts to the autonomy of their members, but their facilities for its full flowering are often very limited. Obviously some balance is required. One traditional solution has been to participate in both large and small communities, seeking to insulate one from the other. The family is an obvious example of a smaller grouping, though in its contemporary nuclear form it has not been equal to the demands placed on it. Size, of course, is not the only factor. Groupings of whatever size may have ends which in practical terms require subordination of the many to the few. The issue is one of degree. Not every limitation on autonomy carries the same disvalue, and there are other aspects of human welfare besides autonomy which may sometimes override certain expressions of it. We need an argument which will justify the importance of autonomy and will indicate the weight it should be accorded in the balancing of interests. This will be attempted later. [11]

Conclusion

In so far as we speak of autonomy as an educational aim, we imply that it is not some genetic endowment like legs, or product of biological maturity such as the ability to procreate. The view that we are born autonomous but tend to be gradually taken over by others because of our biological dependence, seems to be premissed on the dubious view that like the seed which bears within its chemical structure the programme for the tree into which it will grow, so too does the embryonic human organism. This is not to say that there is an absence of *all* structure, but that the most significant aspects of human development are socially learned. Learning to be autonomous takes place in a social context, and autonomous desires, decisions and behaviour presuppose a continuation of social relations. However, some social relations are more friendly to the development, preservation and expression of autonomy than others, and some may favour the autonomy of some at the expense of others. In some ways, autonomy is more likely to be enhanced and preserved in small groups where there is a mutuality of concern, though some autonomy-expanding resources require more extensive social arrangements. Larger social arrangements, however, are likely to have strong autonomy-diminishing as well as some autonomy-enhancing features.

It does not seem possible to point to a social arrangement which will not involve some sacrifice of autonomy or advantage, but this does not mean that improvement is impossible. From where we *are* we can identify a range of social factors that are inimical to the development and preservation of personal autonomy, we can engage in some kind of cost-benefit analysis of various strategies for their removal, and we can work towards that end. The 'we', however, is problematic. Cost-benefit analyses of change do not take place on neutral ground, and those who have most to lose and those who have most to gain are likely to come to different conclusions about alternative strategies. Solutions are more likely to be brought about by political means than by social agreement. In fact, even solutions which appear to express social agreement may be political, in that those in power frequently control the social mechanisms most responsible for maintaining an ideological *status quo*. This has been generally true of the schooling system. Not only are schools particularly susceptible to a hardening of the arteries, whereby they become rigid and self-serving, but they are for the most part oriented to the ends of only a segment of the population. The unbridgeable gap between their professed and actual ends is largely responsible for the perpetual state of crisis in which schools appear to find themselves. As intermediate institutions between the family, which might be anticipated to have educationally-oriented expectations, and industry, which expects a certain kind of person for its workforce, schools express the dilemma of a society which has contradictory goals and finds it increasingly difficult to support a unified and partisan ideology.

NOTES

1. R.F. Dearden, 'Autonomy and Education', in R.F. Dearden, P.H. Hirst & R.S. Peters (eds.), *Education and the Development of Reason*, London: Routledge & Kegan Paul, 1972, p.461.
2. See *infra*, Ch.20.
3. J.S. Mill, *On Liberty*, ed. D. Spitz, New York: W.W. Norton, 1975, Ch.3, pp.55-56.
4. In his introductory chapter to *On Liberty* Mill writes these words:
   > Wherever there is an ascendant class, a large portion of the morality of the country emanates from its class interests, and its feelings of class superiority. The morality between Spartans and Helots, between planters and negroes, between princes and subjects, between nobles and roturiers, between men and women, has been for the most part the creation of these class interests and feelings: and the sentiments thus generated react in turn upon the moral feelings of the ascendant class, in their relations among themselves (p.8).

   But there is little in Mill's later discussion which suggests that he realised the significance of what he was saying. However, his posthumous 'Chapters on Socialism' (reprinted in J.M. Robson (ed.), *Collected Works of John Stuart Mill*, Vol.V: *Essays on Economy and Society*, University of Toronto Press/Routledge & Kegan Paul, 1967) display a much greater awareness of the point.
5. R. Poole, 'Freedom and Alienation', *Radical Philosophy*, 12, (1975), 13.
6. ibid.
7. See R.M. Zingg, 'Feral Man and Extreme Cases of Isolation', *American Journal of Psychology*, LIII (1940), 487-517; H. Lane, *The Wild Boy of Aveyron*, Cambridge, Mass.: Harvard U.P., 1976; C. Maclean, *The Wolf*

Children, London: Allen Lane, 1977.

8. There is a good deal of disagreement about the extent, if any, to which human development is innately structured. For a useful discussion of some aspects of the debate, see D.W. Hamlyn, *Experience and the Growth of Understanding*, London: Routledge & Kegan Paul, 1978.

9. For an extended discussion of this model, see H. Frankfurt, 'Freedom of the Will and the Concept of a Person', *Journal of Philosophy*, LXVIII, 1 (14 January, 1971)), 5-21. There is some discussion of Frankfurt's views in G. Watson, 'Free Agency', *Journal of Philosophy*, LXXII, 8 (24 April 1975), 205-20, esp. 217-19. See also W. Neely, 'Freedom and Desire', *Philosophical Review*, LXXIII, 1 (January, 1974), 32-54.

10. For a more detailed discussion of authenticity, see M. Bonnett, 'Authenticity and Education', *Journal of Philosophy of Education*, XII (1978), 51-61.

11. See *infra*, Ch.7.

Chapter 7

THE JUSTIFICATION OF EDUCATION

Earlier it was suggested that central to education is a person's development as a rational agent, where this includes the development of authenticity, self-awareness, consistency, sensitivity, perseverance and a realistic grasp of the world in which he/she is productively active.[1] Although we have alluded to certain conditions which would need to be met if this ideal of education is to be realised, we shall attempt to make some of the contours a little clearer before considering the kind of justification that might be appropriate to education so conceived.

Education and social structure

Our task here is complicated by the fact that any attempt to cash the conception of human living and being that is envisaged in education is bound to be historically conditioned. We are creatures of a particular time, place and cultural tradition, and what we are in a position to bring to bear on an issue such as this is limited by what is available to us. Should our situation change substantially, we could anticipate that it would be accompanied by changes of emphasis and even content. Thus, what we posit will not have the character of a timeless *a priori* but an open-ended and revisable impression. Nevertheless, we shall endeavour to map out some of those characteristics which are likely to be most resistant to social change.

Any account of what human life might and ought to be like can hardly leave out of account the basic pre-requisites for survival. A form of human life, then, which institutionalises disparities in basic survival needs such that some are unable to survive, whereas others have a surplus, will be severely deficient as a form of life appropriate to human beings. Forms of socialisation which perpetuate or reinforce such institutions will be educationally defective. The business of human survival, however, involves more than a fair distributional structure.

Human survival is closely associated with human learning: more than most other animals, humans need to be taught the art of survival. Even in very simply structured communities, the first few years of life need to be spent in a dependent relationship, and continued survival thereafter is likely to require a fair measure of co-operative (or at least joint) endeavour. [2] So some form of social existence would appear to be pretty essential if there is to be a reasonable probability of basic survival needs being met. Mere survival does not of course constitute the *raison d'être* of human existence. But the conditions of survival indicate a number of more or less inescapable ingredients of a desirable form of life. Poverty, disease and isolation cannot be ignored where the means or possibility of the means of their alleviation exist.

Human life, considered as something of worth, involves more than the satisfaction of survival needs. Indeed, if it didn't, the normative point of nominating poverty, disease and isolation as enemies would largely vanish. It is not mere human *survival* that concerns us, but a certain form of life in which people are enabled to form, make and express a range of attitudes, decisions and desires which enrich their experience in a way which allows for continuing elaboration. This is part of what we have previously described as an autonomous mode of living. [3] The conditions for this are considerably more difficult to articulate. In general they are represented in what we refer to as human welfare interests – those interests which are more or less indispensable to the pursuit and fulfilment of those human interests which help to constitute human life an object of dignity and respect. [4] Here we have in mind a certain level of bodily and mental health, a reasonable degree of intellectual development, adequate material security, stable and non-superficial interpersonal relationships, and a fair degree of liberty. To satisfy these welfare interests we need a social formation which is not only directed to the production and fair distribution of those pre-requisites of bodily health, but also displays and encourages a quality of human interaction which will promote cognitive, affective and volitional growth. For this it will need to support sensitive and co-operative relationships between people.

It is, I think, pretty clear that there are many aspects of our present social formation which work against the general satisfaction of people's welfare interests. Radical critics argue, not unreasonably, that these antagonistic aspects are symptomatic of major structural features of our society – its commitment to a form of economic relation in which the means of production are controlled by a minority whose interests are incompatible with the full welfare requirements of the majority of members of that society. To the extent that this is true, then programmes directed to helping people simply to fit into the existing structures will be defective as education.

If, therefore, we understand education to include the development of people whose involvement in the world is that of autonomous agents, we are committed, in broad terms at least, to the support of a social structure which does not deny such opportunities to people. Persons are beings who persist through time, and it is foolish to suggest an account of autonomy or its conditions which fails to take this into account. It would appear that this is what lies behind Mill's paternalistic solution to the paradox of liberalism. The person who voluntarily sells himself into slavery 'defeats, in his own case, the very purpose which is the justification of allowing him to dispose of himself... The principle of freedom cannot require that he should be free not to be free. It is not freedom to be allowed to alienate his freedom.' [5] The paradox arises where autonomy is thought to attach primarily to isolated choices, and not to persons whose persistence over a substantial stretch of time places certain limitations on the kinds of choices, etc. which are compatible with autonomy.

R.S. Peters and the justification of education

The question, 'What justification is there for education?' may appear redundant or excessively sceptical. After all, if education is constituted by the bringing into being of persons who exemplify in some measure an ideal of human living and being, it would seem that there is little more to be said. Certainly, few writers have done more than assert, as though it were obvious, some justifying aim of education. However, if, as we have suggested, our ideals are historically conditioned, we must resist attempts to give them an unquestionable sacrosanctity. We need only to remember how many different ideals of education have flourished to see that a simple appeal to educational value can be misleading. Moreover, even if we have no doubts whatever about the justifiability of education, we should nevertheless be able to provide grounds for our confidence.

One of few to have explored the justification of education in any detail is R.S. Peters. In his case, because education is an ideal somewhat narrower than a worthwhile life, there is a further reason for considering its justification. For education will constitute only one of a number of desirable human goals and may need to be weighed against them, particularly if they come into conflict or if resources are scarce. If that is to be done in a non-arbitrary manner, we need to know what can be said on its behalf.

It will be recalled that Peters' earlier understanding of an educated person was of one (a) whose knowledge and understanding transforms the way he/she sees things, (b) whose understanding is not narrowly specialised, but has

breadth and connects up to form some kind of cognitive
perspective, and (c) who is capable of engagement in
activities and the pursuit of knowledge for their own
sakes.[6] It is education so conceived that he attempts to
justify. His earlier attempt to do so in *Ethics and
Education* has been superseded by the paper 'The
Justification of Education', first published in 1973.[7] In
that paper, Peters still works with the somewhat narrower
conception of education developed in *Ethics and Education*,
and accordingly, that is the view we shall be considering
here.

In 'The Justification of Education', as in *Ethics and
Education*, Peters raises, only to reject, various
'instrumental' justifications; that is, justifications
which would show the value of (a) - (c) in terms of their
advantage to the individual, society or whatever.[8] He does
not deny that there is some instrumental value in the
qualities constitutive of an educated person. 'Knowledge
... is essential to the survival of a community in which
processes of communication are very important.'[9]
Understanding makes prediction possible and facilitates
'control over and utilisation of the natural world for human
purposes', of particular importance in a rapidly changing
technological society.[10] The possession of a broad cognitive
perspective does, perhaps, improve the quality of political
involvement. And it is at least possible to argue that
where people are committed to activities and the pursuit of
knowledge in a non-instrumental way, then efficiency and
usefulness is maximised. However, he is clearly not
persuaded that these add up to a strong enough argument for
education as he conceives it. The benefits are not
substantial enough to bear the weight of his whole
conception, and, in his view more importantly, being
instrumental, they are fundamentally incomplete as
justificatory reasons. For the problem of justification now
shifts to the ends to which the various elements in his
account of education are instrumental. Only if the ends are
non-instrumentally justifiable can a regress of
justificatory questions be halted.

In consequence, Peters turns his attention to possible
'non-instrumental' justifications of education. Two are
presented. The first, which might be called eudaemonic,
claims that education must be an ingredient in any happy and
worthwhile life. Activities constitutive of education allow
of continuous development and variation, minimising *ennui* by
enabling the transformation of 'natural activities', like
eating and sex, into ones of great skill, sensitivity and
understanding. Yet Peters remains less than confident that
education is the only path to a happy and worthwhile life:

Evanescence is essential to the attraction of
some pursuits.... And is there not something

> to be said for excursions into the simple and
> brutish? ... [Moreover,] in relation ...
> to the arguments in terms of the
> open-endedness and progressive features of
> the pursuit of knowledge it might well be
> said that the vision of life presented is
> altogether too exhausting. .. It takes too
> little account of the conservative side of
> human nature, the enjoyment of routines, and
> the security to be found in the well-worn and
> familiar. [11]

Thus the eudaemonic possibilities of education are neither
exclusive to it, nor, for that matter, assured by it.
Further, and this seems to weigh heavily with Peters, the
eudaemonic argument does not give sufficient reason for a
person, once educated, to continue to devote him/herself to
the activities constitutive of education.

However, the force of Peters' argument remains only so
long as we construe it as narrowly as he does. If education
is not construed simply as a possible and partial path to a
satisfactory life, but is identified as bringing it into
being, then the hiatus that bothers him does not occur. If
this should be thought to embrace, as educationally
valuable, activities which are not included among the stock
offerings of the school curriculum, this should not perturb
us greatly. The school curriculum gives at best a distorted
picture of what is educationally valuable, since it is not
the bare product of educational interests. This is not
intended to suggest that *some form of* the activities
answering to Peters' criteria might therefore be left out
altogether. It is fairly clear that a life which did not
encompass some of these activities in some form would be
considerably impoverished. But there is no reason why
education should be limited to an engagement in such
pursuits.

Peters' second non-instrumental justification is a
transcendental one. A transcendental argument is one in
which a conclusion is justified by showing that it is in
some way presupposed in the demand for its justification.
At least since Kant, transcendental arguments have been used
in attempts to bring to a halt the potentially sceptical
regress of questions that instrumental justifications appear
to generate. In Peters' case, the transcendental argument
gathers its plausibility from the central significance given
in his account of education to the pursuit of knowledge and
truth.[12] In seeking a justification for education, one is
seeking reasons for engaging in some activities rather than
others. In other words, one is asking a question of the
form, 'Why do this rather than that?' If this question is
seriously asked, there is presupposed a commitment to
distinguishing 'this' from 'that', and this, he claims, will

involve one in the various 'forms of understanding' constitutive of education, lest 'this' and 'that' be misrepresented. Thus a concern for truth and breadth of understanding is presupposed in the serious posing of the justificatory question. Further, the question presupposes that there are features inherent in the activities in question which are relevant to their worthwhileness. Exploration of these features may lead to questions about 'the existence and status of ultimate ends.' [13] Here again we are involved in inquiries which require a concern for truth and a breadth of understanding. There is one further presupposition. The person who seriously asks the question 'Why do this rather than that?' is committed to a non-instrumental answer. Such a person

> has already reached the stage at which he sees that instrumental justifications must reach a stopping place in activities as providing end-points for such justifications. To ask of his pattern of life 'What is the point of it all?' is to ask for features internal to it which constitute reasons for pursuing it. [14]

Thus, in posing the justificatory question, we presuppose a commitment to those activities and attitudes implicit in education. These Peters identifies as including science, history, literary appreciation and philosophy, since they 'have a more far-reaching influence on conceptual schemes and forms of understanding' than other activities. [15]

In an earlier chapter we noted Peters' tendency to identify 'worthwhile activities' with the subjects of the traditional curriculum, thus obscuring the extent to which the form in which these subjects *are* taught and practised is inimical to the values which they are supposed to realise. Certainly in his later writings Peters shows greater awareness of this point,[16] though I suspect that his implicit acceptance of the Hirstian 'forms of knowledge' thesis[17] prevents him from questioning the school curriculum more radically than he does. It must further be observed that the worthwhileness of science, history, etc. does not belong to them in isolation, but as much by virtue of their location within a complex of human activity. To some extent, science, history and literary appreciation have their 'internal' standards of assessment, but they are also subject to 'external' standards of assessment.

'Science for science's sake', 'art for art's sake' and similar slogans unacceptably detach these activities from the rest of life. They 'justify' the spending of huge sums of money on enormously expensive and sophisticated equipment and artifacts which may advance knowledge, give pleasure to a few, and perhaps save the odd life, while millions suffer and die from diseases whose investigation and eradication hold no interest for those in financial control. In fact, the use of such slogans often masks the pursuit of knowledge and art for the sake of status and power. The obvious good which knowledge is is detached from that which constitutes its point and goodness: a certain desirable form of human life. Here, too, Peters' views have undergone some transformation since they were first published. In 'Ambiguities in Liberal Education and the Problem of its Content', the slogan 'knowledge for its own sake' is held to be unhelpfully ambiguous, and Peters is more willing to see the value of certain kinds of knowledge and understanding in the ends to which they are directed. [18]

The use of a transcendental argument to justify education is problematic. It only trivialises education if it is argued that a commitment to certain activities deemed to be educationally valuable is presupposed by the justificatory question. For such an argument does not tell us why education is justified except in the sense that it is necessary to answering justificatory questions. What is needed is an account which will display for us the importance of justificatory questions. And this, presumably will lead us to a consideration of the importance of rationality in human life. In itself, then, the transcendental argument is hollow. It stops the question, but gives nothing away. To some extent this lack is made good in 'The Justification of Education'. In a section on 'The value of justification', [19] Peters points out, correctly, I believe, that human life is not internally programmed towards the means of its survival and enhancement. These things are learned, and the form of learning appropriate to them involves conceiving of ends, deliberating about them and about the means to them. The activities which constitute people as agents - able to take initiative and accept responsibility for what they do, bearers of wants and sensitivities which display a realistic grasp of their situations, and capable of maintaining internal coherence and cohesion in the face of changing circumstances - are activities which demand the development of our ratiocinative potential.

However, it must be noted that we are now moving beyond a view of education in which the values of knowledge and understanding are seen as somehow intrinsically desirable independently of some reasonably determinate conception of the good life. What Peters speaks of baldly as 'human life' trades on an implicitly normative understanding of 'human'. It is a life in which the activities for which reason is an essential prerequisite are held to be not simply necessary, but valuable. Hence there is no virtue in encouraging a situation in which some are encouraged simply to rely on the authority of others.

87

The form of justification towards which Peters is moving can be explicated by reference to the importance of autonomy in a critically valuable account of education.

We have already argued the importance of autonomy to education. What we should now consider is the value of autonomy itself. To many it has appeared self-evidently valuable, but clearly this will not do. Indeed, its value has been challenged by a number of writers. John Wilson, for example, queries its value because he is unable to get a grip on it.[20] More interestingly, to B.F. Skinner and the inhabitants of Aldous Huxley's *Brave New World*, autonomy is considerably overrated.[21] It is an unnecessary, even dangerous, luxury. The end of human life (which is seen as happiness) is attainable without personal autonomy, and, moreover, is more likely to be so, since human autonomy has been responsible for so much misery and waste. It is argued that as long as autonomy is abrogated 'non-aversively' for the happiness of all, no wrong is done.

The expectation of autonomy implicit in Skinner and *Brave New World*, that if it is to be accorded any value, it will need to be in virtue of its contribution to happiness, has its roots in utilitarianism, particularly of the Benthamite variety, but it also has links with Mill's anti-paternalism. In opposing interference with the liberty of adult citizens 'for their own good', Mill argues, among other things, that they are more committed to and more likely to be able to judge their own happiness than some external agent, and should therefore be left to pursue their lives as they see fit (within the limits imposed by the rights of others).[22]

Mill, however, links only an aspect of autonomy – liberty from interference – with the *causal* precondition of happiness, and there are a number of passages where the connection is seen more compositely. His stated view in *On Liberty*, that he regards 'utility as the ultimate appeal on all ethical questions; but it must be utility in the largest sense, grounded on the permanent interests of man as a progressive being',[23] is to be taken in conjunction with the claim that the 'human faculties of perception, judgment, discriminative feeling, mental activity, and even moral preference, *are exercised only in making a choice*'.[24] Or, as he puts it later: 'If a person possesses any tolerable amount of common sense and experience, his own mode of laying out his existence is the best, not because it is the best in itself, but *because it is his own mode*.'[25] Mill recognised what Bentham, Skinner and the inhabitants of *Brave New World* fail to see, that if happiness is to have the quality of *human* happiness it cannot be divorced from autonomous activity. In divesting the inhabitants of *Brave New World* of their autonomy, its architects also divested them of their personhood/humanity. It is only Bernard Marx and the Savage who show themselves able to display the range of sensitivities which command our respect. The rest are no longer capable of self-respect or the respect of others, nor do they command it. They can take no real credit or blame for their ideas, attitudes, feelings or achievements. They lack the initiative, responsiveness, and accountability which is crucial to autonomy and the respect which is due to persons. Unlike infants, we cannot even feel that they will grow towards it, they have been so thoroughly tampered with. The happiness they have is only a pale reflection of the happiness which is set up as the end of human life. As Mill would have put it, it smacks too much of the pig satisfied, an end surpassed even by Socrates dissatisfied.[26]

Conclusion

The justification of education is ultimately the justification of a particular form of human life. What its contours will be depends very much on where we are situated at the time of posing the question. To the extent that social reality changes, and our knowledge of it, to that extent our conception of a desirable life may need to undergo revision, as will our arguments in its favour. At this point of time, however, there would appear to be strong reasons for seeing the development of (a suitably articulated) personal autonomy as central to a desirable life, and its suppression as an assault on the very conditions of life which make questions of justification significant to us.

NOTES

1. See *supra*, Chs. 2, 6.
2. For a fascinating example of a 'limit situation', see C.M. Turnbull, *The Mountain People*, London: Jonathan Cape, 1973.
3. See *supra*, Ch.6.
4. For a more detailed discussion of welfare interests, see N. Rescher, *Welfare: The Social Issues in Philosophical Perspective*, Pittsburgh U.P., 1972, Ch.1, and my 'Crime and the Concept of Harm', *American Philosophical Quarterly*, XV, 1 (January, 1978), esp. 30-32. See also *infra*, Ch.17.
5. J.S. Mill, *On Liberty*, ed. D. Spitz, New York: W.W. Norton, 1975, Ch.5, p.95.
6. See *supra*, Ch.2. This rendering is based on that found in the paper discussed below.

7. 'The Justification of Education' in R.S. Peters (ed.), *The Philosophy of Education*, London: O.U.P., 1973, pp.239-67.
8. We have already commented on the instrumental/non-instrumental distinction in Ch.2, *supra*.
9. Peters, p.243.
10. ibid., p.244.
11. ibid., p.250.
12. It is, he notes, a pursuit which necessarily involves a range of intellectual virtues: 'truth-telling and sincerity, freedom of thought, clarity, non-arbitrariness, impartiality, a sense of relevance, consistency, respect for evidence, and people as the source of it' (ibid., p.252).
13. ibid.
14. ibid., p.262.
15. ibid., p.257.
16. See, e.g. his 'A Reply to R.K. Elliott', *Proceedings of the Philosophy of Education Society of Great Britain*, XI (July, 1977), 31-32.
17. For a discussion of Hirst, see *infra*, Ch.12.
18. 'Ambiguities in Liberal Education and the Problem of its Content' in *Education and the Education of Teachers*, London: Routledge & Kegan Paul, 1977, Ch.3.
19. 'The Justification of Education', pp.253-56.
20. J. Wilson, *Philosophy and Practical Education*, London: Routledge & Kegan Paul, 1977,, Ch.7.
21. B.F. Skinner, *Walden Two*, New York: Macmillan, 1948; idem, *Beyond Freedom and Dignity*, New York: Knopf, 1971; A. Huxley, *Brave New World*, London: Chatto & Windus, 1932.
22. Mill, Ch.1, p.14; Ch.4, p.71.
23. ibid., Ch.1, p.12.
24. ibid., Ch.3, p.55, my italics.
25. ibid., p.64, my italics.
26. J.S. Mill, *Utilitarianism*, etc., ed. M. Warnock, London: Collins Fontana, 1962, Ch.2, p.260.

Chapter 8

THE INSTITUTIONALISATION OF EDUCATION

Public schooling has its origins in the sixteenth century, though it was not until the late nineteenth century that it was introduced on a wide scale. Since then it has rapidly expanded to become the major 'industry' of technologically advanced societies. Schools display considerable variety of purpose and format, and it is difficult, if not impossible, to provide any general characterisation which will encompass everything going under that name. Even if we restrict ourselves to what we familiarly know as schools (primary and secondary schooling), we are still confronted with a wide variety of accounts. Perhaps we need to distinguish accounts which characterise schools by reference to what the writer believes they ought to be from accounts which attempt to characterise them in terms of what they are and accounts which endeavour to indicate what they minimally must be. Michael Oakeshott belongs most comfortably in the first group in representing 'School' as 'a serious and orderly initiation into an intellectual, imaginative, moral and emotional inheritance', an undertaking which requires 'effort' and 'detachment from the immediate, local world of the learner'. It is '"monastic" in respect of being a place apart where excellences may be heard because the din of worldly laxities and partialities is silenced or abated'.[1] Everett Reimer belongs to the second group, in cold-bloodedly characterising schools as 'institutions which require full-time attendance of specific age-groups in teacher-supervised classrooms for the study of graded curricula'.[2] However, Reimer's account makes no mention of any specific purposes or effects of schooling, surely matters of considerable importance in understanding contemporary schooling and the particular constellation of features that Reimer has chosen to include in his account. Minimalists usually settle for an account of schooling in which it is seen vaguely as an institutionalised arrangement directed to supervised learning. Such accounts tend not to be very helpful in understanding the phenomenon as it is found.

Our purpose in this chapter is to comment on schooling as it is found. This will help keep our discussion on the ground, and as well will indicate the possibilities for a form of schooling which might satisfy some idealised account such as Oakeshott's. It is not much good setting up an account of schools-as-they-ought-to-be if there are practically insuperable barriers to moving in that direction - at least within the particular social formation for which they are envisaged.

Schooling and education

Talk of 'the institutionalisation of education' suggests that the point, even if not always the effect, of schooling is to provide an education for children, and that indeed is a part of popular sentiment, or, as I would prefer, mythology. It is only in the most attenuated sense that schools are organised for education. However, the illusion is an important one, for, in the face of a succession of 'crises' in schooling, it diverts attention from the fundamental structures, relations and processes of schooling onto matters of detail, as though these were alone responsible for inadequacies in the system. The illusion is supported by the ambiguity which pervades our language of education. The idea that education has something to do with 'preparation for life' is interpreted as preparation for a steady, remunerative job - preferably 'with prospects' - for males, and still, for the most part, as development of skills and attitudes which will make one a desirable and successful wife and mother, in the case of females. In other words, education is interpreted in a way which leaves unquestioned the prevailing personal and social relations.

It is doubtful whether the provision of education in any critically valuable sense was ever the main purpose of public schooling. It originated in Prussia in response to pressures of a politico-religious kind,[3] and it has continued to be most responsive to political and economic demands. However the point is not one of some plurality of functions which schools have served and might come to serve: the main issue is one of compatibility. Are the various purposes which schools advance compatible with education? Those who have entered the schools desirous of promoting education in some critically valuable sense have generally found their hopes frustrated by the prevailing structures and relations. They have found the constraints of fixed syllabi, class sizes, teacher-pupil relations, staff hierarchies, and financial priorities incompatible with their educational ends. This was noticed long ago by anarchist writers; but even 'conventional' liberals such as Mill saw clearly enough the effect of a public (state-run) education system - a despotism over the mind leading to one over the body.[4]

Illich's critique

The anarchist critique of schooling has been recently
revived by Ivan Illich, who has argued with great vigour
that 'all over the world the school has an anti-educational
effect on society.'[5] Illich's critique provides a useful
structure for displaying the problems of contemporary
schooling.
       Central to his discussion is a distinction between two
kinds of institution – 'manipulative' and 'convivial'.
Their fundamental difference can be located in the effects
they have on 'personal growth' – the latter, for Illich, a
continuing process functionally equivalent to education.
Manipulative institutions, among which Illich includes law
enforcement agencies, gaols, modern warfare, mental
hospitals, nursing homes, welfare agencies, orphanages, and
most importantly of all, schools, are inimical to personal
growth. Convivial institutions, on the other hand, provide
for and encourage autonomous and creative intercourse
between people, and between people and their environment.
They include 'telephone link-ups, subway lines, mail routes,
public markets and exchanges.'[6] They are subject to
regulation only to the extent of safeguarding their
accessibility.
       Illich's critique of schools and of manipulative
institutions generally operates at two levels. At one level
he wishes to argue (in traditional anarchist fashion) that
any bureaucratically organised institution into which people
are compulsorily inserted will be manipulative. At another
level, however, it seems to be his view that capitalist
values are responsible for the manipulative character of
certain institutions. Although much of his argument is
conducted at the second of these levels, it is the first
level which most nearly expresses Illich's position.
       Illich's writing tends to be racy and loosely
organised. It is often suggestive rather than argued,
rhetorical rather than supported by evidence. Nevertheless,
the total effect of his critique is powerful and in
important respects convincing. His discussion of
manipulative institutions belongs to the more convincing
part of his argument. In it, I think we can discern four
characteristics by virtue of which manipulative institutions
frustrate 'personal growth' – their addictiveness,
coerciveness, divisiveness and counter-productivity.
(a) *Addictiveness*. Human interaction and behaviour occurs
in a context of socially acquired meanings. It is Illich's
contention that in societies such as our own these meanings
are suffused with the values of and necessary to
consumption; further, that these values have been
institutionalised, in that their realisation is believed to

be dependent on the deliverances of some institution. In these factors lies the basic addictiveness of manipulative institutions. In the case of schools this is exacerbated by the fact that the promulgation of these values and beliefs is accomplished, not overtly, but by means of what Illich calls the 'hidden curriculum': beliefs, values and attitudes implicit in the structures, relations and processes of schooling. It is the covert message of schooling that one 'should have school, and more and more of it'; 'that valuable learning is the result of attendance; that the value of learning increases with the amount of input; and ... that this value can be measured and documented by grades and certificates.' [7] Being part of a hidden curriculum, such beliefs tend to be assimilated unconsciously, forming an unarticulated basis for action. Moreover, 'only school is credited with the principal function of forming critical judgment and, paradoxically, tries to do so by making learning about oneself, about others and about nature depend on a prepackaged process'. [8] Thus the instrument of criticism is itself shaped by the institution which it is asked to assess.

(b) *Coerciveness*. Our association with manipulative institutions tends to be *required*. Conscription into the army, involuntary incarceration in gaols and mental hospitals, and compulsory schooling represent the typical background to involvement with these institutions. Of course, we may not see it that way. The triumph of ideology lies precisely in commitment to such institutions, so that they are perceived as merely required only by rebels, deviants and the ignorant. For most of us, schooling has become so integral to our way of life that we do not know what we would do without it. Nevertheless, Illich claims, it remains coercive. Coercion does not stop with compulsory attendance. School regulations, covering almost every significant act of participation, the authoritarian character of most teacher-pupil relations, the competitive framework into which pupil-pupil relations are cast, and the limitations on curriculum choice, teaching methods, and assessment, make schooling almost totally coercive, made tolerable (sometimes) by the fact that we are brought up to believe in it.

Illich is surely right to see in schooling, and in manipulative institutions generally, the evidences of coercion. Nevertheless, his argument is vitiated by an unwarranted conflation of compulsion with coercion. That schooling and its various activities are required or compelled does not show pupils to be coerced. We may willingly do what we are compelled to do, whereas if we are coerced, what we do we do not do willingly but under threat. It is the effect of ideology to transform what may have involved coercion into something which, though compelled, is done willingly. [9] But this confusion aside, it cannot be

gainsaid that those who are the prime objects of the
activity of manipulative institutions frequently have little
option about their participation. And because of this their
activities stand in need of justification. No doubt there
are circumstances in which both coercion and compulsion can
be justified, but whether and in what circumstances they are
justified in relation to schooling is not something on which
we can presume. Indeed, such is the power of our ideology
of schooling that we fail to appreciate how weak many of the
reasons for such compulsion actually are. [10]

(c) *Divisiveness*. The certification provided by schooling
is believed to be the only acceptable entrée to most
positions within the social hierarchy. The self-taught
person is viewed with suspicion, an oddity not to be
trusted, and those who pass through the system are sorted
into groups having varying status. Further, given the
escalating cost of schooling, schooling for all, or at least
schooling of equal quality for all, will never become a
reality. This is particularly critical within an
international context, where, on the one hand, Third World
countries are heavily influenced by a 'necessity for
schooling' mentality, even though only a tiny percentage of
the population are likely to receive it, and, on the other
hand, the extent of schooling is used as a criterion for 'an
international caste system'. [11]

(d) *Counterproductivity*. Illich argues that as the size of
manipulative institutions increases, the cost of their
achieving the same results as previously rises
disproportionately; moreover, and more importantly, the
likelihood of those results being achieved tends to
decrease. It is not made clear why this should be so,
though certain well-known characteristics of bureaucratic
institutions might be invoked. First of all, as
bureaucratic institutions expand, more and more of their
resources are devoted to their internal machinery, and
proportionately less to the ends for which the institution
was set up or is being maintained. Secondly, the growth of
institutions is normally accompanied by unresponsiveness, an
increase in regulation, a depersonalisation of relations and
a diffusion of responsibility. People relate to each other
not personally but as positions, categories or cases via
regulations and procedures. Thirdly, increasing regulation
brings with it increasing pressure for conformity, creating
new patterns of deviance: it is a source of the
institutionalised values which Illich believes destructive
of personal growth. Finally, most bureaucratic institutions
tend to be malignant: the relations and temptations of
power which they embody find expression in expanded ends and
increasing encroachment on personal life. They may even
come to support incompatible ends. It takes little
imagination to see how well these characteristics are
exemplified in our public schooling systems, so that even if

the provision of an education were among their purposes, its accomplishment would be unlikely.

In this critique of schools, Illich does not naively consider them to be independent of the social context in which they function. He pictures them as a major service industry, reflecting and reproducing the dominant values, structures and relations of the society. Perhaps, as Herbert Gintis argues, he concentrates too much on the consumption orientation of capitalist society, to the neglect of its productive forces and relations.[12] But at bottom it is not capitalism but bureaucracy which is the villain. Capitalist social relations are simply the form taken by bureaucratic structures in our society. Whether socialist or capitalist, these bureaucratic structures prepare people for alienation: divesting them of an incentive to grow in independence, diminishing the attractiveness of relatedness, instilling an acceptance of prevailing authority structures, and providing criteria for self-perception which distort the way in which they see their needs and capacities.

Lines of response

There is, I think, ample evidence that the general drift of Illich's critique of public schooling is correct. Whatever the status of his own theoretical position (a theologically motivated anarcho-socialism?), his efforts to understand schooling by reference to its place within a set of social and political institutions with characteristic structures, relations and values gives a more accurate representation of the character *and* possibilities of public schooling than one which sees it as the concretisation of some ideal of education. The latter position is taken by Hirst and Peters.[13]

Each institution, they argue, has 'some over-all purpose or purposes without which the behaviour of its members would be unintelligible'.[14] In the case of schooling, this over-all purpose is education, though they allow that it has come to acquire certain 'subsidiary' purposes, such as 'training for occupations' and 'selection ... for higher education and employment.'[15] As well, they note a variety of 'factors of both an external and internal sort that can militate against [its] effectiveness'.[16] The Western ideal of consumption, on the one hand, and authoritarian organisation, on the other, both make the achievement of the school's purposes more difficult.

What Hirst and Peters fail to recognise is that it is only by reference to such 'subsidiary' and external factors that public schooling is intelligible. Rather than being later additions or contingent intrusions into an educational situation, socio-political factors have been and are largely determinative of the form and content of schooling. When we look at the particular form of classroom organisation – the relations which are expected to exist between teachers and students (classroom organisation, the marking system, the daily rituals, class size, etc.), between teachers and the school hierarchy, between schools and the Education Department or Local Education Authority, and between the Department and Government – we find a variety of constraints which are so pervasive and so unrelated to education in anything like the sense that we have so far outlined, that it seems at least self-deceptive if not mystifying to describe these as contingencies which tend to frustrate the school's educational *raison d'être*. Only the *appearance* of education is maintained. The language of documents on public schooling is suffused with educational terminology: 'personal growth', 'the development of individual potentialities', 'cognitive development', 'enhancement of individual powers', etc. And the curriculum itself possesses at least the form of an educationally-oriented enterprise. But closer inspection shows these to be only appearances. Competition, grading, the form of class stratification employed, the selective direction of curricula and syllabi, the styles of teaching that predominate, etc., cut across any vaguely educational hopes, except, perhaps, for children whose backgrounds and abilities enable them to rise above or challenge the system without being unduly constrained by it. The appearance of education serves the important ideological function of providing a 'public justification' for the institution – and also for changes to the institution which have the effect of aligning it only more closely with hegemonic demands.

Were the institution of schooling not geared to the labour needs of highly industrialised societies such as our own (or, as politicians now like to put it, to 'the economy'), the maintenance of existing forms, levels, structures and directions of production would not be possible. This is not an implied argument for a return to pre-technological conditions. Technological advances have provided opportunities for educationally valuable development that would not otherwise have existed: they have been instruments through which humans have been able to exercise beneficial control over their environment. But they have also taken a form and direction which has been educationally counterproductive. [17] The domination of most labour by *technique* (in Ellul's sense) – in many ways a function of the magnitude of particular technologically-dependent enterprises – coupled with a social formation in which profit has come to dominate or even determine usefulness, has been dehumanising rather than agency-enhancing. Thus, what we have tended to embody in schooling is not an institution devoted to education and certain subsidiary purposes such as selection and vocational training (though I wouldn't want to argue that vocational training as such is anti-educative), but an institution directed more or less to the labour and ideological needs of a questionable social *status quo* under the guise of providing an education. It is the tension between this direction and what people vaguely feel ought to be the point of education which is responsible for one aspect of the continuing 'crisis' in schooling.

Generally, Marxist critics of schooling do not oppose schooling as such, but its class-character in societies where there is unequal access to control over the means of production. They are reluctant to pass judgment on 'the institutionalisation of education', abstracted from particular modes of production. However, this overlooks the fact that *public* schooling is itself an expression of a social formation which has reached a certain size, degree of sophistication and measure of centralisation. It is not a social necessity in the way in which a certain degree of self-restraint may be. Only certain societies have what we would call public schooling, whereas it would be difficult to imagine a persisting social arrangement in which self-restraint had no place. The practice of schooling in countries which eschew a capitalist mode of production should have raised suspicions that because of the way in which public schooling is related to reproduction of the structures, attitudes and labour needs of the society, it will inevitably tend to treat as secondary the needs of those who participate in it. What is fondly called 'the national interest' or 'the socialist régime', even if it is not partisan (directed to the interests of a particular class, or the Party) can lead only to the treatment of individuals as natural resources: the raw material necessary for the maintenance and modification of a particular large-scale *status quo*. It is sometimes replied that those countries professing to be socialist are only distortedly so, and that it is only because of this that the reproductive and supportive functions subserved by their schooling systems are no more humanising than our own. But this argument has the same air of unreality about it as those to the effect that a genuinely free-market society would maximise social justice and human advancement. In their own ways both arguments are ahistorical and overlook the historical character of public schooling as a social institution, and its operation in a social context where certain of the ingredients are likely to be highly resistant to rapid and predictable change, even where radical methods are employed. The availability of natural resources, national and geographical boundaries, population size and cultural traditions will all have a marked influence on the form and content of a schooling system. If we add to this a commitment to large-scale industrialisation as part of a nation-wide economic plan, then it is difficult to see how to avoid a public schooling system which will stream and stratify consciousness according to some general plan, whether or not it is graced with the name of 'the will of the people.'

This is not intended to be unduly pessimistic or a vote for the *status quo*. It is simply a warning against utopian fantasising. Clearly there are a number of directions in which we can and should move: for example, in the direction of more small-scale rather than large-scale technology;[18] in the direction of greater participation by people in the institutions which regulate their activities; in greater public access to information relevant to decision-making on matters of public policy, and so on. None of these moves would be problem-free, but if we can see that the defects of schooling are not a simple function of, say, capitalism, we may be more willing to see whatever changes we struggle for as the result of weighing present advantages and disadvantages against future advantages and disadvantages: allowing of course that such 'weighing' or deliberating is not a neutral enterprise.

Illich shows some awareness that the problem of schooling goes beyond the question of the mode of production, but his own alternative bases itself in an unacceptable and asocial understanding of human autonomy. His theological understanding of personhood is illictly desocialised and read into the natural structure of the individual, who thus needs only room to move and access to various resources if the acorn is to develop into the oak. Illich thus proposes (surely unrealistically) that schools be replaced by an arrangement of reference services, skill exchanges, and peer-matching networks distributed throughout society, of which individuals can avail themselves if and when they are interested. This sounds fine so long as we assume that the users of these services have acquired the ability to discriminate between them and to choose those best suited to their interests. But this assumption, which Illich hardly raises for consideration, is less than obvious. It is not, in the first instance, adult 'education' which is the focus of Illich's critique but institutions for those of age four and upwards, and it is not at all clear that they have the kind of control over their feelings and judgment which will enable them to make decisions of the kind envisaged by Illich. No doubt we credit children with too little ability; but equally, Illich credits them with too much. This is particularly crucial given the small-scale entrepreneurial character of the educational arrangements he suggests. We are presented not with a library of relatively uniform volumes, differing only in their content, and eliciting our response on the basis of that content, but with a supermarket or sideshow in which the brightness of the packaging or the persuasiveness of the huckster or barker can be decisive. Even adults are notoriously susceptible to irrelevancies, as advertisers are well aware. Further, in the educational market-place envisaged by Illich, the inequalities with which he damns the present institution will not be eliminated. Those who use the present set of arrangements to the best advantage will continue to do so under the new arrangements. And here we note that although Illich acknowledges the close links between schools and the dominant social structures, he neglects the role of the family in personality development. Schools do not work on unformed clay, but in many respects simply expand on and fix a process of personal formation which has already begun. In so far as families transmit the dominant social values (few families object to compulsory schooling), Illich's alternative networks represent a much less radical alternative than he supposes.

There does not seem to be any simple solution to the educational deficiencies of schooling noted by Illich and other radical critics. The problems of school are the problems of society. In our society at least there is little reason to think that Illich's belief in the inevitability of deschooling[19] is more than whistling in the wind. At best we may expect that the complaints of critics will gradually seep into social consciousness and lead to a certain amount of internal reorganisation of schools. This at least may counteract some of their more harmful consequences. At this point, perhaps, some further initiative may be possible. But unless such changes go hand in hand with change at a more general level they will be short-lived or turned to other ends. To hope for anything else is to fail to understand schooling.

NOTES

1. M. Oakeshott, 'Education: Its Engagement and Frustration' (1971), reprinted in R.F. Dearden, P.H. Hirst & R.S. Peters (eds.), *Education and the Development of Reason*, London: Routledge & Kegan Paul, 1972, pp.23-25.
2. E. Reimer, *School is Dead*, Harmondsworth: Penguin, 1971, p.35; cf. I. Illich, *Deschooling Society*, London: Calder & Boyars, 1971, p.32.
3. Luther, frequently considered the originator of modern schooling, wrote in 1524:
   Dear Rulers ... I maintain that the civil authorities are under obligation to compel the people to send their children to school. ... If the government can compel such citizens as are fit for military service to bear spear and rifle, to mount ramparts, and perform other material duties in time of war, how much more has it a right to compel the people to send their children to school, because in

　　　this case we are warring with the devil, whose object
　　　it is secretly to exhaust our cities and
　　　principalities of their strong men
　　　(quoted in W.F. Rickenbacker [ed.], *The Twelve Year
　　　Sentence*, New York: Dell Publishing Co., 1971, p.12).

4. J.S. Mill, *On Liberty*, ed. D. Spitz, New York:
   W.W. Norton, 1975, Ch.5, p.98.
5. Illich, p.8.
6. ibid., p.59.
7. ibid., p.44; cf. pp.77, 78.
8. ibid., p.52.
9. On this, see M.S. Katz, 'Compulsion and the Discourse on
   Compulsory School Attendance', *Educational Theory*,
   XXVII, 3 (Summer, 1977), 179–85.
10. See my 'Compulsory Schooling', *Journal of Philosophy of
    Education*, XV, 2 (1981).
11. Illich, p.17.
12. H. Gintis, 'Towards a Political Economy of Education: a
    Radical Critique of Ivan Illich's *Deschooling Society*',
    Harvard Educational Review, XLII, 1 (February, 1972),
    70–96; partially reprinted in I. Lister (ed.)
    Deschooling, Cambridge U.P., 1974, pp.24–33. A defence
    of Illich against some of Gintis's criticisms can be
    found in C.G. Hedman, 'The "Deschooling" Controversy
    Revisited: A Defence of Illich's "Participatory
    Socialism"', *Educational Theory*, XXIX, 2 (Spring, 1979),
    109–16.
13. P.H. Hirst & R.S. Peters, *The Logic of Education*,
    London: Routledge & Kegan Paul, 1970, Ch.7; for a
    discussion of Peters' views as presented in his *Ethics
    and Education*, see K. Harris, 'Peters on Schooling',
    Educational Philosophy and Theory, IX, 1 (April, 1977),
    33–48.
14. Hirst & Peters, p.107.
15. ibid., p.109.
16. ibid., p.107.
17. For a more general critique, see I. Illich *et al.*,
    Disabling Professions, Boston: Marion Boyars, 1978.
18. See, e.g. E.F. Schumacher, *Small is Beautiful: A Study
    of Economics as if People Mattered*, London: Blond &
    Briggs, 1973.
19. 'The disestablishment of schools will inevitably
    happen – and it will happen surprisingly fast. It
    cannot be retarded very much longer, and it is hardly
    necessary to promote it vigorously, for this is being
    done now' (Illich, *Deschooling Society*, p.104).

Chapter 9

NEUTRALITY IN EDUCATION

In recent years, liberal educational theory and practice has come under increasing attack from both radical and conservative sources. In response to these attacks, and as an expression of its own position, it has sought support by appealing to a range of values. These have included tolerance, impartiality, open-mindedness, the disinterested pursuit of truth, and neutrality. The last of these, in particular, has been the focus of public discussion. Some liberal educators have argued that with respect to party politics, political theory, religious belief, and controversial moral issues, the school, schooling authorities, and/or teachers *ought* to remain neutral. But in reply to this it has been charged that they *cannot* and *do not* remain neutral on these and other issues, and that the demand for neutrality is ideologically motivated.[1] As Paulo Freire writes: 'Those who talk of neutrality are precisely those who are afraid of losing their right to use neutrality to their own advantage.'[2] The defenders of neutrality have generally remained unpersuaded. They argue that those who claim neutrality to be impossible pave the way for totalitarianism, not liberation. Where neutrality is deemed impossible, actions are immediately polarised into 'friendly' and 'hostile'. So, Leszek Kolakowski:

> The totalitarian conception of the university implies that no human values exist that transcend the particular interests of one or other of the conflicting political groups. This principle obviously entails that whatever in the existing spiritual culture cannot be used as a tool for the pursuit of 'our' political goals is necessarily a tool for 'our' enemies.[3]

We have, then, two broad issues to consider: first, whether, and if so, what kind of neutrality is possible; and secondly, whether, and if so, under what circumstances it should be sought. The kind of answer we give to these questions will be closely linked to the account we give of neutrality, and it is to this that we shall give initial consideration.

What neutrality involves

There is no generally accepted account of neutrality, and it is evident from the literature that substantially different understandings operate. As a preliminary move, therefore, it will be helpful to provide an organising schema for neutrality claims. The following will suffice:

X is neutral with respect to M.

X, which we will consider in more detail later, may be a person, organisation, country, policy, theory, statement, concept, etc. M represents some specifiable matter about which differing, generally conflicting, opinions, policies, practices, etc. are possible. To speak of being neutral *simpliciter* is unintelligible. To say anything is to be non-neutral with respect to something. Nevertheless, it is intelligible to claim that, given some M, X may be neutral with respect to some or all of the alternatives it embodies. This is not to deny that there may be circumstances in which it is impossible to be neutral in the relevant respects. That these circumstances are more numerous than recognised is what the radical critics claim.

In what, then, might X's neutrality with respect to M consist? Consider the following three possibilities:

(a) X is uninterested in M;
(b) X is indifferent to M;
(c) X takes no stand on M.

In each of these accounts it is natural to restrict the scope of X to persons or quasi-persons. To be uninterested in M is to have no psychological attraction or inclination to M. To be indifferent to M is to have no personal preference one way or the other with respect to M. To take no stand on M is to refrain from giving expression to a particular position concerning M. Now there are, I believe, senses of 'neutrality' which correspond to each of these possibilities, and in some cases the debate about neutrality *seems* to concern them. For example, the demand for neutrality in certain schooling contexts sometimes takes the form of a demand that teachers do not give expression to their own position on some controversial issue, and it may therefore appear that what is in question is neutrality (c).

103

But I think it would delay us unnecessarily if we considered the debate about neutrality to be about neutrality$_{(a)-(c)}$. In the case of neutrality$_{(c)}$, it is only because taking a stand is believed to have some causal relation to the *advancement* of some particular position that it has been an object of controversy. In other words, the debate about neutrality has been a debate about the *influence*, actual or possible, which X exercises in relation to some outcome with respect to M.

To capture this, we may try the following:

(d) X does nothing which tends to favour a particular position with regard to M;

(e) X tends to help or hinder to an equal degree the alternatives in M under consideration;

(f) X refrains from requiring that a particular course of action be adopted concerning M.

In schooling contexts, it is because taking a stand on M is likely to favour a particular outcome (what students will come to support), that teacher neutrality is sometimes demanded. In other words, neutrality$_{(c)}$ is at issue only because of its link with neutrality$_{(d)}$. But (d) can be interpreted negatively or positively. Negatively, it is taken to mean that X does not act in any way which contributes to a resolution of the conflict embedded in M. As such, it amounts to a policy of non-involvement or silence. Positively, it is taken to mean that such influence as there is is even-handed − it is not slanted in favour of or against one particular position. In practice, this would be thought to display itself as follows. On a controversial issue such as homosexuality, a teacher who endeavoured to be negatively neutral would avoid all discussion of it, or would discuss only those aspects which did not appear to bear on the question of legitimacy. The positively neutral teacher, however, would endeavour to present as fairly as possible the various arguments for and against homosexuality, leaving it up to the students to evaluate them. Now, what we have called the positive interpretation of neutrality$_{(d)}$ is substantially the same as neutrality$_{(e)}$, and we shall henceforth refer to it as such. Both neutrality$_{(d)}$ and neutrality$_{(e)}$ have support in the literature, but we should notice a confusion that often besets the defence of neutrality$_{(d)}$. This is, that by not 'buying into' some controversial matter, one is not favouring a particular position. We can influence opinions and other outcomes not only by what we positively *commit* but also by what we *omit* to do. Religious people often complain that the omission of religious studies from the curriculum does not indicate neutrality but leaves the impression

104

(because it already finds social expression) that religion is unimportant. Likewise homosexual people complain that the refusal to consider homosexuality as a possible form of sexual orientation only perpetuates the social opprobrium which they experience. What is presented as a policy of neutrality is in fact a form of support for the *status quo*. At this point of the argument I do not want to consider whether neutrality as non-involvement is ever possible. It is enough to indicate that negatively interpreting neutrality$_{(d)}$ does not automatically imply that some particular position is not thereby favoured.

I think it is best to see (e) and (f) as existing on a continuum of influence. In the case of (e), X's non-neutrality might be expected to have favourable consequences for one particular position. Non-neutrality$_{(f)}$ would more or less guarantee it. Consider again the schooling context. A non-neutral$_{(e)}$ teacher could be expected to influence the views of his/her students by taking up a particular position on a controversial matter – say, the rights of trades unions. This influence would come about because of the socially accorded authority of the teacher. In the case of a non-neutral$_{(f)}$ teacher, these views might be required by making their 'acceptance' or regurgitation a condition of examination success. Here the continuum of influence between non-neutrality$_{(e)}$ and$_{(f)}$ is clear. It is less clear if we take the extremes: at the one end something like genuine non-involvement, and at the other coercive techniques like brainwashing. Most schooling contexts lie towards the middle of this continuum. They are not neutral, though the form taken by their influence varies. More of this later.

It has already been noted that there is some question about whether neutrality$_{(d)}$ is ever possible. The reason for this, we suggested, can be found in the causal power of omissions.[4] Where I fail to intervene in some M to whose outcome my intervention would have been causally relevant, my failure to intervene itself influences that outcome. This appears to have the consequence that neutrality$_{(d)}$ is possible only where a person is not capable of influencing an outcome – whether because of (non-culpable) ignorance or lack of power. In view of the claim by defenders of neutrality that it is a position which one can responsibly adopt towards some M, this is hardly an encouraging conclusion. One solution is to see neutralists simply as confused; but another possibility is that the account of neutrality implicit in neutralist writings is not (d), even though it is sometimes confused with (d). Before we look at further possibilities, consider (e). This position, too, seems to run into similar difficulties. All we have to do is to assume that the alternative positions embodied in M are of unequal strength – hardly an unusual occurrence. Then, if the alternatives are helped or hindered to an equal

105

degree, the supposedly neutral person simply helps to maintain the dominance of the stronger position. Alan Montefiore, from whom (e) is derived, expresses the dilemma as follows:

> Two children may each appeal to their father to intervene with his support in some dispute between them. Their father may know that if he simply 'refuses to intervene', the older one, stronger and more resourceful, is bound to come out on top. If he actively intervenes with equal help or hindrance to both of them, the result will necessarily be the same. If he wants to make sure that they both have roughly equal chances of success (that is, if he wants to render the outcome of their conflict as nearly unpredictable as possible), then he has in practical terms, to help one of them more than the other. In other words, the decision to remain neutral, according to the terms of our present definition, would amount to a decision to allow the naturally stronger child to prevail. But this may look like a very odd form of neutrality to the weaker child. [5]

Here neutrality$_{(e)}$ involves helping each to the same degree and thus helping the stronger to prevail, hardly the sort of thing intended by the neutrality doctrine. But the alternative, that of rendering the outcome as unpredictable as possible, by helping one more than the other, doesn't look too promising either. Whatever form the intervention takes, one of the children is likely to feel that neutrality was not displayed. Adoption of (e) thus appears to have the consequence that only where the alternatives are evenly balanced will a policy of neutrality$_{(e)}$ be possible. And this, too, is hardly encouraging.

Are any further alternatives possible? We can leave (f) aside, not because it lacks currency, but because the form of neutrality it articulates is not strong enough to capture the whole of the neutralist position. The following suggestions presume rather than deny causal influence:

(g) X in intervening in M, treats the alternatives with the same concern and respect;

(h) X does not actively (i.e. positively) participate in M because the alternatives are presumed to be equally meritorious. [6]

The advantage of (g) is that it does seem capable of

exemplification. Its drawback is similar to that of the alternative in Montefiore's example: treating the two children with the same concern and respect may manifest itself in rendering the outcome of their conflict as nearly unpredictable as possible, and this will involve aiding one of them more than the other. To the stronger child, 'this may look like a very odd form of neutrality'. Indeed it is, and it is better to see (g) as an expression of impartiality rather than neutrality. Alternative (h) also seems capable of exemplification, though less frequently. It also has some currency. But the problem with (h) is that unless some form of value relativism is presupposed, it will have only limited application in some of the contexts where it has been most frequently advocated. Controversial though matters of politics, morals and religion may be, those involved in them do not usually consider the various alternatives to be equally meritorious. So, either neutrality$_{(h)}$ is put forward as a political principle (i.e. because of the fuss that will otherwise be caused, it is expedient to grant equal status to all positions and stay out of disputes), or as the expression of a particular form of relativism.

If nothing else, this brief discussion has suggested that a variety of distinct positions are at stake in the neutrality debate. I do not think that there is any *one* which captures the neutralist position fully, simply because there is no single neutralist position. Different writers press for different things, and a single writer may slide from one understanding to another.

The possibility of neutrality

Clearly those who advocate neutrality believe that it is possible. However, the critic needs to do more than argue for its impossibility if a Pyrrhic victory is not to be the only achievement. For the neutralist can amend his/her stand to the demand that X be *as neutral as possible*. As our discussion of (e) and (f) implied, causal influence admits of degrees, and even if it is impossible to extract oneself from the causal matrix surrounding a particular outcome, it may at least be possible to minimise the effect one will have on the outcome. This seems to be the somewhat confused truth which lies behind the view that omissions have a different status to commissions. Although the point cannot be generalised, the probability of a particular outcome often appears to be related to one's activity or passivity in a situation. If you are bleeding profusely, and I leave you be, you may die. But the chances of your dying are much greater if I add to your wounds. How well this sort of analogy can be applied to the neutrality debate remains to be seen.

We have before us neutrality $_{(d)-(h)}$. There does not seem to be much hope of adopting neutrality $_{(d)}$ as a practical policy. Where X is in a position to influence the outcome with respect to M, then, whether X positively contributes to its resolution or allows it to take its course, X has acted in a causally significant way. We are not much better off where neutrality $_{(e)}$ is at issue. Where the alternatives under consideration are equally positioned, then helping or hindering them to an equal degree generates no paradox. Equal positioning, however, is hardly the norm, and equal help or hindrance will leave X in the same situation as the person who, though able to affect the outcome, allows things to take their course. In some matters, at least, neutrality $_{(f)}$ would seem to be possible, though the extent to which the schooling context allows room for this kind of neutrality is probably less than we suppose. Although it is often stated that certain outcomes are not required, the system operates in ways which make it otherwise. Neutrality $_{(f)}$, however, does not occupy as much of the stage as neutrality $_{(d)}$ and $_{(e)}$. We shall leave neutrality $_{(g)}$ out of account, since it is only dubiously described as a form of neutrality. Our best prospect for the possibility of a neutralist policy appears to be neutrality $_{(h)}$. But, as we have seen, if it is to have the scope normally accorded to such policies, some form of value relativism needs to be presupposed. That indeed is the view taken by certain writers. However, they fail to work through its implications consistently. Not only must they refrain from advocating neutrality $_{(h)}$, but they surely fail or refuse to recognise how deeply schooling in all its aspects actively promulgates particular values.

If neutrality is unlikely or impossible of achievement, what, then, can be said for 'being as neutral as possible'? Those accounts of neutrality which imply no more than a negative causal impact on M (neutrality $_{(d)}$ and $_{(h)}$) may appear to pick out situations in which those who act accordingly will exercise the least possible influence on the outcome. Thus, a teacher who makes no mention of homosexuality may be considered to have contributed less to the attitudes adopted by students than one who sets out to create or confirm a particular outcome. But there is a confusion here between the extent of a person's causal impact and the extent to which a particular outcome is favoured. Although a person's causal impact may be less if he/she allows matters to take their course, this may have a greater influence on the likelihood of a particular outcome than if some positive action is taken. Where, for example, there is already a strong disposition towards a particular outcome, a teacher's passivity may render it more probable than certain forms of active intervention. If strong tendencies towards a certain attitude to homosexuality already exist, a teacher who does not want his/her causal

influence to favour one position rather than another, may do
more by positively investigating the rationales behind such
tendencies than by allowing them to persist unquestioned.
Thus the neutralist is in something of a dilemma. If 'being
as neutral as possible' is construed as having as little
causal impact as possible, a particular outcome with respect
to M may be more likely than would be the case were there
certain forms of increased causal influence. In other
words, non-participation may appear less neutral than active
participation of a certain kind. On the other hand, if
'being as neutral as possible' is construed as organising
one's causal influence in such a way that the outcome is
left as open as possible, then a form of involvement is
likely to occur which will look anything but neutral.

Much of what we have said about neutrality$_{(d)}$ and $_{(h)}$
is equally applicable to neutrality$_{(e)}$. Here, 'being as
neutral as possible' will involve being$_{(e)}$ as even-handed as
possible, but this may have the consequence of making some
particular outcome more likely than a policy which allows
for differential treatment. So the advocate of
neutrality$_{(e)}$ is also confronted with a dilemma in trying to
explicate what 'being as neutral as possible' will involve.

The desirability of neutrality

The preceding discussion has suggested a very limited range
of application for a policy of neutrality, and further
discussion of what is so unpromising may appear superfluous.
However, I think that some insight into schooling is gained
by examining the background of ideas against which
neutralism operates.

It is common for proponents of neutrality in schooling
contexts to distinguish a number of levels at which the
question of neutrality can be raised - the level of the
'education' department or local schooling authority, the
level of the individual school (or its principal), and the
level of the individual teacher. The usefulness of
distinguishing these different levels is a moot point. It
obviously depends on the degree of independence which exists
between them. Radical critics may complain that it allows
for a separation where there should be none, with consequent
obscuring of the important issues. For example, most of the
debate about neutrality focuses on the neutrality of the
individual teacher. But this, it may be objected, draws
attention away from the much more substantial departures
from this supposed ideal of neutrality in the operations of
the 'education' department or local schooling authority.
Their responsiveness to governmental and other social
pressures does more to influence particular outcomes than
anything which individual teachers do or are likely to do.
This is an important point, which must not be lost sight of.
If it is heuristically useful to distinguish between the

109

operations of the 'education' department, the school, and the individual teacher, care is needed lest it degenerate into an ideological separation.

Before passing on to arguments in favour of neutrality, some comment on the scope of *M* in schooling contexts is called for. Although, as we have noted, the question of neutrality might be raised with respect to any matter on which there are conflicting views, the actual discussion is much more limited. Generally, the debate concerns issues of a moral, political or religious nature. But why these and not other issues on which conflict exists? It is sometimes suggested that because value judgments are inextricably involved in these areas, no rational conclusions are possible. This being so, non-neutrality will lead to indoctrination. Proponents of this argument conveniently forget that neutrality as they understand it often helps to perpetuate an already existing indoctrination. But we can leave this aside for the moment. For there is a speciousness about the argument's premises. Value judgments are by no means the preserve of morality, politics, and religion. History, literary criticism, art, domestic science - indeed, almost, if not every subject in the traditional curriculum - is suffused with value judgments. And of course the same might be said for the whole organisational structure of schooling. Moreover, as we noted earlier, there is something self-defeating about an argument in favour of neutrality which bases itself on the thesis that matters of value belong beyond the rational pale. It is, at best, a highly contentious thesis, needing much more to be offered in its support than the prevalence of disagreement.

Alternatively, the neutralist may limit the scope of his/her demand by reference to the subject-matter's contentiousness: we should not expect neutrality about sadism, but we may on the matter of gambling. But this will not do. Homosexual behaviour, the right to private property, and the use of marijuana are highly controversial issues, yet few of those who proclaim the virtues of neutrality are prepared to argue for it in these cases. And these represent only the tip of the iceberg. The existing curriculum is loaded with materials that are contentious. The likely response here, that it is not their 'intrinsic contentiousness', but only their 'public contentiousness' which is in view, is a piece of politics at best, and moral conservatism at worst. If contentiousness is to have any bite as a basis for differentiating issues on which neutrality would be appropriate from issues on which it would not, it will need to be more solidly grounded. It has been suggested that where issues are such that informed or equally informed and rational people are disagreed, neutrality would be an appropriate response. But ploys of this kind raise more problems of interpretation and

110

application than they are worth. There are relatively few matters on which all/most informed/rational people agree, and the structure and content of schooling belong to those about which informed/rational people are strongly disagreed.

At this point the neutralist may talk instead of the relevance of particular issues to schooling/education. Where something falls 'within the curriculum' or 'within the school's institutional *raison d'être*', it would be self-defeating to argue for neutrality. On other matters, however, neutrality would be a reasonable policy. But what is and what is not relevant? If, as neutralists generally claim, educational relevance is at issue, this will include many of the issues that at present generate the call for neutrality. It is more likely that relevance is determined by certain institutional purposes whose relationship with education is tenuous at best. These purposes relate to the maintenance and reproduction of the dominant *status quo*. It is important to the smooth running of any social system that it have the support of a large proportion of those who make it up. This will be expressed in the moral, political and religious ideas and practices of the society. Where serious fragmentation occurs in these, the dominant *status quo* will be threatened. For that reason it is important to those in power that divergent views be kept in bounds. The principle of neutrality is a device for doing this. It keeps discussion on certain volatile issues to a minimum, and thus helps to preserve the existing order. But this of course offers no good reason for thinking neutrality appropriate in some cases rather than others. At best it offers an explanation of the way in which the differentiation is in fact made.

Attempts to justify neutrality commonly confuse two issues. One concerns the desirability of neutrality as a method of operation. The other concerns the desirability of enforcing or attempting to enforce what is believed to be a neutral approach. What might justify the former will not necessarily justify the latter. It is, moreover, likely to be much more difficult to justify the latter. Here we will not expect an argument to do more than justify the former.

It is sometimes argued that the various agencies which make up the public schooling system (the 'education' department and school being the main ones) ought to remain neutral as an expression of the democratic values of toleration, liberty and equality. A democratic community, it is said, is pledged to tolerate the greatest possible diversity of viewpoints, and for that reason these agencies should not favour one alternative over another. The obvious question to ask here is: 'What alternatives are in mind?', because the public schooling system as such is a remarkably monochrome institution, and gives very strong if covert support to certain attitudes and values. And where there are alternatives, these are carefully chosen and fairly

111

limited in range. What a policy of neutrality in these contexts amounts to is not neutrality but a form of non-interference with respect to a limited range of alternatives. The schooling authority may thus leave it up to individual schools to decide whether or not to prescribe a uniform or to include Latin in the curriculum, etc., the argument being that decisions on these matters are dependent on local circumstances. It should of course be observed that it is only rarely that there is any call for the schooling authority to remain neutral. Patterns of preferment and appointment generally ensure that it is closely aligned with the dominant *status quo*, and since what it does, though not neutral, does not pose a challenge to that dominant *status quo*, those to whom the ideology of neutrality is important have little to worry about.

At first blush, the very arguments which might be said to favour a measure of neutrality on the part of schooling authorities tend in the opposite direction as far as schools are concerned. If the health of a liberal democracy depends in part on the availability of alternatives in schooling, then it is arguable that there should be readily available a diversity of types and contents of schooling, reflecting distinctive standpoints.[7] For practical reasons the unit for such alternatives would probably be the school, since it would be organisationally impossible, and no doubt also frustrating, to attempt to provide within a single school the diversity which would be desired. However, it is not for this reason that arguments in favour of the neutrality of schools are rarely heard. The public school as it presently exists is closely aligned in essentials to the schooling authority, and hence to the dominant *status quo*, and thus it not only lacks Millian diversity but also conforms to the expectations of those for whom neutrality is claimed to be a value.

To some extent the situation is different in the case of universities and research establishments. Here there is often a strong commitment to independence from governmental and other powerful interests, and there is an argument for neutrality which is often expressed as part of this commitment. It is, roughly, that the purpose of these institutions is to discover and disseminate truth, and that this is best achieved if, as institutions, they remain neutral on matters of public controversy. If, as institutions, they do not remain neutral on such matters, they pre-empt the question of truth, a question which must remain open to contest in a world of fallible beings. There is, of course, a good deal of distortion and hypocrisy in such claims. If, as institutions, universities declare themselves on certain matters, this does not 'pre-empt' the question of truth. Nor need it close the matter to contest. More importantly, such arguments overlook the already deep connections between the directions taken by much university research and the dominant *status quo*. As most modern universities have learned to their cost, funding does not usually come without some strings attached. The attempt to achieve some independence from such strings is not helped by an argument for neutrality which threatens to make a eunuch of the pursuit of truth. [8]

The neutral teacher

As we have noted, neutrality is most commonly demanded of individual teachers. The form of neutrality sought is generally of a *procedural* kind. It is not really expected that teachers will have no views of their own on the matters about which they are expected to be neutral. Several arguments have been offered for teacher neutrality. They are not entirely disconnected, though it will be useful to look at them individually, in the first instance.

(1) It is said that if teachers do not maintain neutrality they are likely to impose their prejudices on students. Two assumptions underlie this claim. The first concerns the effect of teachers on students. The second concerns the assumption that those issues on which teachers ought to remain neutral are likely to be ones on which they are prejudiced. The first assumption we shall leave till later (see (6) below). The second stands in need of argument. It is not at all obvious that on issues which generate the demand for neutrality teachers have views which have been adopted prior to examining or even in the face of the relevant evidence. For that is what is involved in prejudice. It is prejudging. Non-neutrality, however, is quite compatible with the assessment and presentation of relevant evidence, and perhaps it is this rather than neutrality that is called for. The fact that some teachers might abuse their position and impose their prejudices is not, in the absence of certain additional evidence about its frequency and some consideration of the disadvantages of neutrality, sufficient to justify a demand for it.

(2) Somewhat nearer the mark is the claim that if teachers do not maintain procedural neutrality on controversial issues they are likely to transmit their biases to students. Bias, in its pejorative sense, differs from prejudice in that it is based on a consideration of relevant evidence. But there is an unjustifiable selectivity in relation to that evidence, such that some distortion is introduced. That teachers are often biased is a fair assumption, though of course they need not be, and for the conclusion to follow there needs to be an argument to the effect that procedural neutrality is preferable to the attempt to minimise teacher bias. That argument will be considered later (see (6) below).

113

(3) There is a related argument to the effect that non-neutral teachers are likely to indoctrinate their students. Again, we need to inspect the data on which such a claim is based, considering, among other things, the extent to which students are already indoctrinated. As well, we need to keep fairly distinct the concepts of indoctrination and impartiality. Indoctrination I take to be the passing on of beliefs, attitudes, etc. such that they are no longer open to full rational assessment.[9] This is not to be identified or even closely associated with impartial support for one particular point of view, no matter how controversial the issue. May not students be encouraged to assess that view critically?

(4) A further argument is that non-neutral teachers depart from some ideal of impartiality and objectivity. But this involves a confusion of distinct concepts. An impartial person is not necessarily one who is neutral, but one whose approach to a matter does not involve an unfair representation of a position in relation to its alternatives. Impartial representation involves no caricature or distortion. The objective person, too, is not necessarily neutral, but rather one whose approach to issues of truth is transparent. It is self-aware and not affected by irrelevant considerations. Only if the evidence on some matter is conflicting and equally balanced could we expect the impartial or objective person to be neutral. In other circumstances neutrality might well constitute a perversion of impartiality or objectivity: a form of half-truth or deception.

(5) It would appear that the reason behind demands for neutrality is frequently no more than the fear that if teachers show favour towards one particular position students will be taught the wrong (or is it dangerous?) ideas. If that is so, then we should ask why the demand is made so selectively. After all, many of the ideas which students are taught, be they in mathematics or history are, or are quite likely to be, incorrect. Yet only minimal concern is shown about this. As we have already noted, it is most commonly when behaviour contradicts the dominant ideology or the ideology of those in power that the demand for neutrality is heard. Consider, for example, how much of the neutrality discussion has been against the background of issues such as Vietnam, nuclear power, homosexuality, religion and trade unionism, and how little it has been heard in connection with the issues of competition, nationalism, marriage and success, which are no less contentious but are nevertheless openly supported in schooling contexts. What I am suggesting is this: if the demand for procedural neutrality is taken at all seriously, hardly any aspect of schooling would be exempted. The fact

114

that it is so restricted in its scope strongly suggests that for the most part it is a ploy to safeguard the dominant *status quo*.

(6) However, the abuse of a position is not the same as refuting it, and there is one argument which I have not yet considered, and which lends powerful support to demands for neutrality. Earlier I noted that some well-worn arguments for neutrality stood in need of a further premiss if they were to carry conviction. This premiss can now be suggested. It is a pedagogical one. It is argued that only if teachers (for the most part, at least) proceed in a neutral manner on controversial matters will students develop that independence, vitality of thought, and creativity which is integral to education. Such is the teacher's *de facto* authority in the classroom that the likelihood of views being adopted simply because 'teacher says so' - no matter how much the teacher tries to play down his/her authority - is very high, and with that the possibility of indoctrination. It is argued that only if the teacher proceeds in a neutral manner will students come to give due consideration to evidence, reasons, etc. for the various views which they will meet in the course of their studies.

In some respects, this is a powerful argument. Yet it should not blind us to the objections which we have so far raised. For one thing, if it is correct that students are inclined to believe what their teachers tell them just because their teachers tell them, we should think seriously of extending the demand for procedural neutrality beyond the issue of morality, politics and religion to every other subject/issue in the curriculum. And far beyond that to the hidden curriculum. There, no less than elsewhere, it is important that beliefs be held and discussed in an open, rational manner. Furthermore, if the reason for neutrality is simply the excessive authority of teachers, we have strong reason to amend those features of the teaching situation which give rise to such excess. There is little doubt that the fact that teachers are judges as well as resources contributes much to the deference which their word is given.

In addition to these considerations, we might wonder whether neutrality, if taken as a procedural policy rather than as a device for particular pedagogical occasions might be anti-educative. The skills involved in weighing diverse and conflicting evidence and opinions may be taught most effectively by example. This is particularly so in the controversial areas of the curriculum where rational skills and sensitivities are not likely to be taught by the cold-blooded techniques which procedural neutrality is likely to encourage. Nevertheless, this educational benefit of a non-neutral approach is premissed on a change in

115

existing teacher-student relationships, in which teaching comes to have the form of genuine dialogue.

Conclusion

The last two sections have been premissed on the possibility of a much greater neutrality than we have seen reason to acknowledge. Even so, we have found little to support such a policy, at least in the form in which it comes to us from the public schooling context. Where it has some minimal plausibility - as a counter to the power which a teacher's word is accorded, we do better to press for impartiality. For the most part, the argument is a tool of conservatism, a means whereby those who see the schools as instruments of their own values can further their dissemination without hindrance. Liberals, for all their solicitude about the influence of teachers, would do better to recognise neutrality for what it is, a conservative value.

NOTES

1. I leave to one side the complexities of the 'ought' implies can' issue. For a detailed exploration, see M. Stocker, '"Ought" and "Can"', *Australasian Journal of Philosophy*, XLIX, 3 (December, 1971), 303-16.
2. P. Freire, *Education : the Practice of Freedom*, Harmondsworth: Penguin, 1976, p.147.
3. L. Kolakowski, 'Neutrality and Academic Values', in A. Montefiore (ed.), *Neutrality and Impartiality : the University and Political Commitment*, Cambridge U.P., 1975, p.77.
4. I have discussed this issue further in 'Good Samaritanism', *Philosophy & Public Affairs*, V, 4 (Summer, 1976), 382-407, esp. Sect.3. But see also the reply by Eric Mack, 'Bad Samaritanism and the Causation of Harm', *Philosophy & Public Affairs*, IX, 3 (Spring, 1980), 230-59.
5. Montefiore, p.7.
6. These possibilities were suggested in a paper presented by John Harris at the Conference of the Philosophy of Education Society of Australasia in Perth, August, 1978, a revised version of which appears in *Violence and Responsibility*, London: Routledge & Kegan Paul, 1980. Harris's paper has been very helpful in revising the present script.
7. See J.S. Mill, *On Liberty*, ed. D. Spitz, New York: W.W. Norton, 1975, Ch.V.
8. For a more detailed discussion of the foregoing, see my 'Academic Freedom', *Educational Philosophy and Theory*, XIV, 1 (March, 1982).
9. This account is defended *supra*, Ch.5.

Chapter 10

EQUALITY, SCHOOLING AND EDUCATION

For many people, schooling is or should be 'the great equaliser of the conditions of men',[1] and what is termed 'educational equality' is seen as the major evaluative hoop through which schooling must pass. For others, such equality is the harbinger of totalitarian mediocrity. This divergence is only partly explained by differences of *Weltanschauung*. Equality, like freedom, is referentially incomplete, and until it is made clear by reference to what equality is being invoked or rejected, its invocation or rejection amounts to little more than political sloganeering. Talk of 'educational equality' is too vague to satisfy this condition. Referential incompleteness has been accompanied by referential diversity, and thus the literature in praise or condemnation of equality reveals an almost endless variety of principles parading under its banner. In this chapter we consider several of these principles, relating them where appropriate to the theory and practice of schooling.

It should first be pointed out that there are very few writers who reject equality *altogether*. For to speak of inequality (as distinct from non-equality) is already to imply criticism of some arrangement. The rejection of equality is, rather, the rejection of some concrete principle of equality. Loudest condemnation is usually reserved for an interpretation of equality for which advocates are hard to find.[2] Yet this critique has carried a good deal of weight in the political debate about equality, for it focuses on one of the few senses in which the term 'equality' can be straightforwardly applied. The critique encompasses two distinct principles of equality:

(1) *The principle of identical treatment*

It is in a mathematical context that equality finds its home. There, 'A is equal to B' is equivalent to 'A is identical with B' or 'A is the same as B'. If this is

117

transferred to the social sphere and made a principle of treatment, it might be understood as involving identical treatment for all to whom it applies. Now, as both conservative *and* radical writers have been quick to observe, the operation of this principle - particularly if given some overriding significance - would be disastrous. As things presently stand, people differ substantially with respect to their interests, needs and resources, and to treat them identically would, in many cases, be to frustrate those interests and to leave their needs unsatisfied. Or, to put it another way, it would be to sacrifice their individuality to a formula. Not only would this be incompatible with the respect we owe to others, but it would also diminish the social and personal resources on which we might both individually and collectively draw. In a schooling context, it would leave out of account the differences between people in respect of their backgrounds, interests and abilities. Moreover, it would require for its implementation the centralisation and regimentation of schooling on a scale which would far exceed even what we presently have: besides the insistence on compulsory schooling, there would need to be identical curricula, buildings, staff-student ratios, teaching methods, an effacement of the teacher's personality, and so on. There is nothing of educational merit in such a procedure, and its advocacy could be seen only as increasing that 'despotism over the mind' which John Stuart Mill saw as the political consequence of a state schooling system.

(2) *The principle of identical outcomes*

Like the previous principle, this, too, involves a translation of the mathematical notion of equality into the social sphere. There it prescribes a form of treatment in which the outcome, in each case, is identical. Unlike the principle of identical treatment, this one acknowledges and takes account of people's differing interests, needs and resources, and thus in pursuit of its end will almost surely involve treating different people differently. But this should not make us think that it is any more acceptable than the first principle. In effect, if not in appearance, it, too, sacrifices individuality to a formula. The accommodation to individual differences is not grounded in any respect for the person, but simply in the requirements of the formula. But to object in these terms may be criticised as premature: until we specify the end-state we are in no position to pass judgment on the principle. This response is revealing, for it shows a crucial lack in the principle: without the specification of some end-state, there is little to be said for such equality. Any virtue that it has is likely to be parasitic on the desirability of the end-state. But even if we ignore this problem for the

118

principle, we can reject the charge of prematurity. Of *any* outcome that might be considered, there is no reason for thinking desirable its *identical* realisation, and, for the reason mentioned earlier, good reason to think that it evidences scant respect for individuality and personal autonomy. Marx sees the principle as an expression of generalised envy, a levelling down which negates 'the entire world of culture and civilisation, the regression to the *unnatural* simplicity of the *poor and undemanding* man who has not only failed to go beyond private property, but in fact has not yet even reached it'.[3] For if the principle of identical outcomes is to be satisfied, it, like the previous principle, would require nothing less than totalitarian control over people's lives, in this case to rein in the tendencies – whether innate or socialised – which would differentiate them in the respects envisaged by the principle. In its application to schooling, the principle of identical outcomes would have the effect of limiting the curricula to those activities in which it would be feasible to expect everyone to reach an identical standard; or alternatively, regulation of the depth to which any subject could be pursued to a standard that every person might feasibly be expected to achieve. Should it be argued that the principle is not intended to override other important social principles – such as liberty and justice, for instance – we might respond by asking what practical role would remain to the principle once these other principles had been satisfied. Even if some practical role could be found for the principle, we would still lack a rationale for it. Why should identity of outcomes be an ideal?

It is little wonder that most writers react strongly against such principles. In the case of conservative writers, what they are reacting against is usually a caricature of what their opponents are seeking. However, this reaction may not be wholly undeserved, since it is notoriously difficult to determine exactly what is being sought in the demand for equality. If we look carefully at egalitarian claims which appear to move in the direction of (1) and (2), what we find, I believe, is a reaction against certain inequalities in power, which result in exploitation. Because these inequalities of power come to be displayed in differential wealth (income, ownership of property, etc.), egalitarian claims are sometimes formulated in terms reminiscent of (1) and (2). But this would be to misconstrue them.

Before we take up this point again, we shall consider a number of other possible principles of equality.

(3) *The formal principle of equality*

The ancient dictum that we should treat equals equally and unequals unequally is formal in that it cannot be used as a guide for action unless it is supplemented by material principles which specify those factors which make for equality and inequality. Indeed, even to see it as a formal principle of *action* is to allow it greater specificity than is warranted. It is really only a constitutive principle of rationality – a demand for consistency, whether in thought or action: 'One would violate this more general principle by ascribing different geometrical properties to two identical isosceles triangles,... as much as by denying equal protection of the law to those citizens who have black skins.'[4] Since this principle is formal, it need not detain us. Although it is uncontroversial, it provides no guide to action unless supplemented in ways that we shall later consider. Nevertheless, it is often confused with a somewhat different principle, from which it must now be distinguished.[5]

(4) *The presumptive principle of equality*

In *Ethics and Education*, R.S. Peters formulates and defends a principle of equality which he expresses in these terms: 'No one shall be presumed, in advance of particular cases being considered, to have a claim to better treatment than another.'[6] This principle is presumptive in the sense that it places a burden of proof on any who would treat people differently without good reason:

> It does not prescribe positively that all human beings be treated alike; it is a presumption against treating them differently, in any respect, until grounds for distinction have been shewn....The onus of justification rests on whoever would make distinctions.[7]

Like the previous principle, from which he does not clearly distinguish it, Peters believes this one to be formal. There are three respects in which this might be so. First, in the absence of some statement of those factors which would give one person a claim to better treatment than another, the principle lacks the completeness it needs for confident application. Secondly, to be told that people ought, in the absence of relevant differences, to be treated equally, is not to be told very much about how they ought to be treated – whether they are to be treated equally badly or equally well. The principle is comparative rather than substantive. And thirdly, of central importance to the justification Peters offers, the principle is taken to be a presupposition of practical discourse. It is considered to be *a priori*.

120

Before considering Peters' justification, we should notice that the principle is not as formal as Peters suggests. What the presumptive principle demands is that where relevant similarities or differences are not known, those concerned should be treated in the same way, and that where relevant similarities or differences are known, those concerned should be treated differently. It thus provides a decisive guide to action (at least in respect of identical or differential treatment) in each case. In this respect it differs significantly from the formal principle of justice. With regard to the latter, where relevant similarities or differences are unknown, we are given no guidance as to whether identical or differential treatment is appropriate.[8]

Peters' argument for the presumptive principle goes roughly as follows: Any person seriously committed to practical discourse will ask the question, 'What ought I to do?' The question supposes that there are alternatives and that there are reasons for adopting one alternative rather than any other. These reasons must lie in the features of the alternatives. In other words, presupposed by the practical question is the very formal principle of no distinctions without differences. However, not only is this presupposed. There is also presupposed the relevance of general principles which distinguish between good and bad reasons for doing something. Their generality entails that whatever constitutes a sufficient reason in one situation constitutes a sufficient reason in another unless the situations are relevantly different.[9]

This, Peters believes, is sufficient to yield the presumptive principle of equality. But is it? I think not. If I am wondering whether to become a landscape or a portrait painter, then I am seeking reasons for adopting one alternative rather than the other. We may suppose that there are reasons of the kind Peters wants, and further that they instantiate general principles which would render my decision to be one rather than the other, correct or wise. But it would be odd to say that my engagement in this piece of practical deliberation presupposed the presumptive principle of equality. More, then, is required than the bare claim that 'what ought to be done in any particular situation or by any particular person ought to be done in any other situation or by any other person unless there is some relevant difference in the situation or person in question.'[10] What this might be is suggested a little later, when Peters claims that the principle assumes that there is an additional rule 'stipulating that people generally ought to have something or be treated in some way or another'.[11] In other words, it is only in contexts in which the alternatives concern the distribution of benefits and burdens to people that the principle of no distinctions without differences assumes the character of the presumptive principle of equality. But this is not the same as saying that the practical question 'What ought I to do?' *presupposes* the presumptive principle of equality.

But there is a more significant defect in Peters' argument. The presumptive principle of equality prescribes equal treatment in the absence of reasons for unequal treatment. But there is no basis in the formal principle of 'no distinctions without differences' for *that* conclusion. At best, the principle of 'no distinctions without differences' can yield the Aristotelian formal principle that 'equals should be treated equally, and unequals treated unequally', a principle which, as we have seen (*pace* Peters) involves no presumption of equality. We can put the point as follows: Peters' presumptive principle presupposes the category of persons and then claims that any differential treatment requires justification. But on what basis is it decided that there are similarities between people which are more significant than their differences, and more significant than their similarities to other animals? It is all very well to argue, when one has got a relevantly differentiated category, that differential treatment requires justification. But until that has been established, the onus of proof has not been placed on those who would give unequal treatment. The presumptive principle of equality thus presupposes (without providing any justification) that being human is relevant to determining the treatment that should be received. Whether or not that presupposition is justified, it destroys the *a priori* character of Peters' principle.

(5) *The principle of equal humanity*

The normative assumption lurking behind Peters' presumptive principle of equality, namely, that in respect of our humanity we are all equal, is sometimes advanced (as it covertly is in Peters' case) as an egalitarian principle. By reference to it racism, sexism, élitism, and other forms of discrimination are scrutinised and rejected. Thus, unlike the previous principles, this one is morally significant and widely held.

Support for the principle is generally considered to lie in some attribute or set or attributes possessed by all (or nearly all) human beings, an attribute (or set of attributes) possessing moral significance. The identification of this attribute or set of attributes is a matter of continuing controversy and cannot be pursued here. Suffice it to say that rationality, self-consciousness, free will, the possession of interests, consciousness and productive capacity are some of the more popular candidates.

Let us allow that we succeed in identifying some shared attribute of moral significance sufficient to ground the principle of equal humanity. Do we have a principle of equality? Only in a trivial sense. The basis for the principle of equal humanity is simply that attribute(s) a, having moral significance, is possessed by each human being, and therefore, as a matter of consistency, the moral significance it possesses in one case is possessed in all cases. It is a matter of consistency rather than some independent equality which gives the principle of equal humanity its force. Another way in which the point is sometimes put is as follows: attribute(s) a, having moral significance, constitutes the criterion by which we distinguish the category of persons, where the category of persons may or may not be identical with the (biological) category of human beings. Whichever way we put it, the reference to equality can drop out, as it does in its traditional title: the principle of respect for persons.

It is to be noted that there is little of 'equal' treatment prescribed by this principle. It is, in many ways, a negative principle - functioning as a reason for not humiliating, exploiting, torturing or interfering with others. It is not, however, wholly negative. Particularly, though not exclusively, in the case of children, it should manifest itself in relationships which encourage the fullest expression of the attributes on which the principle is based. But this does not mean sameness of treatment, except contingently. Here, then, we have a principle with obvious implications for the schooling context, but only dubiously regarded as a principle of *equality*.

(6) *The principle of equal consideration of interests*

This is related to the previous principle as, perhaps, a particular specification of it. However, its supporters (e.g. S.I. Benn[12]) claim that it is a truly egalitarian principle. A principle which simply *considered* the interests of everyone would, it is said, be compatible with élitism. However, the principle of equal consideration of interests rules this out. By 'interests' Benn understands those 'conditions necessary to a way of life or to forms of activity that are endorsed as worthwhile, or (what probably amounts to the same thing) as conditions necessary to the process of making oneself something worthy of respect'.[13] The principle, then, requires that each person's interests be considered equally with the interests of others in the distribution of benefits and burdens. Like the principle of equal humanity, it too is grounded in a conception of human beings as having capacities or potentialities for moral freedom, self-appraisal, or whatever.

But despite its egalitarian appearance, it is not immediately clear what the force of its appeal to *equality of consideration* amounts to. For Benn does not deny that the principle is compatible with one person's interest taking priority over another's - as when the wealthy are taxed to assist the poor.[14] So the point of equal consideration is not equal weighting of all interests. So what, then, is involved in equal consideration? Perhaps this, that X's interest in A is to be given the same consideration as Y's interest in A, even though an interest in A is to be weighted more heavily than an interest in B. The argument against élitism would thus be that it involves the favouring of one group with respect to a particular interest (say, intellectual development) over another group. In a schooling context, élitism would be shown in giving privileged treatment to the intellectually able at the expense of the intellectually handicapped. The principle of equal consideration of interests would require instead that the intellectual development of the intellectually handicapped be given the same consideration as that of the intellectually able. And, because of the practical difficulties involved, the principle might justify a greater expenditure of resources on the handicapped than on the able.

So interpreted, I think the principle of equal consideration of interests constitutes a valuable foil to certain élitist tendencies. In the sphere of schooling this is frequently manifest in the debate about equality v. quality.[15] Time and again it is argued that you can't have both, and, since the value of quality is difficult to dispute, the demand for equality is rejected as mediocritising. Notoriously, qualitarians tend to be élitist, and so the debate tends to loom large in élitist apologetics. The value of the principle of equal consideration of interests is that it denies a key assumption of élitism without rejecting quality. Individual differences are recognised, as too is the value of quality. But what is insisted upon is that in the pursuit of quality no person or group of persons' interest in some particular sphere be accorded privileged consideration. This does not involve a levelling down or up. What it means is that the interest of the intellectually handicapped in, say, intellectual advancement is to be given the same weight as that of the intellectually able. In the interests of quality with respect to both groups, some differential treatment may be justified. It is true that where resources are limited excellence may not be maximised, but that is a problem to be tackled on the level of access to resources; it does not reflect on the principle of equal consideration of interests.

(7) *The principle of equal opportunity*

It would be fair to say that this principle, or some variant of it, is the one most frequently invoked in discussions of schooling. For example, the 1960 UNESCO 'Recommendation Against Discrimination in Education' stated that

124

> The Member States should formulate, develop
> and apply a national policy which ... will
> tend to promote equality of opportunity and
> of treatment in the matter of education and
> in particular:
> (a) To make primary education free and
> compulsory; make secondary education in its
> different forms generally available and
> accessible to all; make higher education
> equally accessible to all on the basis of
> individual capacity ...[16]

Most official documents make similar gestures. But what do
they amount to? The principle of equal opportunity remains
hollow until the nature of the opportunity is specified. In
this case the opportunity is limited to 'the matter of
education', where it seems to involve access to schooling
resources. But for many egalitarians this is far too
restrictive, since it ignores the effects of family and
socio-economic background on the ability to utilise those
resources effectively. Thus James S. Coleman, the architect
of a major U.S. study on equality in 'education', has
argued that the concept of 'equality of educational
opportunity' is a mistaken and misleading one:

> It is mistaken because it locates the
> 'equality of opportunity' within the
> educational institutions, and thus focuses
> attention on education [i.e. schooling] as
> an end in itself rather than as properly it
> is, a means to ends achieved in adulthood.
> It is misleading because it suggests that
> equal educational opportunity defined in
> something other than a purely formal (input)
> way, is achievable, while it is not. [17]

If Illich's critique of schooling is roughly correct, not
even equal 'educational' opportunity of a 'purely formal'
sort is likely to be achievable, given the economics and
politics of schooling. However, we shall not pursue this,
since it should be clear that the pursuit of a policy of
equal access to schooling resources abstracted from the
other social factors which affect people's lives is a
pointless exercise, 'justified' only as a piece of public
rhetoric.

Several variants of the principle of equal opportunity
have been noted, and bear examination: [18]

(a) On one version, the principle amounts to the view that
there should be available to all opportunities of equal
worth. Those who support this variant recognise that for a
whole range of reasons the opportunities available to *X* are

125

not going to be identical with the opportunities available to Y. But, it is argued, what should be available to both X and Y are opportunities which are of equal value. This of course supposes that the value of opportunities is susceptible of interpersonal comparison, a position which, if correct, is hardly obviously so. But even if it is possible to compare opportunities in terms of their value, this principle does not escape from the fate previously mentioned. It is all very well to speak of X and Y having equally valuable opportunities available to them. But unless they are similarly capable of making use of those opportunities, it does little good to have them available. This might not be unduly worrying if the differential capacity to make use of the opportunities could be shown to be genetic, but since this is unlikely,[19] and there is good reason to think that social environmental factors play an important role in the development of people's capacities to make use of the opportunities presented to them, we should be suspicious of a principle which demands no more than opportunities of equal value.

(b) According to a second, less ambitious version, the principle requires only that certain opportunities be equally available to all at an appropriate stage of life. These might be to secure employment, to receive some form of tertiary education, to have access to a certain standard of health care, etc. One problem here would be to identify those opportunities which would be covered by the principle. This might not be beyond us if they are limited to what can be regarded as people's welfare requirements. To such, people have a right.[20] Once again, this principle tends to be understood asocially: something must be said about the capacity to make use of these opportunities. Even so, this variant does not take into account that 'secure employment', 'some form of tertiary education', etc. each cover a wide range of situations of varying value. In fact, the reference to equality in this formulation is otiose, even misleading, since the emphasis is not really on some equality of access to secure employment, etc., but on unimpeded access to them.

(c) Restriction of the principle of equal opportunity to access to welfare requirements is considered by many to be too limiting. It is asserted that there are many goods to which people should have equal access, not in the sense of being able to have them for the asking, but in the sense of being able to compete for them on equal terms with others. Unequal terms would be involved if, for example, the conditions of competition included factors which were irrelevant to a utilisation of the scarce resource. This principle of equal competitive opportunity makes explicit the social context which has generated the call for equal opportunity:

126

one in which a limited number of valued resources are to be distributed by means of competition. For this reason it is often seen as a servant of capitalism, distributing resources and individuals as efficiently as possible within its hierarchical structure. That, for radical critics, is its most serious inadequacy. It poses as a system of fair distribution of benefits and burdens, but leaves the nature of those benefits and burdens and the causes of scarcity unquestioned or obscured. In this respect it does not differ substantially from the view which sees a form of justice realised in equality before the law - not much advantage if the laws themselves are unjust.[21]

Supporters of the principle of equal competitive opportunity often fail to appreciate the complexities involved in determining relevant factors relating to the distribution of a limited resource. Suppose, for example, that the scarce resource is a university place. In that case, it might be argued that academic performance is a relevant factor, but religious affiliation and socio-economic background are not. In a sense that is so, but the isolation of academic performance as a relevant factor in the fair allocation of university places overlooks the causal connections which exist between religious affiliation, socio-economic background and academic performance. A person's religious affiliations and socio-economic background may directly affect his/her motivation, industriousness, social acceptance, access to resources, extent of experience, etc., all of which are likely to enter into academic performance. This of course is not a reason for making religious affiliation and socio-economic background criteria in themselves for allocating university places, but it indicates a serious inadequacy in the view that competition on equal terms with others is determined via a simplistic appeal to factors apparently directly relevant to the utilisation of a scarce resource.

It is in recognition of this weakness in the principle that programmes of 'affirmative action' or 'reverse discrimination' have been introduced - in the face of considerable opposition - in the United States. We might see such programmes as an elaboration of the principle of equal competitive opportunity - an attempt to compensate for interference with academic performance by factors which should be irrelevant to it (sex, skin colour, etc.). At this point of time, however, most people would not see it that way, an indication, perhaps, of the conservative-reformist background of the principle of equal opportunity. 'Affirmative action' is seen as the thin edge of a wedge in which all those factors relevant to the successful acquisition of a scarce resource will become subject to manipulation. Handicapping no less than positive discrimination will be the order of the day, resulting in a

massive erosion of liberty. The rationale goes as follows:
if the conditions of access to every scarce resource are to
be equalised, then intervention will be required, not only
prior to competition, but also after, to maintain equality
in respect of succeeding competitions. But this argument
relies on the difficulties in separating relevant from
irrelevant factors in order to deny that differentiation is
possible. Moreover, it assumes that equality of competitive
opportunity is to be given priority in every conflict with
liberty, and that the importance of the scarce resource does
not need to be taken into account in deciding whether
intervention for the purpose of equalising opportunities is
justified. Moreover, those who put forward the objection
tend to see liberty as having uniform value, whereas this is
not the case. Like economic security, some liberty is
essential, but beyond a certain point it becomes less
central to one's person, and one's claim to it is more
easily overridden. Nevertheless, I do not wish to claim
that these rejoinders suffice to justify affirmative action
programmes. The issues are more complex than my comments
have been able to indicate.[22]

(8) *The principle of procedural justice*

In *A Theory of Justice*, John Rawls defends a substantive
principle, according to which 'all social primary
goods - liberty and opportunity, income and wealth and the
bases of self-respect - are to be distributed equally unless
an unequal distribution of any or all of these goods is to
the advantage of the least favoured.'[23] Rawls acknowledges
that within such a conception conflicts will arise, and so
he provides an ordering of primary goods such that first
priority is to be given to providing each person with an
equal right to the most extensive basic liberty compatible
with a like liberty for others. Only then can social and
economic inequalities be justified, provided that two
further conditions are met: first, that they are accessible
to all 'under conditions of fair equality of opportunity',
and then, given that this is the case, that they assign the
greatest benefit to the least advantaged. This account is
defended by reference to a hypothetical situation in which
normally self-interested rational choosers have to decide on
principles of social organisation behind a 'veil of
ignorance' about their own personal situations. The
relevance of the veil of ignorance is that it excludes from
consideration those facts about ourselves which are not
relevant to decisions about the fairest way of distributing
social primary goods.

The general success of Rawls' case need not concern us
here.[24] The argument is complex and sophisticated. What is
of primary interest to us at this point is the kind of
social order which Rawls' believes will emerge from the

application of his principle. From the various examples he gives, it would appear that a moderately amended version of the American *status quo* might come as reasonably close as we could expect. On the surface, this is surprising, since it is surely obvious that those with great wealth or control of wealth have considerably greater basic liberty than others: especially when we note that for Rawls basic liberty includes freedom of conscience and religion, political freedom (freedom of speech, the right to vote, etc.), freedom from arbitrary arrest, and the right to hold property. Those with wealth hold a considerable advantage in the media, at law and in the market place, even when they act entirely within the limits imposed by the law. Rawls manages to 'reconcile' this with his principle by introducing a distinction between liberty and the worth of liberty, arguing that what inequalities of wealth, etc. affect is not the equal basic liberty of all but the worth of those liberties. However, as Norman Daniels has shown, this distinction will not do what Rawls requires of it. Among other things, the same reasons which would justify people behind the veil of ignorance choosing equal liberty would also justify them choosing the equal worth of liberty.[25] What we find, in Rawls' case, is that a principle of procedural fairness which appears on the surface to support equality, does so in only the most attenuated form when some of its complications are unravelled.

Conclusion

In this brief survey we have by no means exhausted the range of principles which parade under the banner of equality. Nor have we attempted an exhaustive exploration of those principles we have considered. Like democracy, equality tends to function as a propagandist slogan into which almost any content can be read. Although this vagueness renders it usable by both critics and defenders of the prevailing social order, it is likely to be exploited more skilfully by those who hold the reins of power, for it is they who predominate in the institutions of major ideological significance. This propagandising is particularly noticeable in schooling, where the notion of 'equality of educational opportunity', because it abstracts access to schooling resources from, on the one hand, grossly discrepant initial social conditions, and, on the other, a social order which, statistically, requires the perpetuation of those discrepancies, functions as an agent of inequality rather than as its enemy. If we are to make use of a principle of equality at all, it needs to be one concerned with social equality, for only so can it amount to anything. And even then, as we noticed in the case of Rawls, it may be so explicated and defended that the justice it is intended to embody is subverted.

1. H. Mann, 'Twelfth Annual Report (1848)', in *The Republic and the School : Horace Mann on the Education of Free Men*, ed. L.A. Cremin, New York: Teachers College, Columbia University, 1959, p.87.
2. Perhaps Babeuf can be charged with this extreme form of egalitarianism, but Marx strongly rejected it. See the discussion in F. Feher & A. Heller, 'Forms of Equality', *Telos*, 32 (Summer, 1977), 6–26, esp. 9–11.
3. K. Marx, *The Economic and Philosophic Manuscripts of 1844*, ed. D.J. Struik, trans. M. Milligan, New York: International Publishers, 1964, p.134, as quoted in ibid., 10.
4. J. Feinberg, *Social Philosophy*, Englewood Cliffs, N.J.: Prentice-Hall, 1973, p.99.
5. For a valuable discussion of this confusion, see L.I. Katzner, 'Presumptivist and Nonpresumptivist Principles of Formal Justice', *Ethics*, LXXXI, 3 (April, 1971), 253–58; cf. idem, 'Presumptions of Reason and Presumptions of Justice', *Journal of Philosophy*, LXX, 4 (22 February, 1973), 89–100.
6. *Ethics and Education*, London: Allen & Unwin, 1966, p.121.
7. S.I. Benn & R.S. Peters, *Social Principles and the Democratic State*, London: Allen & Unwin, 1959, pp.127–28.
8. See Katzner, 'Presumptivist and Nonpresumptivist Principles of Formal Justice', 255–57.
9. Peters' argument is found in *Ethics and Education*, pp.121–22. It is examined in greater detail in my 'R.S. Peters' Use of Transcendental Arguments', *Proceedings of the Philosophy of Education Society of Great Britain*, VII, 2 (July, 1973), 149–66. There is a reply by Peters (167–76) and two postscripts (177–80); see also D.E. Browne, 'The Presumption of Equality', *Australasian Journal of Philosophy*, LIII, 1 (May, 1975), 46–55.
10. *Ethics and Education*, p.122.
11. ibid., p.123.
12. S.I. Benn, 'Egalitarianism and the Equal Consideration of Interests' in J.R. Pennock & J.W. Chapman (eds.), *Nomos IX: Equality*, New York: Atherton Press, 1967, pp.61–78 (reprinted in H.A. Bedau (ed.), *Justice and Equality*, Englewood Cliffs, N.J.: Prentice-Hall, 1971, pp. 152–67).
13. ibid., p.76 (p.166).
14. ibid., p.68 (p.159).
15. For various perspectives on the debate, see M. Young, *The Rise of the Meritocracy*, London: Thames & Hudson, 1958; J.W. Gardner, *Excellence: Can We be Equal and*

Excellent too? New York: Harper, 1961; B.S. Crittenden & J.V. D'Cruz (eds.), *Essays on Quality in Education*, Richmond, Vic.: Primary Education, 1976; D.E. Cooper, T. O'Hagan & R.F. Atkinson, Symposium: 'Quality and Equality in Education', in S.C. Brown (ed.), *Philosophers Discuss Education*, London: Macmillan, 1975, Pt. IV; M. Warnock, *Schools of Thought*, London: Faber, 1977, Chs. 1, 2; D.E. Cooper, *Illusions of Equality*, London: Routledge & Kegan Paul, 1980.

16. From Sect.4, adopted by the General Conference of UNESCO on 14 December, 1960; reprinted in *Yearbook on Human Rights for 1961*, New York: United Nations, 1963, p.440.

17. J.S. Coleman, 'What is meant by 'an Equal Educational Opportunity'?' *Oxford Review of Education*, I, 1 (1975), 28–29.

18. I have based the distinctions which follow on D.A. Lloyd Thomas, 'Competitive Equality of Opportunity', *Mind*, LXVI (July, 1977), 388–404.

19. See the discussion and references in Ch.12 *infra*.

20. I have discussed these notions and connections in greater detail in 'Crime and the Concept of Harm', *American Philosophical Quarterly*, XV, 1 (January, 1978), 27–36, esp. 30–34. See also *infra*, Ch.15.

21. For a critique, see D. Lyons, 'On Formal Justice', *Cornell Law Review*, LVIII, 5 (June, 1973), 833–61.

22. For further discussion of this issue, see B.R. Gross (ed.), *Reverse Discrimination*, Buffalo, N.Y.: Prometheus, 1977; Marshall Cohen, *et al.*, *Equality and Preferential Treatment*, Princeton U.P., 1978; A.H. Goldman, *Justice and Reverse Discrimination*, Princeton University Press, 1979.

23. J. Rawls, *A Theory of Justice*, Cambridge, Mass.: Harvard U.P., 1971, p.303.

24. Valuable discussions on Rawls' theory can be found in N. Daniels (ed.), *Reading Rawls : Critical Studies on Rawls'* A Theory of Justice, London: Blackwell, 1975.

25. N. Daniels, 'Equal Liberty and Unequal Worth of Liberty', in ibid., 253–81.

Chapter 11

INTELLIGENCE

In 1950, (Sir) Cyril Burt spoke for a sizeable body of opinion when he stated, with a disarming lack of self-consciousness:

> Obviously, in an ideal community, our aim should be to discover what ration of intelligence Nature has given to each individual child at birth, then to provide him with the appropriate education, and finally to guide him into the career for which he seems to have been marked out.[1]

The techniques for discovery lay close at hand: 'intelligence' or 'I.Q.' tests. The 1938 English Spens Report, which proposed the tripartite division of schooling into grammar, technical and modern (shades of Plato's *Republic*!), observed that 'with few exceptions, it is possible at a very early age to predict with some degree of accuracy the ultimate level of a child's intellectual powers'.[2] Growing public awareness of 'environmental disadvantages' and their probable effects, coupled with scepticism about the validity of the tests themselves, has led to a decreased reliance upon their results. However, the economic and political climate of the past decade has proved fertile ground for the reassertion of earlier views, albeit in a more sophisticated form. In the United States, in particular, the argument from 'nature' has been applied in the context of 'racial' differences, where it has functioned to give some respectability to the deeply ingrained racial prejudice of many white Americans.

Interest in the 'measurement' of intelligence goes back to Francis Galton's *Hereditary Genius* (1869), though it was not until 1905, when Binet and Simon constructed their test for detecting mentally defective children, that substantial advances were made. Binet, it would appear, did not see the tests as providing anything more than an index of the

132

child's present condition, [3] though their later use has tended to be predictive rather than simply diagnostic. The reason for this has been the conviction that 'intelligence tests' measure an innate or inherited characteristic about which nothing substantial can be done. Nor did Binet make any pronouncements on the nature and structure of 'intelligence', though these matters have exercised other writers. Of considerable influence in this regard has been the work of Charles Spearman, who, in 1904, argued that intellectual performance depended on a combination of two factors, one general and one specific to the particular kind of activity. The general factor (or, as it has become known, g) permeated all intellectual activities and was to be identified with 'intelligence'. Just what the nature of g is remained and remains in dispute, so much so that Boring's 1923 claim that 'intelligence is what [intelligence] tests test'[4] has continued to attract support. This is in fact a *reductio ad absurdum*, though Boring and many others did not see it as such.[5] A more generally accepted view sees 'intelligence' as including 'the grasping of relationships, the use of information for induction [and] some capacity for assimilating new information', though even this position is put forward cautiously, with Boring's claim acting as a backstop.[6]

'Intelligence' and intelligent behaviour

The psychometric investigation of 'intelligence' extrapolates from and reifies the everyday characterisation of people or behaviour as intelligent. It is seen as a fixed, innate endowment which places a ceiling on what people can expect to achieve in life. As Burt put it, 'the degree of intelligence with which any particular child is endowed ... sets an upper limit to what he can successfully perform, especially in the educational, vocational and intellectual fields'.[7] Of course, there *are* limits to what we can achieve in life; but what we achieve at any point of time – say, in an I.Q. test – is simply an index of what we can achieve at that time. It marks out no ceiling or upper limit which need obstruct us for the rest of our life. When the view of 'intelligence' as a fixed deposit is combined with the evaluative associations of our everyday characterisation of people or behaviour as intelligent or unintelligent, the effects can be pernicious. The burden or presumption of an I.Q. score can, in the manner of a self-fulfilling prophecy, come to determine a person's future course in life. Some psychometricians insist that they are aware of the difference between psychometric 'intelligence' (I.Q.) and our ordinary concept, and that they do not import into their own judgments the evaluative aspects implicit in the latter, but the ease with which they slip from the language of I.Q. scores into talking of people as 'clever', 'smart', 'dull' and so on, should make us suspicious of such disclaimers.[8]

Our everyday understanding of intelligent behaviour is marked by two overlapping sets of contrasts - the contrast between intelligent and non-intelligent behaviour, and that between intelligent and unintelligent behaviour.[9] Roughly, behaviour which is intelligent (v. non-intelligent) is purposive and adaptive, whereas behaviour which is intelligent (v. unintelligent) conforms to certain *standards* of purposiveness and adaptation (among other things). The intelligence debate focuses on the latter.

In comparing psychometric 'intelligence' with our ordinary ascriptions, we shall confine our remarks to the questions of range and measurement. In ordinary discourse, the semantic field of the adjective 'intelligent' includes 'clear-headed', 'quick-witted', 'smart', 'bright', 'talented', 'clever', 'sharp', 'adroit', 'astute', 'discerning', 'thoughtful', 'wise', 'logical', 'creative', and 'prudent', among many others. There is considerable diversity here, and in relation to them 'intelligent' functions as one of the more general characterisations. As such it is ascribable to almost any task that has significance for us, be it weeding the garden, solving an algebraic equation, designing a machine, making a bed, writing an essay, running a race, counselling someone in need, singing an aria, playing the stock-market or mending a tear.[10] To see intelligence as broadly as this is not to deny that it has some necessarily cognitive dimension, though it is to affirm that cognitive skills are not limited to the kind of informational and verbal skills which tend to predominate in standard I.Q. tests. What I.Q. tests tend to assume is that there is some fairly specific quality, 'intelligence', which manifests itself in these various activities and can be gauged by means of a standardised testing procedure.

But, as Ryle has pointed out, 'intelligent' is 'a highly generic, not a specific adjective'.[11] That is, it does not pick out a narrowly definable but widely dispersable behavioural property or genetic deposit. Intelligent behaviour in one area may not be highly correlated with intelligent behaviour in another. A footballer who displays intelligent ball-handling skills may be stupid when it comes to driving a car, or pedestrian when planning a garden. A highly intelligent academic may be oafish or unperceptive in interpersonal relationships, or muddleheaded when it comes to household repairs or budgeting. The fact that we sometimes speak of 'intelligent people' may suggest that intelligence is not all that generic. But this overlooks the cultural and other contextual factors that are implicit in such general judgments. An intelligent person can be understood to be a person who shows that in a number of the activities which standardly characterise everyday life he/she can participate intelligently. Often, of course, we understand it more restrictively to mark intelligent performance of what might be called scholastic tasks, thus reflecting a certain social ranking of activities. But it is doubtful whether such a restriction can be justified. It reinforces and is reinforced by the psychometric understanding, and, coupled with the idea of innateness, has been a long-time weapon of racists.[12]

The generic character of the noun 'intelligence' serves to make nonsense of the idea that intelligence can be subject to generalised measurement, just as it would be nonsensical to judge a person's *overall* goodness. Judgments of a person's moral, athletic, mathematical, argumentative, etc. goodness cannot be combined into a single estimate, let alone a numerical one. Judgments of intelligence, though less general than judgments of goodness, are nevertheless not sufficiently specific for overall assessments to be made. Ryle's trenchant comments deserve quotation:

> 'Intelligence' is so generic a noun, and such variations exist in the species of intelligence, in the degrees and mutabilities of each of these species and in the conditions of their acquisition and exercise, that the How much? question, which would fit pools, reservoirs and other static containers (even some metaphorical ones) cannot begin to fit the notion of a person's intelligence ... How *much* Efficiency is there in British Railways? There are thousands of specific ways in which we can indeed sensibly and often numerically compare today's operations, etc., of British Railways with last year's, or with those of the Belgian Railway system, e.g. in respect of train-punctuality, accident-rates, timetable legibility, etc., etc. But these do not congregate into a stock or pool such that we can then nominate an absolute or relative size for it.... With this point there goes another. We can in principle often count the tributaries from which a river or a reservoir gets its water; and we can compare the sizes of the water-contributions made by these different tributaries. For these contributions are all contributions of *water*. But if asked what fraction of British Rail efficiency derives from its nationalised status, and what fraction from electricity, we can only gasp.[13]

What, then, do 'intelligence' tests measure? Presumably they tell us something about how well a person at time t can cope with an artificially constructed test which makes limited use of a limited number of skills which he/she may have acquired. That *may* be correlated with later achievements, though any such correlations are not likely to reveal much about the causal factors involved. But we need to explore this more thoroughly.

'Measuring' intelligence

Because 'intelligence' is a generic noun, talk of 'measuring intelligence' as though it were a unified property, is out of place. But this need not daunt the psychometrician. Psychometricians might argue that their aims are more limited. All they wish to measure is 'intelligence' as it relates to 'the educational, vocational and intellectual fields'; and these modest(!) purposes allow for the application of commensurable criteria of assessment. But do they, even granting that such bombast is indeed modesty? Surely this depends on our having a 'theory of intelligence' (in such matters) which will show that I.Q. test-results adequately reflect the abilities which make for judgments of (such-and-such) intelligence in a person. But a satisfactory theory of such intelligence is notoriously lacking. Indeed, efforts are made to avoid the necessity for a theory. Psychometricians assume that if they can show a correlation between I.Q. tests and 'intelligence', the pressure for a 'theory of intelligence' is relieved. But such correlations beg the question. Unless there is some independent means of 'measuring' intelligence we cannot validate such tests. Such validation cannot be adequately provided by the traditional technique of prescientific measurement – the judgments of individual teachers and others – for such judgments are notoriously inconsistent, or, if consistent, reflect cultural or class conventions. Excessively scholastic criteria (themselves controversial enough), what are taken to be desirable personality characteristics, and the quality of pre-existing relationships, all tend to affect such judgments. The further suggestion, that they represent a valid gauge of an innate and fixed capacity, is even more controversial, reflecting the Galtonian pre-occupation with biological explanations of social phenomena. In recent years, this tradition, so powerfully represented by Burt, has lost some of its hold, and a number of psychometricians have allowed for greater flexibility of individual intelligence. But even so, particularly in view of the predictive and selective role still played by I.Q. tests, the subjective character of validating judgments undermines the credibility of claims to objectivity for such tests. Some writers, of course, have acknowledged the difficulty of validation, but

136

since they have been unable to find an alternative basis possessing better credentials, the practice has persisted, albeit more subtly: the validation of tests by standardising them against other tests only conceals (and perpetuates) their subjectivity.[14] Thus it can be seen that if we are to have reasons for believing that I.Q. tests adequately represent (a particular kind of) individual intelligence, we require first of all some theory of (that kind of) intelligence by reference to which I.Q. tests can be evaluated, lest they measure other variables as well as, or more than, intelligence.

In this connection, Block and Dworkin point out that the development of I.Q. tests, unlike the development of the thermometer (with which they have often been compared), has been almost wholly technological rather than scientific. Whereas the development of thermometers has gone hand in hand with the development of a theory of heat phenomena, there have been few significant developments in the 'theory of intelligence' since Binet's first intuitively based tests.[15] In the absence of a defensible and clearly worked out 'theory of intelligence', there is no reason to believe that the refinement and sophistication of techniques have improved the measurement of what they are intended to measure. It is true that some of the more recent tests have gone some way towards removing some of the variables which have undoubtedly biased test results in the past, but this piecemeal elimination of extraneous variables is no substitute for a positive theory of (a particular kind of) intelligence. Ironically, given his place in recent controversy and refusal to reflect on the implications of his own words, the position is well summed up by H.J. Eysenck:

> It is often believed that intelligence tests are developed and constructed according to a rationale deriving from some scientific theory.... In actual fact ... intelligence tests are not based on any very sound scientific principles, and there is not a great deal of agreement among experts regarding the nature of intelligence.... Because the intelligence tests, originally constructed in the early years of this century, did such a good job when applied to various practical problems, psychologists interested in the subject tended to become technologists eager to exploit and improve these tools, rather than scientists eager to carry out the requisite fundamental research, most of which still remains to be done. Society, of course, always interested in the immediate application of technological

advances and disinterested in pure research,
must bear its share of the responsibility for
this unfortunate state of affairs.[16]

This quotation prompts the question 'What did intelligence
tests do such a good job *at*?' There is, as we have seen,
little *reason* to think that they were good at 'measuring
intelligence'. Eysenck suggests that they were recognised
to have a certain 'practical' value, and that this has been
responsible for their continued popularity. If this is the
case, then, in the absence of a theoretical structure which
links the practical value said to be possessed by I.Q.
tests with (a particular kind of) intelligence, it is quite
misleading, and indeed positively discriminatory, to
continue to refer to them as 'intelligence tests'.[17] This
much granted, what practical value have the tests had?
Binet, we observed, found them diagnostically useful. They
indicated something about a child's present 'intellectual
powers, in order to establish whether he is normal or if he
is retarded', without implying anything about aetiology or
prognosis.[18] Leaving aside Binet's intuitive stipulation
that the tests indicated something as general and specific
as the child's 'intellectual powers', and the problems
attaching to notions of normality, it is clear that this
represents a much more modest view of their usefulness than
has been taken by those who have subsequently built on his
foundations. Later testers have considered the tests to
predict reliably scholastic success or occupational status.
They have therefore been used as a basis for streaming in
schools and as an occupational entry requirement.

In the absence of a developed 'theory of intelligence',
this predictive function is perhaps the most pernicious
aspect of I.Q. testing, quite apart from whether it is
reliably predictive, itself a controversial claim.[19]
Prophecies are frequently self-fulfilling, and it is
well-known in schooling contexts how a teacher's early
impressions may determine judgments of a child's future
performance. Thus, children who come from a lower
occupational status background, and who, for one reason or
another, do not conform to the predominantly middle-class
expectations of the school, are likely to find reinforcement
for that background status within the school. I.Q. tests,
though they may avoid the vagaries of individual teachers,
nevertheless focus on abilities or competencies considered
desirable by the decision-makers within society, who use the
results of such tests to maintain a social stratification in
which those abilities and competencies retain their dominant
position ('maintaining standards'). I.Q. tests 'tell' both
the teacher and child where the child can be expected to
'get to', and, such is their standing, they become a causal
factor in the fulfilment of such prophecies. The importance
of casting this in terms of the child's *intelligence* is that

it serves to locate the reason for treatment within the child him/herself. The demands of a particular socio-economic or socio-political order are thus relieved of possible responsibility for what later happens to the child.

However, it may be argued that the link between (a particular kind of) intelligence, I.Q. tests and social position is not as artificial as I have suggested it may be. For, it has been argued, it is precisely because certain people have less 'native intelligence' that they have tended to occupy a particular social position and so perform less well in I.Q. tests. So, if I.Q. tests tend to reflect social position, and also to reinforce it, this is not something which is independent of 'intelligence'. Can such claims be supported?

Support is supposed to be given via *correlations* with I.Q. tests. However, the only relation for which we have correlation figures is that between I.Q. and social position (as measured by income or a combination of average educational level and income within a particular occupational grouping). Since that is the case, it is only by assuming that there is a high correlation between social position and 'intelligence' that a high correlation between I.Q. and 'intelligence' might be anticipated. But, as Block and Dworkin show, even if it is assumed that there is a perfect correlation between social position and 'intelligence', then, given the best correlation figures for the relation between I.Q. and social position (.5), we could expect no more than a .5 correlation between I.Q. and 'intelligence'. What this means is that *'at most* 25 per cent of the variance in I.Q. scores is due to variation in intelligence.... That is, .. quantities other than intelligence would account for at least 75 per cent of I.Q. variation.'[20] The claim that I.Q. scores measure 'intelligence' is thus supported only weakly, if at all, by the correlation between I.Q. and social position. Block and Dworkin reinforce the inadequacy of the initial argument by showing that even if it is assumed that there is a perfect correlation between I.Q. and 'intelligence', there is little basis for it in the established correlation between I.Q. and social position. For, given a 1.0 correlation of 'intelligence' with I.Q., and a .5 correlation of I.Q. with social position, there will be a .5 correlation of the latter with 'intelligence'. But a correlation of .5 between I.Q. and social position and 'intelligence' and social position is compatible with there being a correlation of .5 between social position and two other variables such that there is a zero correlation between I.Q. and 'intelligence'.[21]

Even such weak reasons for believing that I.Q. measures 'intelligence' are further weakened when the factors behind the correlation between I.Q. and social position are investigated. Such correlation as there is between I.Q. and social position is brought about via schooling. However, the correlation between I.Q. and schooling may be in part attributable to the causal effect of I.Q. scores on schooling: in deciding whether to admit students to particular schooling institutions, in advising them whether to leave such institutions, in streaming them into programmes of a terminating or an ongoing kind, or by influencing teachers' grading decisions. It may also be in part attributable to factors unconnected with 'intelligence', such as the socio-economic status of parents and a social environment which is conducive to extended schooling.[22] For these and other reasons discussed by Block and Dworkin, it is doubtful whether any of the correlations that have been established can be used to validate I.Q. tests as measures of 'intelligence'.

It was noted earlier that many psychometricians identify 'intelligence' with g, Spearman's general factor, an ability common to every activity, and supplemented by a variety of special abilities. Despite its influence, there has been little to confirm such a division, and the view that there is a multiplicity of abilities has just as much claim to acceptance. Certainly if psychometricians believe that they are dealing with something analogous to intelligence as we ordinarily understand it, the multifactorial approach of Guildford and others has much more to commend it. Yet most I.Q. tests seem to presuppose something like g. That this is so is strongly suggested by the practice of eliminating from tests those items which do not correlate highly with the whole, the assumption being that they do not measure what the tests measure − 'general intelligence'.[23]

The point of the foregoing arguments is that we have little reason to believe that I.Q. tests measure some 'general intelligence', and not a geat deal more reason to believe that they measure a specific kind of intelligence. In the absence of a clearly articulated and established 'theory of intelligence', and in view of the dubious inferences made from the correlation of I.Q. tests and other factors such as social position, schooling, etc., we are forced back to Boring's empty observation that the tests measure what they measure. But we can go further than this to suggest that whatever I.Q. tests do measure, it is not intelligence. In part this is because intelligence, like goodness and efficiency, is too diverse in its manifestations to enable such general judgments to be made. In part it is because I.Q. tests take certain achievements as accurate gauges of abilities without reference to additional features such as background, motivation and personality (or only the crudest appreciation of them). But it is also because, as tests, they limit those achievements in certain ways which may unfavourably influence judgments about the particular abilities which they have the best claim to measure. They are, for example, speed tests, and do not provide opportunities for sustained thought. And they do not offer much scope for creative activity. Indeed, the well-known Wallach and Kogan 'creativity tests' (an idea hardly less absurd than 'intelligence tests') show only a low correlation with I.Q. tests. In view of all this, and the use to which such tests have been and are being put, there is clearly a serious moral problem in their continuing use. Indeed, were it not for the fact that they reflect and help maintain the *status quo* with moderate efficiency(!), we might have expected their abandonment long ago.

I.Q. and heritability

Nowhere are the moral difficulties in using I.Q. tests more pronounced than in recent discussions concerning the heritability of intelligence, which have been coupled with the observation that blacks in the United States score on average some fifteen points lower than whites on I.Q. tests. Taken in conjunction with the belief that 'intelligence' is in large measure genetically determined, the consequences are potentially serious. Various programmes designed to compensate blacks for environmental disadvantages have been called into question, since, it is claimed, the disadvantages are largely genetic. At the same time, old fears about an increasing population of 'genetically inferior' people have been revived, typified in William Shockley's much publicised suggestion that people with low I.Q.s be encouraged to undergo sterilisation.[24] Even though heritability is a population statistic,[25] and not strictly transferable to particular cases, there is a strong tendency for such statistics to be applied individually. This, no doubt, was partly responsible for the strong reaction to Jensen, Shockley and Eysenck.

Yet, possibilities of misuse aside, heritability as it relates to intelligence is hardly less controversial than the I.Q.-intelligence relation. Attempts to determine the heritability of 'intelligence' (or, more correctly, I.Q.) via studies of twins have been less than satisfactory,[26] and although there is evidence that I.Q. is to some extent heritable, it is unlikely that 80% of the population variance in I.Q. is attributable to genetic factors. However, it is not the quality of evidence alone which makes heritability estimates controversial. Those who use such estimates tend to work with a distinction between genetic and environmental factors which is not mirrored in the estimates themselves. For the conditions under which genetically transmitted dispositional advantages are determined already include an environmental overlay which probably magnifies any advantage that is present. A child with an advantage in genotypic 'intelligence' may magnify it either by creating its own learning opportunities or by attracting them to itself; likewise a child with a genetic disadvantage may find that it steadily increases through discouragement, etc. This introduces an element into heritability estimates which is environmentally determined. As Block and Dworkin point out,

> Prima facie, one would suppose that genes affect intelligence by some sort of internal biochemical process. A process by which genes affect a person's intelligence by affecting the behaviour of other persons toward him is quite different. But the methods used to assess the heritability of I.Q. automatically count variance produced by genetic variation as genetically caused variance even if it is also environmentally caused.[27]

It has not been possible to separate the effects of these two factors, and since this is so, it is not possible to base recommendations for the withdrawal of compensatory programmes on claims about heritability. Until the causal mechanisms involved are determined, any such recommendations can be based on little more than speculation. Even then, there would be difficulties in deriving recommendations, since they tend to assume that the effects of environment on different I.Q. genotypes will be parallel. 'They suppose that for I.Q., unlike many human traits, a given environmental change produces the same phenotypic effect for every genotype.'[28]

Conclusion

The history of the use of I.Q. tests is not one to inspire much confidence in their use. Although they might have possessed some diagnostic value as an index of achievement with respect to certain limited skills under certain conditions, their traditional association with a theory of 'innate intelligence' has instead constituted them an instrument of racism or a dominant *status quo*. Like much research, research into I.Q. tests has been conditioned more by the needs of an élitist and competitive social structure than by an interest in understanding and ameliorating the human condition. Under the guise of being scientific, they have served to reinforce the values of a particular form of society, locating within individuals and groups the reason for their station in life rather than the changeable socio-economic and socio-political structures which they inhabit. Even though it is reasonable to assume that genetic factors play *some* part in the capacity of individuals to develop various skills, we have no basis for believing that I.Q. tests provide a reliable index of such factors. Indeed, given the generic character of intelligence, it is doubtful whether talk of *separating out* genetic and environmental factors makes any sense at all.

NOTES

1. C. Burt, 'Testing Intelligence', *The Listener*, XLIV (16 November, 1960), 543.
2. Report of the Consultative Committee on Secondary Education (Spens Report), London: H.M.S.O., 1938, p.42.
3. See the quotation in S. Wiseman (ed.), *Intelligence and Ability: Selected Readings* [2], Harmondsworth: Penguin, 1973, p.11. (This collection contains selections from Galton and Spearman.) A relevant quotation from Binet is also included in J. Hirsch, 'Jensenism: The Bankruptcy of "Science" Without Scholarship', *Educational Theory*, XXV, 1 (Winter, 1978), 19.
4. E.G. Boring, 'Intelligence as the Tests Test It', *New Republic*, XXXV (6 June, 1923), 35-37.
5. Shown in detail by N.J. Block & G. Dworkin, 'I Q, Heritability, and Inequality', reprinted in N.J. Block & G. Dworkin (eds.), *The IQ Controversy : Critical Readings*, New York: Pantheon, 1976, pp.414-16. This chapter owes much to Block & Dworkin's paper.
6. R.J. Herrnstein, *I.Q. in the Meritocracy*, London: Allen Lane, 1973, p.43.
7. C. Burt, 'The Evidence for the Concept of Intelligence', reprinted in Wiseman (ed.), p.281.
8. Noted by Block & Dworkin, p.429-32.
9. Cf. rational/non-rational/irrational; moral/non-moral/immoral.
10. In *The Concept of Mind*, Ryle suggests that routine or 'single-track' behaviour is not characterisable as intelligent/unintelligent (London: Hutchinson, 1949, p.44ff), but this is criticised in J.P. White, 'Intelligence and the Logic of the Nature-Nurture Issue', *Proceedings of the Philosophy of Education Society of Great Britain*, VIII, 1 (January, 1974), 36-38.
11. G. Ryle, 'Intelligence and the Logic of the Nature-Nurture Issue: Reply to J.P. White', *Proceedings of the Philosophy of Education Society of Great Britain*, VIII, 1 (January, 1974), 55. Block & Dworkin go further to suggest that the criteria for intelligence may also be culturally relative (p.412).
12. See the essay by C.J. Karier, 'Testing For Order and Control in the Corporate Liberal State', reprinted in Block & Dworkin, pp.339-69; also S. Rose, 'Scientific Racism and Ideology: the I.Q. Racket from Galton to

Jensen', in H. & S. Rose (eds.), *The Political Economy of Science : Ideology of/in the Natural Sciences*, London: Macmillan, 1976, Ch.7.

13. Ryle, 'Reply to J.P. White', 56.
14. This problem is discussed in detail in B. Simon, *Intelligence, Psychology and Education : a Marxist Critique*, London: Lawrence & Wishart, 1971, pp.72–81; cf. Block & Dworkin, pp.414ff.
15. Of course, there have been numerous discussions in the literature as to what intelligence is, but there has been nothing like consensus on the issue, and I.Q. tests have continued fairly much as they were, independently of such theorising. See Block & Dworkin, p.424.
16. H.J. Eysenck, *Know your Own I.Q.*, Baltimore: Penguin, 1962, p.8, as quoted in Block & Dworkin, pp.423–24.
17. The noises to this and similar effect by some psychometricians do not appear to have affected their own practice or the practice of others in any substantial measure. Cf. Block & Dworkin, pp.430–32.
18. As quoted in Wiseman, p.11.
19. Cf. S. Bowles & V.I. Nelson, 'The "Inheritance of I.Q." and the Intergenerational Reproduction of Economic Inequality', *Review of Economics and Statistics*, LVI, 1 (February, 1974), 39–51.
20. Block & Dworkin, p.434.
21. ibid., pp.434–36.
22. See ibid., pp.439–44.
23. See ibid., pp.462–73. Block & Dworkin quote Butcher as observing that

> there is little doubt that on the whole, with a few conspicuous exceptions, theories of general intelligence as the prime mover, perhaps modified or "perpetuated" by subsidiary influence, have flourished in Britain, whereas the generally preferred picture in the United States has been of multiple abilities of more or less equal status and influence.

(p.466).
24. W. Shockley, 'Dysgenics, Geneticity, Raceology: A Challenge to the Intellectual Responsibility of Educators', *Phi Delta Kappan*, LIII, 5 (January, 1972), 297–307.
25. 'The heritability of a characteristic in a population is the proportion of the characteristic's variation in that population which is due to genetic differences. The measure of variation is variance, the average of the squares of deviations from the population average. Thus heritability is the variance caused by genetic differences divided by the total variance' (Block & Dworkin, p.474).
26. See the discussion in ibid., pp.447–79. Since Block & Dworkin's study, Jensen has admitted that the data on

which Burt based his findings cannot be fully relied
upon, and this has been reinforced by Dorfman. In his
careful and restrained re-examination, Dorfman concludes
that Burt 'fixed' some of his results. See A.R. Jensen,
'Kinship Correlations Reported by Sir Cyril Burt',
Behaviour Genetics, IV, 1 (March, 1974), 1-28; D.D.
Dorfman, 'The Cyril Burt Question: New Findings',
Science, CCI (29 September, 1978), 1177-86. There is a
revealing essay by Burt, 'Francis Galton and his
contributions to Psychology', in *British Journal of
Statistical Psychology*, XV, 1 (May, 1962), 1-49.
27. Block & Dworkin, p.480.
28. ibid., p.54.

Chapter 12

CURRICULUM CHOICE

If it is the purpose of education, as a valuable enterprise, to bring into being people with activated and developing capacities for autonomous agency, how is this best achieved? Questions of this general form naturally conceal several sub-questions. One of these concerns the structure/content to be communicated in prosecuting the educational task. Within institutionalised contexts, this has become a question of curriculum, though we may have serious reservations about the value of curricula in the achievement of educationally significant ends. By 'curriculum' I understand a synthetic structure of diverse learning activities unified by the ends or objectives which they subserve.[1] The curriculum is to be distinguished from two other institutional concepts – the syllabus and lesson. The syllabus is limited to an outline of the structure/content to be deliberately communicated within some 'subject' (numbers of which generally occupy an important place in the curriculum). Lessons are one means by which a syllabus may be implemented: the syllabus material is broken up into manageable portions for presentation by a teacher.

Most contemporary curriculum theorists see the curriculum as embodying four elements: a set of ends or objectives, a content or subject matter to be learned, a set of procedures or methods by which the content is communicated, and some means of evaluating the content and methods of the curriculum against its objectives. Each of these elements generates a number of issues and problems which are easily overlooked. In this chapter, however, our focus will be on the first two of these elements.[2]

Ends or objectives

The ends or objectives of curricula in traditional schooling are generally characterised as 'educational'. It is to be wondered whether this amounts to more than a piece of pleasing rhetoric, since it is not uncommon for curriculum

146

planners to think of education in terms of preparing children to fill pre-set social and vocational slots. Little thought is paid to the acceptability of such an understanding, and the dominant *status quo* provides little basis for confidence in it. The needs of industrial capitalism find expression in curricula which pay limited regard to the personal needs and interests of learners. But even if curriculum theorists and planners are not wedded to the dominant *status quo*, it may be overly generous to see their objectives as educational. This may be because the conception of education underlying their objectives is too wanting in theoretical tightness to sustain a ranking of objectives. A good example of this failure is to be found in B.S. Bloom's enormously influential *Taxonomy of Educational Objectives*, which divides educational objectives into three domains: cognitive, affective and psychomotor. [3] A large number of objectives is discriminated within each domain but little help is given to establishing their relative importance, or even their educational relevance, though Bloom appears to give some sort of educational priority to objectives in the cognitive domain. This, however, is never shown, and even so remains too vague to constitute a practicable basis for curriculum construction.

There is, however, a deeper problem which faces the characterisation of traditional curriculum objectives as 'educational'. At first blush, this presents itself simply as the failure to maintain a causal link between the mediate curriculum objectives and the education to which they are related as means. But it is not as simple as this, because of the fundamentally different character of the mediate and ultimate objectives. Put briefly, the tendency in traditional curriculum theory to characterise objectives in some terminal fashion sits awkwardly with a conception of education which focuses on the ongoing development of insights and relations, in which objectives come to be autonomously determined and not merely complied with. The idea of education as brought about through the attainment of certain pre-set terminal objectives runs in sharp contrast to the autonomous character of the educated person. There is something overly manipulative about traditional statements of curriculum objectives – no doubt a reflection of their roots in behaviourism. We are not arguing here that the requirements of 'being educated' are totally unspecifiable, since autonomy itself presupposes the existence and development of certain capacities and relations; but many traditional curricula do not locate their objectives within such an open-ended context. Nor must our criticism of specific terminal objectives be taken as advocacy of 'education for change', which has recently become fashionable in curriculum theory. 'Education for change' merely echoes the changing technological demands of industrial society. It is the agent of a dominant *status*

147

quo whose maintenance demands flexibility rather than autonomy, and the purpose of curricula which are geared to this is to develop people who can 'fit into' this process of change rather than exercise control over it.

The problem posed by specific terminal objectives is made more acute when these objectives are interpreted behaviourally (in the behaviourist's sense of that word) - still, perhaps, the major temptation of curriculum theorists. Because the development of curricula in contemporary schooling is so closely bound up with 'measurement' - to satisfy the school's function of social stratification - objectives 'need' to be expressed in some 'measurable' form. This, however, invites serious distortion.[4] Although educationally valuable learning can be expected to have some behavioural expression, it is not constituted by this or that specific behavioural outcome, but by understanding. Of course, understanding manifests itself in behaviour, but the particular behaviour which is indicative of understanding is neither sufficient to constitute that understanding, nor (generally) sufficiently specific for the standard techniques of 'measurement' to provide a valid or reliable indication of the level of understanding attained. Where the claims to validity and reliability are strongest, the link between the objective and education (in a critically valuable sense) tends to be most problematic. However, claims to validity are themselves problematic, since even behaviourally defined objectives are somewhat recalcitrant to measurement.[5]

A further difficulty for the traditional approach to curriculum construction arises from its understanding of the relationship between curriculum objectives and curriculum content. Objectives, it is usually claimed, precede and determine content. In institutional contexts, this means that basic curriculum decisions are generally made by teachers/committees prior to and without direct consideration of and consultation with those who are to be subject to those decisions. But why should we think that curriculum objectives can be established prior to involvement with those for whom they exist? The 'progressive' slogan (for that is all it is) - 'We teach children, not subjects' - at least has the merit of recognising that education is basically about people and their development as autonomous, responsible agents. That end is not easily resolved into a set of *curriculum* objectives capable of being articulated in anything but the most provisional fashion prior to an acquaintance with the particular child(ren). Nevertheless, it is not difficult to see how curriculum objectives have come to be thought of as determinable prior to any involvement with the children who are making their way through the institution. For the purpose of schooling generally is to produce and reproduce in the coming generation those values, attitudes and attributes consistent

148

and continuous with the values, etc. prized by the dominant stratum within the present generation. To view schooling in this way is to secure the almost total dependence of children on adults for yet another aspect of their development.

Content: P.H. Hirst

The views expressed in the previous paragraph do not coincide with the current orthodoxy, and will need to be argued for. We shall attempt to do this taking as a reference point two philosophically articulate exponents of the orthodox position, P.H. Hirst and J.P. White.

A general survey of theoretical discussions of school curriculum content reveals a strong concentration on 'cognitive' objectives, to the neglect of 'affective' and 'psychomotor' objectives. Most probably this is due to the inherent constraints of a *school curriculum*, but it is unfortunate nevertheless, since it overlooks the profound interplay between these various aspects of the human person. Some awareness of this one-sidedness in school curricula appears to be shown by Hirst, who explicitly acknowledges that the 'liberal education' for which he is an advocate 'is only one part of the education a person ought to have, for it omits quite deliberately ... specialist education, physical education and character training'.[6] But a close reading of Hirst's work leaves the overwhelming impression that even if there is more to education than induction into various 'forms of knowledge', it plays very little part in his thinking. Nevertheless, Hirst's defence of the externally determined curriculum is instructive, and repays investigation.[7]

For Hirst, the ultimate objective of a liberal education curriculum is the development of a rational mind, this being accomplished through an individual's initiation into each of the logically distinct forms which constitute the realm of human knowledge. These forms are, contingently, 'mathematics, the physical science, knowledge of persons, literature and the fine arts, morals, religion and philosophy'.[8] They are distinguished in virtue of three (or four) features. First, each form is characterised by certain concepts which are unique to it, including some which are categorically fundamental. These categorical concepts, say, space, time and causality in the physical sciences, ought in morals, intention in knowledge of persons, and God in religion, are characterised by 'logical uniqueness, mutual irreducibility'.[9] Secondly, the network of concepts and propositions which go to make up each form have a distinctive logical structure. Aesthetic knowledge will be structured differently from mathematical knowledge, historical knowledge from that in the physical sciences, etc. Thirdly, each form possesses distinctive truth criteria. The kinds of tests appropriate to demonstrating the truth of mathematical claims are logically distinct from those appropriate to the demonstration of moral or scientific claims. And finally (though Hirst now sees this as secondary), each form has its own methodology, whereby advances can be made within it.[10]

It is difficult to read Hirst's earlier writing as other than a defence of the traditional grammar or 'public' (i.e. private) school curriculum. Matthew Arnold, one imagines, would have warmly approved, though the sterility of Hirst's account of literature and the fine arts[11] betrays the legacy of what C.P. Snow described as 'the two cultures'.[12] But in later defences of his position, Hirst is more circumspect. The forms of knowledge, we are told, are not intended to endorse the typical 'public' school curriculum: they represent different classes of true propositions and not curriculum subjects. A particular form may 'have little in common with what elsewhere falls under the same label',[13] and there is no implicit reason why 'the organisation of the curriculum should mirror the fundamental categories of knowledge'.[14] Nevertheless, Hirst's discussion of curriculum planning strongly favours a division of material which recognises the 'primacy of achieving cognitive development in the distinct forms'.[15] Though inter-form relationships are important, approaches which are multi-form in character (so-called integrated curricula) invite confusion and superficiality: 'attention to forging inter-form links must be at the price of systematic attention to the development of understanding within the separate forms'.[16]

The adequacy of Hirst's position obviously depends on, though it is not wholly determined by, its epistemological underpinnings. But these, it turns out, are sketchy at best. In 'Liberal Education and the Nature of Knowledge' the Western cultural tradition is frozen into the necessary conditions of human understanding, but in later work he dissociates himself from the view that 'in elucidating the fundamental categories of our understanding we reach an unchanging structure that is implicit, indeed *a priori* in all rational thought in all times and places'.[17] At best, 'we pick out those concepts and principles which are necessary and fundamental to anything we could at present call understanding, as well as to the understanding we presently have'.[18] There is, however, more appearance than reality to Hirst's concessions to an evolutionary or possibly revolutionary view of human knowledge. For our present situation is that 'all intelligibility that we can have is tied to the creation of concepts within a setting that being given, we cannot escape, and which is in large measure not of our creating'.[19] When we ask, 'To whom does the "we" refer?' it becomes clear that Hirst is urging the reader to see things from the point of view of a *particular* tradition, whose theory and practice can lay no irresistible claim to exhausting or even correctly delimiting the presently available epistemological possibilities. We are *bound* only in so far as we fail to recognise the socially and historically conditioned 'interests' which have influenced the development of the various 'forms of knowledge' articulated by Hirst. His approach recalls Wittgenstein's self-critical observation that 'a *picture* held us captive. And we could not get outside it, for it lay in our language and language seemed to repeat it to us inexorably.'[20] Although Hirst concedes that his forms of knowledge are historically contingent, he focuses on them so resolutely that it is difficult to avoid the impression that they are the very eyes through which beings like us must comprehend reality, rather than spectacles whose structurings are not given but imposed. A curriculum which sees the forms as primary and neglects their conditioning by social interests is no less dogmatic than a theology for which the question of God's existence cannot (in practical terms) arise, and an emphasis on 'achieving cognitive development in the distinct forms' risks locking its subjects into a mental straitjacket from which escape will be nigh impossible. Unless the so-called forms of knowledge are seen in the context of their socio-historical development - in other words, in terms of their 'inter-form relationships', they come to acquire an aura of permanence and unquestionability to which they can have no proper claim. Theoretical discussions within the various 'forms' now recognise this, though Hirst does not take such developments into account. An illuminating, if controversial example from the area in which he feels most comfortable is Thomas Kuhn's *The Structure of Scientific Revolutions*,[21] which sets the development of scientific theory and discourse into the context of wider social changes, and casts something of a shadow over the claim to distinctive criteria of testability. Even if Kuhn's own position represents something of an over-simplification and distortion of scientific change, it nevertheless draws attention to the interconnectedness of the enterprise which makes up the large and uneven patchwork of human knowledge.

The schooling system, with its professional cast of teachers (those who know) charged with the responsibility of passing on as established beliefs and practices which confirm or appear to confirm social reality, is well suited to the Hirstian understanding. For, by laying primary emphasis on 'achieving cognitive development in the distinct forms', Hirst encourages and reinforces the view that knowledge is something given, and the knower a more or less passive recipient of this given. Since this conception of knowledge is imposed on us at crucial points in our development, it comes to dominate our epistemological framework. The crucial importance of interests in the

151

production and structuring of knowledge is all but ignored, and the distinction between epistemological and institutional authority gets blurred. Hirst's account diverts attention from the character of cognition as an active enterprise, in which the knowing subject must continually reflect on and test what is presented to it, and in which the social context of the knower prompts a particular focusing of attention, and substitutes for it a receptiveness to what are in practice unquestionable 'facts', theoretically neutral and externally validated by objective methods.

Once we recognise the dynamic character of knowing, and the social determinants of knowledge, we are free to reflect on and question the supposedly fundamental forms of intelligibility, to see how well they stand up to the scrutiny of the reality they supposedly represent. Obviously this is an ongoing enterprise rather than a once-off operation. We cannot, nor should we expect to, detach ourselves from the social determinants of knowledge. Nevertheless, some social determinants tend to distort, whereas others enable us to focus more clearly on the world. Without a continuing process of testing and reflection which will enable an exposure and examination of the interests at work in the structuring of our knowledge, we can have no real grounds for confidence in what we come to hold. To suggest, as Hirst does, that induction into the 'forms' is the precondition for this process of testing and reflection, on the contrary subverts it.

However, it is not enough to emphasise the historical and social contingency of Hirst's forms. It is, as we have seen, something which he theoretically if not practically concedes. We need to go on to ask whether the forms as he outlines them provide a fruitful epistemological schema. Here we must express considerable reservations. Several alternatives to Hirst's position have been offered. Some of these have been limited, amounting to no more than slight structural modifications. More ambitious has been the attempt to argue that there are only two forms of knowledge (conceptual and empirical) and that Hirst has elevated superficial differences into fundamental structural distinctions.[22] But since even that dualism is itself highly contentious (for reasons developed by Quine[23]), we shall not explore it further here. More impressive, I think, have been attempts to show, from our experience of the world and recognition of the role played by interests in structuring our understanding of it, that positing a determinate number of distinct 'forms' only conceals that world from us, or, what amounts to the same, distorts our perception of and involvement in it.

Here it may be helpful to look first at some of the internal difficulties faced by the 'forms of knowledge' thesis. Consider, for example, the tension between Hirst's

152

four criteria for a 'form' and the diversity that exists within each of his posited 'forms'. The discipline of mathematics, for example, has to accommodate (more or less) arithmetic, calculus, Euclidean and Riemannian geometry; the physical sciences have to accommodate (more or less) geology, astronomy, biology and thermodynamics; religion presumably includes not only Christianity but Mahayana Buddhism, Orphism and Theosophy; and so on. Even if we allow, what Hirst casually acknowledes, that 'many of the disciplines borrow from each other',[24] we should, I think, find it impossible to bring them into line with the criteria as outlined. Take religion, for example. Hirst argues that each 'form' involves 'certain concepts that are peculiar in character to the form.' And he offers 'God, sin and predestination' in religion. Well, that might tell us something about Christianity, but it doesn't help much with Mahayana Buddhism. Not even the concept of 'god' is common to all religious belief. It is significant that in his 'Forms ... Revisited' article, Hirst modifies the boldness of his original thesis with the observation that in religion the concept of God is only 'widely regarded' as categorial.[25] A similar qualification is made with respect to the other 'forms'. As noted earlier, there is evidence that Hirst now wishes to shift the weight of his thesis to the third criterion, relating to testability. But we are no better off. Even if we leave aside the substantial differences between religions in this regard, we cannot discover within a religious tradition such as Christianity such a distinctive test. Religious claims are not all of a piece, and support for them may take the form of appeals to history, religious experience, revelation, natural theology, and so on. I do not of course wish to suggest that such appeals are unproblematic. They are not, but what Hirst's thesis does is to pre-empt the issue by suggesting that there must be some distinctive test. The point, really, is this: the so-called disciplines are not concerned with 'one logically distinct form of expression or test'. To suggest that they must be is to emasculate them.

Hirst's difficulties do not stop with the internal complexities of the 'forms'. The enumeration of 'forms' is itself problematic, as Hirst has found.[26] He has tried to overcome this problem by distinguishing 'forms of knowledge' from 'fields of knowledge', the latter including geography, engineering, law, politics and education. Why do these not qualify as 'forms of knowledge'? It is not simply that they 'make use of several forms' (for even the 'forms' do that), but that they 'are not concerned, as the disciplines are, to validate any logically distinct form of expression. They are not concerned with developing a particular structuring of experience.'[27] When you think about it, this is pretty vague. But it provides no obvious reason for calling, say, law a 'field' rather than a 'form' of knowledge. Nor, for that matter, do the four criteria for 'forms'. It is a matter of some importance for Hirst that a distinction between 'forms' and 'fields' of knowledge can be sustained, since he can see 'no reason why ... 'fields' should not be endlessly constructed according to particular theoretical or practical interests'.[28] What would happen to a compulsory liberal education if it required induction into all of these enterprises!

The last quotation betrays the fundamental wrongheadedness of the 'forms of knowledge' thesis. For the 'forms', no less than the 'fields' of knowledge, are products of human interests, and it is the human interests involved which give the so-called 'forms'/'fields' their specificity and distinctiveness. The structuring of knowledge is a function of the interests which are operative in our interactions with the world, and attempts to relocate these in a set of formal criteria of the kind suggested by Hirst distorts our understanding of the growth and differentiation of human knowledge. We come to the world, not as passive recipients of logically distinct 'forms', but as active bearers of interests, who, in the prosecution of those interests, find it fruitful to gain mastery over our world by structuring our interactions with it in certain ways.[29] Physics, law, sociology, mathematics, naturopathy, geology, economics, psychology, religion, etc. simply express some of the ways in which some people have found it helpful to structure their understanding. Others may not find it helpful to structure their understanding in these ways; indeed, they may even believe the interests which express themselves in a particular enterprise to be misconceived or confused. Religion has come in for a battering on this score, but there is no special reason why the same could not be true of the others. Indeed, when one looks at the transformations which have occurred within, say, physics, chemistry and law over the centuries, it becomes apparent that there have been fundamental shifts of interest as well as of conceptual schemata. The linking of knowledge to interests is thus crucial to the criticism of knowledge, for it reminds us that the body of knowledge which is transmitted to us as a part of our acculturation is neither theoretically neutral nor incontestably 'given'. The Hirstian thesis, by diverting our attention from 'the social construction of reality',[30] locks us into an approach to knowledge which obscures its origins and inflates its claims. In the curriculum context, it becomes dogma, to be indoctrinated.

Content: J.P. White

Looked at in one way, Hirst and White belong together: White has been greatly influenced by Hirst. Yet he wishes to argue for a more broadly conceived curriculum than Hirst,

one which does not focus narrowly on an induction into the
'forms of knowledge', but rather has as its ultimate end the
realisation of a personally constructed good life. For this
to be possible, White argues, we must ensure

> (a) that [a person] knows about as many
> activities or ways of life as possible which
> he may want to choose for their own sake, and
> (b) that he is able to reflect on priorities
> among them from the point of view not only of
> the present moment but as far as possible of
> his life as a whole.[31]

In (a), White sees the distinction between 'activities' and
'ways of life' as being of sufficient significance to
justify separate discussion. With regard to the former, a
distinction is drawn between (i) those activities in which a
person (logically) must engage if there is to be any proper
understanding of what it is to want to engage in them, and
(ii) those for which this is not necessary.[32] A 'proper
understanding', in White's view, is constituted by the
ability to give 'either a correct verbal account, sufficient
to distinguish the [activity] from other things, or correct
identification of cases of [the activity]'.[33] Activities
falling within category (i) are justifiably incorporated in
a compulsory curriculum, and, according to White, include
communication in general, pure mathematics, the (exact)
physical sciences, art appreciation, and philosophy. With
regard to 'ways of life', White notes their great variety,
and argues that in order to free people from the pressures
of conformity and thus to help them rationally judge between
the various 'ways', they should be required to study
history, religious studies (of a general sort), literature
(especially the novel and drama), and (again) philosophy
(especially ethics). If condition (b) is to be satisfied, a
person's ability to integrate various activities into 'ways
of life' and to give them effect must be developed. Moral
development, economics and politics, careers information and
the social sciences become indispensable here.

White's distinction between category (i) and (ii)
activities is not meant to relegate the latter to an
inferior status, but simply to justify compulsion with
respect to the former. Compulsion is justified in terms of
the greater freedom it is supposed to enable in respect of
life choices. The same consideration is intended to justify
compulsory exposure to activities designed to satisfy
condition (b).

We should note three problems with White's account.
First, by virtue of what criteria do we determine which
activities will satisfy condition (b)? Though there is a
surface plausibility to the inclusion of history, religious
studies, literature and philosophy, the list is very

open-ended. What in the last century was called 'travel' might easily be included, as would political science, social anthropology and sociology. But we need not stop there. Very few activities are so detached from the rest of everyday life that they would have no relevance to questions about 'the good life'. It is eminently arguable that if we gave more attention to bushwalking, nutrition, sex education, and the creative use of leisure, our perceptions of and ability to pursue 'the good life' would be greatly improved. White's response to this problem of choice is to leave it in the hands of government authorities, in so far as they are democratic (where the latter is understood as 'more or less like our own').[34] This does, I believe, represent an overly optimistic appreciation of both the will and the competence of government authorities. Inescapably social 'the good life' may be, but the power of special interest groups in our society is far too pervasive to justify any formalistic approach to the delegation of responsibility. As things stand, governments, in response to the various pressures under which they find themselves, *will* take the major curriculum decisions. We do not need to argue that they *ought to*; instead, it is necessary to do what one can to ensure that whatever decisions are made, they are the best achievable. This is in no way guaranteed or even rendered more likely by (what we call democratically elected) government control.

The second problem is related. The idea that some involvement with history, religious studies, economics, etc. will make an important and acceptable contribution to our decision-making about 'the good life' has much to commend it. But to a degree this is because we idealise these activities. We overlook the deep theoretical commitments which inform such investigations, in particular the form taken by such commitments in the schooling situation. You can be pretty sure that school texts in history will not approach the subject in a way which undermines or challenges the existing order. It is not a matter of truth, but of the purpose of schooling, which is to prepare people for the dominant *status quo*. Some criticism there can be, but it is criticism premissed on the structural soundness of that dominant *status quo*. Teachers who take a more radical position soon learn what the system is all about. A serious fault with White's position, no less than with Hirst's, is that those who take them seriously will not see the need to do anything very different from what is presently going on. True, White argues for considerably more compulsion than we presently tolerate (as though that is not more than enough!); but basically what he wants is just more of the same. Talk of a self-chosen good life remains empty rhetoric while its conditions are packaged and dispensed in the schooling system. We see this clearly enough when we look at Soviet schools, but we have been carefully shielded

156

from seeing it in our own.

The third problem concerns the distinction between category (i) and category (ii) activities. It is, I believe, an artificial one. Consider the position of a child who is not sent to school, but who grows up in accommodating and caring surroundings. Through its interactions with parents, friends and others it will acquire basic skills of communication and will develop and learn to articulate a variety of interests. What these interests are and how they are expressed will depend to a considerable extent on the resources of the environment and their availability to the child's emerging understanding. Suppose, however, that the child comes to acquire an interest in collecting rocks, shells and plants, in making music, in asking questions about why this or that happens, and why it is permitted to do some things and not others. If it is to pursue these questions at any depth, then there is some case for saying that it should undertake studies in geology, conchology, botany, music, chemistry, physics and any other studies presupposed by a serious involvement in these. The point of the example is this: the interests necessary to choosing between various 'curriculum subjects' may and frequently do exist prior to schooling in them. Such curriculum subjects are prefabricated sophistications of interests developed informally as part of everyday experience. Therefore, to claim that 'no understanding of [category (i) activities] is logically possible without engaging in [them]' is hardly true if it is intended to justify compulsory participation in the activities of an institutional curriculum. White has failed to distinguish the kinds of interest which give rise to investigational foci from the conceptual apparatus developed in consequence of such investigations. Perhaps it could be argued that these interests may sometimes not exist independently of an engagement in the activities, but this is true only in the sense that elementary studies in communication in general, pure mathematics, the (exact) physical sciences, art appreciation, and philosophy may introduce people to dimensions of their cultural world that had not till then been available to them. Arousal of their interest, however, need not require initiation into the complexities of these areas, their so-called formal apparatus. Indeed, if there is no interest prior to such initiation, we are more likely to inhibit than to encourage it.

White, like Hirst, is fundamentally aligned with the dominant *status quo*. Both are committed to compulsory schooling, and both believe that they can produce arguments for a compulsory curriculum. What they turn up with looks suspiciously like what we've already got, or at least not different enough to trouble those with institutional oversight. This wouldn't matter if the existing institution was better than it is. But it is in many ways a repressive

157

and oppressive institution, one which distances children from the world in which they live, one which pigeonholes their learning in ways that prevent them from using it and transferring it to other areas of concern to them, and one which so mistrusts them that their interests are legitimised only when they fall within the prescribed curriculum.

Conclusion: the hidden curriculum and beyond

Compulsory schooling, at least in its present form, comprehends not simply an overt or explicit curriculum of the kind we have been discussing, but also a covert or hidden one.[35] The structure, organisation and social standing of compulsory schooling is such that it effectively and systematically conveys a message beyond that which is explicitly acknowledged. For example, it teaches people to believe that school is necessary if one is to get on in the world; that schooling and education are identical; that what is taught in school is worthwhile, and what is not is not really important; that what is taught in school is the way things are; that teachers know, as do others in authority; that learning requires teaching; that school provides a proper index of one's abilities; that one's education finishes with one's schooling; and so on. Proposals for curriculum reform cannot ignore the hidden curriculum.

If our arguments in relation to Hirst and White have been at all to the point, there would appear to be few grounds for a compulsory curriculum. The idea of a necessary core of knowledge or of a core set of forms of knowledge, attainable through schooling, seems hard to sustain. This is not to say that one need learn nothing, only that what is necessary cannot be determined in advance of one's immersion in the life of the world, and cannot be determined for all. No doubt we can help to make that immersion intelligible and productive through basic literacy programmes, though there is no reason why this should take place in schools or with the sorts of materials that are presently in use for such purposes. There is also an important place for giving children access to the ongoing activities of society: entry to factories, offices, the theatre, executive suites, small businesses, slums and mansions, parks and zoos, farms and abbatoirs, helping them to understand what they see, letting them ask questions, showing them how they can find out more. This, after all, is their world, not a world of 'subjects' or of isolated, unconnected events, but of complex interactions between people, groups, institutions and structures. Would compulsion be necessary for this sort of immersion? Probably very little. Of course it would need to be organised, but it would not be schooling in the accepted sense. It would not need to be tested or graded. It would be enough that it was taken seriously. Perhaps by the age of twelve (maybe earlier, maybe later - it doesn't really matter) we could expect children to be developing some sense of direction, a view about where their interests and abilities lie, and we could point them to institutes or resource centres where they could pursue these interests at greater depth and get a better idea of their aptitudes. There would of course still be the problem of scarce resources, of the limited marketability of certain skills and talents, of dashed expectations, and so on, because that is a function of the larger social structure and its resources. But we might hope that children who have had a broad experience of the world in their earlier years will be a bit more sensitive to their common humanity and more willing to move in directions compatible with the personhood of others.

NOTES

1. John Wilson defines 'curriculum' more stringently as 'planned, sustained and regular learning, which is taken seriously, which has a distinct and structured content and which proceeds via some kind of stages of learning' (*Philosophy and Practical Education*, London: Routledge & Kegan Paul, 1977, p.68). I see no virtue in being as tight as this, though his account provides a welcome contrast to the excessively vague descriptions offered by many curriculum theorists.
2. Chs. 3, 4 contain some discussion of the third, and Ch.14 relates to the fourth.
3. B.S. Bloom (ed.), *Taxonomy of Educational Objectives : the Classification of Educational Goals, Handbook I: Cognitive Domain*, New York: David McKay, 1956; D.R. Krathwohl, B.S. Bloom & B.B. Masia (eds.), *Taxonomy of Educational Objectives : the Classification of Educational Goals, Handbook II: Affective Domain*, New York: David McKay, 1964; for critical discussion, see H. Sockett & R. Pring, 'Bloom's Taxonomy: a Philosophical Critique, I & II', *Cambridge Journal of Education*, I, 1 (Lent, 1971), 16-25 and I, 2 (Easter, 1971), 83-91; B.K. Nelson, 'Hierarchy, Utility and Fallacy in Bloom's Taxonomy', and R.H. Ennis' response, 'Eight Fallacies in Bloom's Taxonomy', in C.J.B. Macmillan (ed.), *Philosophy of Education 1980*, Proceedings of the Thirty-sixth Annual Meeting of the Philosophy of Education Society, Normal, Ill.: Philosophy of Education Society, 1980, 260-68, 269-73.
4. Cf. Ronald Hyman: 'Though behavioural objectives have the manifest functions of facilitating measurement and evaluation and of permitting the marketing of profitable

materials and machines, their latent functions of restricting learning to a mode of dependence and expectedness are important enough in themselves to warrant opposition to them' ('Means-End Reasoning and the Curriculum', *Teachers College Record*, LXXIII, 3 (February, 1972), 398).

5. See further, Ch.14, *infra*.
6. P.H. Hirst, 'Liberal Education and the Nature of Knowledge', reprinted in *Knowledge and the Curriculum*, London: Routledge & Kegan Paul, 1974, p.51.
7. 'Liberal Education and the Nature of Knowledge', the paper which brought Hirst into prominence in 1965, is reprinted, with later pieces which modify the original thesis, in *Knowledge and the Curriculum*. All references are to this volume. In the account which follows, I have endeavoured to incorporate his later views.
8. Hirst, 'The Nature and Structure of Curriculum Objectives', p.25.
9. Hirst's original statement of the distinguishing features appears on p.44, but the quoted phrase comes from 'The Forms of Knowledge Re-visited', p.89.
10. I understand that Hirst now wishes to place most emphasis on the third of these distinguishing features.
11. Hirst's essay 'Literature and the Fine Arts as a Unique Form of Knowledge', pp.152-64, does not do anything to remove this impression.
12. C.P. Snow, *The Two Cultures : and a Second Look*[2], Cambridge U.P., 1974. Hirst started off in the sciences, majoring in mathematics.
13. Hirst, 'The Forms of Knowledge Re-visited', p.87.
14. Hirst, 'Curriculum Integration', p.137.
15. ibid., p.151.
16. ibid., p.149.
17. Hirst, 'The Forms of Knowledge Re-visited', p.92.
18. ibid., p.93.
19. ibid.
20. L. Wittgenstein, *Philosophical Investigations*[2], trans. G.E.M. Anscombe, Oxford: Blackwell, 1958, §48e.
21. Chicago: University of Chicago Press, 1970. A general survey of developments in this area, including criticism of Kuhn, can be found in A.F. Chalmers, *What is this thing called Science* ? University of Queensland Press, 1976.
22. See, e.g., A.J. Watt, 'Forms of Knowledge and Norms of Rationality', *Educational Philosophy and Theory*, VI, 1 (March, 1974), 1-11; R. Barrow, *Common Sense and the Curriculum*, London: Allen & Unwin, 1976, pp.45ff.
23. Quine's original critique of the analytic/synthetic distinction can be found in 'Two Dogmas of Empiricism', in *From a Logical Point of View*[2], New York: Harper, 1961, Ch.2.
24. Hirst 'Liberal Education and the Nature of Knowledge',

    p.46.
25. Hirst 'The Forms of Knowledge Re-visited', p.92.
26. See the whole essay, 'The Forms of Knowledge Re-visited'.
27. Hirst, 'Liberal Education and the Nature of Knowledge', p.46.
28. ibid.
29. As my later remarks are meant to suggest, these interests may not originate with us, and may not even be in our interests. Sometimes the form in which our (acquired) interests structure the world needs to be changed before it proves beneficial to our interests as persons.
30. The phrase comes from P.L. Berger & T. Luckman, *The Social Construction of Reality: A Treatise in the Sociology of Knowledge*, Garden City, N.Y.: Doubleday, 1966.
31. J.P. White, *Towards A Compulsory Curriculum*, London: Routledge & Kegan Paul, 1973, p.22.
32. ibid., p.26. For a critique of White's position, see J.E. McPeck, 'Can J.P. White's "Categories of Activity" Support a compulsory Curriculum?' in I.S. Steinberg (ed.), *Philosophy of Education 1977*, Proceedings of the Thirty-third Annual Meeting of the Philosophy of Education Society, Urbana, Ill.: Philosophy of Education Society, 1977, pp.138-45.
33. White, p.27.
34. See J.P. White, 'Teacher Accountability and School Autonomy: a Reply to Hugh Sockett', *Proceedings of the Philosophy of Education Society of Great Britain*, X (July, 1976), 58-78.
35. The term 'hidden curriculum' owes its present currency to Ivan Illich (see *supra*, Ch.8). Cf. I. Lister, 'The Whole Curriculum and the Hidden Curriculum', in I. Lister (ed.), *Deschooling: A Reader*, Cambridge U.P., 1974, pp.92-93; J.R. Martin, 'What Should we do with a Hidden Curriculum when we Find One?' *Curriculum Inquiry*, VI (1976), 135-51; D. Gordon, 'The Immorality of the Hidden Curriculum', *Journal of Moral Education*, X, 1 (1980), 3-8; 'The Hidden Curriculum and the Latent Functions of Schooling: Two Overlapping Perspectives: 1. Why the Hidden Curriculum is Hidden (D.C. Phillips); 2. Who Hides the Hidden Curriculum? (N.C. Burbules)', in C.J.B. Macmillan (ed.)., 274-80, 281-91.

Chapter 13

COMPETITION

It is a commonplace that most schooling is structured round competitive models of interaction. It is equally a commonplace that in this it reflects and helps to prepare people for the dominant model of interaction in the wider society. So much taken for granted are these commonplaces, that they have attracted comparatively little attention from philosophers of education. Attempts to characterise competitive interactions and to consider their compatibility with the educative task are few and far between. Yet this is curious, given the very sharp divergences of opinion among the few who have considered the question. There is, on the one side, strong support for the view that people are innately competitive, that competition is the precondition of personal development and social progress, that a competitive framework is the only one in which benefits and burdens can be distributed fairly and freely, and that a non-competitive framework of distribution breeds apathy, indolence and stagnation. On the other side, competitive attitudes are said to be socially induced, threats to co-operation and other worthwhile personal and social relationships, the basis for a vicious distinction between winners and losers, built on a false idea of progress, and the source of much envy, despair, selfishness, pride and callousness. Perhaps the paucity of discussion shows only that most philosophers of education have found the commonplace untroubling.

What is competition?

For most writers, competition is a form of interaction which is normatively ambiguous; that is, its desirability or undesirability is thought to depend on the features of a particular competitive situation – the object being competed for, the motives of those involved, the consequences of success and failure, etc. However there are exceptions. In particular, Michael Fielding has recently argued that

162

competition is an 'essentially contested' normative concept.[1] In other words, the normative considerations which delineate its boundaries derive from incompatible evaluative frameworks, making the term irresolvably astigmatic. No single coherent analysis is thus possible. In what follows I will take issue with this aspect of Fielding's account, while following him in a number of other respects.

In common with most recent commentators, we will use R.F. Dearden's analysis as our starting point.[2] According to Dearden, A and B are interacting competitively if and only if (i) there is some X which they both want, (ii) it is not the case that both A and B can gain possession of X, and (iii) the knowledge that by gaining possession of X one would deprive the other of it does (or would) not deter either A or B from seeking it.[3] Several problems are raised by this account.

First, a minor point, but symptomatic of Dearden's methodological rigidity, there is no place in this account for the idea of 'competing with oneself'.[4] Taken literally, Dearden claims, this involves a contradiction. What is being conveyed, namely, the effort to improve oneself, is better expressed in those terms, and the only reason for continuing to speak of 'competing with oneself' (in a schooling context) is the political one of clothing a more acceptable practice (self-betterment) in the well-entrenched terminology of a less acceptable but widely accepted practice (competition against one's fellow students).[5] But why do we need to define 'competition' so rigidly? One reason is methodological. Dearden appears to hold that a definition is constituted by a set of necessary conditions jointly sufficient for the use of a term. But this is too inflexible, deriving from a model of definition in which technical terms are taken as paradigmatic.[6] A further and, for Dearden, related reason, is that if 'competing with oneself' is an acceptable manner of speaking, we will be left without any way of distinguishing competition from emulation. Like the competitive person, the emulous person also 'strongly wishes to approach, or match, or even perhaps excel another person in some respect'.[7] It is only condition (ii) – safeguarded by the exclusion of 'competition with oneself' – which distinguishes them, since success in emulation does not require the exclusive possession of what was sought. However, quite apart from the question of flexibility in analysis, we are not restricted to Dearden's possibilities. Emulation may be more usefully seen as a species of rivalry, the latter to be distinguished from competition in virtue of its focus. In a competitive interaction A and B attempt to gain X, whereas in a rivalrous relationship A and B attempt to outdo each other. In one the focus is on winning, in the other it is on worsting. There is of course nothing to stop a particular interaction from being both competitive and rivalrous. [8]

Secondly, as Dearden outlines it, competition is a form of conflict, but it is not made clear how it differs from other forms of conflict. If A and B both want X, and stop at nothing to get it, we may not wish to regard what they are doing as competing. The reason is concealed within Dearden's discussion, where he suggests that competition requires 'co-operative observance of its own shared ethic'. [9] Underlying competitive interactions are conventions limiting the moves available to A and B in their pursuit of X. The point of such conventions, presumably, is to ensure fairness, though this may not in fact eventuate. In such cases we qualify the competition as unfair. This aspect of the competitive situation is particularly vulnerable to ideological pressures. People are led to believe that they are participants in a fair competition when they are not. They may, for example, believe that because all the participants are competing according to the rules, they are in fair competition. But the rules themselves may be arbitrary or improperly slanted in favour of some of the participants. They give a mystique of fairness to the proceedings. [10] Dearden himself is not free from this form of ideological contamination. He speaks of competition requiring 'the co-operative observance of its own shared ethic' (a much more endearing word than 'rules'!) by way of claiming that competition may be compatible with, nay, 'normally requires various forms of co-operation'. Strategically, this is important, for it is perhaps the most persistent criticism of competition that it is incompatible with co-operation. Towards co-operation we are, for the most part, warmly disposed. However, it is a misleading overstatement to refer to a mutual acceptance of (or acquiescence in) the conventions governing a competition as a form of co-operation. Even if it can be argued that all co-operation presupposes some such mutual acceptance of conventions, that is hardly sufficient to constitute it. Co-operation must also involve a harmony of ends, and on a direct level at least, this is normally absent from competitive interactions.

Thirdly, Dearden fails to make certain distinctions which might be thought important to the assessment of competition. For one thing, 'to compete' can mean either 'to take part in a competition' or 'to act competitively', depending on the attitudes or motives of those involved. Schoolchildren are often forced into competition with each other for academic, athletic, psychological or other rewards. Some merely take part in the competitive interaction, others act competitively in it. Dearden's account manifests, without clarifying, the ambiguity. Condition (iii), for example, acknowledges that A and B may compete for X without realising it (though the counterfactual is a poor attempt to diminish the significance of this). Yet it is not adequate to determine whether *A* and *B* are acting competitively or are merely in competition. If *A* wants and applies for a particular job vacancy, he/she may do so in the knowledge that *B* has also applied. To that extent both *A* and *B* are in competition. Whether or not they are acting competitively depends on how they see what they are doing. If *B*'s seeking the job is for *A* simply an unhappy or irrelevant fact, then *A* is merely in competition with *B*. But if *A* views his/her participation in the competitive situation as an attempt to win/come first/be at the top of the list, then *A* is acting competitively. In assessing competition, we need to keep these distinct. We can assess competition as a structural arrangement whereby benefits are distributed, or we can assess acting competitively.

Cutting across the distinction between being in competition and acting competitively is a further distinction between optional and compulsory competition. Children in schools do not usually elect to enter into competitive interactions; they are thrust into them. Even involvement in sporting activities is often compulsory. Once engaged in them they may or may not act competitively. In Dearden's account, optional competition appears to be paradigmatic. It is, however, considerably less common than compulsory competition, and this must have a bearing on its assessment. By concentrating on optional competition, Dearden distorts the practice he professes to be helping us to understand and assess.

Having noted these defects in Dearden's analysis, we can now consider Fielding's contention that competition is a normative and essentially contested concept. Unfortunately, Fielding does not venture much past an assertion and appeals to authority. With regard to its normative character, he does no more than quote two definitions in which competition is regarded as essentially selfish.[11] This, however, is no substitute for argument. Fielding's failure here stems from his interest in establishing a wider and a narrower thesis. The wider thesis is that some act-descriptions are inherently normative, and (*pace* Dearden[12]) where this is so the search for a neutral analysis will be in vain. The narrower thesis is that competition is one such concept. We cannot establish the narrower thesis by establishing the wider one, and a mere recital of those who accept the narrower thesis does not settle the matter. In so far as he takes his sample to be typical of the socialist tradition, there may be some reason for thinking that embedded in the notion are features which within that tradition have a particular normative significance. Yet his own later references to internal disputes about the possibility of 'socialist competition'[13] suggest that the normative factors may not be embedded in competition as such, but in a

165

particular form of it - individualist competition.[14] Perhaps we could strengthen his thesis by arguing that the form of competition found in our society is irreducibly individualistic. But even this would not show it to be impossible to provide a non-normative account of competition; what it would properly do is to warn us that there was little moral mileage to be made out of such a possibility.

If the claim for normativeness cannot be made out, neither can the claim for essential contestability. Essential contestability depends on the presence of competing normative elements within a concept, something which Fielding believes he has shown in the case of competition. But his demonstration shows only that just as there are writers in the socialist tradition who regard competition as essentially undesirable, so there are writers in the individualist tradition who regard it as essentially desirable. Without a close scrutiny of the competing accounts their evidential value must remain minimal.

We might sum up the discussion so far as follows: the verb 'to compete' is ambiguous between 'to take part in a competition' and 'to act competitively'. Where only the former is in view, we may generally suppose that A and B are engaged in a rule-governed activity which is so structured that its intended outcome will be the exclusive possession of X by either A or B. A and B may or may not want X, but if either does, it is not under its description as a prize, etc. that it is wanted. Where A and B are acting competitively, they must not only want X but also want it as a prize, etc.

Competition: pro and con

We shall now examine some of the arguments for and against competition, leaving open the possibility that it may yet turn out to be an essentially contested concept. If it is an essentially contested concept, we should expect to find that some of the reasons for or against competition are inseparable from our conception of it, and that included in such reasons are some drawn from competing normative frameworks.

(1) We can start with the claim that competition is 'essentially selfish'. Presumably this charge is directed at those who act competitively (though it is also a possible criticism of those who set up competitive structures). In relation to the former, the criticism implies that those who look for competitive success are motivated by self-regarding desires which have no regard for the legitimate interests of others. But is this so? In particular cases, no doubt, it is, but as a conceptually essential or even universal feature it seems to be based on confusion. First of all, it is quite possible for the rules which govern a competition

166

to reflect a concern for the interests of those who compete, particularly if they have been formulated with the informed consent of those who are to participate in the activity.[15] In many spheres this will not be very common, since the competition is virtually compulsory and the stakes are high. In schools, children are made to compete for prizes which go far beyond a place in the class or an end-of-the-year book. Their self-identity and future prospects are to some extent also at stake. In these circumstances, it may be difficult to find people competing non-selfishly. But it would be improper to generalise by making competition inherently selfish. Secondly, the criticism may be based on an understandable but illegitimate inference from the connection between acting competitively and being motivated by a desire to win. The person who acts out of a desire to win usually acts self-interestedly: there is something at stake for him/her. This, however, is not the same as acting self-regardingly, that is, for the sake of personal enhancement. The self-interested actor may act self- or other-regardingly. For example, A may enter into a competition with a desire to win so that B, A's friend, might benefit. Where that is the case, A acts self-interestedly but not out of self-regard. But even if A acts out of self-regard, A does not necessarily act selfishly. Selfishness is disproportionate self-regard, self-regard in which the interests of others are left out of account, except, perhaps, negatively. We should not, however, allow this conceptual wedge between competition and selfishness to blind us to the extent to which the forms of competition so prevalent in our society appeal to self-regarding if not blatantly selfish desire. Those who argue against all competition rightly perceive the extent to which *our* participation in competitive activities is infected by selfish motives.

(2) The claim that those who act competitively act selfishly lies behind the further charge that competition breeds suspicion, despair, greed, cunning, hatred, jealousy, pride, hardness of heart and fear. These are the products of a social context so structured that basic personal goods are made dependent on competitive interactions. If, for example, self-esteem, acceptance by others, and a sense of achievement come to be partially constituted by competitive success, then, on the one hand, those who fail will easily succumb to feelings of despair, hatred, jealousy, or fear, those who win to feelings of pride and hardness of heart, and all who compete will tend to become suspicious, greedy and cunning. It is sometimes protested that this picture over-simplifies the competitive structure of our society. Every person, it is said, is good at something, and failure in one area is counter-balanced by success in another. Thus, each person will find a context in which he/she will

find self-esteem, acceptance, and a sense of achievement. This competitive pluralism must be acknowledged; no doubt it serves to ameliorate the effects of competition for personal goods. Nevertheless, the argument overlooks the differential status which is accorded to these competitive arrangements. Success in certain kinds of competition is accorded considerable social standing, giving those who do well wide acceptance and manoeuvrability, whereas those who succeed in less vaunted enterprises may find their acceptance limited to a very small group of people, who anyway wish for success in the more highly ranked enterprises. The point of this is not to deny that some activities are to be more highly rated than others (though it is to be doubted whether the prevalent ranking adequately reflects this); it is rather to question whether, on the one hand, they have to be structured competitively, and, on the other, whether, if they do, self-esteem, acceptance, etc. should be made to depend on success in them. Thus, even if this general argument will not serve to condemn competitive interactions as such, it may carry sufficient weight to bring into question much familiar competition.

(3) On the other side, those who support competition see the defects noted as unfortunate contingencies, outweighed in significance by various benefits brought about by competition. It is claimed that competition breeds self-reliance, enterprise, perseverance, and industry. It roots out apathy, indifference, indolence, aimlessness and stagnation. Our first response to this should be to question the value attributed to self-reliance, enterprise, etc., on the one hand, and apathy, indifference, etc., on the other. If, for example, enterprise and apathy express different responses to the competitive commercial rat-race, it is not clear to me that the former is to be regarded as desirable and the latter undesirable. We need to know how the rat-race fits into an ideal of human living and being, and to what extent the *status quo* in terms of which people are judged to be enterprising or apathetic is properly describable as a rat-race. But suppose we allow that the form in which enterprise, etc. is valued and encouraged, and apathy, etc. is disvalued and discouraged, is found to be linked with competitive structures. Does this show those structures to be desirable? Our second response is to consider whether such structures represent the only or best way to achieve these ends. The experimental literature is sometimes made to read in this way.[16] However, crucial unstated assumptions underlie such experiments/surveys. In particular, it is assumed that the social context in which the comparative value of competitive and co-operative structures for activity is measured is not one in which people have already been socialised according to competitive models. Obviously, people will perform better under

competitive conditions if it is only under those conditions that they have been *taught* to expect rewards. Given different conditions, different results could probably be expected. The functioning of this unstated assumption is very obvious in Richard Lynn's defence of competition. He cites approvingly an early study carried out by Pearl Greenberg:

> She worked with pairs of children between the ages of two and seven. She took both the children into a room and showed them a table with some bricks on it and she asked them to build something with the bricks. The children began to build and when they had finished their efforts were assessed for general sophistication, e.g. size, structural ingenuity, etc. Then she pushed all the bricks into the middle of the table and said 'Now this time I would like to see who can build prettier.' This introduction of the competitive element seemed to have no effect on the two- and three-year olds, but among the six- and seven-year-olds, there immediately appeared what the author described as a 'really appreciable increase in interest, in spontaneity and in energy, and the quality of their building work'. The author concluded that by the age of six at least 90 per cent of children have well-developed competitive impulses which motivate them to perform better than they do when these competitive feelings are absent.[17]

It is, admittedly, not clear whether the comparable performance in the case of the two- and three-year-olds is due to their inability to grasp the idea of competition or to their relative freedom from the need to compete. What is clear is that by the ages of six and seven, children have been sufficiently exposed to competitive structures for it to make a significant difference to their performance. Such results say little about how we *should* structure people's activities. Lynn's facile conclusion, that 'psychologists have demonstrated what common sense had already dictated, namely that children will work harder for success in competitive situations', assumes that the world as psychologists describe it is a world of brute and not social facts and further that 'common sense' can stand as some neutral or impartial judge of the way things should be.

(4) Perhaps the most loudly proclaimed virtue of competitive structures is their recognition of individual freedom. Their absence is seen by defenders of competition as

tantamount to domination by custom or an authoritarian régime. This argument is most frequently heard in defence of *laissez-faire* capitalism, though it is not absent from the schooling context. There it is often associated with the further claim that competitive structures enable the distribution of benefits to be made on the basis of merit/achievement rather than some end-state principle which is irrelevant to what is being distributed. This, it is said, leads to a fairer distribution than would otherwise be possible. Several problems confront this argument. First, what is the nature of the freedom said to be recognised by competition, and who benefits from it? Those who defend competition on account of its freedom almost invariably have in mind only an individualistic form of freedom from interference, sometimes spoken of as negative liberty. Competition allows the individual to find his/her own level of achievement, unimpeded by others. But any freedom worth having is inescapably social, and liberty which is not associated with autonomy is truncated and of greatly diminished significance.[18] Those who benefit from such freedom are frequently the meritorious only in the sense that they have had the privilege of a better start. Competition in schools does not take place against a background of 'equal opportunity', except in the most superficial sense, and so the resulting distributions can hardly be represented as fair or fairer than alternative distributions. Secondly, competition often frustrates freedom in the sense that it enables and to some extent encourages cheating, it breeds insecurity, feelings of failure and impotence, and traps people into a form of motivation for activities which diminishes their intrinsic enjoyability, debases those activities, and leaves alternatives unappealing. Thirdly, the view that the alternative to a competitive framework is a custom-dominated or authoritarian one is historically and socially myopic, depending for its power on the acceptance of an ideology which restricts the possibilities of social and political interaction to two: capitalist or communist. The crudity of this way of setting up the alternatives as well as the naiveté of its characterisations and the simplistic manner in which it is applied, testifies, by virtue of its wide acceptance, to the power of the dominant ideologies. Its fragility is shown in the feeble attempts of its promulgators to assimilate into a competitive framework that range of interactions which stands as its natural alternative: co-operative relations.

(5) One further argument for competition associates it with progress, invention, productivity, and efficiency. To meet this, we need not deny that competition has been an enormous stimulus to human endeavour. We may, however, question the value of much of that endeavour. Entrepreneurial genius has

170

frequently exhausted itself in the production of unnecessary products which have wasted valuable resources.[19] Economic gain rather than human need has, in the name of progress, motivated a squanderous or corrupting approach to human and natural resources. The school is no exception to this, since it is for the most part locked into the dominant *status quo*. Attitudes are developed in the school which are incompatible with autonomy, knowledge is converted into a scarce resource and material is learned which serves little purpose beyond the stratifying one of examinations. Only on a very limited basis is there fostered the co-operative endeavour which is crucial to autonomy and a worthwhile life. Talk of competition fostering creativity, spontaneity, originality, etc. is counteracted by the hard facts of conformity, stereotypes and motivation only by the hope for external reward or fear of failure. The authority structure of the school and the traditional 'teacher knows best' pattern of schooling ensure that those who get on are generally those who conform, or whose dissent takes a non-threatening form.

(6) One final objection concerns the location of competitive structures. Where particular resources or benefits are scarce yet desired, then people will find themselves inevitably in competition for them. This doesn't show competition to be inevitable (though it is not my purpose to deny that it may sometimes be), since the availability of a particular resource or benefit, and the prevalence of a particular desire, is often within human control. If, for example, children have to compete for schooling opportunities because the government has chosen to limit the schooling budget in favour of defence technology, the competition is not inevitable (whether or not it is justifiable). What frequently happens in our society is that benefits which should never be made matters of competition are assimilated to that framework. This is particularly (though not exclusively) so in the case of what I have called basic personal goods such as self-esteem, acceptance, a sense of identity, etc., which are not scarce resources in the sense in which gold is a scarce resource, but have been made scarce by the form of social organisation in which we have become embedded. They have become unnecessarily linked with prestige, status and competitive success. For such benefits we can say that competition is always wrong, since it places an unnecessary limitation on the distribution of what, because it is an ingredient in their welfare, belongs to people by right. The socialist critique of competition, in so far as it detects the contingent connection between such benefits and competitive success of the familiar sort, carries greater weight here than the individualist defence.

171

Conclusion

Our argument has not supported the claim of 'essential contestability'. We have not found within the competitive relation *as such* the elements of antagonistic normative frameworks. Nevertheless, we have seen reason to believe that the concrete expressions of competition in our society are frequently suffused with attitudes which are not compatible with co-operative and autonomy-enhancing endeavour. The domination of much schooling by competitive structures and attitudes, neither of which is necessary to education, and both of which so easily frustrate it, strongly suggests that the school's major role lies elsewhere. As indeed it does. The strong conviction held by many supporters of competition that the minimisation of competition will lead to a decline in excellence, if true, is true because it has been made so by those who believe the desire for excellence cannot be separated from the desire to win. I would suggest that a closer reading of the history of capitalism suggests otherwise.

NOTES

1. M. Fielding, 'Against Competition: in praise of a malleable analysis and the subversiveness of philosophy', *Proceedings of the Philosophy of Education Society of Great Britain*, X (July, 1976), 124-46. The idea of 'essential contestability' is developed in W.B. Gallie, 'Essentially Contested Concepts', *Proceedings of the Aristotelian Society*, LVI (1955-56), 167-98, and A.C. MacIntyre, 'The Essential Contestability of some Social Concepts', *Ethics* LXXXIV, 1 (October, 1973), 1-9; but see also A. Hartnett & M. Naish, *Theory and Practice of Education*, London: Heinemann, 1976, Vol. I, pp.79ff; J. Gray, 'Contestability of Concepts', *Political Theory*, V (1977), 330-48. My account owes a great deal to Fielding's scholarly discussion, both in the above article and in his M.A. dissertation, 'Competition and Education', University of London, 1975.
2. R.F. Dearden, 'Competition in Education', *Proceedings of the Philosophy of Education Society of Great Britain* IV, 1 (1972), 119-33.
3. ibid., 120-21. I have paraphrased Dearden's account.
4. Dearden is not the only person to hold this view. See also J.W. Keating, *Competition and Playful Activities*, Washington, D.C.: University Press of America, 1978, p.3.
5. Dearden, 122-23.

6. See the discussion in my *Punishment and Desert*, The Hague: Martinus Nijhoff, 1973, pp.15-16. As a further indication of the problems generated by attempts to provide a rigid account we can observe that where the prize is a perpetual trophy, condition (ii) needs a qualification to the effect that *A* and *B* cannot *simultaneously* gain possession of *X*. But even this will not be good enough. For in the case of a dead heat they might share it.
7. Dearden, 123.
8. Keating misses the essentially distinct foci of competition and rivalry in his criticisms of Georg Simmel's observation that competitive conflict is 'indirect' (Keating, pp.3-5).
9. Dearden, 122.
10. Cf. H.L.A. Hart, *The Concept of Law*, Oxford: Clarendon Press, 1961, pp.156-57, 202; for criticism, see D. Lyons, 'On Formal Justice', *Cornell Law Review*, LVIII, 5 (June, 1973), 833-61.
11. Fielding, 'Against Competition', 133-34.
12. 'There are ... at least two conceptual questions which can be rationally pursued, and with some profit, before the value question is faced. These two conceptual questions concern what competition is, and what things can in consequence be competed for.' (Dearden, 119). The wider thesis has been commented on in Ch.1, *supra.*
13. See, e.g. I. Deutscher, '"Socialist Competition"', *Foreign Affairs*, XXX, 3 (April, 1952), 378-90.
14. Fielding, 'Against Competition', 137 and fn.29.
15. This will often be the case in athletics.
16. See R. Lynn, 'Competition and Co-operation', in C.B. Cox & R. Boyson (eds.), *Black Paper 1977*, London: Temple Smith, 1977, pp.107-13, for such a reading.
17. ibid., p.108, citing P. Greenberg 'Competition in Children', *American Journal of Psychology*, XLIV (1932), 221-48.
18. Cf. D.G. Ritchie's trenchant comments on Herbert Spencer's individualistic reading of freedom:

> In this country no one is hindered by law from reading all the works of Mr. Herbert Spencer. This is negative liberty. But if a man cannot read at all, or if he can read but has not any money to spare for the purpose if buying so many volumes, or if he has no access to any public library, or if the managers of any library to which he has access refuse to permit such works on their shelves, or, if having access to them, he has no leisure in which to read them, or if he has not had such an education as enables him to understand what he reads, he cannot be said to get much good out of the fact that the law of the land does not prohibit him from reading Mr. Spencer's

works.
(*Natural Rights*, London: Allen & Unwin, 1894, p.139).
See also Chs.6, 7, *supra*.

19. Nicely summed up in the attitude if not the achievement
    of Thomas Edison: 'Anything that won't sell, I don't
    want to invent' (in R. Conot, *A Streak of Luck : The
    Life and Legend of Thomas Alva Edison*, New York:
    Seaview, 1979).

Chapter 14

ASSESSMENT AND GRADING

Each element within the institutionalised teaching/learning process - the curriculum, administrative procedures, teaching methods, teacher competence, student performance, etc. - is open and increasingly subject to assessment of some kind. But without doubt, the predominant preoccupation has been with the assessment of students, ostensibly with respect to what they have learned. Robert Paul Wolff goes so far as to suggest that 'for most American students, the dominant educational fact for the first eighteen years of schooling - if they last that long - is the *Grade*'.[1] He is not far wrong. The school has become one of our society's most important sorting mechanisms, and as the demands of a technologically-based economy have become increasingly specialised, so too have the selection and sorting techniques used in schools, universities and similar institutions. Schools and universities do not always see themselves in this role, preferring to see their goals as education or the increase of knowledge. To the extent that this is so, assessment is seen in a different light. The result has been frustration and endless confusion - a confusion manifest in the multiplicity of terms that have come to be indiscriminately thrown around in the seventy-year-old debate.[2] We need to clarify some of the terms of that debate before we can expect to advance very far in our consideration of the topic.

The terminology of assessment

Students are not merely assessed, they are appraised, evaluated, criticised, examined, inspected, tested, judged, marked, classified, selected, graded, scored, sorted, tagged, scaled, ordered, measured ... and so on. To attempt a thorough explication of all these different notions would be unnecessarily distracting; nevertheless, it is important that we endeavour to provide an account of some of them. What follows is an effort to mark out useful distinctions: it makes no attempt to represent a consensus (of which there appears to be little anyway). For convenience I have restricted the context of my descriptions to that of learning.

Assessment, as I understand it, is a very general term, implying no more than some estimation of what has been learned. It is sufficient to constitute an assessment that we be able to say: 'Your attribution of the "Trumpet Voluntary" to Purcell was incorrect, but you managed to remember that it was originally titled "The Prince of Denmark's March".' Assessment need not be directed to any specific end. However, when it takes the form of *criticism*, it is teleological with respect to the learning process. According to Wolff, 'criticism is the analysis of a product or performance for the purpose of identifying and correcting its faults or reinforcing its excellences'.[3] Sometimes, assessments like the one provided are sufficient for the purpose of criticism; but it is often considered appropriate to add a further dimension, so that questions like, 'Was it a bad mistake to attribute the "Trumpet Voluntary" to Purcell?' or 'Given the answer as a whole, did it display an intelligent grasp of the topic?' can be answered. Good criticism requires not only a sense of error and excellence but also of importance. Questions like those just raised call not merely for an assessment but for an *evaluation* of the person's learning. Evaluations are qualitative judgments in which what is learned is considered under some description whose criteria function as a standard of comparison.[4] They are normally indicated by expressions such as 'good', 'poor', 'thorough', 'weak', 'excellent', etc., and the descriptions under which they are made can be either internal or external to the learning. An internal evaluation might consider the learning with respect to its breadth, depth, retention, the extent to which it is linked with evidence or argument, the facility with which it can be defended, whether it is able to be applied or transferred, its independence, presentation, etc. Where the learning is evaluated with respect to some description which is external to the quality of learning, I shall speak instead of its *appraisal*.[5] If a committee asks for an appraisal of a candidate's work, its interest is in the candidate's work in so far as it bears on the issue of employment, promotion, sale, the award of a degree, etc. Where these are the controlling descriptions, the standards by which the work is appraised may not be identical with those by reference to which it is (internally) evaluated.

Assessment, criticism, evaluation and appraisal are not comparative notions (which is not to say that they cannot be employed for comparative purposes). Sorting, ordering and ranking, however, necessarily involve a class of comparison. *Sorting*, the simplest of these operations, requires only the grouping of learners on the basis of some rule or property.

176

Thus, students may be sorted into groups according to whether they know the answer to some question. Nothing need be implied about the relative merits of the different groups. Unlike sorting, which distinguishes learners in order to group them together, *ordering* requires the application of a rule or the isolation of a property which results in their serial or linear arrangement. No hierarchy is implied by an order, though most orderings are directed towards hierarchical ends. Where this is the case we speak of *ranking*. A person's ranking is group dependent. *A* and *B* may perform identically on a learning test, but be ranked differently because they belong to different groups. As well, rankings are ordinally related. The ranking 1, 2, 3, 4... implies nothing about the intervals between 1 and 2, 1 and 3 or 3 and 4. Nor does a ranking convey any information about the degree to which the ordering criteria are satisfied by the individual rank-holders. The ranking 1, 2, 3 is as applicable to test scores of 40, 20 and 5 as it is to scores of 100, 99 and 98. In the schooling system, sorting, ordering and ranking are generally holistic. That is, they focus on a comparison of individuals, and not on the individual criteria by which an individual's learning may be assessed. Students are ranked with respect to their overall place in class or in a particular subject, but not generally with respect to the individual learning skills that might be required within a subject. It would not be usual to rank a person 5th in respect to his/her grasp of the detail of Tokugawa Japan and 8th in respect of his/her ability to discern its continuing influence. Most rankings, therefore, presuppose a commensurability of the criteria of assessment, thus enabling individuals to be ranked on some linear scale.

A holistic approach to what is learned is also evident when students are graded, marked and 'measured', though this is a reflection on our practices rather than on the ideas themselves. *Grading* involves the use of a conventional symbol to represent an evaluation of what has been learned. In schooling contexts, the grading labels A, B, C, D and F have wide currency, and detailed procedures for their use may, and often do, accompany them. Because they tend to have some official status, efforts are often made to standardise their application.[6] Grading represents one form of *marking*, where the latter generally involves the resolution of an assessment into a single numerical or quasi-numerical expression: a percentage mark, fraction, or grade. Without contextual factors, a mark need not imply an overall evaluation, though where it remains 'raw', that is, entails no commensurability with respect to the items tested, it may be preferable to speak of a *score*. Marking and grading, unlike ordering and ranking, are not necessarily comparative, though in contemporary schooling practice they are often made so by being linked with a system of distribution of marks or grades. Institutions sometimes require that marks or grades be 'normally distributed' (i.e. on a bell curve). In the literature, non-comparative marking/grading is sometimes referred to as 'absolute' as distinct from 'relative', which is comparative.[7] The term *measurement* has come to be used quite generally of any arithmetic or symbolic representation of what has been learned – no doubt because it suggests a 'scientific' status for assessments. However, we should limit its use to the arithmetic representation of magnitudes. Mass, volume, length and period constitute the most familiar context of measurement. Whether learning and other human capacities can be measured is a moot point. Even though such capacities may be reasonably said to possess magnitude, it is difficult to see how such magnitudes can be arithmetically expressed without arbitrariness, and even more difficult to devise arithmetically expressible criteria for commensurability.[8]

The assessment of learning may be accomplished in a variety of ways. It may be sufficient to observe how a person conducts his/her affairs to determine how much has been learned about a particular aspect of human experience. In institutional contexts, however, a more deliberate or structured approach generally prevails. Learning is *tested* by means of set essays, projects, interviews, and, still most commonly, by means of *examinations*. The format of an examination may vary, but generally it comprehends an artificially constructed limited-time test performed under closely supervised conditions. The purported value of an examination is that it removes from the process of testing variables which are extraneous to what is being tested. But it may be more accurate to see its function as providing a semblance of comparability with respect to the assessment of a number of learners.

Learning and assessment

With these working definitions behind us, we can now look in more detail at the assessment of learning, particularly as it occurs in institutionalised contexts - schools, universities, etc. My focus will be primarily on secondary and tertiary schooling. At the outset, it is as well to remind ourselves that in some measure, all our learning is socially conditioned. The individual learner is and generally remains very dependent on others for what is learned, whether through personal communication or via some social product: newspapers, books, films, etc. Even what is learned in isolation tends to rely for its conceptualisation on a previously learned public language. Autonomy in learning is not impossible, but it cannot be thought of asocially.[9] Some autonomy in learning is important when we are thinking about *education*, since educationally significant learning requires much more than the memorisation and absorption of what others pass on to us. A developed sense of what is and what is not important is required, as well as a critical mastery of at least some of those matters considered important.

How is educationally valuable learning achieved? We do not need to fall back on any very precise view of human nature to propose that unless there are opportunities for learners to subject their ideas and practices to the scrutiny of others, it is most unlikely that they will come to be educated in any critically valuable sense. Our fallibility and limitations are such that we can have little basis for confidence in what we believe independently of its exposure to the assessment of others. Not any old others, of course, since some of those others may not themselves possess the requisite skills of assessment. To avoid the difficult task of determining *who* the appropriate others should be, we might suggest that the degree of confidence we can have in our ideas and practices is dependent on their openness to the scrutiny of others, particularly those who would disagree with us.[10] In so far as we take learning seriously, such assessment must be willingly sought. In the institutionalised teaching/learning process, such assessment should embrace not only what is 'learned' but also what is 'taught'. Where the professed aim is education, neither teacher nor student can afford to insulate him/herself from the assessment of others.

I think it is fair to say that this much is not greatly disputed in the current discussion, although careless expression sometimes gives the impression that certain writers are opposed to all assessment. A more careful reading suggests that it is some contingency in or around the assessment situation - an inflexible teacher/student relationship, its competitiveness, marking unreliability, its stratifying effect or invalid holistic character - which is responsible for the reaction. Nevertheless, the problems embedded in most institutionalised assessment are so deep-seated, it is not surprising that opposition to it is sometimes expressed with a vehemence which suggests total rejection. It must be admitted that a good deal of the continued popular support for institutionalised assessment rests on the belief that it is *educationally* justified. Not only is it believed to be motivationally necessary, but it is also thought to be a valid and reliable indicator of educationally relevant achievement. Even in much academic writing on the subject, this is assumed to be the case. The attainment of various 'educational objectives' is thought to be appropriately gauged by means of the stock-in-trade of institutional assessment - examinations and similar instruments. Such beliefs belong in the realm of mythology, along with the view that the purpose of schools is education. Schools are public facilities, designed to produce, reproduce and reinforce in the coming generation those skills, attitudes and values necesssary to the maintenance and furtherance of the dominant social order. If at points that coincides with the education of the oncoming generation, well and good. But it is only too apparent that in most existing societies, including our own, the educational value of schooling and of its assessment techniques is seriously deficient. The economic and socio-political functions of schooling so intrude upon any educational ideals that they are often all but extinguished.

That the schooling context is not well adapted to educationally worthwhile assessment can be seen from a consideration of some of its aspects. Take, for example, the rigid teacher/student distinction which operates. In the schooling context, the identities of teacher and student are fixed and exclusive: within a particular relationship, a person isn't seen as both teacher and student. What Freire speaks of as 'the banking concept of education' predominates. The teacher passes on a pre-packaged and relatively fixed 'body of knowledge' to the student, and then determines how well that 'knowledge' has been assimilated. The assessment system thus leaves little room for a recognition of the social form and content of that knowledge, or for an exposure and questioning of its presuppositions and value. Yet these are necessary if assessment is to have educational value. School knowledge functions as a more or less 'neutral' given, whose successful acquisition is unilaterally determinable. As such it constitutes (in many cases) a substantial constraint on the exercise or development of the learner's autonomy.

Another aspect of institutional assessment which betrays its educational inadequacy is its individualism. Only rarely is co-operative work encouraged in schools (particularly at higher levels), and even more rarely is co-operative assessable work encouraged, despite what appear to be the obvious educational advantages. Both education and the growth of knowledge are social processes, yet schooling encourages an individualistic and competitive approach to both. The reason is simple: the grading/ranking process, so important to the social purposes of schools and universities, would break down were people to submit co-operatively produced work for assessment. There would be no way (it is said) of determining each individual's contribution. Institutional authorities regard this as a defect, not because of a high moral regard for the individual (giving to each his/her due), but because the ranking/selective function of the institution would be thwarted by its occurrence. In primary schools the situation tends to be somewhat different. Because the 'workforce' is still some way off, a more relaxed and co-operative work and assessment system sometimes operates.

Universal compulsory schooling and the boom in higher and further 'education' have generated an industry dedicated to its maintenance and elaboration. Assessment has not escaped the attention of its promoters, and there is even a journal devoted to its study.[11] Yet, despite a somewhat bewildering variety of proposals designed to improve institutionalised assessment, the terminal examination has remained its mainstay. It is not too hard to see why. In institutions built on a rigid teacher/student division, in which teachers have academic responsibility for a large number of students, the terminal examination represents the least exhausting method of assessment. If plagiarism is a coping mechanism employed by students, terminal examining is one employed by staff. Alternative schemes of assessment, some of which are quite sophisticated and likely to be valid and reliable, presuppose a staff-student ratio considerably less than any government is prepared to countenance.

We should make one qualification to this picture. In recent years, the problems associated with terminal examinations have become so apparent that they are now frequently supplemented with or even replaced by some form of progressive or 'continuous' assessment - assessment which takes place while a course is still in progress. However, even continuous assessment has proved problematic, and the greatest weight is still borne by the final assessment - usually an examination.

Examinations do not comprise an undifferentiable class. Several cross-classifications of sub-forms might be distinguished: objective, essay-type, oral and practical constitute one classification; open and closed book, another; public/external and internal, yet another; and so on. In what follows, I shall not attempt to discuss each of these sub-forms in detail, but will focus on what should be recognisable as a typical examination, commenting on particular sub-forms only where it seems useful to do so. Most of my criticisms will be generally applicable.

Like other forms of assessment, examinations are usually evaluated within two dimensions: their validity and their reliability.[12] An examination (or other form of assessment) is regarded as *valid* if it assesses what it is supposed to assess. According to the familiar justificatory rhetoric, that is 'educational achievement' - as objectified in something like Bloom's taxonomy. We have suggested elsewhere[13] that Bloom's taxonomy may not be a very satisfactory guide to 'educational achievement', but even if some such taxonomy were satisfactory, there would be good reason to doubt whether the typical examination would passably achieve that purpose. There are several reasons for this.

(1) It is said that examinations provide evidence of various abilities - e.g. the ability to understand, to organise and to evaluate certain materials, issues, etc., to display independence of thought, subtlety of argument, depth of knowledge, and so on. Yet it may be able to do this only *indirectly*. All the examiner sees is how the student performs under certain limited and artificial conditions, and the assumption is made that this performance, under these conditions, is non-contingently or at least regularly related to the student's possession of the relevant abilities. Frequently, however, the assumption cannot be made with any confidence. Few examiners have the time or experience necessary to construct questions which will test all and only those abilities which the examination is designed to assess. What is intended to assess a student's depth of knowledge may instead display the student's ability to cram or to predict questions, and a student's failure to perform well may show only that the student was tired, nervous or indisposed. The point is this: even if examination performance sometimes provides a rough-and-ready indication that the student possesses the abilities in question, the variables (and exceptions) are too numerous to justify the weight that is frequently accorded to them. This problem tends to be exacerbated where the examination is external to the institution, since there is a tendency (for reasons of reputation, etc.) for teachers to gear their material and techniques to 'examination success', and examination performance, rather than the development of 'educationally relevant' abilities, becomes the focus of teaching. Where this occurs, as indeed it often does - in the attention of students, even if not their teachers - the examination may not even function as a rough-and-ready indicator. The obvious reply to this, that it should be possible to construct questions which are not sufficiently predictable to allow for a 'backwash effect', or which will provide a direct assessment of the relevant ability, is easier made than implemented. No doubt every teacher could improve his/her performance in this respect, but it would be surprising if the relevant abilities could be adequately assessed via examination questions.

An alternative response to this criticism might be that examination questions are not intended to provide evidence of anything as 'pure' as abilities. They are geared to an assessment of *performance*, and this is a function of ability, interest and application, as well as a number of other things. But such a reply does nothing to relieve the situation. For, entering into the examination performance of students, we may not have evidence only of their ability, interest and application (and we may not have much evidence relating to them), but also of how well a course was taught, the students' health and predictive talent, the temperature and atmosphere of the examination room, and so on. How should we determine which of these and other factors played the greatest part in their performance, and if we cannot, what justification do we have for giving their results the academic and social function they are usually accorded? It is only because some connection is generally believed to exist between examination results and socially significant abilities, that they are able to persist as socially valued indicators.

(2) We have noted that it is not simply the indirectness of examinations which brings their evidential value into question, but also the presence of other variables. Because examinations are not intended merely (if at all) to assess this or that educationally relevant ability, but function instead as mechanisms for ranking, selection and accreditation, and hence as major instruments for social stratification, they frequently place students under enormous psychological pressure, leading to a deterioration of performance, or, even worse, to ill-health or suicide.[14] Alternatively, students may 'cope' by simply opting out, endeavouring to gain self-esteem and social recognition in some other way. Even routine fluctuations in health - due, say, to influenza or menstruation, may markedly affect examination performance, and even though provision is sometimes made for this to be taken into account, there are various reasons why people do not always take advantage of it. Even the aseptic surroundings and artificial constraints of an examination room, plus, of course, the constraint of time, can have a psychologically powerful effect on some examinees.

Against such negative assertions, defenders of examinations (as an educationally valid instrument) sometimes argue that it is only in the context of (the expectation of) examinations that education can thrive.[15] The prospect of an examination acts as an important incentive to learning, maximising the chances that a high standard of performance will be achieved or maintained. Moreover, such prospect forces students 'to sort out their thoughts and ideas, to organise their time and to adopt systematic study habits'.[16]

In responding to such arguments, it is not necessary to deny that for many students the prospect of an examination does constitute an incentive, and, moreover, may cause them to review their work in a way which enables them to achieve a holistic and coherent grasp of the source material. Rarely are social practices so limited in possibilities that nothing of worth can come out of them. But against this, several other factors have to be set. For one thing, the claim that the prospect of an examination acts as an incentive warrants closer scrutiny. Incentives of course vary, and different incentives will have different effects on performance. Granted that education would not thrive

183

without incentives, what needs to be considered is whether the prospect of an examination, with all its socio-psychological associations, is the appropriate form for an educationally justifiable incentive. This is to be doubted. Should it be replied that without the prospect of an examination (or some form of graded/ranked assessment), students will not be motivated to learn (what they are taught in school), this will not of itself suffice to justify the use of examinations. Quite apart from the question of the costs (personal, academic, social, economic, etc.) of the examination system, the need for this form of incentive should first lead us to question what is taught, and how it is taught. Is the content of most courses so irrelevant to the needs and interests of students, are the demands made by competing courses so heavy and time-consuming, and is the manner of their teaching so divorced from personal involvement, sympathetic rapport, and so on, that only the threat of examination (with the stigma or loss attaching to failure) will provide those who (are required to) engage in them with sufficient motivation? In many cases, this would appear to be so. And if not, is it that we bring children up in such a way that the form of motivation to which they will most readily respond is material and competitive? Again, our answer must often be in the affirmative. Or, if we do not ourselves bring them up to be motivated (in the main) by such factors, our social milieu will soon 'rectify' the matter. So pervasive are such attitudes that we are wont to regard them as 'natural' or 'inborn'. In sum, the argument which relies on the incentive value of examinations is in large part an affirmation of the dominant *status quo*. It says: if we're to keep things going as they are, we will need to rely on the incentive value of examinations.

But, as we have already observed, such (in some respects dubious) benefits have associated costs. What is a challenging incentive for some is a paralysing threat to others. C.B. Cox, like many other defenders of examinations, appears mesmerised by the way *he* (as a generally successful examinee – like most of those who write on the topic) reacted in an examination context into thinking that this is how it generally is or should be. There is a strong tendency (by those who succeed) to see those who have wilted as victims of their own making – through laziness, preoccupation, procrastination, etc. But such disparagements put the cart before the horse: they presume that what is on offer in the (compulsory?) curriculum *ought* to absorb the attention and energies of participants. Someone whose sensitivities are assailed by a particular course (or its method of teaching), or who believes it to be irrelevant to his/her goals – though it has been made administratively necessary, and who cannot participate in it with the requisite enthusiasm, may display

184

much more of that emotional and discriminative capacity which is partially constitutive of education than someone for whom the course is merely a means to some competed-for and not especially desirable end.

Finally here, the merits of intellectual discipline and of 'sorting out' one's ideas need to be contextualised. Teachers who have abandoned terminal examinations for continuous assessment have often sensed some loss, in that student involvement in courses often becomes fragmented and over-specialised. They do not acquire a coherent overall perspective on the course subject matter. The usefulness of terminal examinations in bringing this about makes teachers reluctant to abandon them. Yet how necessary are examinations for such purposes? Might not an end-of-course critical overview do just as well? Is not part of the difficulty caused by the competition for the student's time within the institution? There is a tendency for teachers to think their subject of sufficient importance to justify a large slice of the student's time. Students engaged in a number of courses thus find that they must play one off against another if they are to cope. Where a teacher takes a liberal approach to assessment, he/she is thus likely to find a diminishing involvement on the part of students (whatever the merits of the course). The temptation to reintroduce examinations 'for the sake of the subject' then becomes considerable. But, like most expedients of this kind, it avoids the underlying causes, and perpetuates rather than solves any problems. It may not even achieve these limited ends given the practice of examination prediction. Furthermore, we should not see the matters of intellectual discipline and acquiring an overall perspective on course subject matter in isolation from the content of the syllabus. Where set in the context of questionable material, and examined for questionable purposes, much of their value may evaporate. Discipline may be infected by docility, coherence may express indoctrination.

(3) We have already noted that the form taken by assessment in schooling contexts generally presupposes a rigid teacher/student distinction and a more or less static and asocial view of knowledge. Nowhere is this more evident than in examinations. Here the only response a student usually receives to his/her ideas is an enigmatic mark or grade - enigmatic because, apart from indicating that his/her work was/was not considered satisfactory, nothing else is directly conveyed. The student is left to his/her own conjectures as to why this was so. Terminal examinations cannot really be construed as check-points in an ongoing dialogue. If there was dialogue, then examinations generally signal its end.

But the mark or grade which expresses an examination result is not unsatisfactory only for these reasons. It bases itself on a highly problematic notion – that of the commensurability of educational (or whatever) objectives. Let us suppose that a particular examination paper is designed to assess the following items: (a) independence of thought; (b) knowledge of the French Revolution; (c) ability to identify the major issues; and (d) ability to marshal diverse materials in arguing a position. Let us also suppose (somewhat optimistically) that the examination paper does test these and (even more optimistically) only these items. Now, how do we rate these different items? Are they of equal value? Or is (a) twice as important as (b)? We know how people differ with respect to such judgments. Can they be rationally settled? Let us suppose they can. How does this help us with the concrete practice of examining where teachers differ in the estimates they give (and no doubt also in the items they test), and are normally too pressured to carry out the fine computation which would be required? A grade or mark, by its very simplicity, obscures matters of great complexity and controversiality, lending to the assessment process an aura of objectivity and definiteness to which (in practice) it can lay no claim.

To this point we have premissed our comments on the supposition that examinations are designed to give a *valid* determination of 'educational achievement'. Were that their purpose, it would at least provide a backdrop of legitimacy to the discussion of their validity. But, as we have already observed, the purposes of examinations, like those of schooling, are not only, if at all, educational. Those who, like C.B. Cox, argue that examinations 'prepare children and students for the realities of adult life',[17] do not have in mind the kind of preparation for life that is implicit in a critically valuable understanding of education, but only a tailoring to the dominant *status quo*.[18] Examinations constitute a socially sanctioned obstacle course which serves to toughen up those who complete it successfully, and to weed out those not 'fitted' for a high place in the existing hierarchy. Thus is the psychological misery of examinations justified. 'Most employers', writes Chadwick in defence of the examination, 'would like to be warned if a prospective employee can only be trusted provided he has plenty of time and no pressures on him. In most professions, life is not like that.'[19] Pidgeon and Yates chorus similarly: 'The damage to morale or even to mental health that might result from unfavourable comparisons is often stressed by those who object to examinations but it may sometimes be in an individual's best interests to discover his true status.'[20] True status! We are not far from the law of the jungle.

Whose interests, then, do examinations serve? It is difficult to answer the question generally, but Oppenheim, Jahoda and James give a partial list which summarises the various functions which examinations (and other forms of graded assessment) may have:

1. *Examination purposes concerning past or present achievement*

(a) *vis-à-vis* the student: to give a reward and a sense of achievement; feedback on own strengths and weaknesses; a changed self-concept; improved earning powers; admission to graduate work; an incentive, to make sure that the students work;
(b) *vis-à-vis* university staff: feedback information concerning effectiveness of their teaching, and the extent to which teaching objectives are being reached ('knowledge of results'); inducing harder work in students; selective and diagnostic purposes, to help the staff to adjust their teaching more effectively to the student's needs, or to select students for particular courses;
(c) *vis-à-vis* parents: a return on investment, both personal and financial.

2. *Predictive examination purposes*

(a) *vis-à-vis* employers: a guarantee of standards;
(b) *vis-à-vis* 'knowledge': the training of future contributors to its expansion;
(c) *vis-à-vis* the government: to provide the necessary number of doctors, technologists, etc;
(d) *vis-à-vis* schools: a target to aim at, and feedback information on which success claims can be made to future parents;
(e) *vis-à-vis* the postgraduate schools: information predictive of future performance;
(f) *vis-à-vis* professional bodies: minimum qualifications for admission;
(g) *vis-à-vis* the university administration: the convenience of a pattern of regular entries and exits; enhancement of the status of their own particular institution in the community.[21]

Some caution must be exercised in relation to such lists. Note, for example, how 1(a) reports only on 'beneficial' functions. Those who pass may indeed get 'a reward and a sense of achievement'. But what about the many who fail? There is also a tendency for such summations to obscure the incompatibility of some of the purposes. What an employer is looking for in examination results may not be what a postgraduate selection committee needs; but the same set of results is frequently used to serve both the employer and the selection committee. This may lead to real conflict. Where those who wish to use the results possess the necessary power, there is frequently some attempt made to influence the examining process so that it subserves *their* purposes more effectively. And thus examinations come to embody a variety of institutional and ideological struggles, as 'standards', 'relevance', 'return on public money', 'comparability' and so on, attempt to stake their frequently incompatible claims.

If, for the sake of argument, we grant that the foregoing list picks out a range of acceptable functions which examinations (and other forms of graded assessment) may be called on to fulfil, we still need to ask whether they are the only or best means whereby they can be accomplished. In most, if not all, cases, it must be doubtful whether this is so, but the examination mentality is so deeply ingrained in many quarters that those who rely on examinations would feel insecure about any alternative. This can only reflect great ignorance about their dubious validity and lack of reliability. To argue, as Hardie does,[22] that all the successful work accomplished by accredited engineers, doctors, teachers, accountants, and so on, shows that examinations couldn't be *that* bad, is hardly convincing. Not only might we reflect on all the 'unsuccessful' work done by such people, but we need also to be reminded that it is not really known how things would go under an alternative system.

So much for the validity of examinations. What about their *reliability*? A given mark or grade is said to be reliable if it is consistent with the mark or grade which another competent examiner would give, or which the same examiner would give on another occasion. Strictly speaking, there is more to reliability than consistency of judgment. A reliable assessment gives an accurate estimation of the various aspects of the work being considered. However, in the absence of agreed criteria for assessment, consistency is taken as a gauge of reliability.

Defenders of examinations usually acknowledge the difficulties in achieving such consistency, but believe that on the whole it is an attainable ideal. Thus C.B. Cox confides:

> Those who know examiners for professional qualifications in this country will agree that standards of fairness are high, and based on wide experience. University dons are notoriously meticulous, and will spend hours arguing about borderlines.[23]

Such pieces of impressionistic self-justification have to be set beside the almost unrelievedly gloomy picture given by

188

controlled studies of examiner reliability. The early work
of Starch and Elliott,[24] followed by that of Hartog and
Rhodes,[25] and others since then, has indicated not only the
enormous differences which exist between examiners, but also
a multitude of factors which enter into their assessments.
Their marking is affected by handwriting, tiredness,
carelessness, sex, changing expectations, judgments about
the effort and attitude of the student, class origins,
whether the views expressed agree with or differ from their
own, and so on. Thus Roy Cox, to whom C.B. Cox refers, sums
up his depressing survey of studies on examiner reliability
with a quotation from Pieron:

> All the experimental data has shown that for
> a particular performance expressed in terms
> of an exam script, assessment by different
> examiners produces marks with considerable
> variability such that in the determination of
> these marks the part played by the examiner
> can be greater than that of the performance
> of the examinee.[26]

It is probably *logically* possible to counteract the
various factors which lead to examiner unreliability. But
this is not really the issue. The issue is whether we can
have any confidence that this is likely to be achieved. And
here we can hardly avoid being pessimistic. One further
factor indicates why. Examinations, we have seen, can be
used to assess many things, and thus, even with the best
will in the world, two examiners are likely to work with
differing criteria of assessment. One may be looking for
comprehensiveness, coherence and clarity. The other may be
more interested in evidence of independence, critical
ability and depth. Both may be interested in comprehension,
but weight it differently. Even if they are agreed about
the criteria, and their weighting, there are usually so many
that the task of keeping them constantly in mind while
reading a script (particularly if it is handwritten at
examination speed), against a deadline, proves well-nigh
impossible. Coupled with the problems of quantifying such
judgments, there is as much reason to be surprised at their
agreement as at their differences.

Other forms of assessment

The problems confronted by terminal examinations, some of
which we have outlined, have prompted a variety of
alternative instruments of assessment, sometimes to
supplement, sometimes to replace examinations. Even
terminal examinations have been modified in various ways:
open-book, open-question, and take-home examinations can be
instanced. But the most popular supplement/alternative has

been some kind of continuous assessment. Though this can take the form of an examination, its most characteristic form is that of a written assignment (one or several), generally on a predetermined topic or problem, worked and written on at a relatively unhurried pace, and allowing access to resource materials. Feedback is normally involved in the form of detailed comments.

But continuous assessment has not proved the panacea it was supposed to be. The problems of validity and reliability are still there, even if not in as aggravated a form. The psychological trauma associated with terminal examinations has been ameliorated, but by no means eliminated. As Anthony Ryle observes (though not in this connection), 'any alternative system is likely to produce its own crop of casualties and its own varieties of stress.'.[27] Because continuous assessment is still attached to the grading/ranking system, and because this is still yoked to the accreditation function of schooling, thus serving to distribute life chances, social status, and (for many) ingredients of self-esteem, some of the major causes of stress remain. Teacher/student relations continue to be threatened by the power which the teacher's judgment is accorded, narrow conformism is still encouraged, and as a means of coping various forms of cheating flourish.

But defenders of terminal examinations may not even see continuous assessment as an improvement. While acknowledging that terminal examinations have their problems, they argue that there is no better alternative. It is observed that 'continuous assessment means continuous pressure. Concentrating that pressure into two weeks ... makes it much more intense, but it does allow a great deal more freedom at other times.'[28] Furthermore, it is too open to cheating,[29] too disruptive of teacher/student relations, and too time-consuming. Drawbacks though these are, they hardly outweigh the possible improvement constituted by continuous assessment. Perhaps what we need to ask is: For what purpose(s) is there no better alternative to examinations? If it is said to be educational, then examinations hardly figure among the alternatives. Education is furthered through dialogue, whether of a verbal or practical nature, and in terminal examinations this is severely truncated. We might argue that people become educated despite rather than because of examinations. It is more likely that those who see terminal examinations as the best alternative have in mind the various selecting functions which examinations have been given. They may not accomplish any of these very well, but because they have been given so many, and because people believe that they are tolerably valid and their results for the most part reliable, it is difficult to think of any better substitute. And of course there is no better substitute, because there is nothing, not even examinations, which can do all that

190

examinations are believed capable of doing!

A way forward?

The schooling machine is not likely to vanish overnight, but this is no reason to persevere with the assessment *status quo*. Continuous assessment is one advance, and now that it is well established we can work towards some further modifications.[30] Here we may utilise a distinction initially made by Michael Scriven and subsequently developed by Bloom *et al*. The distinction is between 'summative' and 'formative' assessment.[31] Summative assessment takes place 'only at the end of the unit, chapter, course or semester', and 'has as its primary goals grading or certifying students, judging the effectiveness of the teacher, and comparing curricula'.[32] It is what I earlier spoke of as appraisal, and terminal examinations constitute the prime example. Formative assessment, on the other hand, 'intervenes during the formation of the student, not when the process is thought to be completed. It points to areas of needed remediation so that immediately subsequent instruction and study can be made more pertinent and beneficial.'[33] What we have called continuous assessment is on the way to satisfying the conditions for formative assessment. But there is a crucial difference. Formative assessment (what we earlier identified as criticism) is directed exclusively to the improvement of learning, whereas continuous assessment, though it improves the learning environment, at present remains yoked to certification and selection. These two purposes cannot be properly reconciled. The purposes of certification and selection introduce into the learning and assessment situation psychological factors and other criteria (e.g. for ranking and grading purposes) which are not necessary to, and tend to be incompatible with, the learning process (particularly if it is to be educationally significant). What now needs to be done is for these two functions to be separated as much as possible. What this means is that accreditation should become the responsibility of employers, professional boards, etc., who can then conduct their own appraisals of potential employees, members, etc. Schooling certificates (and basic degrees) might then indicate only satisfactory or unsatisfactory participation in courses. There would not need to be any pass/fail quotas, grading or ranking. Not only would this improve the educational possibilities of schooling, but it would also lead to more efficient selection, since employers, etc. would not have to put up with an assessment system pointed in a dozen different directions.[34] Such a move could not be expected to occur easily or quickly. While school institutions are financed by governments whose interests are primarily those of employers, professional groups, etc., they will not readily

191

permit the erosion of the assessment *status quo*. But the social contradiction posed by the present arrangement creates the possibility that some advances might be contemplated and reasonably striven for.

NOTES

1. R.P. Wolff, *The Ideal of the University*, Boston: Beacon Press, 1969, p.58.
2. For a brief historical survey, see A.Z. Smith & J.E. Dobbin, s.v. 'Marks and Marking Systems', in C.W. Harris (ed.), *Encyclopedia of Educational Research*[3], New York: Macmillan, 1960, pp.783-91.
3. Wolff, p.59.
4. For a detailed development of this account of evaluation, see J. Kovesi, *Moral Notions*, London: Routledge & Kegan Paul, 1967, Ch.V; idem, 'Valuing and Evaluating', in B.Y. Khanbhai, R.S. Katz & R.A. Pineau (eds.), *Jowett Papers 1968-1969*, Oxford: Blackwell, 1970, pp.53-64; and G.H. von Wright, *The Varieties of Goodness*, London: Routledge & Kegan Paul, 1963.
5. 'Appraisal', like the other terms discussed, has a number of senses besides the one I have attributed to it. In this context, however, it is convenient to limit it as I have suggested.
6. For discussion of grading terminology, see J.O. Urmson, 'On Grading', *Mind*, LIX (April, 1950), 145-69. There are criticisms of Urmson in LX (October 1951), 526-29, 530-35; LXVIII (October, 1958), 485-501; *Australasian Journal of Philosophy*, XXXVIII, 3 (December, 1960), 234-45; XL, 2 (August, 1962), 187-203.
7. Cf. criterion- and norm-referenced testing.
8. Difficult, though not impossible. For valuable discussion of measurement, see special issue, 'Quantification: A History of the Meaning of Measurement in the Natural and Social Sciences', *Isis*, LII (December, 1961); C.W. Savage, *The Measurement of Sensation*, Berkeley: University of California Press, 1970. For a brief, recent contribution to the discussion of measurement in schooling contexts, see C.D. Hardie, 'Measurement in Education', *Educational Theory*, XXVIII, 1 (Winter, 1978), 54-61.
9. See *supra*, Ch.6.
10. These matters are usefully discussed in J.S. Mill, *On Liberty*, ed. D. Spitz, New York: W.W. Norton, 1975, Ch.2: 'Of the Liberty of Thought and Discussion'.
11. *Assessment in Higher Education*, University of Bath, Educational Services Unit.
12. Some writers would also add two further dimensions, precision and accuracy.

13. See *supra*, Ch.12.
14. The psychological effects of examinations are documented in A. Powell & B. Butterworth, *Marked for Life: A A Criticism of Assessment at Universities*, privately published, c/- A. Powell, Institute of Classical Studies, 31/4 Gordon Square, London, W.C.1, n.d. [c.1972], and references therein; also D. Mechanic, *Students Under Stress: A Study of the Social Psychology of Adaptation*, Glencoe, Ill.: The Free Press, 1962; A. Ryle, *Student Casualties*, London: Allen Lane, 1969; and J. Heywood, *Assessment in Higher Education*, London,: John Wiley, 1977, pp.8–9, and references.
15. See the opening sentence of C.B. Cox, 'In Praise of Examinations', in C.B. Cox & A.E. Dyson (eds.), *The Black Papers on Education*, London: Davis-Poynter, 1971, p.71.
16. J.D. Nisbet, 'The Need for Universities to Measure Achievement', in *The Assessment of Undergraduate Performance*, Report of Conference, Committee of Vice-Chancellors and Principals and Association of University Teachers, London, 1969.
17. C.B. Cox, p.77.
18. Whether they accomplish even that task efficiently may be doubted. As it is often pointed out, the pressures peculiar to an examination are commonly not duplicated in real life (see, e.g. Powell & Butterworth, pp. 5–6).
19. J. Chadwick, 'The Cambridge Classical Tripos: a reply', *Didaskalos*, III, 2 (1970), 275.
20. D. Pidgeon & A. Yates, *An Introduction to Educational Measurement*, London: Routledge & Kegan Paul, 1969, pp.5–6.
21. A.N. Oppenheim, M. Jahoda, & R.L. James, 'Assumptions Underlying the Use of University Examinations', *Universities Quarterly*, XXI, 3 (June, 1967), 342.
22. Hardie, 59. Hardie's failure to be impressed by the Hartog & Rhodes study (see fn.23) ignores the many years of 'pre-selection', making the pool of students considered in the Hartog & Rhodes study such that even a chance determination of grades (at this level) might be expected to produce a good number of successful engineers, doctors, etc.
23. C.B. Cox, p.73.
24. D. Starch & E.C. Elliott, 'Reliability of the Grading of High-School Work in English', *School Review*, XX (September, 1912), 442–57; idem, 'Reliability of Grading Work in Mathematics', *School Review*, XXI (April, 1913), 254–59; idem, 'Reliability of Grading Work in History', *School Review*, XXI (December, 1913), 676–81.
25. P. Hartog & E.C. Rhodes, *An Examination of Examinations*, London: Macmillan, 1935; also P. Hartog, E.C. Rhodes & C.J. Burt, *The Mark of Examiners*, London: Methuen,

1936.

26. H. Pieron, *Examens et docimologie*, Paris, 1963; quoted in R. Cox, 'Examinations and Higher Education', *Universities Quarterly*, XXI, 3 (June, 1967), 300.

27. Ryle, p.103.

28. Chadwick, 275.

29. It is not usually asked why students cheat. It is simply assumed to reflect laziness. But it may just as frequently indicate the effects of competitive pressures or the failure of teachers to present a course which inspires interest. See W. Bowers, *Student Dishonesty and its Control in College*, New York: Bureau of Applied Behavioural Science, 1964.

30. In this connection I have found suggestive and helpful the Ed.D. thesis of D.R. De Nicola, 'Evaluation and Grading: a Philosophical Analysis', Graduate School of Education, Harvard University, 1973, Part II.

31. M. Scriven, 'The Methodology of Evaluation', in R.W. Tyler, R. Gagné & M. Scriven, *Perspectives of Curriculum Evaluation*, AERA Monograph Series on Curriculum Evaluation, No.1, Chicago: Rand McNally, 1967, pp.43ff.; B.S. Bloom, J.T. Hastings & G.F. Madaus, *Handbook on Formative and Summative Evaluation of Student Learning*, New York: McGraw-Hill, 1971.

32. Bloom *et al.*, p.20.

33. ibid.

34. It could also help to free the curriculum from its sometimes narrow pre-occupation (as, e.g. in many law courses) with vocational needs.

Chapter 15

CHILDREN AND RIGHTS

That children are frequently recipients of great tenderness and affection is not to be denied. Yet their powerlessness and dependence has also made them vulnerable to oppressive treatment, and it is this which has been highlighted in recent demands for children's rights. Such demands have been made in the face of a long tradition within which children have been viewed as having a justifiably inferior status within the community, a status which gives others the right (and duty?) to mould them more or less as they wish, limited only by the most compelling requirements of humanitarian instinct.

Even the most liberal writers have felt persuaded by the central thrust of this tradition: children are different, and not to be accorded most of the rights, freedoms, privileges and immunities considered essential by adult members of society. They cannot vote or act in ways that are legally binding; they are compulsorily schooled and must do as they are told; within fairly broad limits they may be assaulted without redress by parents; they have little freedom of movement; and such choice as they have in the matter of what they eat, wear, say and with whom they associate is dependent on the discretion of parents, teachers and others deemed (without consultation) *in loco parentium*. Can this state of affairs be justified?

The received tradition

J.S. Mill provides an instructive defence. In his essay *On Liberty* we find consciously combined one of the most eloquent defences of liberalism and at the same time an unequivocal commitment to paternalism in the case of children. Mill's basic thesis is that

> the only purpose for which power can be rightfully exercised over any member of a civilised community, against his will, is to

prevent harm to others. He cannot rightfully
be compelled to do or forbear because it will
be better for him to do so, because it will
make him happier, because, in the opinion of
others, to do so would be wise or even
right.[1]

With respect to that part of a person's life which 'merely
concerns himself, his independence is, of right, absolute.
Over himself, over his own body and mind, the individual is
sovereign.'[2] Inserted into this statement of principle is a
crucial qualification, namely, that independence rightfully
belongs only to members of a 'civilised' community. And so,
in the very next paragraph he almost casually observes that

it is hardly necessary to say that this
doctrine is meant to apply only to human
beings in the maturity of their faculties.
We are not speaking of children, or of young
persons below the age which the law may fix
as that of manhood or womanhood. Those who
are still in a state to require being taken
care of by others, must be protected against
their own actions as well as against external
injury.[3]

The restriction is not limited to children. As the essay
proceeds, he excludes 'barbarians',[4] 'those who are delir-
ious or in some state of excitement or absorption incompatible with the full use of the reflecting faculty',[5] those
who would sell themselves into perpetual slavery,[6] and
possibly others[7] from the purview of the principle of
individual liberty from interference.

Of course, whenever exceptions are made to a principle,
there is a problem about where to draw the line. And the
problem of the slippery slope clearly bothered Mill. Into
the mouth of a detractor he puts the question: 'If
protection against themselves is confessedly due to children
and persons under age, is not society equally bound to
afford it to persons of mature years who are equally
incapable of self-government?'[8] He attempts, somewhat unsuccessfully, to answer the question by observing that

Society has had absolute power over them
during all the early portion of their
existence: it has had the whole period of
childhood and nonage in which to try whether
it could make them capable of rational
conduct in life.... If society lets any
considerable number of its members grow up
mere children, incapable of being acted on by
rational consideration of distant motives,

196

society has itself to blame for the consequences. [9]

From his reply, this much at least is clear: children are
the paradigm exclusions from the liberal principle.

In excluding children from the purview of the liberal
principle, it is not Mill's purpose to deny all 'rights' to
them (though, on a certain account of rights in which rights
are viewed as discretionary powers, his exclusion might have
that effect). They have 'rights' not to be mistreated, and
the 'rights' which others have over them allow interference
only to the extent of providing for their welfare. [10] And the
latter, for Mill, included as an important ingredient the
child's development as a 'self-governing' being.

Mill's position regarding children is well-entrenched
in current social ideology. Like other aspects of that
ideology, it misleads us into thinking that what it is used
to justify (schools, a certain form of parental domination,
etc.) is *actually* directed towards the ends which Mill
recites (particularly individuality/autonomy), when it
generally does not. But even if we ignore that aspect of
its functioning, it is not without its problems. Chief
amongst these is the use of the category of childhood to
exclude some people from (some of) the rights, liberties,
privileges and immunities enjoyed by others.

The concept of childhood

What constitutes childhood? No simple answer is available,
for indeed there is no unified concept of childhood. We
might make a start, however, by distinguishing *institutionalised* and *normative* concepts of childhood. The former type
categorises according to some customary or legal-like
criterion – whether it is some age to be reached or some
rite to be passed through. Mill makes use of an institutionalised concept when referring to those in their 'nonage'
or as 'below the age which the law may fix as that of
manhood or womanhood'. The normative type categorises
according to some feature which has normative
significance – some capacity which is believed relevant to
treatment which the categorisation is intended to sanction.
Again, we find that Mill employs a normative concept when he
speaks of children as those not in 'the maturity of their
faculties', and uses this to exclude them from the scope of
the principle of individual liberty.

The relationship between institutionalised and normative concepts of childhood is often thought to be close,
since it is generally believed that the institutionalised
concept is *based on* the normative concept. Yet the correspondence is frequently less than supposed. There is, for
example a very untidy relation between those not in 'the
maturity of their faculties' and those 'below the age which

197

the law may fix as that of manhood or womanhood', yet Mill gives them equal status in determining those who fall into the category of childhood.[11] This is morally suspect, for two reasons. First of all, it will result in some who qualify morally not having their rights recognised since they do not qualify institutionally, and, presumably, it may qualify institutionally some who do not qualify morally. Given the attractiveness which institutionalised procedures tend to have in our society, it is very likely that institutional categorisations will dominate. Secondly, the institutionalised concept may reflect and perpetuate a form of repression in which the period of normative childhood is extended. For example, it is arguable that most humans *could* attain 'maturity of their faculties' (whatever Mill means by that) by the time they are thirteen years old, but because they are legally children until they are eighteen or twenty-one, we do not give them the opportunities to be 'mature' until they are a good deal older than thirteen. Childhood can, to some extent, be manufactured and prolonged.

The position on childhood is rather more complicated than I have so far suggested. The institutionalised/normative distinction picks out types of concepts of childhood rather than specific concepts of childhood. There are, for example, several distinct institutionalised concepts in common use. In law, the term 'child' may refer to any person below some determinate age, such as eighteen or twenty-one (a minor), or to an offspring of two people (whether natural or by adoption). Other institutions have their own criteria: a theatre management may consider as children those between the ages of five and eighteen, the proprietors of a bus service those between the ages of three and fifteen, and so on. In what I have called the normative sphere, the situation is not substantially different, except that the different concepts tend to be regarded as being in competition. Thus, in line with a number of recent writers, David Wardle has claimed that it is 'almost reasonable to say that childhood was invented in the eighteenth and nineteenth centuries'.[12] Talk of 'invention' is something of an exaggeration, but Wardle is probably correct in thinking that the last few centuries have spawned an alternative concept of childhood, one which exists in tension with more traditional understandings. Within the traditional understanding, childhood is dominated by the idea of immaturity: it is something to be grown out of, the start of the road to adulthood. But the more recent trend, Wardle claims, has been to view it as 'a stage having characteristic needs and interests which have a value of their own regardless of their role in preparing for adult life.'[13] This is supposedly evidenced in (though I think it hardly demonstrated by) the growth of child-oriented and child-populated institutions, distinctive clothes and books for children, legal protections specifically for children, and so on.

The situation regarding the so-called normative concepts of childhood is further complicated by the academic industry which has grown up around childhood. This has led to a 'refinement' of categories, and in the academic discussion we find, instead of the simple dichotomy of children and adults, a trichotomisation of the former into infants, children and youths or adolescents. A possible gain from this 'refinement' is a greater sensitivity to relevant differences with a consequent improvement in relations between people, but this of course depends on how the discriminations are made, what treatment they are used to sanction, and whether they lead to the formation of new institutionalised concepts whose rigidity is self-defeating. In this area, the studies on which such discriminations are made frequently do little more than articulate unquestioningly patterns of development observable within a particular society or social grouping. In so far as these observations are then made the justification for programmes of treatment, they may do little more than maintain a repressive existing pattern of development. These discriminations, moreover, may be based on criteria which are not directly relevant to the treatment they are used to sanction. Whereas the notion of childhood has traditionally been conceived in a quasi-moral manner, the academic discussion of childhood has been dominated by developmental psychologists, whose criteria have not been restricted to those from which morally significant conclusions can be drawn. And yet the categorisations arrived at are made the basis for compulsory treatment of certain kinds.

The foregoing observations on 'the concept of childhood' are intended to suggest that any simple appeal to childhood in relation to the matter of right-ascription is likely to be morally suspect or opaque. However, we might attempt to redeem the situation by stipulating a refined or technical sense of 'childhood' which bases itself solely on features which are thought relevant to right-ascription - whether in general, or in relation to some particular right. Something like the latter appears to have been in the back of Mill's mind. The right to liberty from interference presupposes certain capacities which children, by definition, do not have. They are, therefore, justifiably subjected to paternalistic interferences. Although the link between the presuppositions of some particular right and the concept of childhood may raise the spectre of a multitude of concepts of childhood, each one associated with the presuppositions of some particular right, it is not unreasonable to see the right to individual liberty as being sufficiently central in the constellation of rights to make alternatives less attractive.

What are the capacities or conditions which a person must satisfy if he/she is to possess the right to liberty from paternalistic interference? On this Mill and other writers are less than clear.

(1) One suggestion has regard to mobility and linguistic competence. In so far as our ability to survive might well depend on our being able to move around and communicate with others, then, once a certain level of competence has been reached in that regard, enabling the person to take his/her own initiatives in survival, no further paternalistic interferences would be justified (except, perhaps, in exceptional circumstances). If this is accepted as the basis for the child/adult distinction, it would require a radical redrawing of our present boundaries.[14] While I do not consider this an irrelevant factor in determining the extent of freedom children might justifiably claim, it might be too narrow a basis for full liberty of self-regarding action. It is, after all, not mere survival which is of importance, but the capacity to enjoy and secure a certain kind of life.

(2) More plausible might be the reaching of puberty. The physical and psychological changes associated with puberty might be thought sufficient to equip a person, not merely for survival, but for the kind of relations and pursuits which constitute a worthwhile life. I believe that there is a good deal to be said for giving this point in personal development considerable weight. In many traditional societies puberty is the signal for initiation rites into adulthood, but in contemporary Western society, with the specialised demands of its workforce, that recognition of adulthood is withheld until people have been trained to take what is fondly called 'a responsible part in society'. The period between puberty and 'adulthood' is consequently a time of more than usual frustration as people seek to establish and gain recognition for their personal integrity. Yet there is relatively little interest in according children full adult rights and responsibilities at puberty. One reason for this has been mentioned earlier: because we locate the passage from childhood to adulthood at about eighteen or twenty-one, we create a social environment in which many people do not, and are not encouraged to, acquire the maturity of outlook that is possible at puberty; and so we still see post-pubertal adolescents as 'too young' to be given the same rights, liberties, privileges and immunities enjoyed by the rest of us.[15]

The criterion of puberty is a useful one because it has a certain visibility and is therefore not as easily distorted by social pressures. However, as we have seen, puberty can function as a criterion only because it is associated with a variety of changes, and some of these may be delayed till well after puberty, given a particular social formation. This contingency makes it a somewhat unreliable criterion. We should, therefore, look more closely at that to which puberty is thought to point.

(3) Here we can start with Mill's account. As we have noted, Mill speaks of 'maturity of faculties' as a condition to be satisfied if liberty of action is to be claimed as of right. But what could be meant by this exceptionally vague phrase? By what standard is maturity to be determined? What 'faculties' are in view? Some clarification, but no substantial advance, is made when he goes on to speak of those who are 'still in a state to require being taken care of by others.' This looks like an appeal to the 'survival' criterion we first considered, though I expect that Mill did not mean anything as basic as this. Whatever it is, as he states it it places in jeopardy the rights of the infirm to liberty from interference. More importantly, it is not clear how being in such a state disqualifies a person from liberty from interference. As Herbert Spencer had already pointed out, the parent's maintenance of the child established at most a claim to 'like kindness toward himself should he ever need it'. The parent does not establish a 'title to dominion'.[16] To be sure, although Mill recognised the 'absolute power' which parents had over children, he (unlike many parents) did not consider that they had a 'title' to it, and it may be that his inbuilt limitation on the use of that power – the protection of welfare interests – would come close to meeting Spencer's objection. Nevertheless, Mill's appeal to those still in a state of dependence does not seem to warrant his conclusion that dependent children are therefore to be *excluded* from the liberal principle.

(4) As Mill's argument progresses, he becomes more specific about the nature of the deficiency which leaves children properly subject to paternal interference. They, like 'barbarians', are not yet 'capable of being improved by free and equal discussion'.[17] Improvement of a praiseworthy kind, that is, improvement fitting to the kind of beings we are, is possible only for those capable of autonomous judgment. The child, lacking autonomy, can improve only as a result of chance or the intervention of others. Since the former cannot be relied upon, the latter is justified.

The capacity for self-improvement, however, is not an all or nothing affair. Autonomy is a matter of degree. Certainly it is not something we suddenly come by at a specifiable age, such as eighteen or twenty-one. But neither is it something that we acquire at *about* that age.

A six-year-old child may have, within certain parameters, a capacity for self-improvement, and a twenty-five-year-old adult may find spheres of operation within which he/she is unable to operate in a constructive way. The passage from childhood to adulthood is not like crossing the border from one country to another. It is a matter of continuous development in which capacities for self-improvement to some extent in evidence from very early in life, are gradually extended and developed. Thus, if we adopt a criterion such as Mill's, we would need to be more specific about the kinds of liberties to which children are or are not entitled. There will need to be a progressive freeing of the child from paternalistic interference as capacities for choice increase. A six-year-old child may be capable of deciding whether and what game it will play but not whether and who to marry.

To some extent our society and its laws give evidence of recognising this development. But they do so, I believe, in a fairly inflexible, repressive, and disrespecting way. It is not the interests of the child - its own self-development and the development of a pattern of relationships conducive to the achievement of a worthwhile life - which determines the lifting of paternalistic restrictions, but the child's preparedness for some set of pre-established social or economic pigeon-holes. The cult of childhood, of seeing childhood as a way of life to be fostered and pandered to, serves to keep people young until they have had impressed upon them where they belong in our present society. Rapid change has not affected this: we now 'educate children for change', without giving much thought to whether the change is good for them or us.

What we seem to have come to is this: if the child/adult distinction is used to justify paternalism of a fairly total kind in the case of the former, it must be based on considerations relevant to the ability to make use of liberty. However, when we spell out those considerations, we find that they are not such as to allow for a workable distinction between child and adult, since they are manifested in varying degrees in respect of a range of contexts, and their development covers a time-span which does not allow for the location of any precise or even approximate point at which it can be said that paternalism is justified before but not after it.

As a matter of practical politics, of course, it may be advisable to have a publicly recognised point after which the onus is on the state to justify any paternalistic interference in which it wishes to engage or which it seeks to support (i.e. the rights of parents over children). However, we should endeavour to make that point as early as possible rather than as late as possible, lest children become so indoctrinated with the values and expectations of an exploiting group that they never become capable of the kind of life which exemplifies that ideal of human living and being which is the justifying point of education.

Rights

To this point, not a great deal has been said about *rights*. The focus has been on the substance of what is claimed or rejected as *a* right of children – the right to pursue their lives without unconsented to interference by others or their agents, in so far as those pursuits do not violate the legitimate interests of others. What is the significance of claiming this as *a right*? To what extent ought we to be concerned for the rights of children? It is to these questions that we now turn.

Rights-talk finds its natural home in a politico-legal context. Historically, its extension into the moral sphere was the function of a number of factors.[17] Most importantly, the rise of individualism in the sixteenth and seventeenth centuries, in the wake of the renaissance of Greek humanism and the Reformation, needed to express itself in terms which carried some kind of political significance. Rights-talk did just that, and the background vocabulary of the natural law tradition provided a favourable environment for this linguistic transplant. Natural rights became the rallying cry of revolution and of the individual against state and church. The language of natural rights began as the language of the oppressed. Bentham spoke of it as 'terrorist language', thus showing where he stood. Others might call it 'freedom fighter language'.

However, there is now a danger that the point of rights-talk will be lost. More and more, rights-talk has become the medium of moral exchange, and other important dimensions of our moral transactions have been edged out of the picture. The political value of such talk has been emphasised to the point of obscuring those values which made such rhetoric appropriate. There has been an extension of rights-talk to future generations, the unborn, animals, plants and rocks; and within the sphere of children's rights there are references to the right to play, to be loved, to choose one's parents, to be consulted about decisions which affect oneself, to eat what one likes, to dress how one likes, to be breast-fed, to competent teachers, to all kinds of knowledge, to free ante-natal care, and so on. I do not want to say that there is something bogus about all these claims, but the rapid expansion of rights-talk may easily lead to its trivial-isation if it becomes a mere political husk.

What, then, is the distinctive character of rights-talk? The issue is a controversial one. H.L.A. Hart represents one important tradition in his view that the distinctive feature of rights-possession is being morally in a position to determine by one's choice how another will

act, and in this way to limit the other's freedom of choice.
Rights on this view are discretionary powers, and,
consequently, not possessed by babies and animals.[18] We may
have duties *regarding* babies and animals, but we cannot have
duties *to* them. According to another tradition, rights are
to be distinguished as an advantage to which we have some
claim, whether or not the capacity for choice is present.
On this view, babies and animals *may* be right-holders,
depending on how the advantage is explicated. It is the
latter view which I consider most acceptable.

According to the discretionary view, if A has a right
to x against B then B's duty to A rests on A's exercising
his/her right. A's right is simply his/her being in a
position to require the forbearance or contribution of
another. Hart puts it thus: 'The precise figure is not
that of two persons bound by a chain, but of *one* person
bound, the other end of the chain lying in the hand of
another to use if he chooses.'[19] There is an ambiguity in
Hart's figure which is symptomatic of an underlying confusion in the discretionary position. It is not clear
whether in the latter figure B is simply bound, or bound *to*
A. The context suggests that Hart wants to say that B is
bound *to* A. Yet the picture of the chain simply 'lying' in
A's hand, to be used only 'if he chooses', suggests that B
is not bound to A *unless* A grips the chain. Put more
schematically, the statement form, 'A has a right to x
against B', may be thought to entail either 'B has a duty to
give x to A unless A chooses otherwise', or 'B has a duty to
give x to A only if A chooses.' It may be questioned whether
either of these is entailed (contented slaves still have
their rights violated), but if we are to choose that which
most nearly approximates to the discretionary element in
rights-talk, the first formulation seems more accurate.
Your duty to respect my rights does not have to wait for my
assertion of them, and if I waive them I release you from
what is *already* due me. Thus, if I have a right against
you, the chain which binds you does not merely *lie* in my
hand. I have a firm grip on it, though I may release it.
However, advocates of the discretionary position tend to
adopt the second formulation, and this explains their
exclusion of babies and animals from the company of
right-holders. For the second, though not the first,
formulation presupposes the right-holder's actual ability to
choose. There is no reason, therefore, why the
discretionary aspect of rights-talk needs to be tied
directly to the interests possessed by *actual* choosers.

In my view, it is preferable to see human rights, at
least, as representing those minimum conditions under which
human beings can come to exemplify some ideal of human
living and being.[20] These conditions we may term their
welfare interests. Such interests are possessed not only
by actual but also by potential choosers. Against this

view, Hart argues that in some cases the right-holder does not benefit from the exercise of his/her right – not because of some unexpected intervention, but because the beneficiary is a third party.[21] Thus if B promises A in return for some favour that he/she will look after A's aged mother, A has a right against B, though it is not A, but A's mother, who benefits. Two comments may be made about this. First, if Hart is right, then it is because this case is exceptional. Its being exceptional flows from the kind of right it is – what Hart elsewhere refers to as a 'special' rather than a 'general' right. Promises, contracts and agreements create rights in respect of particular individuals, but should not be invoked as paradigmatic of human rights. Secondly, the plausibility of Hart's case depends on an excessively narrow conception of advantage as benefit. In the case under consideration, A's mother will certainly benefit if B keeps his/her promise. But this does not show that A is not also substantially advantaged; quite the contrary. A's advantage will reside in the securing of his/her interest (stake) in his/her mother's welfare. Were A to have no interest at all in his/her mother's welfare, B's promise would be pointless, as would be the ascription of a right to A.

We still have to explain the connection between the advantages and the appropriateness of talking about them as *rights*. As noted, rights-talk was originally intended to serve a politico-moral purpose. In their primary politico-legal context, A's right to x against B amounted to A's legally guaranteed capacity to compel B to give x to him/her, should any compulsion be required. This connection with force was taken over into the moral sphere, where human rights were appealed to as *justification* for the use of force. This justification was possible because of the *importance* of the interests rights-talk was designed to secure, namely people's welfare interests. Welfare interests, those more or less indispensable conditions for the pursuit of a worthwhile human life, are of such importance that their coercive protection or securing is justified.[22]

On this account, the rights of children will be identical with those of adults. If we assume, for the sake of argument, that human welfare interests can be roughly identified as bodily and mental health, normal intellectual development, adequate material security, stable and non-superficial interpersonal relationships, and a fair degree of liberty,[23] then we can see little difference between children and adults in respect of the kinds of claims they may make of others. Greater effort may sometimes be needed to secure children's welfare interests, and in certain cases this may result in a diminution of their liberty. Where that is the case there needs to be a balancing of interests. Where, as in the case of a very young child, liberty has little value since the child is in no position to make constructive use of it, the compulsory securing of welfare interests is not too difficult to justify. But where the interference with liberty would also constitute an interference with a person's autonomous projects, harmful though they may be to that person, interferences of a paternalistic kind are much more difficult to justify. Between these two situations there is a continuum of cases in which a person's liberty and other welfare interests may come into conflict and in relation to which the question of paternalism will pose a difficult balancing problem. Nevertheless, I believe that the balance lies in favour of the child's freedom far more frequently than we conventionally recognise.

It is against this background that we can view some aspects of the question of 'compulsory education'.[24] Some measure of education is fairly clearly implied by the earlier catalogue of welfare interests. To that extent, then, education is a human right. Yet the very young child is not in a good position to secure it. It must be secured for it. The compulsory nature of this is justified by pointing to the valuelessness of the child's liberty, prior to its ability to make that liberty count for something. This appears to be Mill's view. He sees the value of liberty against a background of individuality. Individuality, however, is not innate but a product of nurture, and so the child must be brought to that position where it 'becomes capable of self-improvement'. Education, therefore, is a precondition of the right to liberty. Mill, at least, was reasonably sensitive to the differences between compulsory education and compulsory (state) schooling. Others have not been.

Conclusion

So far we have been seeking to establish the importance of rights to children. To conclude, I want to suggest that they can be over-emphasised. In an attack on 'children's rights', Paul Goodman argues that the unhappy situation of children

> is not something to cope with polemically or to understand in terms of 'freedom', 'democracy', 'rights', and 'power', like bringing lawyers into a family quarrel. It has to be solved by wise traditions in organic communities with considerable stability, with equity instead of law, and with love and compassion more than either.[25]

He goes on to claim that 'the key terms are not children's rights' or 'democracy', but their 'spontaneity, fantasy, animality, creativity, innocence'.[26]

We do not have to accept Goodman's romanticism to see the point of his attack. The priority given to the securing of rights in recent discussion has all but obscured other dimensions of our relationships. There is much more to adequate moral relationships than the bare recognition of rights, a point frequently forgotten in the course of campaigning. Unless there is love, care and concern for others as individuals, *in addition to* the recognition of rights, there remains a moral lack in interpersonal relationships.[27] Action done for another, simply because it is the other's due, remains morally truncated. This is because actions motivated simply by the rights of others remain anonymous or impersonal, whereas, if motivated by love, care or concern for the other, their focus is on the other's particularity. Only relations of the latter kind are morally adequate. They are person-specific, whereas rights are category-specific.

This is not intended to underrate the importance of rights as politico-moral requirements. But it is intended to suggest that rights-talk, if it is not to be abused, must be seen in a wider moral context and not permitted to get out of hand. The wider context is one in which the primary moral relations of love, care and concern have broken down, and we need to fall back on the auxiliary apparatus of rights. That at least demands the basic minimum. On the other hand, where people do love and care for each other, there is no need for recourse to rights-*talk*, since what is due to the other will be encompassed within the loving or caring relationship.[28] Where that is no longer the case, or where love and care have been distorted, as in bureaucratic or class-based societies, then the language of rights must be appealed to in order to maintain or recover the minima of interpersonal morality.

NOTES

1. J.S. Mill, *On Liberty*, ed. D. Spitz, New York: W.W. Norton & Co., 1975, Ch.I, pp.10–11.
2. ibid., p.11.
3. ibid.
4. ibid.
5. ibid., Ch.V, p.89.
6. ibid., p.95.
7. ibid., Ch.IV, p.70, where he excludes those without 'the ordinary amount of understanding'.
8. ibid., p.75.
9. ibid., p.77.
10. Cf.: 'Despotism is a legitimate mode of government in dealing with barbarians, provided the end be their

improvement, and the means justified by actually effecting that end' (ibid., Ch.I, p.11). Mill, it is to be noted, does not make any considerable use of the terminology of rights, since it tends to be more closely associated with a rival tradition.

11. ibid., Ch.I, p.11; Ch.IV, pp.70, 75, 77. To be strictly accurate, Mill distinguishes two categories of people 'under age' - children and youths (those in their nonage).

12. D. Wardle, *The Rise of the Schooled Society*: *the history of formal schooling in England*, London: Routledge & Kegan Paul, 1974, p.27. Cf. Philippe Ariès, *Centuries of Childhood*, ET, London: Jonathan Cape, 1962, p.125 *et passim*.

13. Wardle, p.30. Cf. also romantic conceptions of childhood, with their emphasis on innocence, *joie de vivre*, etc.

14. Francis Schrag cites research which suggests that basic competence in these areas has been developed by age six ('The Child in the Moral Order', *Philosophy*, LII (April, 1977), 170). Amongst the Ik of Northern Uganda, children are left to fend for themselves from age three (see C.M. Turnbull, *The Mountain People*, London: Jonathan Cape, 1973).

15. This is not to suggest that the *status quo* with respect to the rights, etc. enjoyed by the rest of us is some sort of ideal. Far from it. Nevertheless, with respect to the ability to order their own lives, many children seem to be considerably worse off than most of us.

16. H. Spencer, *Social Statics* (1851), London: Williams & Norgate, 1868, p.194. I explore Spencer's views in more detail in 'Mill, Children & Rights', *Educational Philosophy and Theory*, VIII, 1 (April, 1976), 8-9. In later years Spencer appears to have changed his views. See the discussion in Margaret Spahr, 'Mill on Paternalism in its Place', in C.J. Friedrich (ed.), *NOMOS IV: Liberty*, New York: Atherton Press, 1962, pp.164-65. For a modern-day version of Spencer, see K.R. Paton, *The Great Brain Robbery*, privately published, 102 Newcastle St., Silverdale, Newcastle-under-Lyme, Staffordshire, ST5 6PL, U.K. 1971.

17. The material in this and succeeding paragraphs is developed further in my 'Human Rights, Legal Rights and Social Change', in E. Kamenka & A.E.-S. Tay (eds.), *Human Rights*, London: Edward Arnold, 1978, pp.36-47.

18. 'If common usage sanctions talk of the rights of animals or babies it makes an idle use of the expression "a right", which will confuse the situation with other different moral situations where the expression "a right" has a specific force and cannot be replaced by other moral expressions' (H.L.A. Hart, 'Are there any Natural Rights?', *Philosophical Review*, LXIV (1955),

181).

19. ibid.

20. The notion of a welfare interest is pursued at greater depth in my 'Crime and the Concept of Harm', *American Philosophical Quarterly*, XV, 1 (January, 1978), 27-36.

21. Hart, 181.

22. In Ch.V of *Utilitarianism* Mill gives a utilitarian twist to this by talking instead of 'general utility' as justifying that which rights are designed to secure. See D. Lyons, 'Human Rights and the General Welfare', *Philosophy & Public Affairs*, VI, 2 (Winter, 1977), 113-29.

23. A more detailed discussion is provided by Nicholas Rescher in *Welfare: The Social Issues in Philosophical Perspective*, Pittsburgh U.P., 1972, Ch.1.

24. For a more detailed discussion, see my 'Compulsory Schooling', *Journal of Philosophy of Education*, XV, 2 (November, 1981).

25. P. Goodman, 'What Rights Should Children Have?' *New York Review*, (23 September, 1971), 20.

26. ibid., 21.

27. On the centrality of love, etc. to morality, see my 'Moral Schizophrenia and Christian Ethics', *Reformed Theological Review*, XL, 1 (January-April, 1981), 11-19, and 'Moral Education and the Nature of Morality', *Journal of Christian Education* (forthcoming).

28. Love and care, it may be objected, are sometimes stifling. But this, I think, is true only of distorted love. What is done in the name of love is not necessarily done in love. Love and care must have regard to the particularity of the thing that is their object, and that, in the case of love and care for another human being, will involve an acknowledgement of the other's welfare interests, including the other's interest in liberty. Love and care which stifle are defective as love and care. Those whose 'love' commits them to acts knowingly or negligently harmful to the other are evidently acting out of love for something else: some ideal or their own egos.

Chapter 16

EDUCATION AND AUTHORITY

Discussions about the place of authority in education have a tendency to degenerate into slanging matches, one side accusing the other of 'abdicating authority', and the other replying with charges of 'authoritarianism'. As is often the case with such disputes, there is something to be said on each side, and what is wanted more than anything is a sensitivity to the opposition viewpoint and a willingness to reconsider one's own. This is no guarantee of agreement, since some of the differences are deeply rooted in opposed ideologies. Nevertheless, a cool reappraisal of the issues should at least serve to locate the differences more usefully than is achieved via namecalling. In brief, proponents on the one side argue that the teaching/learning relationship implies authority, that the recognition and exercise of authority is a causal precondition of an effective teaching medium, and that those who reject authority confuse liberty with licence. On the other side, it is argued that the exercise of authority in teaching stifles creativity and the development of autonomy, leads to indoctrination, and substitutes for relationships of mutual respect and interest, relationships of domination and subservience. Not surprisingly, such polarised claims oversimplify the situation. The debate cannot be properly conducted in terms of two sides, despite the public convenience of doing so. Moreover, it is not simply a debate about the place of authority in education (or schooling). Different understandings of education, teaching, the role of schools, the nature of autonomy, and the capacities of children also tend to be involved. Nevertheless, differences concerning the nature, justification and location of authority also play a part, and it is on these that we shall concentrate in this chapter.

In the recent philosophical literature, it has become customary to distinguish three kinds of authority – positional or *de jure* authority, actual or *de facto* authority, and expert authority. The first two have been linked with power or influence, and the third with the claim to be heard/believed.[1] In some ways these have been helpful distinctions, but I believe that they have sometimes led, on the one hand, to a fragmentation of the notion of authority, and, on the other, to an overemphasis on institutional factors. There is some value, then, in attempting to re-draw the lines of the debate.

Perhaps the first thing to be said about authority is that it picks out a social relation. When *X* believes or does *A* on *Y*'s authority, there exists a relation between *X* and *Y* with respect to some sphere of knowledge or action such that *X* believes or does *A* because *Y* says or permits so. Commencing with the authority relationship (doing/believing something on authority) helps us to avoid what in some standard accounts appears to be a radical dualism between actual and epistemic authority. Influence is involved in both cases, and what we need to do is to articulate more precisely this relationship between *X* and *Y*, and to reconcile it with the demand for rationality in belief and action.

To say that *X* believes or does *A* because *Y* says or permits so is not sufficient to distinguish (on a conceptual level) a relation of authority from a coercive relation. The armed bandit whose command secures my compliance does not have authority but coercive power over me. I am compelled to comply. I have no real choice. It is central to authority relationships that what is believed or done on authority is believed or done voluntarily. It need not be willingly believed or done, for what we consent to is not always what we approve of or agree with. The point at which agreement or compliance can be achieved only by coercive means is also the point at which authority is replaced by force.

According to a time-honoured account, authority is legitimate power. In the light of the foregoing, two observations are in order. First of all, not all power is coercive power or force, and we should not restrict the traditional account to certain (presumably legitimate) acts of coercion. It might be more appropriate to think in terms of influence, leaving it open whether, in a particular context, the influence is coercive. Secondly, legitimacy in the traditional account can be understood only in the sense of 'consented to', or, what in many contexts comes to much the same thing, 'lawful'.[2] It is not possible, I think, to interpret 'legitimate' as 'justifiable' without unduly narrowing the range of authority relations. In discussing authority we want to distinguish justifiable and unjustifiable uses of it, and a view which limits authority to justifiable influence makes conceptually awkward what should be straightforward.

Is anything more to be said about authority than that it expresses a relationship between X and Y such that X voluntarily believes or does A because Y says or permits so? More must be said. If a friend asks me to buy something for him/her while I am overseas, and I do so, it is not because he/she has authority over me. A further condition is needed. This we can locate in beliefs held concerning the authority-holder. Most importantly, X's believing or doing A because Y says or permits so expresses Y's authority with respect to X when X believes that Y is in a position to *know* whether or not A, or whether or not X should do A.[3]

We can *partially* express the preceding point in more familiar terms by saying that where X ascribes authority to Y with respect to A, it is generally because Y is perceived as being *an* authority or *in* authority. We may clarify these as follows:

(1) An authority. A person is said to be an authority by virtue of the (supposed) extensiveness or intimacy of his/her knowledge. Two limitations are generally implicit in such ascriptions. First, it is with respect to some particular field of inquiry or subject-matter that a person is said to be an authority. Secondly, it is relative to a given group or community that a person is an authority. (This is a consequence of the 'voluntary acceptance' requirement.) We may suggest then, that judgments to the effect that someone is an authority generally have the implicit form:

Y is an authority on A with respect to group Z.

(2) In authority. A person is said to be in authority by virtue of holding an office or position within an institutional structure. The structure may or may not be hierarchically ordered. However, it is not the particular person so much as the office or position which is invested with authority. Occupants may come and go, and the authority which is vested in them is limited to the period of occupancy. Qualification for occupancy may be grounded in custom or institutionally recognised rules.[4] The same limitations which apply to being an authority also hold for those in authority. Such authority is generally limited to specified matters within a community bounded by the sponsoring institution.

212

We may illustrate the foregoing expressions of authority by reference to the schooling situation. In a typical school the principal and teachers are usually considered to be *in* authority – they are authorised to act in a limited number of ways within a particular socially defined context. This authorisation is generally grounded in a complex of laws, departmental rules, internal permissions and prescriptions, and certain societal or local traditions. From time to time, those in authority *act on* that authority by doing or permitting or requiring certain acts. In a limiting case, someone in authority may never, or never need to, act on that authority. He/she may achieve the ends for which the authority is given by other means – manipulation, promises, coercion, inducements, friendship, etc. Or, perhaps, no occasion for acting on authority arises. Acting on authority needs to be distinguished from *having* or *possessing* it. If a principal's directives are ignored by his/her staff and students, then there is a sense in which, despite his/her acting on authority, he/she lacks it. His/her word fails to influence. Moreover, whereas anyone can have authority, only those in authority can act on it. If, instead of the principal, the staff of a school listen only to a junior member, and respond to his/her directives (because he/she is or is believed to be in a position to know), then that teacher has authority, even though he/she is not in (a position of) authority. Someone in a school may have authority (i.e. others may believe or do A on that person's authority) for a variety of reasons. It may be because he/she is in authority, or because he/she possesses certain qualities of personality (what Weber spoke of as charismatic authority), or because he/she is an authority; but these reasons can usually be pressed back to the general reason that the person is believed to be in a position to know whether or not A, or whether or not A is to be done.[5] To be *an* authority one need not be *in* authority. A principal and his/her most junior staff member may be authorities on school administration. Being in authority does not constitute one an authority, though being an authority may be the reason for placing someone in authority. The ability of those in authority to maintain their authority generally depends on their ability to present themselves as authorities (possessors of extensive and/or intimate knowledge and competence in the particular field). As we know, this presentation, in the public, political sphere at least, is often fraudulent.

In introducing the distinction between positional and expert authority, I noted that they only *partially* exhausted the range of authority relations. They should not be taken (as they so often are) as exclusive categories. Instead, they are but two standardised *loci* for the knowledge presupposed by authority ascriptions. What is important is not whether the person with authority is in authority or

213

even an authority, but whether he/she is (believed to be), in some relevant sense, 'in the know'. Thus I may have it on authority that there was a large crowd at a particular cricket match - not because my authority was in authority or an authority, but simply because he/she was *there* - and thus in a position to know. The same is true of the person who exercises charismatic authority. His/her bearing exudes the confidence of one who knows what to believe or do.

Earlier I referred to the fragmentation of authority in standard accounts of its nature. By commencing with a distinction between positional and expert authority, its proponents make any conceptual link between them difficult to see. At best, some causal or justificatory connection might be proposed. What our analysis has suggested is that both 'kinds' of authority express a social relation with a common epistemic basis, in that those with authority *are presumed to be*, in some appropriate sense, 'in the know'.

Authority: critique and justification

There is an important difference between the presumption of knowledge and the possession of knowledge, and on it turns the critique of *authorities*. As we have noted, those who possess authority commonly do so because they are in authority or are regarded as authorities (experts). The presumption underlying such appeals is that those with authority are in a position to know whether or not *A*, or whether or not *A* ought to be done. This presumption is not always justified. Because of the institutionalised form in which *both* these authority-grounds (being in or an authority) now manifest themselves, it is highly possible and all too common that those in authority or who are regarded as authorities have authority on false pretences. Though the 'office' proclaims the office-holder to be in a position to know - a point acknowledged by those who accept the office-holder's authority - the office-holder may in fact lack the knowledge presumed by the office. Such authorities can be notoriously ignorant/deceptive, something which tends to be concealed by the institutionalised procedures for producing and identifying them. This is true not only of what I have referred to as positional authorities, but also of expert authorities. Although we say that an authority is simply a person whose extensive knowledge places him/her in a position to know what to believe within a specified field, the institutionalisation of knowledge (certification procedures, recognition by institutional peers, etc.) has led to the institutionalisation of authorities on particular areas of inquiry. Thus, a professor of history is *eo ipso* an authority on a certain area of historical inquiry. As in the case of positional authority, the institutionalisation of expertise has allowed for a hiatus to develop between the person whose knowledge places him/her 'in the know' and the person who is regarded as an authority. In schooling contexts, this hiatus can be very large in both cases.

The gap between theory and practice in the life of institutionalised authority provides an important clue to the coercive backing which frequently (some would say essentially) goes with being in authority. Those in authority can normally enforce their directives by means of positive or nullifying sanctions. Of course, to the extent that this is necessary, there has been something of a breakdown in authority. But by the same token, the possession of coercive power is also important to the ideological hegemony of institutional authorities. The perpetuation of institutions and their authority structures requires a certain degree of ideological uniformity on the part of those who participate in them. Where there are no constraints on questioning or challenging the authority of those in authority, and there is occasion to do so, the institution itself may appear to come under threat. And where this is so, some control over the agencies of ideological influence will seem necessary. Compulsory schooling, censorship and other forms of media influence are means whereby this ideological hegemony is maintained. Furthermore, they are maintained in a way which sees the use of coercive support as good and necessary. 'Strong government' becomes a plus in the factors determining people's support. Where ideological hegemony is lost, the dominant *status quo* can be maintained only by dictatorship, where rule by force replaces the rule of law. Anarchism is a theory of social relations in which this corruption of authority is seen as endemic to its institutionalisation.

This coercive backdrop is not altogether absent from the authority of the person who is regarded as an authority. The accreditation of someone as an authority is often in the hands of those who have the power to destroy that reputation for reasons which may have little to do with their actual knowledge. People's political or religious affiliations have often been exploited in this way. However, it seems reasonable to argue that the epistemic basis for someone who is an authority is a bit more secure than it is for the person in authority. Precisely because the expert authority calls attention to the dependence of his/her status on the reliability of his/her claims, rather than on a system of authorisation, the possibility of detecting and exposing bogus authorities is somewhat higher. This, presumably, explains why some radical critics of authority (in so far as it emanates from those in authority) are much less sceptical about the possession of expert authority. Nevertheless, lest the two 'grounds' for authority be distinguished too radically, it needs to be remembered that where the accreditation of expertise and institutional authorisation are very closely related, as in schooling contexts, the epistemic basis for an authority's authority may not be very secure at all.

To the extent that the authority possessed by a person
is not grounded in knowledge of the relevant kind, it is
bogus. The complaint of critics of authority is that this
is more often than not the case. The pattern of institutional preferment is partly responsible for this. Y is
appointed to position A (a lectureship) because of his/her
expertise in matters connected with A. If this expertise
continues to be displayed or is increased, Y may find
him/herself promoted to position B (a professorship), for
which his/her expertise is at best a partial qualification.
Position B may give Y a form of authority over others for
which Y's expertise is irrelevant. To the extent that Y is
prepared to use this authority, and if necessary to secure
it by coercive means, to that extent it tends to become
dictatorial.

To this point I have been considering objections which
are directed to the misuse of authority rather than to
authority as such. Even if some of these objections amount
to criticism or suspicion of all authority located within
hierarchically ordered institutions, they do not amount to a
total rejection of authority. A stronger position may be
contemplated, basing itself on an apparent conflict between
autonomy and the appeal to epistemic authority. It is
argued that any situation in which X believes or does A
because Y says so must involve a *sacrificium intel-
lectus* - an abandonment of rational autonomy. To the extent
that autonomous convictions must be rationally grounded, to
that extent appeals to authority must be eschewed. However,
this objection bases itself on a misunderstanding of
epistemic authority and an overly individualistic account of
autonomy. When we are born, we do not come into the world
with highly refined cognitive equipment. The development
and refinement of our cognitive and other psychological
equipment is as much a product of our social interactions as
it is of any maturational processes which occur (indeed,
even the maturational processes are not completely
independent of social environment). Our growth in knowledge
is fundamentally social: 'Others equip us with the
indispensable techniques of knowledge-gathering and
knowledge-processing, with consumable items of singular
information and with more durable theory.'[6] The point is
this: if we are to become rationally autonomous, we must
start off by taking others at their word. We have no
alternative of our own. Later on, with the development of
our ability to articulate and reflect on our beliefs in the
light of experience, we may come to see their source in
others, and thence begin to assess critically those whom we
have taken as our authorities to that point. Even so, we
do not do away with authority entirely. None of us has the
time, energy or ability to pursue every belief to its source
in reality. This is, of course, a contingent matter, and as

time goes on and our experience expands to corroborate or challenge what we have initially accepted on authority, authoritative pronouncements may progressively come to have the character of testimony. But it is not a *merely* contingent matter. The limitations of finitude make the prospect of dispensing with authority altogether an unrealistic one. But we should not see this as a fatal blow to the prospect of autonomy. Our decision to accept this or that authority need not be blindly taken: we may have good reasons for accepting someone's authority which are not at the same time reasons for what is accepted on authority. Further, and most importantly, accepting someone's authority with respect to *A* is not to commit oneself irrevocably to *A*. There is, or at least ought to be, a provisional character about what is accepted on authority. The triumph of ideology and indoctrination lies in concealing this from us. Either we see what is accepted only on authority as 'given' in experience, or, what amounts to much the same, we regard (what we take to be) an authority as unquestionable.

If we cannot get entirely away from authority, this by no means justifies its every use. On this point, radical critics of schooling have a strong case against its conservative defenders. The use of authority in schooling contexts is often defended by reference to educational ends: only if we first accept authority can we learn anything. True, but this does not mean *any* authority. Not everything that is learned is conducive to our development as autonomous agents, and what is authoritatively promulgated in the context of schooling is frequently of questionable value for that development. Most schooling is so structured that opportunities and encouragements for children to recognise the provisionality of authority and to test the claims of their teachers and their texts is minimal. The close association between the teacher's expert authority and his/her positional and grading power gives little scope for an autonomous appreciation and utilisation of authority. Where the encouragement to question is given, it is usually carefully restricted to matters which do not challenge the teacher's structural or expert authority. It may be, of course, though this is unlikely, that our social resources are such that what we've got is the best we can do, given the other demands against which the need for education has to be balanced. But this is not something that we need to take on authority, and such experience as we have suggests that we should not.

Authoritarianism

It may help to clarify the preceding discussion if we distinguish authority from authoritarianism, for it is really the latter against which critics of authority inveigh, and which they see manifested in many, if not most,

217

authority relations. For reasons of convenience, we may distinguish two forms of authoritarianism, personal and structural.

Personal authoritarianism is displayed when someone who poses as an authority or is in authority falls back on that authority status when pressed to defend a claim or directive. An authoritarian teacher is one who, by words, gestures or other actions, discourages any examination of the rationale for his/her claims or directives. 'I'm the teacher, aren't I?'; 'Who do you think you are?'; 'Because I said so!'; etc. reveal an authoritarian attitude. A non-authoritarian teacher will offer reasons for, encourage questions about, and accept challenges to what he/she asks or imparts. This is not a rejection of one's authority so much as a recognition of its provisional character. The teacher who encourages this openness may enhance rather than diminish his/her authority, since the presumption behind the possession of authority, that the one with it is 'in the know', may be strengthened rather than weakened. But the authoritarian teacher refuses to take the risks involved. He/she endeavours to maintain a respect which has not been or cannot be earned.

Structural authoritarianism arises when institutional structures no longer subserve the purposes for which they were set up, nor any subsequent desirable purposes, but are maintained and enforced nevertheless. The 'law and order' mentality is a common symptom of structural authoritarianism. Order is invested with a value independent of any ends which it subserves. Blind obedience/acceptance is another symptom of structural authoritarianism: the edicts/pronouncements of authorities are obeyed/believed just because they are edicts/pronouncements of authority. Even though authority relations involve X taking Y at his/her word, this does not imply and should not involve X's blindly/ unthinkingly/immutably accepting Y as having the requisite authority. Accrediting structures themselves stand in need of accreditation, and when they pretend otherwise by veiling their provisional character they operate authoritarianly.

Conclusion

The defence of authority is not helped by its social expressions. So much of socially recognised authority depends for its acceptance on hidden coercion and ideological manipulation, that it is tempting to oppose it altogether. Yet it cannot be so easily rejected. Our cognitive development depends on it, especially in its early stages, but also later in life. Moreover, it is doubtful whether any complex social organisation could exist without some authority structure, a point which even libertarians somewhat grudgingly admit.[8] However, as opponents of authority have acutely recognised, the ways in which authority comes to be institutionalised almost inevitably gravitate in the direction of authoritarianism. The ends for which authority is necessary are easily frustrated by its institutionalised expressions. In assessing the need and value of authority, therefore, we need to look beyond its institutionalised expressions to the presumptions which maintain them. There, in the presumption that those who possess authority are 'in the know', we have the basis not only for its criticism, but also for its renovation in ways more conducive to the development and maintenance of personal and social autonomy.

NOTES

1. R.S. Peters has been influential in popularising this position. See his contribution to the symposium on 'Authority', *Proceedings of the Aristotelian Society*, Supp. Vol. XXXII (1958), 207-24.
2. The gunman view of law (John Austin) fails for exactly the same reason as the gunman view of authority. For a directive to have force of *law* (rather than mere demand) it must be seen as obligatory, i.e. it must have the recognition (consent) of those to whom it is applied.
3. In some cases, it might amount to little more than the belief that *Y* knows what he/she is about - e.g. a boss who gets an employee to fetch something. My formulation is based on that in Gary Young's valuable paper, 'Authority', *Canadian Journal of Philosophy*, III, 4 (June, 1974), 563-83.
4. What Max Weber refers to as traditional and legal-rational authority respectively (*The Theory of Social and Economic Organisation*[2], trans. A.M. Henderson & T. Parsons, rev. edn., London: W. Hodge, 1947, pp.324ff).
5. As a limiting case, a person may *blindly* believe or obey some authority: where the person's social position in authority or recognition as an authority is sufficient for obedience or belief. Though a limiting case, it is not uncommon.
6. A.M. Quinton, 'Authority and Autonomy in Knowledge', *Proceedings of the Philosophy of Education Society of Great Britain*, V, 2 (July, 1971), 201-15.
7. Cf. Wittgenstein: 'The child learns by believing the adult.... I learned an enormous amount and accepted it on human authority, and then found some things confirmed or disconfirmed by my own experience' (*On Certainty*, Oxford: Blackwell, 1974, §161).
8. See, for example, R. Nozick, *Anarchy, State and Utopia*, Oxford: Blackwell, 1974, Pt.I: 'State-of-Nature Theory, or How to Back into a State without Really Trying'.

Chapter 17

SCHOOLING, EDUCATION AND DISCIPLINE

There is, we are regularly informed, a 'discipline problem' in schools. The evening tabloids, prompted by the report of some 'incident', self-righteously investigate 'the collapse of discipline in our schools'. Committees of Enquiry are set up 'to determine the nature and extent of disciplinary problems' in schools, 'to ascertain factors contributing to these disciplinary problems' and 'to recommend measures for their resolution'.[1] Opinion polls regularly identify 'lack of discipline' as one of, if not the major problem confronting the public schooling system. And from the pens of educationalists there now pours forth an ever-growing stream of books and articles designed to prepare and pacify the teacher on the front-lines or the school principal at the control post. Classroom discipline, the teacher is told, is essential if he 'expects to rise above mediocrity in his profession'.[2] And the principal is usually made all too aware that 'discipline can be the difference between a good or poor image in the community', vital in relation to 'the community's willingness to provide adequate financing and other types of support'.[3]

At the same time, there is a certain nervousness about the term 'discipline'. One writer tells us that 'in the enlightened vernacular of the contemporary educator, the word *discipline* has been supplanted by the word *control*'.[4] The reason for this, presumably, is to avoid its identification with those harsh and repressive practices of yore. Instead, it is to be seen as 'the process whereby student and staff relationships are structured to maximise the educational, social and emotional well-being and attainments of students, to attain the most effective and efficient use of human and material resources and to facilitate the maximum satisfaction of needs for all members of the school'.[5] The emphasis is to be on prevention, promotion and therapy rather than correction.

220

Several distinct concepts of discipline can be discerned within the literature. All of them imply some idea of limitation or constraint, though it goes too far to claim with Vredevoe that 'all organisms and most of the things in our universe are subject to some form of discipline.... The very struggle for existence or survival demands discipline.'[6] Discipline always refers to an agent-imposed constraint and cannot be usefully made to cover all those adaptations which an organism must make in the 'struggle for survival'. What distinguishes the various concepts of discipline is the way in which these agent-imposed constraints manifest themselves.

In the educational literature, the scope of discipline is variously circumscribed. Sometimes it focuses on individuals, but more often it is classroom or school discipline which is in view.[7] Generally they are seen in some sort of relation to each other. In mapping out a range of understandings, it is not our intention to provide an exhaustive cataloguing of its various established usages.[8] Our investigation is directed to clarifying aspects of the public debate about school discipline, and to providing a critique, particularly in relation to its educational value.

(1) The most common focus in educational writings is on a form of discipline which, as a first approximation, we can characterise as *observable, hierarchically determined, (mass[9]) control* (hereafter discipline$_1$). If it is claimed that X maintains good discipline$_1$ in his/her class, it is implied that X keeps his/her class under control. This does not necessarily imply regimentation, though it is one form which such discipline may and often does take (cf. prison discipline and discipline in the armed services). More often, it refers to a range of attributes of classroom or school behaviour: a stable quietness, apparent attentiveness and purposiveness, an efficient orderliness, tidiness, punctuality, and so on, achieved through the *authority* of the teacher/principal. This last point is important, for it helps to distinguish a well-disciplined$_1$ class from what is merely a well-controlled class. Control may be achieved in many ways: naked force, drugs, inducements, etc. But discipline$_1$ is hierarchically determined control. There must be *some* estimation that the teacher/principal is in a position to require certain kinds of behaviour of them. In practice, the distinction between a disciplined$_1$ and a merely controlled class is often fine, since, as in the political sphere, consent is often purchased against a backdrop of coercion.

For some writers, discipline$_1$ is so much a preoccupation that it functions almost as an end-in-itself. For such, T.E. Hulme's assertion that 'nothing is bad in itself except disorder; all that is put in order in a hierarchy is good',[10] finds ready approval. It is closely related to the view that there is an obligation to obey the law over and above any obligation we have to obey particular laws.[11] Something like this seems to be the view of John Wilson, who argues that $discipline_1$ should be seen as 'an educational objective in its own right – not just as a facilitator for education'.[12] Wilson's argument is that the conditions of our survival are such that we must spend some years in tightly-structured environments (families, schools). Integral to such environments are 'duties, allotted tasks', etc. and unless we submit to $discipline_1$, i.e. are obedient to 'established authority', our survival and development will be jeopardised.[13] It is not altogether clear what this argument shows. At best it suggests that in situations of recognised epistemic or physical deficiency we should provisionally accept the control of those whom we acknowledge as better placed or fitted to oversee our welfare. But this does not seem to be the same as making a virtue out of $discipline_1$ independently of some quite specific end to which it is directed. This is the usual pattern of justification for $discipline_1$. Any value it has is directly related to purposes which are said to constitute its justification. We shall later consider some of these.

(2) The *means* used to achieve discipline are also referred to as 'discipline' (hereafter $discipline_{1a}$) by many writers – what Gnagey refers to as 'all techniques a teacher uses to increase the proportion of school-appropriate behaviours'.[14] The educational books are replete with techniques for achieving control. Suggestions about seating arrangements, the structure and content of lessons, the teacher's attitudes and 'presence', the use of aids, preparation, means of conflict resolution, and so on, fill page upon page, all designed to enhance the teacher's authority in the classroom, to enable him/her to operate efficiently and effectively. Generally such books assume that failure to achieve $discipline_1$ is the fault of and is remediable by the teacher. Home/socio-economic background is sometimes made to carry part of the weight, but syllabi, authoritarian structures and the compulsory nature of schooling, only rarely.

It might be wondered whether there is a distinct sense of 'discipline' in which it refers generally to those techniques used to bring about $discipline_1$, whether or not they succeed. I am somewhat dubious, for much the same reasons that I am dubious whether we should regard as teaching what does not bring about learning, and as indoctrination what does not result in beliefs held being open to full assessment. Not too much, perhaps, hangs on the point, though it might be argued that the current tendency to emphasise 'non-aversive' techniques of discipline deflects attention from the real moral issue – their outcome. If $discipline_1$ is made to bear most of the logical weight, the sugar-coating comes to be of secondary, even if not negligible, importance.

(3) I suspect that the tendency to see $discipline_{1a}$ as conceptually distinct arises through its conflation with a *more limited* range of techniques which may, though need not, be used to achieve $discipline_1$. In this sense (hereafter $discipline_2$), if X disciplines Y, X purposively imposes on Y in some way considered unpleasant to Y. It is the traditional associations of this use of 'discipline' (beatings, scourgings, etc.) which have prompted some writers to prefer alternative terms such as 'order', or 'control' when referring to $discipline_1$ and $_{1a}$.

Discipline$_2$ has often been thought synonymous with punishment. But despite close similarities, they are distinct notions. Punishment is a deliberate, presumably unpleasant, imposition on or interference with a person because of (that is, as a retribution for) that person's moral failure.[15] Discipline$_2$ also involves a deliberate, presumably unpleasant, imposition. And, like punishment, it is occasioned by (and to some extent justified by reference to) some (usually) moral failure. However unlike punishment, its essential orientation is not retributive but teleological. Its main, immediate purpose is reform or correction, and it is therefore sometimes referred to as *chastisement*. This teleological dimension to discipline$_2$ affects not only its justification, but also, to some extent, its occasioning. Whereas punishment is justified by and restricted to instances of moral failure (otherwise it amounts only to penalisation), discipline$_2$ may sometimes be directed to awakening a sense of moral failure: we chastise, rather than punish, very young children.

There are several broad differences between discipline$_2$ and $discipline_{1a}$. Discipline$_2$ is essentially 'corrective', whereas many of the techniques referred to as $discipline_{1a}$ are 'preventive'. Further, discipline$_2$, though it may focus on actions disruptive of $discipline_1$, is generally oriented towards individuals, whereas the techniques used to bring about $discipline_1$ are mostly group oriented. And the end of discipline$_2$ is only contingently $discipline_1$. Unlike $discipline_{1a}$, its immediate focus is not $discipline_1$ but some other end: reform, correction or moral development. Though $discipline_1$ is sometimes a further end of discipline$_2$, the latter's unwantedness generally makes any reference to $discipline_1$ otiose. Instead, its importance for 'socialisation, personality maturation, conscience development, and the emotional security of the child' is emphasised.[16]

223

(4) Those concerned to justify discipline$_1$, or, for that matter, discipline$_2$, often do so by appealing to its supposed causal connection with self-discipline (or discipline$_3$):

> Were every product of the school-room a perfectly disciplined product, the pupil would be self-controlling and the prophecy that perfect discipline would annihilate prisons, reforms and courts of justice would become a fact. A human being self-controlled after experience under a sound system of discipline would offer little difficulty as a subject of school management.... Discipline is a training in self-control and self-direction.... The true end of discipline is none other than the achievement of self-control. [17]

Though somewhat dated, this statement expresses well and revealingly the thrust behind much disciplinary activity. The end of discipline$_1$ and discipline$_2$ is discipline$_3$ – here spoken of as self-direction or self-control. Discipline$_3$ substitutes self-regulation for regulation by others, and in that lies its justification. But we need to notice that what is meant *here* by self-control is little more than the internalisation of external norms. A self-disciplined person will 'offer little difficulty as a subject of school management' and will conform to the social *status quo*. This amounts to no more than indoctrination, and is quite inadequate to justify discipline$_1$ or discipline$_2$. Self-discipline, if it is to constitute a valuable personal characteristic, an end, must be explicated in ways compatible with personal autonomy. Indeed, self-discipline, properly understood, and personal autonomy are very closely related. They are mutually dependent. This obviously creates some sort of tension for those who wish to support discipline$_1$ and discipline$_2$ by virtue of their relation to discipline$_3$. What tends to happen, even among those who recognise the links between self-discipline and autonomy, is that the latter is modified in the direction of the dominant *status quo*. Staten Webster, for example, outlines as his particular understanding of discipline$_3$,

> the development within individuals of the necessary personal controls to allow them to be effective, contributing members of a democratic society and of the human community at large. The self-controls of behaviour,

> feelings, and desires must function to
> enhance the individual's realisation of his
> unique personal goals in a way which is
> compatible with the similar efforts of
> others.[18]

There is, here, a salutary acknowledgement of the inter-
relatedness of the individual and social dimensions of
autonomy. However, by embedding it so firmly in the
dominant *status quo*, Webster introduces a serious tension
into his account. What he understands by 'a democratic
society' and 'the human community at large' are the
prevailing social and political structures, and it does not
occur to him that the dominant forms of their organisation
may be incompatible with the individual's 'realisation of
his unique personal goals'. *Pace* Webster, the person who
reacts against the prevailing structures (i.e. is undis-
ciplined$_1$) is not necessarily undisciplined$_3$.

There is, I think, little doubt about the value of
self-discipline, and it is therefore hardly surprising that
classroom discipline$_1$ is frequently justified by reference
to the contribution it is supposed to make to its development. Yet, as we have briefly noted, this form of argument
is not entirely unproblematic. Apart from the more
particular problem of indoctrination, there are general
points that need to be considered. Not every means to a
justifiable end is itself justifiable: even if the end is
realised, the costs of realising it may have been too great,
or they may have been greater than some alternative means.
And of course the means may not realise the end which is
invoked to justify them. These shortcomings are all evident
in the attempt to justify school discipline$_1$ by reference to
discipline$_3$. The classroom (as usually structured) is not
the only or best context for developing discipline$_3$: it is
much better suited to passive conformity. And, as Maria
Montessori recognised, there is a long distance to travel
between discipline$_1$ and discipline$_3$:

> We do not consider an individual disciplined,
> only when he has been rendered as arti-
> ficially silent as a mute and as immovable as
> a paralytic. He is an individual
> *annihilated*, not *disciplined*. We call an
> individual disciplined when he is master of
> himself, and can therefore regulate his own
> conduct when it shall be necessary to follow
> some rule of life.[19]

Montessori may not have fully seen the extent to which power
has been transmuted into authority in the classroom, but her
general point still holds. Classroom discipline may express
a blind, uncritical consent to a form of organisation and

teaching which is remote from the achievement of self-discipline. And here it is important to recognise that the form which classroom discipline$_{1-2}$ take is a function, not simply of their conduciveness to discipline$_3$ (whether or not they do contribute to it), but of various structural features of schooling: the traditional teacher-student relationships, the size of classes, the nature and content of the curriculum. What discipline$_1$ does is enable teachers to survive as they carry out (wittingly or otherwise) the social functions of schooling.

Discipline and the conditions of learning

Self-discipline is not the only proffered justification for discipline$_{1-2}$. The 'desire to learn', we are told, 'must be taught'.[20] And this is possible only where there is effective discipline$_1$. 'Classroom control is a prerequisite to classroom learning ... its real purpose ... is to prepare the moral atmosphere for the achievement of instruction from a teacher.'[21] It is doubtful whether the desire to learn has to be taught. What probably has to be taught is the desire to learn much of what is included in the school curriculum. For that frequently does not connect up with the needs and interests of students. A single curriculum imposed on a group of 30-40 students in a classroom context is bound to require conventional discipline$_1$ and probably discipline$_2$ if it is to be implemented. And note also the implicit recognition in the second quotation that it is not learning but classroom learning which requires classroom discipline$_1$. Whether discipline$_1$ is necessary for learning is left unexplored. This is a serious hiatus in the argument for discipline$_1$. But even if some learning does require discipline$_1$, the question of its educational (or other) value can still be raised. The usual indicators of 'good discipline$_1$' - quietness, apparent attentiveness, etc. - manifest an educationally questionable model of knowledge and teaching. Knowledge is seen as something to be handed down, something which only the teacher has. Students are to be the more or less passive recipients of what the teacher has to offer. When the students acknowledge this, and all eyes and attention are focused on him/her, then good discipline$_1$ reigns. Although there is some over-simplification here, the architecture and social structure of schools do not allow for a great deal of variation. 'Noise' is disruptive of other classes, and teachers have to remain in good standing with their colleagues and principal.

Discipline and moral education

Classroom discipline$_1$ is frequently regarded as having a moral dimension. The last quotation spoke of discipline as preparing 'a moral atmosphere'. Vredevoe speaks of it as 'a standard of conduct which is reasonable and essential to society'.[22] Hogg goes further. Classroom discipline, she argues, involves self-limitation in the pursuit of a common purpose, such self-limitation constituting morally good behaviour. The point and justification of this is not simply the establishment of good conditions for learning but as part of moral education.[23] This is related to Wilson's view of discipline$_1$ as a virtuous behavioural trait, and it suffers from similar weaknesses. It is true that co-operative activities require on the part of their participants a reasonable level of moral awareness, and that regular involvement in such activities may help to develop that awareness. But to see classroom discipline$_1$ in this light is to mystify it. For the kind of moral education implicit in classroom discipline$_1$ is one which takes for granted the basic pattern of schooling: 'the age-specific, teacher related process requiring full-time attendance at an obligatory curriculum'.[24] The scope of such moral education is implicitly limited to certain aspects of the interpersonal relations of those in the classroom, the larger pattern remaining unexamined. To speak, as Vredevoe does, of the pattern of classroom discipline$_1$ as representing 'a standard of conduct which is reasonable and essential to society' is to confuse 'society' with 'a society'. It is the perpetuation of American society, in roughly its present form, which he has in mind.

Discipline and socialisation

The use of discipline$_{1-2}$ to perpetuate and reproduce the dominant *status quo* is made even more explicit by other writers. In *Discipline: How to Establish and Maintain it*, Robert Schain is quite candid about the purpose of schools:

> Society itself lives according to accepted rules, and since one of our main objectives in education is to prepare youngsters to live in our society, they must be trained to live according to established rules. [25]

The use of discipline$_{1-2}$ in accomplishing this is considered to present no special problems. Indeed, it is especially well-suited to this end. But the end is left unexamined. It is assumed that the 'accepted rules' needed if our society is to persist are the 'established rules' of our society. But the rules required for social persistence are nowhere near as extensive as our own society enforces, and hardly to be identified with many of the petty regulations which crisscross the life of the school.[26] Moreover, it is at least arguable that some of our social rules (e.g. the right to private ownership of the means of production) frequently work in an anti-social fashion. Unless living in our society is first established as worthwhile and not realistically improvable, its invocation in defence of school discipline remains seriously incomplete.

Conclusion

It has not been my purpose here to deny all value to discipline$_{1-2}$, or even to deny that they may have some educational value. My focus has been on discipline in schooling contexts, specifically, though not exclusively in countries such as Australia, the United Kingdom and the United States. But many of the points made would hold equally of school discipline as it is found, say, in Soviet bloc countries.[27] In each society, the public schooling system is oriented to the support and re-creation of the dominant *status quo*, and in large-scale industrialised societies this has uniformly generated a bureaucracy possessing only a limited sensitivity to people's individual and social needs. School discipline has served, both in itself and in what it allows, to prepare people for supportive participation in this dominant *status quo*. If it presents a continuing problem, it is because the demands it makes on people do not take into account their needs and resources.

NOTES

1. e.g. *Discipline in Secondary Schools in Western Australia*, Report of the Government Secondary Schools Discipline Committee (Chairman: H.W. Dettman), Perth: Education Department of Western Australia, 1972, p.v.
2. A.J. Prescott, 'Classroom Control or Classroom Chaos', *Ohio Schools*, XLI (January, 1963), 32; reprinted in J.S. Kujoth (comp.), *The Teacher and School Discipline*, Metuchen, N.J.: The Scarecrow Press, Inc., 1970, p.110.
3. L.J. Chamberlin, *Effective Instruction Through Dynamic Discipline*, Columbus, Ohio: Charles E. Merrill, 1971, p.37.
4. K.C. La Mancusa, *We do not Throw Rocks at the Teacher*, Scranton, Penn.: International Textbook Co., 1966, p.1.
5. *Discipline in Secondary Schools in Western Australia*, p.7.
6. L.E. Vredevoe, *Discipline*, Dubuque, Iowa: Kendall/Hunt Publishing Co., 1971, p.1. Additional criticism of Vredevoe can be found in T. Kazepides, 'Discipline in Education', in I.S. Steinberg (ed.), *Philosophy of Education 1977*, Proceedings of the Thirty-third Annual Meeting of the Philosophy of Education Society, Urbana, Ill.: Philosophy of Education Society, 1977, pp.54-55.

7. It is not my intention here to explore the sense of 'discipline' implicit in questions like 'Is education a discipline?' On this issue see J. Walton & J.L. Kuethe (eds.), *The Discipline of Education*, Madison, Wisc.: University of Wisconsin Press, 1963.

8. A laborious attempt to do this can be found in R.J. Farley, 'Concepts of Discipline in Education', Unpublished Ph.D. dissertation, University of Pennsylvania, 1973. See also Kazepides.

9. This sense of 'discipline' is sometimes used of individuals, but generally of groups.

10. Quoted in P. Nash, *Authority and Freedom in Education*, New York: John Wiley, 1966, p.104.

11. For a useful discussion, see M.B.E. Smith, 'Is there a Prima Facie Obligation to Obey the Law?' *Yale Law Journal*, LXXXII, 5 (April, 1973), 950–76.

12. J. Wilson, *Philosophy and Practical Education*, London: Routledge & Kegan Paul, 1977, p.43.

13. ibid., p.44.

14. W.J. Gnagey, s.v. 'Discipline, Classroom', in L.C. Deighton (ed.), *Encyclopedia of Education*, New York: Macmillan & The Free Press, 1971, Vol. III, p.96.

15. See *infra*, Ch.18, and the discussion in my *Punishment and Desert*, The Hague: Martinus Nijhoff, 1973, esp. Ch.2.

16. D.P. Ausubel, 'A New Look at Classroom Discipline', in C.J. Troost (ed.), *Radical School Reform: Critique and Alternatives*, Boston: Little, Brown & Co., 1973, pp.160–61.

17. R.C. Beery, *Practical School Discipline*, Pleasant Hill, Ohio: International Academy of Discipline, 1916, pp.104–05, quoted in Farley, p.185.

18. S.W. Webster, *Discipline in the Classroom: Basic Principals and Problems*, San Francisco: Chandler, 1968, p.4.

19. M. Montessori, *The Montessori Method*, trans. A.E. George, London: Heinemann, 1912, p.86.

20. C.H. Madsen, Jr. & C.K. Madsen, *Teaching/Discipline: a positive approach for educational development*, expanded second edn., Boston: Allyn & Bacon, 1974, p.18.

21. Sr. Jeanne Marie, 'The Trouble with Discipline', *Catholic School Journal*, LXVII (April, 1967), 50; reprinted in Kujoth, p.197.

22. Vredevoe, p.7.

23. A.C. Hogg, 'The Concept of School Discipline: and a Christian Interpretation', *Journal of Christian Education*, XI, 3 (1968), 123–40.

24. I. Illich, *Deschooling Society*, London: Calder & Boyars, 1971, p.32.

25. R.L. Schain, *Discipline: How to Establish and Maintain it*, Englewood Cliffs, N.J.: Teachers Practical Press,

1961, p.7.

26. Cf. H.L.A. Hart, 'Social Solidarity and the Enforcement of Morality', *University of Chicago Law Review*, XXXV, 1 (Autumn, 1967), 1–13.
27. Cf. A.S. Makarenko, 'Discipline and Régime' (trans. A.R. Crane), *Australian Journal of Education*, X, 1 (March, 1966), 38–44.

Chapter 18

EDUCATION AND PUNISHMENT

The schoolmaster (sic) with his cane upraised remains as
much a symbol of the school as the tea-drinking parson
remains a symbol of the church. Though both are now
somewhat outmoded in their form of representation, to many
people they are still recognisably true with respect to the
content of that representation. School is remembered for
its regimented life, the plethora of petty regulations, the
threats of penalties for non-compliance, the harsh or shrill
tones, the stinging flesh, the detention, etc. We have,
perhaps, become more subtle in the 'management' of
children - generally less willing to justify corporal penalties, but the legalistic/punitive contours remain. In some
ways it is difficult to imagine how it could be otherwise.
Thirty (or more) children with different backgrounds,
temperaments, levels of achievement, interests and
expectations, packed without reference to their own desires
into not very comfortable classrooms, and fed the same
pre-packed formula for intellectual and social growth -
improved maybe, by a teacher's ability to present the
ingredients reasonably attractively, but only within the
constraints of the overriding syllabus, timetable, budget,
and permissions of authority. It is very difficult to
operate a system having these specifications without
coercion figuring fairly prominently. In recent years,
various modifications have been made to the formula,
particularly at a primary level, which have allowed a less
punitive approach to be taken. Nevertheless, the place of
punishment in schools, and its compatibility with education,
have remained topics of considerable interest and importance
to teachers, parents and others whose lives are closely
bound up with children. Of course, punishment is not
problematic only in schools. The latter are but part of a
wider structure of social practices and attitudes, and there
is a rich literature dealing with the problems of punishment. In this chapter, we shall first consider some of
these more general problems, and then return to the educ-

ational issue.

Punishment and related concepts[1]

Discussions of punishment are often separated into problems of definition and problems of justification. But though distinguishable, these issues are not wholly separable. The reason for this is that many of our concepts have developed against a background of interests which already embody moral values. In consequence, what they pick out is already evaluatively-laden. Common moral notions like murder, assault and deception belong to this set, as indeed do many other terms used to describe human behaviour.[2] Punishment, I believe, is also a member; it does not refer to any old reactive interference with another person, but instead isolates a range of interferences which have been discriminated, at least in part, on the basis of morally important criteria.[3] A consequence of this is that the definition of 'punishment' embodies considerations which also enter into its justification (allowing of course, what we shall consider later, that the moral perspective reflected in the concept is itself an acceptable one).

Nevertheless, despite the connectedness of definition and justification, it is heuristically useful to consider first the question of definition. Here I shall offer a proposal, to be defended, in the first instance, by means of a conceptual map which I believe to be more helpful than that standardly offered. This proposal is to describe as *punishments* those deliberate, presumably unpleasant, impositions on or interferences with others, inflicted on account of their (supposed) moral failure. On this view, when speaking of punishment there is a presumption that the person on whom it is inflicted has done something morally reprehensible and that this is the reason for its infliction. Such an account does not rule out the possibility of 'punishing the innocent' (because of mistaken identity or misdescription of 'offence'); what it does necessitate is that where the presumption is successfully challenged we must qualify our description by speaking instead of 'unjust' or 'undeserved punishment'.

The account of punishment I have proposed differs in a number of important respects from another well-known definition, popularised by Flew, Benn and Hart,[4] in which *legal* punishment is taken as paradigmatic. On that account, 'a standard case of punishment' is defined in terms of five conditions:

(i)   It must involve an 'evil, an unpleasantness, to the victim';
(ii)   It must be for an offence (actual or supposed);
(iii) It must be of an offender (actual or supposed);
(iv)   It must be the work of personal agencies (i.e. not merely the natural consequences of an action);

(v)   It must be imposed by authority (real or supposed),
       conferred by the system of rules (hereafter referred
       to as 'law') against which the offence has been
       committed.[5]

    This account seems to me philosophically myopic since
it incorporates into itself, as conditions of punishment,
what properly belong only to one form of it - *legal*
punishment. More importantly, in so doing it has confused
punishment with *penalisation*. What distinguishes
penalisation as a form of imposition is that the person
penalised has broken a rule (irrespective of whether this
also involves moral failure). Hockey players and pupils no
less than legal offenders can be penalised. But such
penalisations can qualify as punishments (whether or not
deserved) only if the ground for penalisation is considered
to involve moral failure. Penalties for being off-side or
for adding up incorrectly do not normally constitute
punishments (though they can, albeit undeserved). The legal
paradigm also leads to confusion over the distinction
between punishment and *revenge*. On that account, revenge is
understood as an unauthorised imposition.[6] However, what
distinguishes revenge is that the revenger has been hurt in
some way (irrespective of whether this expresses or is
believed to express moral failure), and wishes 'to get
his/her own back'. You could take revenge on a teacher who
was recognised to have justly punished a delinquent student,
but you could hardly punish the teacher. It is motive
rather than status which distinguishes revenge from
punishment. Given the psychological complexity of human
beings, a particular imposition might be describable both as
punishment and as revenge.
    To help locate punishment a little better, we might
briefly add to the preceding distinctions several others.[7]
We speak of someone being *victimised* rather than punished
when it is known by the imposer that the person penalised is
guilty of no breach of rules or morals, or, if guilty, is
not imposed on for that reason. The latter is quite common,
and often passes for punishment. It occurs when only some
of a class of offenders are singled out for penalisation,
the reason being some further characteristic (colour, sex,
socio-economic group, religion, etc.) which is concealed by
the fact that the person *is* an offender. *Persecution*, on
the other hand, generally occurs where the ground for
interference is constituted by the beliefs of the person
persecuted. No moral judgment of the beliefs needs to be
presupposed. Where some other morally irrelevant
characteristic (such as race, skin colour or sex) is the
reason for interference, we tend to speak more generally of
discrimination. Discrimination is a broader notion than
victimisation, since it need imply no attribution of guilt
to the person discriminated against. *Vengeance* can be
distinguished as a form of punishment in which the punisher

233

and the person wronged are identical. Finally, punishment can be distinguished from treatment or *therapy*. Four differences might be noted: (a) punishment is inflicted for what people have done or failed to do, whereas therapeutic treatment is administered because of the mental or physical state or condition of those concerned; (b) therapeutic treatment logically must be administered in order to procure some desirable state of affairs, but punishment need not be inflicted with any further purpose in mind; (c) in punishing people for their actions we imply that they could be held responsible for them, something not implied when we treat them; and (d) whereas punishment necessarily involves a presumably unpleasant imposition, therapeutic treatment does not.[8]

Punishment : its general justification

The problems of justification associated with punishment are manifold. In part, this is because there are different kinds of justification – moral, psychological, legal, educational and theological, and though there are some connections between them, they are not identical. As well, there are various contexts of punishment – legal, parental, educational, ecclesiastical, etc., and in each of these contexts different kinds of justification may be sought; e.g. the legal justification of parental punishment, the moral justification of legal punishment, etc. In addition there are questions about the severity and methods of punishment: how much punishment should an offender receive? What can be said for and against corporal, capital and psychological punishment, incarceration, *lex talionis*, etc.? Finally, there are questions relating to particular punishments – whether this punishment of Mary Brown or Bill Jones was/would be morally, legally, etc. justifiable. All of these justificatory questions are important. Nevertheless, in the history of discussions about punishment they have been overshadowed by a more general problem of justification, namely, whether any kind of punishment at all is morally justifiable. This question is critical, because punishment involves an unpleasant imposition on another person as a matter of deliberate principle; it will therefore be the first to occupy our attention.

Traditionally, moral justifications of punishment in general have been classified into consequentialist and retributive. This is not an altogether helpful distinction: too many different accounts can satisfy each description, and it is very difficult to give a satisfactory general characterisation of what would count as a consequentialist or a retributive justification. For present purposes, the following will do: consequentialist justifications of punishment appeal to the actual or supposed consequences of punishing offenders as justification for such impositions, whereas retributive justifications seek to justify punishment by reference to the nature of the offence for which it is inflicted. Here we shall not attempt to recite and evaluate the many different varieties of consequentialist and retributive justification. Instead, I shall attempt to develop an account which goes some way toward showing the general conditions under which punishment would be justified. In its central features, this account belongs to the retributivist tradition, though I shall later indicate ways in which consquentialist considerations are important.

In passing, however, it might be worthwhile just to note the major problem faced by consequentialist accounts.[9] If punishment is justified by reference to its consequences, these provide us with no clear reason why punishment should be restricted to offenders. No doubt, not so restricting it would be a source of disutility, but there does not appear to be any convincing reason to believe that, overall, the total consequences would not sanction occasional or even, perhaps, systematic 'punishments of the innocent'. Consequentialists have a short answer to this criticism: punishment of the innocent cannot be justified on consequentialist grounds since, by definition, 'punishment' is of the guilty. This 'definitional stop', however, serves only to reformulate the problem: consequentialist considerations can be invoked to justify interferences with non-offenders which, when imposed on offenders, constitute punishment. Without additional argument, this possibility evokes a strong suspicion of injustice. Some consequentialists, to be sure, are willing to accept this possibility. Most, however, seek to avoid it.

Now it must be admitted that consequentialist considerations sometimes do justify interferences with innocents. For example, if a person has or carries a dangerous and infectious disease, we consider it morally justifiable to restrict his/her movements to a certain extent. We do this because of the threat posed to the welfare of others. However, there is an important respect in which quarantining is disanalogous to punishment, and which prevents the use of the practice of quarantining as the basis for a consequentialist justification of punishment. The difference is this: punishment involves interference with a person as a matter of deliberate principle, whereas quarantining is simply a regrettable interference contingently necessary to some future benefit. In quarantining we do not set out to interfere with others. We hope the time will come when it no longer involves any or any substantial imposition. However, to interfere with someone as a matter of deliberate principle for consequentialist reasons is to violate the respect due to him/her as an autonomous agent. In Kantian terms, it is to treat that person as a means only, and not as an end.[10]

In seeking to provide an alternative account, it will be useful to recall the normative character of punishment. The concept of punishment already marks out for us a class of unpleasant interferences whose characterisation as punishments is centrally dependent on the supposed moral failure of their recipients. Where there has been no moral failure, it is necessary to qualify the punishment as unjust, or, in cases where it is known that there has been no moral failure, the act must be characterised in other ways - e.g. as victimisation. This feature of the concept strongly suggests that what leads us to differentiate a specific kind of activity, punishment, as a morally positive category, must also be central to its justification. But what is it about moral failure that makes it appropriate to respond in the way punishment implies?

We can briefly answer this question by means of a three-stage argument. First of all, if moral standards and requirements are to mean anything at all, as standards or requirements, we can hardly ignore breaches which occur. Just as it makes no sense to speak of a legal system without sanctions, neither do interpersonal moral requirements make sense as requirements if nothing is done about violations of those requirements.[11] This, of course, is not quite sufficient to show that punishment is the proper response, though it does not fall far short. If, for example, it is argued that no more is implied than, say, blame, reproach, criticism, censure or reproof, in which an appeal is made to the person's conscience, it may be argued that these constitute forms of punishment in so far as they are acts unpleasant to their recipients. Blame, as C.L. Stevenson suggests, is 'a kind of verbally mediated punishment'.[12] Nevertheless, a critic might insist that all that is necessary to satisfy the conditions necessary for moral requirements to be regarded as requirements is that offenders have their breaches drawn to their attention, and this does seem to involve something less than punishment. The second stage of the argument involves an appeal to justice. In so far as moral requirements constitute standards of interpersonal behaviour, an injustice is involved if some can 'get away with' departures from these standards. Punishment, to use Hegel's term, 'annuls' the injustice. It restores a moral balance that would be lacking were offences to go unpunished. It implies that no one's moral freedom is privileged without justification. The third stage is closely related. Punishment constitutes the morally appropriate means of securing justice for wrongdoing because it presumes and acknowledges the responsibility of the person punished. It was this that Hegel attempted to express in speaking of the offender's 'right to punishment'.[13] In imposing on others because they deserve it, because they have acted wrongly, we acknowledge their status as moral agents. As a just response to their wrongdoing,

236

and not simply (if at all) for their/our good, punishment constitutes a response to wrongdoing which treats it seriously without violating the wrongdoer's personhood. Ideally, punishment will be accompanied, on the wrongdoer's part, by a sense of guilt and of the justness of the punishment.

To this point, all we have argued is that the activity of punishment can be justified by reference to considerations which serve to differentiate it from other interferences, viz. the wrong done by the person to be punished. We have not argued that this general justification entitles this or that person or agency to inflict it. The authority to punish, and hence the institutionalised practice of punishment, requires further justification. In many discussions of punishment this is overlooked, since punishment is assumed, by definition, to be an authoritative act. But this need not be the case. Nevertheless, there are good reasons for thinking that punishment ought generally to be left in the hands of some provisional authority. The human condition being what it presently is, we cannot be trusted to punish our fellows justly if left to ourselves. We tend to be too impetuous and fault-finding, too easily swayed by the wrong motives, too uncertain and variable in our moral judgments, and so on. The institutionalisation and authorisation of punishment offers us a possible way out of this. By placing punishment in the hands of those who have access to resources of knowledge beyond those available to us individually, and who are better situated to be impartial in judgment, we increase the likelihood of justice in punishment. This general argument helps to explain and justify the recourse to authorities in punishment, but it needs to be extended slightly to explain the distribution of punishing authority. A person who is authorised to punish is not thereby entitled to punish every wrongdoing. Parents may be accorded authority to punish their children, but not the burglar they apprehend. Governmental authorities may be accorded the authority to punish crime, but not other wrongdoing. Put generally, we can say that the justification for institutionalised punishment is found in and limited by the justifiable functions of the institution concerned and its safeguarding promotion of those functions.

The chief problem faced by the foregoing account is one of applicability. If punishment is justified by reference to a person's moral failure, we have to confront the fact of moral diversity. What is regarded as a moral violation by one may be a matter of indifference to another. Who, then, is to determine whether a particular act or kind of act falls into the punishable category? To reply: 'This is what we have democratic institutions for' is too simple. It can be argued that the major institutions of our society, in particular those which have access to coercive power, are structured in ways which bring about and perpetuate substantial injustice, and that this finds expression in their punishing activity no less than their other operations.[14] We cannot just assume that the present structuring of our social institutions is promotive of justice and that their present punishing activity is more or less acceptable. For example, it is tempting to justify the authority of teachers to punish students by reference to the educational ends of schooling. But this presumes that the *raison d'être* of schooling is education, a presumption which we have questioned elsewhere.[15] Further, when we look at the pattern of punishment in schools, we frequently find that the offences for which children are condemned and punished are system-generated; that is, the institution unjustifiably places children under pressures which dispose them to offend: boring teaching, unnecessary regimentation, competition, and so on. These are serious difficulties with the system of institutionalised punishment as it presently exists.

Education and school-based punishment

With the preceding illustration, we have moved from the more general problems of punishment to a discussion of those problems as they manifest themselves in a specific context. To begin with, we need to consider the possibility that children cannot be punished. In so far as punishment is for wrongdoing it might be argued that children, by virtue of their immaturity, cannot be held accountable for their acts and hence cannot qualify for punishment. Impositions on children are intended to train rather than to punish.[16] There is something to be said for this. Young children tend to be disciplined or chastised rather than punished. In chastisement, impositions are occasioned by evils, but are directed toward moral growth. Nevertheless, I am not as pessimistic about the moral capacities of many, even quite young, children as the objection suggests. It does not seem reasonable to claim that children *cannot* be punished, even if they are sometimes improperly punished by those who attribute capacities to them which they do not yet possess.

Much of the controversy about the punishment of pupils in schools - i.e., the proper authority of teachers to punish - concerns what is viewed as a problematic relationship between punishment and education. For, even if punishment is deserved, it might also be anti-educative. Now this controversy, as we have noted, is based on the disputable premiss that schools are educational agencies; and consequently, the practice of punishment as it is embodied in schools is likely to bear a questionable relationship to education. Nevertheless, there is some point in considering whether punishment is compatible with or can serve the ends of education. This is in part though

238

not wholly an empirical question, and in making some suggestions, I will endeavour to take the empirical data into account. [17]

On one score at least, punishment can be viewed as compatible with the ends of education. Unlike some therapeutic alternatives to punishment, it does recognise, and indeed affirms, the personhood of the person punished. It treats the person as a subject to whom justice is due. However, whether this possibility is realised in practice is contingent on a number of factors. For one thing, unless the person punished shares the judgment of the punishing authority, the punishment may be viewed as an oppressive action, thus breeding resentment, fear or neurosis. Only if the person punished feels the guilt appropriate to his/her wrong, will the punishment restore the moral equilibrium that justice implies. But many of the offences found in schooling contexts reflect interests that are alien to those of the pupils, and they find it difficult to identify with the structure of behaviour into which they have been compulsorily inducted. Explanation accompanying punishment is no doubt some help, but by no means sufficient. Explanations may build bridges, but they can also reveal distance. And it is above all distance which poses the greatest threat to an educationally acceptable practice of punishment. Moral wrongdoing, whatever else can be said about it, involves a breach in the relationships which are appropriate to human beings, and punishment ought to express the loss which such breaches involve. However, in bureaucratic structures, including schools, both offences and their punishment are depersonalised. The whole process is interpreted in terms of institutional rules. Where this is the case there exists little rapport before the offence, and, given that punishment represents an imposition, often less after punishment has taken place. The role-differentiation between teachers and students, and the dominance of this role in their relationships, is not conducive to a healthy climate for punishment, and can help to explain some of the parental opposition to school-based punishments.

A further factor of importance to any educational value which punishment might have, concerns its severity. If punishments are to be just, their severity must be proportionate to the offence for which they are administered. Questions of proportionality are notoriously difficult to settle, [18] but they are sufficiently determinable for it to be clear that many school-based punishments fail to reflect a proper sense of the seriousness or triviality of particular offences. In this way punishment constitutes a confusing or unintelligible response to past behaviour, and the resulting puzzlement or anxiety can interfere with learning of educational consequence. The old view that 'lickin' an' larnin' go together' [19] did not reflect very seriously on the kind of 'larnin'' involved. To some extent, of course, school-based punishments do possess an intelligibility even when they are disproportionate. They reveal the point of many such punishments to be the assertion of power over non-compliant material. To some extent this is seen in the form which school-based punishment takes. Corporal punishment, detention, tongue-lashing, and deprivation of privileges, tend to be negative and unproductive forms of punishment, at least when considered in relation to education.[20] They may achieve an enfored compliance, but they offer little opportunity for constructive rectification or compensation. Quantity and form of punishment thus frequently give the lie to both retributive and educative accounts of school-based punishment.

Conclusion

'The elimination of punishment from social relationships', Paul Wilson argues, 'would only be possible along with the elimination of the whole moral order of life.'[21] This seems to me basically correct. Punishment, or at least the belief in its propriety, is inseparable from a social order in which justice and personal responsibility are valued and pursued. Where this view runs into trouble is in its implementation. What is upheld as the 'moral order of life' bears the strong imprint of a particular social formation, and so what comes to be affirmed in punishment may not be much more than the conditions necessary to support a fundamentally unjust and coercive *status quo*. Certainly there are significant elements of this in the sphere of law.[22] And the same, I believe, is true of school-based punishments. What is problematic about them is to be located not in their character as punishments but in their incorporation into the schooling system. For there they are used to affirm, impress and establish values which have little to do with justice and personal responsibility. Much school-based punishment, it appears, is for 'impertinence', the challenging of a particular authority relationship. But the moral impropriety of impertinence depends, not simply on its character as impertinence but as much on the propriety of the authoritative act or structure which the 'impertinent' behaviour calls into question. The history of schooling provides no grounds for confidence that teachers are particularly well-placed to judge of such matters. The absence of ready-made alternatives is not so much a reason for re-endorsing the *status quo* as for trying to develop some.

1. A greatly expanded discussion of the issues considered in this chapter can be found in my *Punishment and Desert*, The Hague: Martinus Nijhoff, 1973.
2. We have discussed this point in Chs. 1, 2, *supra*.
3. It is for this reason that the common psychological practice of calling the aversive stimulation of rats 'punishment' involves serious confusion – especially when the results of such studies are applied to the punishment of human misdemeanors.
4. A.G.N. Flew, '"The Justification of Punishment"', *Philosophy*, XXIX (December, 1954), 293-94; S.I. Benn, 'An Approach to the Problems of Punishment', *Philosophy*, XXXIII (October, 1958), 325-6; H.L.A. Hart, 'Prolegomenon to the Principles of Punishment', *Proceedings of the Aristotelian Society*, LX (1959-60), 4.
5. I have quoted Benn's version.
6. See, e.g. Flew, 294; cf. G.H. von Wright, *The Varieties of Goodness*, London: Routledge & Kegan Paul, 1963, p.200; R.S. Peters, *Ethics and Education*, London: Allen & Unwin, 1966, p.268; J.P. Day, 'Retributive Punishment', *Mind*, LXXXVII, 4 (October, 1978), 501.
7. Though treated somewhat sketchily, these notions help to illuminate the distinctiveness of punishment.
8. On punishment *v.* treatment, see J.G. Murphy (ed.), *Punishment and Rehabilitation*, Belmont, Calif.: Wadsworth, 1973.
9. There are certain longstanding problems confronting consequentialism which I shall ignore; see, e.g. D. Lyons, *Forms and Limits of Utilitarianism*, Oxford: Clarendon, 1965; D.H. Hodgson, *Consequences of Utilitarianism*, Oxford: Clarendon, 1967; M.A.G. Stocker, 'Consequentialism and its Complexities', *American Philosophical Quarterly*, VI, 4 (October, 1969), 276-89.
10. This Kantian terminology is not, however, wholly perspicuous. For a brief note, see L. Pollock, 'On Treating Others as Ends', *Ethics*, LXXXIV, 2 (January, 1974), 260-61 and for recent discussions of the general issue, see H. Morris, 'Persons and Punishment' *The Monist*, LII, 4 (October, 1968), reprinted in J. Feinberg & H. Gross, *Punishment: Selected Readings*, Encino, Calif.: Dickenson, 1975, 74-87; R.S. Downie & E. Telfer, *Respect for Persons*, London: Allen & Unwin, 1969; D.E. Marietta, Jr. 'On Using People', *Ethics*, LXXXII, 3 (April, 1972) 232-38; E.V. Spelman, 'On Treating Persons as Persons', *Ethics*, LXXXVIII, 2 (January, 1978), 150-61; A. Fleming, 'Using a Man as a Means', and J.R.S. Wilson, 'In One Another's Power', *Ethics*, LXXXVIII, 4 (July, 1978), 283-98, 299-315.

11. See, e.g. J. Charvet, 'Criticism and Punishment', *Mind*, LXXV (October,1966), 573-79; H. Fingarette, 'Punishment and Suffering', *Proceedings of the American Philosophical Association*, L, 6 (August, 1977), 499-525.
12. C.L. Stevenson, *Ethics and Language*, New Haven: Yale U.P., 1945, p.307.
13. G.W.F. Hegel, *Philosophy of Right*, trans. T.M. Knox, Oxford: Clarendon, 1942, 100; a useful discussion of Hegel's point can be found in D.E. Cooper, 'Hegel's Theory of Punishment', in Z.A. Pelczynski (ed.), *Hegel's Political Philosophy* : *Problems and Perspectives*, Cambridge U.P., pp.151-67.
14. See, e.g. J.G. Murphy, 'Marxism and Retribution', *Philosophy & Public Affairs*, II, 3 (Spring, 1973), 217-43.
15. See Ch.8, *supra*.
16. This view is taken by J.D. Marshall, 'Punishment and Education', *Educational Theory*, XXV, 2 (Spring, 1975), 148-55.
17. See, e.g. D. Wright, 'The Punishment of Children: a review of experimental studies', *Journal of Moral Education*, I, 3 (June 1972), 221-29.
18. For some discussion, see Kleinig, Ch.7; J. Kidder, 'Requital and Criminal Justice', *International Philosophical Quarterly*, XV, 3 (September, 1975), 255-78; E. Pincoffs, 'Are Questions of Desert Decidable?', in J.B. Cederblom & W.L. Blizek (eds.), *Justice and Punishment*, Cambridge, Mass.: Ballinger, 1977, pp.75-88; H.A. Bedau, 'Retribution and the Theory of Punishment', *Journal of Philosophy*, LXXV, 11 (November, 1978), Sect.III. There is a useful advance on my views in D.E. Scheid, 'Theories of Legal Punishment', Ph.D. dissertation, New York University, 1977, Ch.12.
19. Quoted in P.E. Harris, *Changing Conceptions of School Discipline*, New York: Macmillan, 1928, p.37.
20. Though see the recent discussion of corporal punishment by E.G. Rozycki, 'Pain and Anguish: the Need for Corporal Punishment', in G.D. Fenstermacher (ed.), *Philosophy of Education 1978*, Proceedings of the Thirty-fourth Annual Meeting of the Philosophy of Education Society, Champaign, Ill.: Philosophy of Education Society, 1979, pp.380-92; reply by D.R. Tunnell, pp.390-96. Cf. P. Nash, 'Corporal Punishment in an Age of Violence', *Educational Theory*, XIII, 4 (October, 1963), 295-308.
21. P.S. Wilson, *Interest and Discipline in Education*, London: Routledge & Kegan Paul, 1971, p.113.
22. Though I would not want to go as far as some radical critics in denying all validity to the criminal justice system. On this, see R.R. Brown, 'The New Criminology', in E. Kamenka, R. Brown & A.E.-S. Tay (eds.), *Law and Society: the crisis in legal ideals*, Pt. Melbourne, Vic.: Edward Arnold (Australia), 1978, pp.81-107.

Chapter 19

MORAL EDUCATION

With each new generation the problem is posed: To what extent and in what ways are we justified in influencing the young? Despite its generality, the question is asked most insistently when the sphere of moral (and/or religious) influence is considered. The reasons for this are not altogether clear. Moral diversity and hence moral disagreement may appear to be sufficient explanation, the assumption being that on controversial matters we ought to be particularly cautious about and in seeking to influence. But a closer inspection of other areas in which influence is commonly exerted on the young reveals a similar diversity. Perhaps the point is not moral diversity as such, but what it symptomatises, namely, an ineradicable subjectivism or relativism attaching to moral issues. But even this, obscurities aside, does not get to the heart of the matter. If there is an 'ineradicable subjectivism or relativism' here, it can be found no less in areas where hackles are not usually raised - aesthetics education, for example. It is only when we take into account the status given to moral considerations in our appraisals of persons and practices that the controversy over moral education becomes readily understandable. The acquisition of a moral character is seen as largely determinant of the kind of person one is. Moreover, what is developed here is thought to constitute the most important regulatory device for governing our pursuits. Thus, those who wish to engage in moral education are seen as exercising an influence not on peripheral but on central aspects of a person's existence. Hence its sensitivity.

Of course, were moral issues not controversial the question of moral education would not be as sensitive as it is. The gradual 'dehomogenisation' of Western culture, due in part to the decreasing influence of a single institutionalised religion, coupled with the rise of mass public schooling, has meant that what was once seen as the important task of 'character training' has had to be

243

tailored to political realities. Character training presupposed no firm separation between morality and religion, whereas the nomenclature of 'moral education' has been introduced into the public schooling arena in fairly clear (though disputed) contradistinction to 'religious instruction'. The enterprise of character training, moreover, presupposed the existence of a relatively fixed and uncontroversial structure of virtuous habits and dispositions into which the young were to be baptised. Moral education, on the other hand, is often said to focus instead on development of the cognitive equipment for autonomous moral judgment. Sometimes this has been expressed as a shift from the content to the form of morality – though, like the distinction between character training and moral education, it has a tendency to break down if pressed. In my view, the effect of the distinction is to make covert what was once overt. The emphasis on developing capacities for autonomous moral judgment turns out, on inspection, to be more aligned to the need for flexibility in rapidly changing social situations than to a heralded freeing of people from a fairly narrowly circumscribed substantive moral position.

Moral expertise

However, before we get further involved in a consideration of the practice of moral education, we must first raise some fundamental questions about its *possibility*. These are not new. Plato's *Protagoras* takes its rise from the question, 'Can virtue be taught?' For Socrates, the problem is occasioned by an apparent absence of recognised and/or successful teachers of morality, but the issue boils down to one about the relations, if any, between virtue and knowledge. We may give it contemporary expression as follows:[1] If moral education is to take place we should expect there to be moral experts who could be consulted, and whose judgments might be expected to be generally correct. However, because moral judgments are ultimately lacking in rational support, the question of correctness and hence of expertise does not arise. Therefore, it is irresponsible to speak of moral *education*.

As stated, this argument relies heavily on the view that moral judgments are not assessable in terms of truth or falsity. To explore this position (in its many versions) in any sort of detail would take us too far afield, though it may be appropriate to comment briefly on what has been its most influential recent statement, the so-called emotive theory of ethics. According to (one standard version of) this view,[2] moral utterances merely express attitudes of approval or disapproval, and as such do not qualify as true or false. But emotivism is phenomenologically and logically dubious. It is more accurate to see the so-called emotive element in such utterances (where, indeed, it can be found) as resultant upon the supposed presence in or absence from a situation of certain determinate morally relevant features, than to regard it as constitutive of their moral character. More formally, the terminology of approval is logically appropriate only in contexts where a grounding in intersubjective features of the object of approval is presupposed. To approve of something is not merely to take a liking (for whatever or no reason) to it.[3] The emotive theory correctly notes that moral judgments are not merely fact-stating; but by concentrating on and misdescribing the 'something more', it overlooks their grounding in the world of human experience.

Nevertheless, more is required to render the case for moral expertise plausible. The reason is concealed in the phrase 'morally relevant features', and can be illustrated by reference to Peter Singer's argument for the moral expertise of moral philosophers.[4] Singer properly recognises that moral decision-making involves rational reflection. It requires the gathering, selection and unbiased assessment of data. In these respects, he argues, the moral philosopher is especially well-placed. He/she is more than ordinarily competent in assessment of arguments, has made a study of moral concepts and of the logic of moral argument, and has the freedom and time to pursue moral issues at depth. This may be true, and to that extent to the moral philosopher's advantage. The problem with it is that this moral discussion takes place in the context of moral theory, and moral philosophers are notoriously divided over the theory. This is no minor issue, for the particular theories, even if to some extent they take their rise from and respond to widely shared convictions, do not support identical practices. On a number of important issues they support incompatible practices. Therefore, in so far as particular moral judgments depend on such theories for their support, and these theoretical differences remain intractable, the view that moral philosophers possess some special moral expertise will fail to carry conviction. It may, however, be premature to see this difficulty as destroying the possibility of moral education. It may do no more than make us wary of leaving moral education in the hands of so-called or self-styled experts.

The stronger conclusion, that moral education is impossible, requires a certain view of the intractability of differences in moral theory. If these differences are considered to be of a kind which excludes all further argument, thus allowing only an articulation of ultimately incompatible world-views, we may well despair of the possibility of moral education. For the implications of moral theory are not confined to moral practice but bear on our very conception of morality and hence of moral education. This pessimistic conclusion may seem to be sufficiently indicated by the lack of neutrality in the meta-ethical arena.[5] If lack of neutrality is taken to imply that there is no possibility of building a rational bridge between competing theories, then we will be left in a position of irresolvable uncertainty about what could count as morality and thus as moral education.[6] However, we have no strong reason to believe that the pessimistic conclusion is warranted. Rationality does not require normative neutrality, and the apparent intractability of moral disagreements may say more about our own limitations than about their amenability to rational discussion. As Renford Bambrough appropriately reminds us: 'A man who sets bounds to reason tends to place them suspiciously near to the limits of his own understanding.'[7] Nor is it irrelevant to be reminded of the 'theory-ladenness' of other forms of inquiry. Scientific inquiry, no less than morality, is 'theory-dependent' and theoretically controversial.[8] But because science is not believed to bear as centrally on our self-identity, we are more ready to ignore its theoretical turbulence.

The nature of morality

Although the foregoing discussion has fallen far short of decisiveness, and I shall henceforth assume that its more sceptical possibilities can be set aside, it functions as something of a caveat in relation to the account of morality and moral education which follows.

As a helpful first move in delimiting the moral landscape, we can observe that moral attributions and appraisals have a point only so long as it is assumed that those of whom they are made could help or could be held responsible for the conduct in virtue of which these attributions or appraisals are made. In other words, to denominate conduct morally right or wrong, just or dishonest, is to presuppose its voluntariness. The chief subjects of such denominations will thus be human beings who have reached a certain level of maturity. For they are not to be regarded merely as the meeting points of external forces, but as possessors of the capacity to stand back from or transcend the various forces which press in upon them, and to choose which path they will follow. In this capacity resides the possibility of morality.[9]

Although moral attributions and appraisals are generally associated with conduct, it would be a mistake to divorce them from the thoughts, intentions, motives, goals, or more generally the character, which inspires it. This is implicit in the voluntariness requirement, but frequently overlooked by those who see morality largely in terms of conformity to rules. More than anything, moral appraisals reflect on character, on the kind of person one is.

To approach morality in this way is to avoid some of the dichotomous thinking that has pervaded philosophical discussion - for example, in the view that morality is essentially other-regarding and not at all self-regarding. On the position I have outlined, it is clearly both. Morality is concerned with what we are, in our relationships with each other. One of the historical sources for the dichotomy has been the post-Kantian focus on duty as the paradigmatic moral notion - a departure from an earlier tradition in which the cultivation of virtue, no less than the performance of duty, was of decisive moral importance. The focus on duty has encouraged a separation of acts from agents and of moral theory from moral practice. [10]

It is a commonplace that moral considerations are accorded a position of pre-eminence in our practical thinking. Why should this be so? Why place so much emphasis on what we are in our relationships with each other? In brief, I would suggest that it is because our relationships with others are not merely optional, irrelevant to our being, and readily detachable: they create, sustain and in large measure determine our self-identity. Without them we would be nothing; in terms of them we have position and our world has meaning. Where those relationships are severely fractured, those involved will be diminished or threatened, or, in the case of those whose self-identity has not yet been established, that identity may be twisted or deformed. Crucial to the kind of person we are are the relationships in which we stand. Morality, then, by virtue of its concern with what we are *in our relationships with each other*, is also concerned with *what we are*. Herein lies its practical significance.

By understanding morality as a concern for what we are in our relationships with each other, we are enabled to accommodate one of the most serious problems facing traditional ethical theories - the problem of moral motivation. [11] Traditional theories, be they utilitarian, egoist, intuitionist, or Kantian, provide rationales for conduct which, if acted upon, undermine the moral worth of the conduct they motivate. If Jack visits Jill in hospital, his apparently charitable conduct is shown to be something else if he offers as his motivation the kinds of reasons associated with traditional moral theories - a desire to maximise happiness in the world, or to advance his own interests, or to do his duty, etc. It is only if his conduct is motivated by love or concern for *Jill*, by his desire to stand in and express a certain kind of relationship with and for *her*, that its moral integrity can be preserved. Otherwise, as occurs when reasons derived from the traditional moral theories are invoked, Jill figures simply as *an occasion for* their being acted upon.

The foregoing remarks, of course, still leave it something of an open question what we ought to be in our relations with each other. And beyond that they do not prejudge whether our so being is consistent with ownership of the means of production, abortion, strikes, and so on. Nor do they advocate some sentimentalised form of love, concern or affection. Nevertheless, by highlighting the character of morality in a certain way, they suggest a starting point for moral reflection which is generally ignored.

Form and content

Writers in ethics and those concerned with moral education tend to be considerably troubled by moral diversity. Perhaps they are sometimes too troubled by it, for there are often deep congruences running through the varied patterns of moral belief and practice. Nevertheless, apparently intractable differences remain, and in a society seemingly committed to a measure of pluralism, this constitutes a problem for moral education, particularly within the setting of public institutions. Indeed, it is often used as an argument for excluding moral education from such settings.[12] Whatever the merits of this argument, it is impossible to exclude moral teaching altogether, since, in the case of schools at least, structure, organisations, example, and course materials inevitably convey an overt or covert moral message. It is better to ask, not: 'Ought there to be a place for moral education in schooling?' but: 'Given that some form of moral teaching/learning will go on, how can we ensure that it is the best possible?'

One way in which some writers have attempted to come to terms with the tension between the fact of moral disagreement and the demands of moral education, is by drawing a distinction between the form and content of morality.[13] By focusing on the former, it is claimed, a generally acceptable basis for moral education can be provided. The distinction can be illustrated by means of an example. Suppose *A* and *B* both believe that civil disobedience is wrong. To that extent their beliefs have the same *content*. But *A* is opposed to civil disobedience simply because it is illegal, whereas *B* argues that civil disobedience threatens the social fabric. To that extent they differ in the form taken by their belief. It is argued by a number of these writers that although beliefs having particular contents may have different forms, one particular form is appropriate to moral beliefs, and this, taking into account the capacities of those to be taught, can be grasped and communicated independently of one particular content. But this is to claim more for the distinction than it can properly bear. There is a subtle connection between form and content which is usually overlooked. The reasons we

248

give for a particular belief - that is, its form - also serve to shape its content. If the reason that I do not steal is its illegality, then what I have a reason not to do is only what the law happens to define as stealing. If the reason why I do not steal is that it would lead to a great deal of insecurity and unpleasantness, then what I have a reason not to do is only taking those things from others whose removal would lead to insecurity and unpleasantness. In other words, form to some extent dictates content.

Even so, it may be argued that a focus on form would significantly diminish the problems caused by moral disagreement. This seems to be R.S. Peters' position. Peters maintains, not unreasonably, that morality is a rational form of thought and life. Moral decisions are not merely private preferences, but are grounded in considerations which anyone might be expected to recognise and acknowledge. This commitment to reason in moral decision-making presupposes a commitment to certain general principles which structure it and can thus function as criteria of relevance in moral deliberation. Put briefly, the derivations go as follows. The commitment to reason presupposes a commitment to drawing distinctions only where there are differences. In the practical sphere this amounts to a principle of fairness or impartiality, whereby people are to be treated the same unless there can be shown to be relevant differences between them. Further, if one is to be at all serious about rationality in decision-making, then no impediments should be placed in the way of any source of reason. Hence, unless there is good reason, others should not be interfered with but be left free to act as they themselves determine. In addition, the commitment to rationality requires for its realisation a general adherence to the principle of truth-telling, lest the whole process of basing practical decisions on reason be subverted. Again, to the extent that morality is concerned with relations between possessors of interests, rationality in practical matters demands that these be taken into consideration, and, further, that it be recognised that others' interests are as important to them as one's own interests are to oneself. The list could be extended, but enough has been said to indicate the nature of the derivations involved.[14]

Were such derivations successful, they would provide a useful, though limited, focus for moral education. But it is doubtful whether they are successful. It has been pointed out that only in conjunction with a number of moral assumptions can they yield anything like their present form;[15] and to that extent they (and the form-content distinction) do not provide the secure ground that was being sought.

A strategically more useful approach to the content of a morality which lends itself to promulgation within a public institutional setting may be to explore and articulate the conditions under which morality, understood as a form of life for which we can be held accountable, is possible. Accountability, as an aspect of autonomy, is not arrived at and sustained in a vacuum, but depends on the creation and maintenance of certain reasonably determinate social relations. Although there is obviously room here for disagreement, some limit to it is set by its focus.

Autonomy and education in the virtues

A major dimension of the foregoing can be cast in terms of education in the virtues. Moral accountability is achieved and preserved through interdependence. And the kind of interdependence appropriate to this requires the development and expression of fairly specific though familiar virtues. The virtues of love, honesty, fidelity, kindness, justice, sympathy, respect for others, humility, self-control and courage, in various ways mark out dispositions of character – ways of caring – which contribute to internal and external relations of an autonomy-enhancing kind. True, such virtues can sometimes be conjoined with ends which are morally unacceptable – damaging to the person of their possessor and others – but to employ this as a criticism of education in the virtues as a centrepiece of moral education is to indulge in unwarranted abstraction. The virtues belong together, as aspects of a total character, and singling them out for scrutiny independent of their association with other virtues is to ignore the interconnectedness of the interests which have given rise to their differentiation.

Progress in the virtues is not intended to comprise an alternative to or substitute for the acquisition of rational skills. The virtuous person, when acting in concrete settings, will need and want to exercise a good deal of rational sensitivity. It is not always clear what love or justice requires. The traditional moral rules represent an attempt to codify the way of virtue, but even these are often too rigid or general to be unquestioningly applied. The cultivation of virtue, therefore, does not represent an abandonment of rationality in favour of blind or non-rational habit; rather, it provides a moral setting for the exercise of reason.

The cognitive developmental approach

In proposing the importance of the virtues I have parted company with the most favoured theory of moral education – the cognitive developmental approach of Lawrence Kohlberg. Kohlberg is highly critical of the 'bag of virtues', as he calls them,[16] though his arguments generally seem more appropriate to a caricature than to a serious study of the place of the virtues in the moral life. It is

Kohlberg's view that when people make moral decisions they seek to bring the situation before them under the umbrella of some moral concept - a process of reasoning which has a determinate structure, and which may differ from person to person. These structures are referred to as 'stages' of development and, according to Kohlberg, full moral development is represented by a passage through six hierarchically ordered and sequentially invariant stages, grouped into three levels. [17] The lowest, or 'preconvention-al' level, encompasses two stages - the 'punishment and obedience' and 'instrumental relativist' orientations. At this level the person's 'moral' classifications follow 'cultural rules and labels of good and bad, right and wrong', but as determined by clearly differentiated considerations. At the first stage the physical power of those imposing the rules or labels is dominant; at the second stage, hedonistic 'What's in it for me?' associations dominate and determine the particular labels or rules followed. The second, 'conventional' level, also comprises two stages - what Kohlberg terms the 'interpersonal concordance or "good-boy - nice-girl"' and 'law and order' orientations. When moving into this level, the individual's criteria of classification shift from a concern with the immediate and obvious egoistic consequences of behaviour to a concern with wider expectations. This concern is not merely conformist, for loyalty to these wider expectations is involved and shown in the person's active maintenance of, support for and justification of the wider order, and identification with the persons or groups who make it up. These third and fourth stages are distinguished primarily by the extent to which relations with the wider 'group' are interpersonal rather than impersonal. Kohlberg regards the form of reasoning involved in the first four stages as being sub-moral, though it is his opinion that many people never progress beyond these stages. It is only at what he refers to as the 'postconventional, autonomous or principled' level that a genuinely moral form of reasoning is involved. The two stages which make up this level are dubbed the 'social-contract legalistic' and 'universal ethical principle' orientations. The former is characterised by reasons of a social contractual or right-based nature, whereas the latter emphasises reasons of conscience grounded in self-chosen universal principles. Kohlberg's characterisation of this last level is heavily influenced by John Rawls, for its intended effect is to establish the priority of justice in ethical theory.

It is Kohlberg's view that this cognitive picture of moral decision-making and moral development is far superior to any in which the virtues are given a central role. In what appears to be his only serious objection to them, he states that virtues and vices have a central significance only at the conventional level of morality, where they function as 'labels by which people award praise or blame to others....[They] are not the ways in which they think when making moral decisions themselves.'[18] Of the postconventional level he says, somewhat curiously, that 'the individual is oriented towards acting to create a moral state of affairs.... The principled virtue "justice", is not a "trait" like honesty; it is a concern about maintaining a just state of affairs.'[19]

Partly, no doubt, as a reaction against emotivist and relativistic views of ethics, Kohlberg's own view is highly intellectualistic. Moral development is seen primarily as a matter of increasingly sophisticated reasoning about matters of right and wrong. It is not understood in terms of character or relations between *persons* but in terms of rules or principles of 'a just order' or right and wrong. This is a very thin and depersonalised understanding. It does not explain why we should *care* to engage in what he calls genuine moral reasoning, nor why, when we have engaged in it, we should care enough to act on it. Moral reasoning does not take place in a vacuum. It is not an intellectual game played by people who have nothing better to do with their time. It is only as people come to care about others in certain ways that the kind of reasoning represented by Kohlberg's third level will have any pull. Learning virtue is learning to care about the kind of life in which 'moral reasoning' has a place. In snubbing the virtues, Kohlberg has all but severed moral development from moral life and reduced moral education to moral philosophy.

One consequence of this reduction is particularly disturbing - the way it masks the real moral sensitivity and achievement of which even young children are capable. They are capable of such achievement because they can come to care for the kind of relations which are the stuff of morality, even though their lack of maturity will in certain situations lead to inevitable failures in the expression of that care. If, as is no doubt the case, the young have not passed through all six stages, then, on the Kohlbergian position, we need not regard their views as morally serious and are given a justification for the extended moral paternalism in which our society indulges, and through which it seeks to perpetuate its dominant values. But if moral education is not just or mostly a matter of moral reasoning, but a growth in our concern for what we are in our relationships with each other, we may encourage, discern and respond appropriately to real moral achievement on the part of children much earlier than Kohlbergian theory would seem to allow.

Moral education and schooling

Over the past two decades there has been a revival of interest in 'moral education' as part of the explicit school

252

curriculum. Its traditional vehicles have shown themselves unable to satisfy the demands of an increasingly industrialised society. Religious instruction, traditionally conceived, is now something of an anachronism, and the nuclear family has wilted under the pressures placed on it. And so, in view of the importance of 'moral education' to a social formation requiring a high degree of co-ordination, responsibility for it has devolved more and more upon the school. But this does not show schools to be a good environment for moral education. Nor does it provide an argument for separate 'moral education' curricula.

One reason for this is hinted at in the slogan 'Virtue is caught, not taught'. Moral education is not merely a matter of learning a whole lot of facts, as one might learn the details of some historical incident or experiment in chemistry. Nor is it just a matter of acquiring a theoretical framework within which such facts can be interpreted, related and tested. Nor is it simply a matter of acquiring a range of skills, whether the argumentative skills of a philosopher or the practical skills of a musician. It is a matter of becoming a certain kind of person - of coming to care in certain kinds of ways, and this is not directly achievable by means of syllabi and classroom techniques of the familiar kind. As much as anything, the development of virtue is a function of the relationships within which people move, and which provide a context for whatever moral reflection they engage in. Moral sensitivity arises through immersion in and reflection upon relationships of an intimate kind, and in this respect schools have been seriously deficient. It is true that through literature and history one *may* get something of a vicarious insight into and appreciation of the moral life, but existing syllabi are generally oriented toward other dimensions of those subjects, and the everyday life of the school unites people through role rather than personal relationships. Competition of a non-innocent kind, unquestionable authority structures, the pressures of school honour, classroom organisation, and the restricted nature of curriculum choice, all constitute impediments to the development of relationships which will be conducive to moral reflection and moral growth. The introduction of an explicit 'moral education' curriculum will do nothing to ameliorate this, unless it can also call into question its embodiment in the existing school curriculum. But this, of course, would be self-defeating from the point of view of those sponsoring such curricula. Better that we seek to restructure family life so that it becomes capable of supporting durable and non-repressive intimacy.

This is not to deny that schools can have anything to contribute to moral education. In one sense their contribution, for good or ill, is unavoidable. The relations of schooling will inevitably create or reinforce attitudes and

253

values which belong to the moral domain. But they might also have a more deliberate role. Just because the nuclear family as presently constituted is often ill-fitted to the task of moral education, the school curriculum *may* provide access to life-styles and relationships which expand the horizons of people trapped in a damaging environment - though if they are to do this effectively, they will need to become less damaging environments themselves. For this, change is required in both their structure and curricular emphases. The erosion of artificial subject distinctions, a recognition of the historical nature of the school and its curriculum, increasing provision for the development of co-operative and non-authoritarian relationships, and curricula which allow for an adequate appreciation of the relational and circumstantial factors involved in the material dealt with, will be necessary if the school is to avoid the moral indoctrination which present curricula encourage. Some movement in this direction seems to be possible, though the prevalent tendency to see moral education in terms of the development of rational skills is not much improvement on the moralism it is designed to replace. Both tend to ignore the relational character of moral development.

Conclusion

We have barely scratched the surface of this vast topic, and it would be misleading to lay claim to any decisive arguments. But I have endeavoured to re-open for further consideration certain commonplaces of contemporary discussion in moral education: the rejection of moral expertise, the neglect of the virtues, the intellectualistic understanding of morality and moral education, and the nature of the school's involvement in moral education. If this has been achieved, there is some scope for an amelioration of the problems of contemporary schooling.

NOTES

1. For recent discussions, see G. Ryle,, 'Can Virtue be Taught?' in R.F. Dearden, P.H. Hirst & R.S. Peters (eds.), *Education and the Development of Reason*, London: Routledge & Kegan Paul, 1972, pp.434-37; R.W. Burch, 'Are there Moral Experts?', *Monist*, LVIII, 4 (October, 1974), 646-58; R.G. Frey, 'Moral Experts', *Personalist*, LIX, 1 (January, 1978), 47-52; B. Szabados, 'On "Moral Expertise"', *Canadian Journal of Philosophy*, VIII, 1 (March, 1978), 117-29, and references therein.
2. A more detailed dicsussion is found in J.O. Urmson, *The Emotive Theory of Ethics*, London: Hutchinson University

Library, 1968.

3. See G.W. Pitcher, 'On Approval', *Philosophical Review*, LXVII, 2 (April, 1958), 195–211; P. Foot, 'Approval and Disapproval', in *Virtues and Vices and Other Essays*, Oxford: Blackwell, 1978, pp.189–203.

4. P. Singer, 'Moral Experts', *Analysis*, XXXII, 4 (March, 1972), 115–17.

5. See my 'Neutrality in Moral Education', *Discourse*, III, 1 (1982).

6. To suggest, as some have, that morality is neutrally definable as that which has overriding significance for us, though true, is also empty. For it is no less true that we may legitimately argue that what some consider to be of moral importance (because of the status they give it), should not be so regarded. The precedence given to moral considerations is not merely formal, but is assigned in virtue of their content. And this content is 'theory-laden'.

7. R. Bambrough, *Reason, Truth & God*, London: Methuen, 1970, p.102.

8. Cf. A.F. Chalmers, *What is this thing called Science?*, Brisbane: University of Queensland Press, 1976.

9. See, further, H. Frankfurt, 'Freedom of the Will and the Concept of a Person', *Journal of Philosophy*, LXVIII, 1 (14 January, 1971), 5–21.

10. For a development of these points, see M.A.G. Stocker, 'Morally Good Intentions', *Monist*, LIV, 1 (January, 1970), 124–41; idem, 'Act and Agent Evaluations', *Review of Metaphysics*, XXVII, 1 (September, 1973), 42–61; and idem, 'The Schizophrenia of Modern Ethical Theories', *Journal of Philosophy*, LXXIII, 14 (August, 1976), 453–66.

11. See Stocker, 'The Schizophrenia of Modern Ethical Theories', and my 'Moral Schizophrenia and Christian Ethics', *Reformed Theological Review*, XL, 1 (January–April, 1981), 11–19.

12. These arguments are considered in greater detail in my 'The Place of the School in Moral Education', *Journal of Christian Education* (forthcoming).

13. See, e.g. Lawrence Kohlberg, 'Stages of Moral Development as a Basis for Moral Education', in C.M. Beck, B.S. Crittenden & E.V. Sullivan (eds.), *Moral Education: Interdisciplinary Approaches*, New York: Newman Press, 1971; R.S. Peters, 'Form and Content in Moral Education', in *Authority, Responsibility and Education*, London: Routledge & Kegan Paul, 1973; John Wilson, Norman Williams & Barry Sugarman, *Introduction to Moral Education*, Harmondsworth: Penguin, 1967; B.S. Crittenden, *Form and Content in Moral Education*, Toronto: Ontario Institute for Studies in Education, 1972.

14. R.S. Peters, *Ethics and Education*, London: Allen &

Unwin, 1966; for an admirably clear and brief development of these derivations, see A.P. Griffiths, s.v. 'Ultimate Moral Principles: Their Justification', in P. Edwards (ed.), *Encyclopedia of Philosophy*, New York: Macmillan & The Free Press, 1967, Vol. VIII, pp.177–82.

15. Some criticisms are indicated in Ch.10 fn.9, *supra*, and adjacent text; cf. also R. Simon, 'Equality as a Presupposition of Morality', *Personalist*, LV, 4 (August, 1974), 388–97; A.J. Watt, 'Transcendental Arguments and Moral Principles', *Philosophical Quarterly*, XXV, (January, 1975), 40–57.

16. See his discussion in 'Stages of Moral Development as a Basis for Moral Education', esp. pp.74–78.

17. He has recently toyed with the idea that there might be seven stages of development. See 'Education, Moral Development and Faith', *Journal of Moral Education*, IV, 1 (October, 1974), 5–16.

18. 'Stages of Moral Development as a Basis for Moral Education', 75.

19. ibid., 77.

Chapter 20

RELIGIOUS EDUCATION

The very mention of religious education is liable to excite strong feelings. On the one side, there are old sectarian animosities which, even in days of ecumenical dialogue, lie uneasily below the surface. Some of the names and faces may have changed, but the potent dichotomy of 'us' and 'them' still persists. On the other side, the very idea of religious education is thought to be incoherent. Religious belief is held to be fundamentally irrational or non-rational ('a matter of faith, not reason'), so that its transmission must be a matter of indoctrination, not education. When considered in the context of a compulsory public schooling system, all these problems are exacerbated. Because sincere religious belief almost invariably colours a person's whole outlook, it is no small matter whether and what religion is included within the curriculum. In this chapter we shall confine ourselves to brief observations on three questions. What is religion? Is religious education possible? Should religion be taught in schools?

What is religion?

Agreement on the nature and scope of religion is notoriously difficult to reach. Perhaps because religion is such a pervasive and multi-faceted phenomenon, it has occasioned 'definitions' or characterisations from a wide variety of perspectives. Some accounts focus on the institutions (e.g. churches) and ritual practices (e.g. kneeling) of religion, some see it in terms of distinctive beliefs (e.g. the existence of a god) or attitudes (e.g. awe, reverence), and others in relation to certain 'ultimate' and synoptic questions (e.g. Why is there something rather than nothing? Does life have a meaning?); more often than not, some combination of these is thought central. In an influential contemporary discussion, Ninian Smart has claimed that religion is best seen as a six-dimensional phenomenon, having doctrinal, mythological, ethical, ritual, experiential and social facets.[1] There is something to be said for a multi-dimensional approach, even though particular religions or instances of religious commitment will not be represented in each dimension. The search for something more precise - say, a set of necessary conditions jointly sufficient for its characterisation - is almost bound to come to grief. For one thing, it is organised round an unnecessarily restrictive and rarely exemplified understanding of conceptual delimitation. For another, like science and art, it functions as a general rather than as a specific concept. For yet another, it overlooks the concept's historical development.[2] Although the different dimensions of religion show a degree of mutual dependence in any particular instance, there is no necessary connection between them; and, as part of the concept's history, characteristic expressions within each of these dimensions have come to possess something of a life of their own, in terms of which religion is identified. Thus, in some accounts, belief in a god or something 'beyond' is made to bear most of the weight; in other accounts it is the attitude of awe or the response of worship; in yet others it is the involvement with matters of ultimate concern or the search for a synoptic understanding of reality which is said to identify a situation as religious. This branching out, somewhat akin to the 'family resemblance' thesis of Wittgenstein,[3] has made it virtually impossible to provide any unified account of religion.

Even so, the concept of religion is not so fluid as to be useless, and in the context of religious education the range of candidates is limited by a variety of practical considerations. We do not need to map the outer reaches of the concept in order to know what will and what will not count as religion. Nevertheless, it is not enough to fall back on some intuitive understanding of religion, since at least two distinguishable ways of conceptualising it appear to be operative in the debate over religious education. We can probably describe these as broad and narrow approaches to religion. Central to the narrow understanding are certain ontological commitments - to the existence of a transcendent being (or beings), or at least to some 'Power' beyond the mundane world. Although this does not suffic- iently characterise the narrow view, it has been a central plank of the predominant understanding in discussions of religious education. The broader aproach, however, is not limited to phenomena which involve this kind of ontological commitment. Instead, religion is understood more functionally, in which it constitites an answer or at least an approach, to certain 'ultimate' and synoptic questions. On this account, Marxism, humanism, and indeed almost any other '-ism' which claims to provide the wherewithal for a comprehensive and practically-oriented world-view, functions as a religion. In contrast, the narrow view sees Marxism, humanism, etc. as alternatives to religion. A preference for one rather than the other of these approaches is bound to be controversial. However, I believe an argument for preferring the functional approach is available.

There are two counts on which it makes better sense to see religion not simply as a metaphysical system in which the existence of some supra-mundane reality is postulated (and responded to), but in relation to certain practical questions that arise out of personal and social existence. First, the process of conceptual differentiation is closely related to shared interests – though not necessarily universally shared interests – interests that reflect our character as active beings; and secondly, the intense feeling and commitment commonly associated with religion is best understood if something like the functional view is correct. Apart from reasons of curiosity, there would be little point to the passionate concern about the existence of supra-mundane beings were it not thought that they possessed great practical significance. The broad approach leaves it open whether the kinds of interests and questions to which religion characteristically addresses itself are most adequately approached via ontological commitments like those which characterise the narrow approach. Our common tendency to approach the concept of religion narrowly should perhaps be seen as a by-product of the dominant position which theism has had in our culture. The gradual erosion of its hegemonic role has enabled alternative world-views to gain a cultural foothold. Secularisation so-called thus represents a change not in the fact but in the form of religion.[4]

Two objections may be briefly considered. First, it may be claimed that the broad approach leaves religion and metaphysics indistinguishable.[5] I am not sure how serious a difficulty this is. Though I consider them to be differentiable, they may sometimes be closely related. Perhaps the difference can be expressed generally as follows: whereas metaphysics is primarily an intellectual concern, the focus of religion is practical. On this view, certain forms of theism and atheism are better seen as metaphysical than as religious positions. Where theism amounts to no more than the postulation of some supra-mundane power, and atheism to no more than a denial of such, this would be the case.[6] It might also be objected that the broad approach has the odd consequence of classifying as religious those who might normally regard themselves as non- or anti-religious, e.g. humanists, Marxists). However, this does not seem to me to be a serious objection. Humanism and Marxism function for their adherents in much the same way as 'conventional' religion does for its devotees.[7] This is overlooked if we make the difference simply one of a particular ontological commitment - a commitment which, in any case, is problematic in relation to some forms of conventional religion. In connection with religious education there is, moreover, an important advantage in adopting a broad understanding of religion. Opponents of religious education frequently argue that schools should remain religiously neutral, the assumption being that the resultant secular humanism or 'Australian way of life' which permeates the school do not themselves constitute religious positions. If we disabuse ourselves of this assumption, then we can discuss the differences between acceptable and unacceptable forms of 'religious education' in a way which does not distort our choices. Moreover, we can then set aside the question of the possibility of religious education for a consideration of more general issues. Too often the discussion of its possibility has been made to hang on debates which arise within a particular tradition of religious education.

Is religious education possible?

Before this question can be explored in any detail, we need to determine what is involved in religious education. Here it has been found useful to distinguish between education *about* religion and education *in* religion. Although both have been commonly termed 'religious education', it is better to reserve that description for the latter. Education about religion (sometimes called 'religion studies') is a conglomerate of sociological, historical, psychological, and philosophical, etc. studies of religious phenomena. In so far as it is educative, this package might more accurately be seen as education in sociology, history, psychology etc., distinguished by its focus on religion. To say this is not to deny its value for education in religion (religious education), but it is not itself religious education.

It is frequently asserted that religious education must involve the promulgation of and participation in some particular religious position. There is some truth in this. Santayana's observation that 'the attempt to speak without speaking any particular language is not more hopeless than the attempt to have a religion that shall be no religion in particular',[8] correctly makes the point that we cannot come to terms with the ultimate and synoptic concerns which comprise the focus of religion except by means of some reasonably specific framework of understanding. However, this does not constitute a justification for what is generally called religious instruction, the uncritical and exclusivist propagation of the tenets and practices of some one religious tradition. What is fundamental to religious education is a serious involvement with the kinds of ultimate and overarching questions and perspectives to which religion addresses itself, and although this cannot be accomplished except via some particular 'tradition', it does not pre-empt the matter in favour of some one tradition. In

260

this respect, religious education is very like a philosophical education. As with religious education, education in philosophy requires a person's constructive engagement with the problems which have preoccupied philosophers, without pre-empting the particular philosophical tradition within which those problems must be approached, or even the particular form taken by those problems. Yet fruitful involvement requires that some specific standpoint or methodology be adopted, albeit one that is innovative or unorthodox.

We can now approach the question: 'Is religious education possible?' Here we shall understand it conceptually rather than practically. Our difficulties in answering it are by and large the difficulties involved in determining the nature of religion and of religious education. However, if we understand religion in the broad manner I have suggested, as picking out a range of human concerns (those of an ultimate and synoptic kind), then I think we can argue for the intelligibility of religious education in roughly the following manner. Human social experience cannot be adequately accommodated by the language of instinct and conditioning. It has a self-reflective dimension which expresses itself in the rational ordering and evaluation of experience and practice. We can distinguish (though not separate) synoptic and analytic aspects to this activity. It is in relation to the former that we come to pose the kinds of questions and provide the kinds of answers which are constitutive of religion – whether of the humanistic, Marxist or theistic variety. We may call them questions about 'the meaning of life', questions which seek a comprehensive and coherent framework for or key to individual and social existence. As studies of puberty suggest, these questions tend to be of considerable importance to the formation of personal identity and autonomy, for they help (or are intended to help), the individual to locate him/herself in the world, to provide bearings by means of which the individual can understand and accept responsibility for his/her life-plans and behaviour. Of course, not everyone reflects in these terms: but equally, not everyone seeks to rise above heteronomy. And, as with other aspects of human experience, synoptic reflection tends to be greatly influenced by cultural factors. I am, nevertheless, impressed by the universality of religion (broadly understood), not as an *argumentum de consensu gentium*, but as evidence of the importance of ultimate and synoptic questions to the human condition. To claim this is not to imply that every form in which questions about 'the meaning of life' arise is legitimate, or even that there is some form of the question which is beyond question.[9] We cannot insulate them or the answers we provide to them from critical scrutiny. Their controversiality need not jeopardise the possibility of

261

religious education, since a serious questioning of the legitimacy of certain ultimate questions may itself reflect a form of the sensitivity and concern to which religious education is directed. Here we need to distinguish the sort of crass attack on ultimate questions which was encouraged by logical positivism and some of the linguistic philosophy which followed it, from the sensitive critique that one finds in Camus [10] and other writers, who display a serious regard for ultimate questions, but cannot discern any intelligible response.

My suggestion, then, is that in so far as ultimate and synoptic questions intelligibly arise out of the self-reflective activity of human beings, and can be answered in ways that are amenable to rational scrutiny, religious education has a strong claim to be seen as a conceptual possibility. Further, I would suggest that in so far as such questions and the answers provided to them can constitute an important element in a distinctively human mode of experience, religious education is to be approached as a matter of some priority.

Faith and reason

Nevertheless, some consideration must be given to a difficulty we have so far ignored. Put briefly, it is that ultimate and synoptic questions do not admit of rational answers. All we can do is to 'lay them out' for people to accept or reject, or alternatively, we must accept them on 'faith' or 'authority'. This is said to follow from their character as ultimate questions. Now, if, as it is said, education involves taking an increasingly rational approach to life, an induction into religion, broadly understood, would appear to be a retrograde step.

We cannot underestimate the problem of making good ultimate and synoptic claims, but we do not ameliorate these problems by ruling them out of court. It is a general feature of the justificatory process that for any set of reasons advanced in favour of a position further reasons can be demanded. Kantian transcendental arguments, designed to halt such a regress, have at best a limited applicability, and the Popperian rejection of justification in favour of criticism need pose no threat to religious beliefs as such. Provided that ultimate and synoptic claims are not given some special status, which insulates them from scrutiny, there is no reason why, in principle, they should not have as secure a place in the rational life as the claims of those who object to them. The problem is that such claims have sometimes been given a special status. The appeal to faith or authority has been made unconditional rather than provisional, though such appeals may, and indeed ought to be only provisional, even if wholehearted and assured. There is no way, apart from dogmatism, in which even the most ultimate beliefs can be secured against critical evaluation, though of course practical considerations usually dictate that we draw a provisional line somewhere. It is the supreme presumption to favour one's own beliefs with an immunity one is not prepared to extend to others. They may be more defensible, less criticisable, but there is no way that they can be legitimately sealed off from the probings of other rational agents. [11]

In our own culture, particularly in relation to what is often understood as 'religious education', the provisional character of basic commitments has not always been appreciated. Some strands of Judaeo-Christian-Islamic belief have endeavoured to insulate themselves against questioning by construing faith as an irrevocable commitment whose reconsideration would be 'sinful', a commitment about which human reason can have nothing legitimate to say. [12] There are some important confusions here, and in view of our common (though hardly essential) cultural association of religious education with programmes having a substantial Judaeo-Christian content, it will be worth saying a bit more about the nature of faith, and its connection with reason. Our comments here will not be directly transferable to religion, broadly understood, though I think they could provide a model for the kind of critique that might be advanced in relation to any ultimate and synoptic commitment which seeks to arrogate to itself a privileged status.

Within the Judaeo-Christian tradition, writers have regularly distinguished different kinds of faith. [13] The dominant distinction is a two-fold one, sometimes represented by the two Latin words, *fides* and *fiducia*. Roughly, *fides* is used to express assent to propositions: it is faith or belief *that p*. *Fiducia* is used to signify trust: it is faith or belief *in X* (where *X* is usually though not necessarily some person). We may see *fides* very largely in terms of an intellectual commitment, whereas *fiducia* refers more generally to a person's whole orientation. The two are not of course completely unrelated: if *A* has faith in *X* then *A* must believe that certain *X*-related propositions are true. In so far as this is the case, *fiducia* may be based on and should be open to rational appraisal.

It should be noted here that the central concept so far as Judaeo-Christian understanding is concerned is *fiducia*, which has as its primary opposite unbelief (lack of trust) rather than disbelief (intellectual doubt). Yet most of the debate concerning the conceptual possibility of religious (i.e. Judaeo-Christian) education has been premissed on the idea that the central concept of Judaeo-Christian understanding is *fides*. While it is true that to have faith in *X* one must believe that certain *X*-related propositions are true, no immediate inference can be drawn as to the rational standing of those *X*-related propositions. My faith in my wife may presuppose certain propositional beliefs that are excellently founded, whereas my faith in the government may presuppose propositional beliefs for which there is at best the flimsiest evidence. Where *fides* is understood not simply as assent to a proposition, but as groundless or non-demonstrable assent (as it is most influentially by Aquinas), then there need be no necessary connection between *fiducia* and *fides*. The difficulty with Judaeo-Christian understanding, and religion in general, is that because it deals with ultimate and synoptic questions the propositional supports are unlikely to carry the persuasiveness that we might expect of claims to knowledge.

There is, nevertheless, a further reason why, at least in relation to Judaeo-Christian understanding, the emphasis on faith has encouraged the view that it is alien to reason. It also helps to explain why, within the history of discussion, there has been a slide from *fiducia* to *fides* and from *fides* to non-demonstrability. There has been a conflation, I believe, of two distinct activities which I shall call 'coming to *fiducia*', and 'continuing in *fiducia*'. An illustration will help make the distinction. Suppose my wife tells me that she is going shopping and will return home at 6.00 p.m. Rather than take her at her word, I have my personal private detective follow her and report her movements to me. At six o'clock I ring up to find out whether she has returned home. If the detective's report is satisfactory, and she answers the phone when I ring, I will have ample reason to believe (*fides*) her assertion about what she was going to do. But do I have faith (*fiducia*) in her? Here, my demand for evidence, my refusal to take her at her word, shows a distinct lack of faith (*fiducia*) in her. It is characteristic of situations in which the activity is one of *continuing* in faith that one is prepared to take another at his/her word. It is easy to confuse this with non-rational commitment. But the contrary may be closer to the mark. Had I taken my wife at her word, I should probably have had good reasons for doing so, since my initial trust, my *coming* to faith in her, was based on a thoughtful assessment of her trustworthiness. I would not have put my faith in her unless I had carefully considered whether and to what extent she could be believed. Otherwise my faith would have been mere credulity. However, having settled the question of trustworthiness in her favour, I cannot legitimately continue in faith and insist on reasons for everything before I believe. This does not make *fiducia* incorrigible. *Fiducia* constitutes a presumption in favour of the object of trust, a provisional even if wholehearted commitment, which might, in appropriate circumstances, be reconsidered. A determination of 'appropriate circumstances' would be no mean task, though it is doubtful whether some of the more extreme demands for unquestioning obedience that are sometimes made in Judaeo-Christian-Islamic circles have much to commend them.

Whatever else may be said about such demands, they seem to involve a dangerous identification of the human perception of the word of God (Allah) with the word of God (Allah).

The conflation we have been discussing has been responsible for much of the disrepute into which 'religious instruction' classes have fallen. Since these have often been staffed by people strongly committed to a particular *Weltanschauung*, there is a temptation to expect those who do not, or do not yet, have any religious commitment,[14] to accept without question what they themselves now (at least) accept without question. But why should others, who do not know my wife like I do, take her at her word like I do?

Before leaving the supposed opposition of faith and reason, a brief comment on 'reason' is in order. The reification of concepts so characteristic of Western philosophy should not blind us to the fact that there is no such thing as Reason. There are simply people who think (i.e. reason), and who do this well or badly. Behind their thinking activity there lurks no parent animal 'Reason', intuitively observed and self-evidently sovereign, but a set of culturally acquired and alterable standards by which that thinking activity can be evaluated. The so-called 'laws of logic', perhaps the most permanent standards of rational assessment, comprise only a small part of the critical apparatus to which we appeal when making rational appraisals. Other parts are highly controversial. Canons of non-deductive reasoning, standards of evidence, and so on do not constitute a fixed 'given' out there, a philosopher's touchstone, but a set of thought-out but not unchallengeable proposals for the conduct of rational enquiry. The upshot of this is that the assessment of ultimate and synoptic positions need not necessarily take the form of a single-directioned attempt to bring those positions into line with a fixed standard, Reason, but may also prompt a reconsideration of the standards of rationality in terms of which assessments are to be made.

Should religion be taught in schools?

The question invites us to consider the purpose and practice of schooling, matters on which we have commented elsewhere.[15] Too often, one feels, the matter of teaching religion in schools has been little more than an expression of wider political struggles. The educational possibilities have been overridden by sectarian politics or the political desire for some form of cultural homogeneity and compliance. Understandably, the whole enterprise has been brought into disrepute. It is unlikely, given the structural location of schooling in society, that what is taught in schools and how it is taught will ever be dissociated from wider socio-political ends; nevertheless, there is at least some room within the existing structure for improvement in the kind

265

and quality of teaching.

Let us suppose, however, that it is possible to take genuinely educational initiatives within a schooling context. Should we reasonably expect religion to be among those initiatives? In terms of the importance of ultimate and synoptic questions, I think there is a good deal to be said for giving religion a place in the curriculum. Yet at the same time it is clear that as it presently exists and is likely to continue, the school environment is particularly unconducive to a thoughtful consideration of these issues. The formation of a life-plan, the integration of one's experience into a coherent and durable framework of understanding, the practical expression and testing of a total way of life, is not easily accomplished in the competitive, prepackaged, depersonalised environment of the school.

The compulsory nature of schooling presents a further problem. P.H. Hirst argues against the inclusion of 'religious education' (narrowly conceived) in the curricula of publicly supported schools by maintaining that since there are no agreed public tests for religious claims, and since no issue of public good is at stake, it would represent a violation of people's freedom to initiate them into a particular religious tradition.[16] The view that religious education is unconnected with public good is surely a superficial one, an unwarranted generalisation from a pietistic tradition, but the civil liberties question is more significant. If there is to be any serious engagement with ultimate and synoptic questions, it will not be possible to remain agnostic in regard to their formulation and the kind of response given to them, and to compulsorily require that children confront one particular tradition on a matter so embracing is difficult to justify.

But the school may adopt a more limited role - not of endeavouring to provide a religious education, but of familiarising students with background material relating to a variety of traditions. This would include not simply the so-called theistic religions but humanism, Marxism and other alternatives that have some cultural significance. The contentiousness of these different traditions should not be seen as an argument against their consideration in schools. Contentiousness is part and parcel of the search for understanding, and it is a condemnation of much schooling that syllabi fail to acknowledge the contentious nature of much of what is ordinarily taught in other subjects. Many of those who oppose some exploration of religious questions in schools would have no objection to the inclusion of philosophy in the curriculum, yet it could hardly be claimed that there exist public tests for philosophical theses which can attract anything approaching universal assent. The issue is not whether religious positions are highly contentious, but whether they can be approached in a manner which allows for their assessment by those who teach and learn. It is a matter of autonomy rather than certainty.

Conclusion

Given the present structure of schooling, it is unlikely that the foregoing suggestions could be very satisfactorily implemented in the classroom. The various political pressures which affect the content of the curriculum would not ignore an area of such ideological significance. Yet the somewhat narrow experience provided by the home in such matters gives one pause lest the attempt to provide some reasonably broad basis for religious understanding be abandoned altogether. To reject all consideration of such issues because any curriculum is likely to excite controversy and opposition is simply to capitulate to a world-view which wishes to maintain its latent hegemony in the school.

NOTES

1. N. Smart, *Secular Education and the Logic of Religion*, London: Faber & Faber, 1968, pp.15ff.
2. See, e.g. W. Cantwell Smith, *The Meaning and End of Religion*, New York: Mentor, 1964.
3. L. Wittgenstein, *Philosophical Investigations*², trans. G.E.M. Anscombe, Oxford: Blackwell, 1958, §§66 ff.
4. Cf. D.C. Hickman, 'Some Popular Ideas of Secularisation: A Critique', *Interchange* (Sydney), II, 4 (1970), 233-39.
5. See J. Wilson, *Education in Religion and the Emotions*, London: Heinemann, 1971, p.13.
6. The distinction is implicit in Normal Malcolm's defence of the ontological argument: 'It would be unreasonable to require that the recognition of Anselm's demonstration as valid must produce a conversion' ('Anselm's Ontological Arguments', *Philosophical Review*, LXIX, 1 (January, 1960), 62).
7. See the discussion in J. Kovesi, 'Marxist Ecclesiology and Biblical Criticism', *Journal of the History of Ideas*, XXXVII, 1 (January–March, 1976), 93-110.
8. Quoted in M. White, 'Religious Commitment and Higher Education', in *Religion, Politics and the Higher Learning*, Cambridge, Mass., Harvard U.P., 1959, p.98.
9. See P. Edwards, s.v. 'Life, Meaning and Value', and 'Why' in P. Edwards (ed.), *Encyclopedia of Philosophy*, New York: Macmillan & The Free Press, 1967, Vol. IV, pp.467-77 and Vol. VIII, pp.296-302 respectively.
10. e.g. A. Camus, *The Myth of Sisyphus and other Essays*,

trans. J. O'Brien, New York: Knopf, 1955.

11. For an extended discussion, which takes a dim view of much narrowly religious commitment, see W.W. Bartley, III, *The Retreat to Commitment*, London: Chatto & Windus, 1964.

12. Cf. that variety of Marxism which sees any radical questioning of its claims as a manifestation of 'bourgeois ideology'.

13. For extended treatments of this question, see J. Hick, *Faith and Knowledge*^{2}, London: Macmillan, 1967, and H.H. Price, *Belief*, London: Allen & Unwin, 1969, esp. pp.426-54.

14. I do not mean to suggest that there is no commitment appropriate to religious education or to those who teach it. See M.H. Grimmitt, 'When is "Commitment" a Problem in Religious Education?', *British Journal of Educational Studies*, XXIX, 1 (February, 1981), 42-53.

15. See Ch. 8, *supra*.

16. P.H. Hirst, 'Morals, Religion and the Maintained School' (1965), reprinted with additions in *Knowledge and the Curriculum*, London: Routledge & Kegan Paul, 1974, pp.173-89, esp. pp.180ff.

The items included here *supplement* the materials referred to in Chapter Notes. It has been my intention to represent a range of viewpoints. The ordering is roughly chronological.

Chapter 1: *Philosophy of Education*

C.J. Ducasse, 'What Can Philosophy Contribute to Educational Theory?', *Harvard Educational Review*, XXVIII, 4 (Fall, 1958), 285÷97; 'Comment' by H.S. Broudy, 297-99.

K. Price, *Education and Philosophical Thought*, Boston: Allyn & Bacon, 1962.

H.S. Broudy, 'The Role of Analysis in Educational Philosophy', *Educational Theory*, XIV, 4 (October, 1964), 261-69, 285; and 'Between the Yearbooks', in J.F. Soltis, *Philosophy and Education*, Eightieth Yearbook of the National Society for the Study of Education: Chicago: NSSE, 1981, Part I, pp.13-35.

J.A. Passmore, *The Philosophy of Teaching*, London: Duckworth, 1980, Part I.

R.S. Peters, (with J.P. White), 'The Philosopher's Contribution to Educational Research', *Educational Philosophy and Theory*, I, 2 (October, 1969), 1-15, and (with P.H. Hirst), *The Logic of Education*, London: Routledge & Kegan Paul, 1979, Ch. 1.

G. Langford, *Philosophy and Education: An Introduction*, London: Macmillan, 1968, Chs. 1,2.

C.J. Lucas (ed.), *What is Philosophy of Education?*, London: Macmillan, 1969.

K. Thompson, 'Philosophy of Education and Educational Practice', *Proceedings of the Philosophy of Education Society of Great Britain*, IV, 1 (January, 1970), 45-60; reply by R. Pring, 61-76.

J. Soltis, 'Analysis and Anomalies in Philosophy of Education' in R.D. Heslep (ed.), *Philosophy of Education*

1971, Proceedings of the Twenty-seventh Annual Meeting of the Philosophy of Education Society, Edwardsville, Ill.: Philosophy of Education Society, 1971, 28–46; replies by G.R. Eastwood, 47–54, and J.E. McClellan, 55–59; also 'Philosophy of Education: Retrospect & Prospect', in R.Pratte (ed.), *Philosophy of Education 1975*, Proceedings of the Thirty-first Annual Meeting of the Philosophy of Education Society, San Jose, Calif.: Philosophy of Education Society, 1975, 7–24; reply by P.G. Smith, 25–29.

I. Scheffler, *Reason and Teaching,* London: Routledge & Kegan Paul, 1973, Pt. I.

A. Edel, 'Analytic Philosophy of Education at the Crossroads', in J.F. Doyle (ed.), *Educational Judgments,* London: Routledge & Kegan Paul, 1973, Ch. 14.

R. Barrow, 'What's Wrong With the Philosophy of Education?', *British Journal of Educational Studies,* XXII, 2 (April, 1974), 133–46.

W. Feinberg, *Reason and Rhetoric: the intellectual foundations of 20th century liberal educational policy,* New York: Wiley, 1975.

H. Freeman, 'On the Nature of Philosophy of Education and its Practice in Colleges and Departments of Education – or – "Does Philosophy of Education Leave Everything as it is?"', *Education for Teaching,* 98 (November, 1975), 37–48.

L.J. Nicholson, 'What *Schooling in Capitalist America* Teaches us about Philosophy', *Canadian Journal of Philosophy,* VIII, 4 (December, 1978), 653–63.

Chapter 2: *Education*

F.N. Dunlop, 'Education and Human Nature', *Proceedings of the Philosophy of Education Society of Great Britain,* IV, 1 (January, 1970), 21–44.

A. Dupuis, *Nature, Aims and Policy,* Urbana: University of Illinois Press, 1970.

R.F. Dearden, P.H. Hirst & R.S. Peters (eds.), *Education and the Development of Reason,* London: Routledge & Kegan Paul, 1972.

P. Freire, *Pedagogy of The Oppressed,* Harmondsworth: Penguin, 1972, Ch.2.

W.K. Frankena, 'The Concept of Education Today', in J.F. Doyle (ed.), *Educational Judgments,* London: Routledge & Kegan Paul, 1973, pp.19–32; reply by A.S. Kaufman, pp.46–56.

A. Edel, 'Analytic Philosophy of Education at the Crossroads', in J.F. Doyle (ed.), *Educational Judgments,* London: Routledge & Kegan Paul, 1973, pp.232–57.

G. Langford, 'The Concept of Education' and 'Values in Education' in G. Langford & D.J. O'Connor (eds.), *New*

Essays in the Philosophy of Education, London: Routledge & Kegan Paul, 1973, pp.3-32, 115-34; reply to the latter by R.S. Peters, pp.135-46; reply to the former by A. Thatcher, 'Education and the Concept of a Person', Journal of Philosophy of Education, XIV, 1 (June 1980), 117-28 (and rejoinder, 129-36).

J. Earwaker, 'R.S. Peters and The Concept of Education', Proceedings of the Philosophy of Education Society of Great Britain, VII, 2 (July, 1973), pp.239-59.

B.A. Cooper, 'Peters' Concept of Education', Educational Philosophy and Theory, V, 2 (October, 1973), 59-76.

P. Herbst, 'Work, Labour and University Education', in R.S. Peters (ed.), The Philosophy of Education, London: O.U.P., 1973, pp.58-74.

C.M. Beck, Educational Philosophy and Theory : An Introduction, Boston: Little, Brown & Co. 1974, Chs. 1, 2.

R.S. Downie & E. Telfer, Education and Personal Relationships, London: Methuen, 1974, Ch. 2.

R.E. Fitzgibbons, 'Peters' Analysis of Education: the Pathology of an Argument', British Journal of Educational Studies, XXIII, 1 (February, 1975), 78-98.

R.K. Elliott, G. Langford & P.H. Hirst, Symposium: 'Education and Human Being', in S.C. Brown (ed.), Philosophers Discuss Education, London: Macmillan, 1975, Pt. 2.

J. Spring, A Primer of Libertarian Education, New York: Free Life Editions, 1975.

J. Wilson, Philosophy and Practical Education, London: Routledge & Kegan Paul, 1977, Ch. 1.

Chapter 3: Teaching and Learning

Teaching

M. Buber, Between Man and Man, London: Kegan Paul, Trench, Trubner & Co., 1947.

J. Wilson, 'Two Types of Teaching', in R.D. Archambault (ed.), Philosophical Analysis and Education, London: Routledge & Kegan Paul, 1965, pp.157-70.

G. Ryle, 'Teaching and Training', in R.S. Peters (ed.), The Concept of Education, London: Routledge & Kegan Paul, 1967, pp.105-19.

G. Langford, Philosophy and Education, London: Macmillan, 1968, Chs. 8, 9.

C.J.B. Macmillan & T.W. Nelson (eds.), Concepts of Teaching: Philosophical Essays, Chicago: Rand McNally, 1968.

B. Bandman & R.S. Guttchen (eds.), Philosophical Essays on Teaching, Philadelphia: Lippincott, 1969.

C.R. Rogers, Freedom to Learn, Columbus, Ohio: C.E. Merrill, 1968.

J.T. Klein, 'Presuppositions of Teaching', Educational

Theory, XIX, 3 (Summer, 1969), 229–307; reply by R.M. Lawson, 308–11.

R.T. Hyman (ed.), *Contemporary Thought on Teaching*, Englewood Cliffs, N.J.: Prentice-Hall, 1971.

T.F. Green, *The Activities of Teaching*, Tokyo: McGraw-Hill Kogakusha, 1971.

J.F. Andris, 'Person X is Teaching', in R.D. Heslep (ed.), *Philosophy of Education 1971*, Proceedings of the Twenty-seventh Annual Meeting of the Philosophy of Education Society, Edwardsville, Ill.: Philosophy of Education Society, 1971, 234–46.

W.A. Hart, 'Is Teaching What the Philosopher Understands by it?', *British Journal of Educational Studies*, XXIV, 2 (June, 1976), 155–70.

J.C.-W. Koh, 'Jones is Teaching', in K.A. Strike (ed.), *Philosophy of Education 1976*, Proceedings of the Thirty-second Annual Meeting of the Philosophy of Education Society, Urbana, Ill.: Philosophy of Education Society, 1976, 71–80.

J.E. McClellan, *Philosophy of Education*, Englewood Cliffs, N.J.: Prentice-Hall, 1976, esp. Chs. 2–4.

D.W. Hamlyn, *Experience and the Growth of Understanding*, London: Routledge & Kegan Paul, 1978, Ch.10.

J.A. Passmore, *The Philosophy of Teaching*, London: Duckworth, 1980, Ch.2.

B.C. Hurst, 'Teaching, Telling and Changes in Belief', *Journal of Philosophy of Education*, XIV, 2 (November, 1980), 215–24.

Learning

J. Hanson, 'Learning by Experience', in B.O. Smith & R.H. Ennis (eds.), *Language and Concepts in Education*, Chicago: Rand McNally, 1961, pp.1–23.

H.S. Broudy, 'Mastery', in B.O. Smith & R.H. Ennis (eds.), *Language and Concepts in Education*, Chicago: Rand McNally, 1961, pp.72–85.

E.R. Hilgard & G.H. Bower, *Theories of Learning*, New York: Appleton-Century-Crofts, 1966.

B.P. Komisar & C.J.B. Macmillan (eds.), *Psychological Concepts in Education*, Chicago: Rand McNally, 1967.

D. Arnstine, *Philosophy of Education: Learning and Schooling*, New York: Harper & Row, 1967.

R.S. Peters (ed.), *The Concept of Education*, London: Routledge & Kegan Paul, 1967.

G. Langford, *Philosophy and Education*, London: Macmillan, 1968, Ch.5; also 'Learning and Knowledge', *Journal of Philosophy of Education*, XII (1978), 41–50.

C.R. Rogers, *Freedom to Learn*, Columbus, Ohio: C.E. Merrill, 1968.

D. Vandenberg, *Teaching and Learning*, Urbana, Ill.: University of Illinois Press, 1969.

B.L. Curtis, 'Learning and Intentionality', *Proceedings of the Philosophy of Education Society of Great Britain* IV (1970), 105-21.

T.F. Green, *The Activities of Teaching*, Tokyo: McGraw-Hill Kogakusha, 1971, Ch.6.

S.C. Brown & J.P. White, Symposium: 'Learning', *Proceedings of the Aristotelian Society*, Supp. Vol. XLVI (1972), 19-58.

D.W. Hamlyn (*et al.*), Symposium: 'Human Learning', in S.C. Brown (ed.), *Philosophy of Psychology*, London: Macmillan, 1973, Pt. 3; also 'The Concept of Development', *Proceedings of the Philosophy of Education Society of Great Britain*, IX, 1 (July, 1975), 26-39 (and reply by R.K. Elliott, 40-48); *Experience and the Growth of Understanding*, London: Routledge & Kegan Paul, 1978 (with discussions and replies in *Journal of Philosophy of Education*, XIV (1980) and XV (1981)).

R.P. Riegle, 'The Concept of "Learning"', in B.S. Crittenden (ed.), *Philosophy of Education 1973*, Proceedings of the Twenty-ninth Annual Meeting of the Philosophy of Education Society, Edwardsville, Ill.: Philosophy of Education Society, 1973, 77-85.

J.C.-W. Koh, 'Paula has Learned', in R. Pratte (ed.), *Philosophy of Education 1975*, Proceedings of the Thirty-first Annual Meeting of the Philosophy of Education Society, San Jose, Calif.: Philosophy of Education Society, 1975, 41-51.

J.E. McClellan, *Philosophy of Education*, Englewood Cliffs, N.J.: Prentice-Hall, 1976, esp. Ch.3.

J. Holt, *Instead of Education: Ways to Help People do Things Better*, New York: E.P. Dutton, 1976, Ch.2.

K.G. Fleming, 'Criteria of Learning and Teaching', *Journal of Philosophy of Education*, XIV, 1 (June, 1980), 39-51.

Chapter 4: *Teaching and Related Concepts*

A number of these references are comparative and might be included under more than one heading.

Instruction

D.P. Ausubel, 'In Defence of Verbal Learning', *Educational Theory*, XI, 1 (January, 1961), 15-25; also, *The Psychology of Meaningful Verbal Learning*, New York: Grune & Stratton, 1963; reply, 'Ausubel on Discovery and Verbal Learning', by C. Clark, *Educational Philosophy and Theory*, XI, 1 (March, 1979),1-15.

I. Scheffler, *The Language of Education*, Springfield, Ill.: C.C. Thomas, 1962, p.76-77.

A.S. Anthony, 'Observations on Verbal and Discovery Learning in the Educational Context', *Educational Theory*, XIV, 2

(April, 1964), 83-92, 98.

R.F. Dearden, 'Instruction and Learning by Discovery', in R.S. Peters (ed.), *The Concept of Education*, London: Routledge & Kegan Paul, 1967, pp.135-55.

W.J. Campbell, 'Studies of Teaching I: Classroom Practices', *New Zealand Journal of Educational Studies*, III, 2 (November, 1968), 97-124.

N. Postman & C. Weingartner, *Teaching as a Subversive Activity*, Harmondsworth: Penguin, 1969.

R.T. Hyman, *Ways of Teaching*, Philadelphia: J.B. Lippincott, 1970, Pt. III.

T.F. Green, *The Activities of Teaching*, Tokyo: McGraw-Hill, Kogakusha, 1971, pp.27-33, 49-50.

A.C. Hogg & J.K. Foster, *Understanding Teaching Procedures*, Victoria: Cassell Australia, 1973, Chs. 12, 13.

J.A. Passmore, *The Philosophy of Teaching*, London: Duckworth 1980.

Learning by discovery

D.P. Ausubel, 'Learning by Discovery: Rationale & Mystique', *Bulletin of the National Association of Secondary-School Principals*, XLV (1961), 18-58.

W.E. Ray, 'Pupil discovery vs. Direct instruction', *Journal of Experimental Education*, XXXIX, 3 (March 1961), 271-80.

L.S. Shulman & E.R. Keisler (eds.), *Learning by Discovery : A Critical Appraisal*, Chicago: Rand McNally, 1966.

R.F. Dearden, 'Instruction and Learning by Discovery', in R.S. Peters (ed.), *The Concept of Education*, London: Routledge & Kegan Paul, 1967, pp.135-55.

S.I. Brown, 'Learning by Discovery in Mathematics: Rationale, Implementation and Misconceptions', *Educational Theory*, XXI, 3 (Summer, 1971), 232-60.

G.H. Bantock, 'Discovery Methods', in C.B. Cox & A.E. Dyson (eds.), *The Black Papers on Education*, London: Davis-Poynter, 1971, pp.101-17.

C. Richards, 'Third Thoughts on Discovery', *Educational Review*, XXV, 2 (February, 1973), 143-50.

A.C. Hogg & J.K. Foster, *Understanding Teaching Procedures*, Victoria: Cassell Australia, 1973, Chs. 8, 9.

Drilling

G. Ryle, *The Concept of Mind*, London: Hutchinson, 1949, pp.42-44; also 'Teaching and Training' in R.S. Peters (ed.) *The Concept of Education*, London: Routledge & Kegan Paul, 1967, pp.105-19.

R.M. Gagné, 'Military Training and Principles of Learning', *American Psychologist*, XVII, 2 (February, 1962), 83-91.

J.P. Powell, 'Education, Training and Drilling', *Australian Journal of Higher Education*, II, 3 (December, 1966), 230-37.

274

H. Schofield, *The Philosophy of Education*: *An Introduction*,
London: Allen & Unwin, 1972, pp.44–48, 171–73.
A.C. Hogg & J.K. Foster, *Understanding Teaching Procedures*,
Victoria: Cassell Australia, 1973, pp.130ff.
J.A. Passmore, *The Philosophy of Teaching*, London:
Duckworth, 1980, pp.121, 132, 139–40, 142, 207.

Training

J. Dewey, *Democracy and Education*, New York: Macmillan,
1916, pp.15–16.
G. Ryle, *The Concept of Mind*, London: Hutchinson, 1949,
Ch.2; also 'Teaching and Training', in R.S. Peters
(ed.), *The Concept of Education*, London: Routledge &
Kegan Paul, 1967, pp.14–16.
M.P. Crawford, 'Concepts of Training', in R.M. Gagné (ed.),
Psychological Principles in System Development, New York:
Holt, Rinehart & Winston, 1963, 301–41.
R.S. Peters, *Ethics and Education*, London: Allen & Unwin,
1966, pp.32–35; also 'What is an Educational Process?'
in R.S. Peters (ed.), *The Concept of Education*, London:
Routledge & Kegan Paul, 1967, pp.14–16.
J.P. Powell, 'Educating, Training and Drilling', *Australian
Journal of Higher Education*, II, 3 (December, 1966),
230–37.
T.F. Green, *The Activities of Teaching*, Tokyo: McGraw-Hill
Kogakusha, 1971, pp.23–29.
L.R. Perry, 'Training and Education', *Proceedings of the
Philosophy of Education Society of Great Britain*, VI, 1
(January, 1972), 7–29.
H. Schofield, *The Philosophy of Education*: *An Introduction*,
London: Allen & Unwin, 1972, Ch. 3.
J.A. Passmore, *The Philosophy of Teaching*, London:
Duckworth, 1980, pp.41–43, 121, 133.

Conditioning

E.R. Hilgard & D.G. Marquis, *Conditioning and Learning*,
rev. G.A. Kimble, New York: Appleton–Century–Crofts,
1961.
R.S. Peters, *Ethics and Education*, London: Allen & Unwin,
1966, pp.41–2; also 'What is an Educational Process?',
in R.S. Peters (ed.), *The Concept of Education*, London:
Routledge & Kegan Paul, 1967, pp.12–14.
G.N.A. Vesey, 'Conditioning and Learning', in R.S. Peters
(ed.), *The Concept of Education*, London: Routledge &
Kegan Paul, 1967, pp.61–72.
J. Langer, *Theories of Development*, New York: Holt,
Rinehart & Winston, 1969, pp.56–64.
T.F. Green, *The Activities of Teaching*, Tokyo: McGraw-Hill
Kogakusha, 1971, pp.25–26.
H. Schofield, *The Philosophy of Education*: *An Introduction*,

London: Allen & Unwin, 1972, Ch.9.

H. Lehman, 'Conditioning and Learning', *Educational Theory*, XXIV, 2 (Spring, 1974), 161-69.

J.E. McClellan, *Philosophy of Education*, Englewood Cliffs, N.J.: Prentice-Hall, 1976, pp.133-39.

Chapter 5: *Indoctrination*

C. Washburne, 'Indoctrination Versus Education', *The Social Frontier*, II (April, 1936), 213; reprinted as 'Arguments against Indoctrination', in J.S. Brubacher (ed.), *Eclectic Philosophy of Education*[2], Englewood Cliffs, N.J.: Prentice-Hall, 1962, pp.339-40.

J. Wilson, 'Education and Indoctrination', in T.H.B. Hollins (ed.), *Aims in Education : the Philosophic Approach*, Manchester U.P., 1964, pp.24-46; Reply 'Adolescents into Adults', by R.M. Hare, pp.47-70.

B.G. Mitchell, 'Indoctrination', in *The Fourth R : Durham Report on Religious Education*, London: S.P.C.K., 1970, Appendix B.

I.A. Snook (ed.), *Concepts of Indoctrination*, London: Routledge & Kegan Paul, 1972.

G. Paske, 'Education and the Problem of Indoctrination', in M.A. Raywid (ed.), *Philosophy of Education 1972*, Proceedings of the Twenty-eighth Annual Meeting of the Philosophy of Education Society, Edwardsville, Ill.: Philosophy of Education Society, 1972, 92-100.

H. Rosemont, jr., 'On the Concept of Indoctrination', *Studies in Philosophy and Education*, VII, 3 (Spring, 1972), 226-37; reply 'Indoctrination and the Indoctrinated Society', by I.A. Snook, VIII, I (Summer, 1973), 52-61.

A.G. Davey, 'Education or Indoctrination?', *Journal of Moral Education*, II, 1 (October, 1972), 5-15; reply by R.G. Woods, 75-76; rejoinder by A.G. Davey, II, 3 (June, 1973), 287-88.

E.L. Pincoffs, 'On Avoiding Moral Indoctrination', in J.F. Doyle (ed.), *Educational Judgments*, London : Routledge & Kegan Paul, 1973, pp.59-73; reply 'Indoctrination and Justification', by K. Baier, pp.74-89.

A.C. Kazepides, 'The Grammar of "Indoctrination"', in B.S. Crittenden (ed.), *Philosophy of Education 1973*, Proceedings of the Twenty-ninth Annual Meeting of the Philosophy of Education Society, Edwardsville, Ill.: Philosophy of Education Society, 1973, 273-83.

P. Smart, 'The Concept of Indoctrination', in G. Langford & D.J. O'Connor (eds.), *New Essays in the Philosophy of Education*, London: Routledge & Kegan Paul, 1973, pp.33-46.

L. Smith, 'Indoctrination and Intent', *Journal of Moral*

Education, III, 3 (June, 1974), 229-33; reply by H. Marantz, IV, 2 (February, 1975), 117-30.

H. Meynell, 'Moral Education and Indoctrination', *Journal of Moral Education*, IV, 1 (October, 1974), 17-26.

W. Feinberg, 'Limits of the Indoctrination Debate: Or How Ordinary can Ordinary Language Philosophy be and still be Philosophy?', in R. Pratte (ed.) *Philosophy of Education 1975*, Proceedings of the Thirty-first Annual Meeting of the Philosophy of Education Society, San Jose, Calif.: Philosophy of Education Society, 1973, 209-21.

R. Barrow, *Plato*, *Utilitarianism and Education*, London: Routledge & Kegan Paul, 1975, pp.114-33.

R.G. Woods & R.St.C. Barrow, *An Introduction to the Philosophy of Education*, London: Methuen, 1975, Ch.4.

J.E. McClellan, *Philosophy of Education*, Englewood Cliffs, N.J.: Prentice-Hall, 1976, pp.139-51.

R.C. Page, 'Epistemology, Psychology and Two Views of Indoctrination', in J.R. Coombs (ed.), *Philosophy of Education 1979*, Proceedings of the Thirty-fifth Annual Meeting of the Philosophy of Education Society, Normal, Ill.: Philosophy of Education Society, 1980, pp.77-86.

M.A. Raywid, 'The Discovery and Rejection of Indoctrination', *Educational Theory*, XXX, 1 (Winter, 1980), 1-10.

Chapter 6: *Autonomy, Community and Education*

D.L. Norton, 'Life, Death, and Moral Autonomy', *Centennial Review*, X, 1 (Winter, 1966), 1-12; also 'The Rites of Passage from Dependence to Autonomy', *School Review*, LXXIX, 1 (November, 1970), 19-41; *Personal Destinies : a philosophy of ethical individualism*, Princeton U.P., 1976.

G. Dworkin,, 'Acting Freely', *Nous*, IV, 4 (November, 1970), 367-83; also 'Autonomy and Behaviour Control', *Hastings Center Report*, VI, 1 (February, 1976), 23-28; 'Moral Autonomy', in H.T. Engelhardt, Jr. & D. Callahan (eds.), *Morals, Science and Sociality*, New York: Hastings Center, 1978, pp.156-71.

S.I. Benn & W.L. Weinstein, 'Being Free to Act and Being a Free Man', *Mind*, LXXX (April 1971), 194-211; reply, 'Freedom as the Non-restriction of Options', by W.A. Parent, LXXXIII (July, 1974), 432-34; rejoinder, 435-38; also S.I. Benn, 'Freedom, Autonomy and the Concept of a Person', *Proceedings of the Aristotelian Society*, LXXVI (1975—76), 109-30.

R.S. Downie & E. Telfer, 'Autonomy', *Philosophy*, XLVI (October, 1971), 293-301.

A.M. Quinton, 'Authority and Autonomy in Knowledge', *Proceedings of the Philosophy of Education Society of Great Britain*, V, 2 (July, 1971), 201-15; reply,

'Autonomy and Education', by M.M. Coady, *Cambridge Journal of Education*, IV, 3 (Michaelmas Term 1974), 114–22.

L.I. Krimerman, 'Autonomy: a new paradigm for research', in L.G. Thomas (ed.), *Philosophical Redirection of Educational Research*, NSSE 71st Yearbook, Part I, Chicago: NSSE, 1972, pp.327–55.

R.F. Dearden, E. Telfer & R.M. Hare, Symposium: 'Autonomy as an Educational Ideal', in S.C. Brown (ed.), *Philosophers Discuss Education*, London: Macmillan, 1975, pp.3–42; for comment, see J. Wilson, *Philosophy and Practical Education*, Routledge & Kegan Paul, 1977, Ch.7.

S.D. Ross, *The Nature of Moral Responsibility*, Detroit: Wayne State University Press, 1973, Ch.6.

R.S. Peters, 'Freedom and the Development of the Free Man', in J.F. Doyle (ed.), *Educational Judgments*, London: Routledge & Kegan Paul, 1973, pp.119–42; response and development, 'The Idea of a Free Man', by J. Feinberg, pp.143–69.

S. Hampshire, *Freedom of Mind*[2], Princeton U.P., 1975.

R. Barrow, *Moral Philosophy for Education*, London: Allen & Unwin, 1975, Ch.8.

D.C. Phillips, 'The Anatomy of Autonomy', *Educational Philosophy and Theory*, VII, 2 (October, 1975), 1–12; reply by N.C. Burbules, IX, 2 (October, 1977), 57–62.

J. Spring, *A Primer of Libertarian Education*, New York: Free Life Editions, 1975, Ch.2.

B. Gibbs, *Freedom and Liberation*, Sussex University Press, 1976, esp. Chs. 6, 7.

B. Crittenden, 'Autonomy as an Educational Ideal', in K.A. Strike & K. Egan (eds.), *Ethics and Educational Policy*, London: Routledge & Kegan Paul, 1978, pp.105–26.

J.A. Passmore, *The Philosophy of Teaching*, London: Duckworth, 1980, Ch.9.

Chapter 7: *The Justification of Education*

W.H. Kilpatrick, *Philosophy of Education*, London: Macmillan, 1951.

I.S. Steinberg, 'On the Justification of Guidance', *Educational Theory*, XIV, 3 (July, 1964), 216–23.

P.S. Wilson, 'In Defence of Bingo', *British Journal of Educational Studies*, XV, 1 (February, 1967), 5–27; reply by R.S. Peters, XV, 2 (June, 1967), 188–94.

R.F. Dearden, 'Happiness and Education', *Proceedings of the Philosophy of Education Society of Great Britain*, II (1967–68); reprinted with slight alterations in R.F. Dearden, P.H. Hirst & R.S. Peters (eds.), *Education and the Development of Reason*, London: Routledge & Kegan Paul, 1972, pp.95–112.

P.A. White, 'Education, Democracy and the Public Interest', *Proceedings of the Philosophy of Education Society of Great Britain*, V, 1 (January, 1971), 7-28; reprinted in R.S. Peters (ed.), *The Philosophy of Education*, London: O.U.P., 1973, pp.217-38.

E. Telfer, 'Education and Self-Realisation', *Proceedings of the Philosophy of Education Society of Great Britain*, VI, 2 (July, 1972), 216-34.

A.J. Watt, 'Conceptual Analysis and Educational Values', *Educational Philosophy and Theory*, V, 2 (October, 1973) 27-38.

P. Herbst, 'Work, Labour and University Education', in R.S. Peters (ed.), *The Philosophy of Education*, London: O.U.P., 1973, 58-74.

B.S. Crittenden, *Education and Social Ideals*, Ontario: Canada Longman Ltd., 1973, Ch.II.

C. Bereiter, *Must We Educate?*, Englewood Cliffs, N.J.: Prentice-Hall, 1973.

J.P. White, *Towards a Compulsory Curriculum*, London: Routledge & Kegan Paul, 1973.

R.S. Downie, E.M. Loudfoot & E. Telfer, *Education and Personal Relationships*, London: Methuen, 1974, Chs. 3, 4.

J. Holt, *Escape from Childhood*, New York: E.P. Dutton, 1974; also *Instead of Education: Ways to Help People do Things Better*, New York: E.P. Dutton, 1976.

J. Burgess, 'Value in Education', *Proceedings of the Philosophy of Education Society of Great Britain*, VIII, 1 (January, 1974), 7-29; reply by L.B. Daniels, VIII, 2 (July, 1974), 237-50.

P.J. Higginbotham, 'Aims of Education', in D.I. Lloyd (ed.), *Philosophy and the Teacher*, London: Routledge & Kegan Paul, 1976, pp.41-52.

J.E. McClellan, *Philosophy of Education*, Englewood Cliffs, N.J.: Prentice-Hall, 1976, Ch.5.

R.K. Elliott, 'Education and Justification', *Proceedings of the Philosophy of Education Society of Great Britain*, XI (July, 1977), 7-27.

Chapter 8: *The Institutionalisation of Education*

A.S. Neill, *Summerhill* (1960), Harmondsworth: Penguin, 1968; commentaries in M. Lawson (ed.), *Summerhill: For and Against*, Sydney: Angus & Robertson, 1973; R.L. Hopkins, 'Freedom and Education: the Philosophy of Summerhill', *Educational Theory*, XXVI, 2 (Spring 1976), 188-213.

P. Goodman, *Compulsory Miseducation* (rev. edn., 1964), Harmondsworth: Penguin, 1971.

J. Ohliger & C.McCarthy, *Lifelong Learning or Lifelong Schooling*, Syracuse University Publications in Continuing Education and ERIC Clearing House on Adult Education,1971.

L. Althusser, 'Ideology and Ideological State Apparatuses (Notes towards an Investigation)', in *Lenin and Philosophy*, ET, London: New Left Books, 121-72.

J. Holt, *What do I do Monday?*, London: Pitman, 1971; also *Freedom and Beyond*, New York: Dutton, 1972; *Instead of Education: Ways of Helping People to do Things Better*, New York: Dutton, 1976.

A. Graubard, *Free the Children: Radical Reform and the Freeschool Movement*, New York. Pantheon, 1972.

E.B. Nyquist & G.R. Hawes (eds.), *Open Education : A Sourcebook for Parents and Teachers*, New York: Bantam, 1972.

R. Hutchings, 'The Great Anti-School Campaign', in *Great Ideas Today, 1972*, Chicago: Encyclopedia Brittanica, 1972.

P. Freire, *Pedagogy of the Oppressed*, tr. M.B. Ramos, New York: Herder & Herder, 1970; also *Cultural Action for Freedom*, Harmondsworth: Penguin, 1971; *Education for Critical Consciousness*, New York: Seabury, 1973; *Education : the Practice of Freedom*, Harmondsworth: Penguin, 1976.

C.J. Troost (ed.), *Radical School Reform : Critique and Alternatives*, Boston: Little, Brown & Co., 1973.

P. Buckman (ed.), *Education Without Schools,* London: Souvenir Press, 1973.

A. Gartner, C. Greer & F. Riessman (eds.), *After Deschooling, What?*, New York: Harper & Row, 1973.

I. Lister (ed.), *Deschooling*, Cambridge U.P., 1974.

R. Sharp & A. Green, *Education and Social Control : A Study in Progressive Primary Education*, London: Routledge & Kegan Paul, 1975.

W.K. Richmond, *Education and Schooling*, London: Methuen, 1975.

D. Nyberg (ed.), *The Philosophy of Open Education*, London: Routledge & Kegan Paul, 1975.

S. Bowles & H. Gintis,, *Schooling in Capitalist America*, New York: Basic Books, 1976.

R. Barrow, *Radical Education: a critique of preschooling and deschooling*, London: Martin Robinson, 1978.

Chapter 9: *Neutrality in Education*

H.C. Hand, *Neutrality in Social Education: an aspect of the educator's world of make-believe*, Los Angeles: College Press, 1940.

R.H. Ennis, 'The "Impossibiity" of Neutrality in Teaching', *Harvard Educational Review*, XXIX, 2 (1959), 128-36; reprinted as 'Is it Impossible for the Schools to be Neutral?' in B.O. Smith & R.H. Ennis (eds.), *Language and Concepts in Education*, Chicago: Rand McNally, 1961, pp.102–11; reply by D.C. Hoffman, *Educational Theory*, XIV, 3 (July, 1964), 182–85; also an interchange between R.H. Ennis and M.A. Raywid, in *Studies in Philosophy and Education*, II, 1 (Winter, 1961–62), 86–96, 96–103.

E.L. French, D.P. Derham, D.H. Monro, E.J. Stormon, & J.D. McCaughey, Symposium: 'Objectivity and Neutrality in Public Education', in E.L. French (ed.), *Melbourne Studies in Education 1963*, Melbourne U.P., 1964, pp.3–80.

J.E. McClellan, 'The Politicising of Educational Theory: A Re-evaluation', in G.L. Newsome, Jr. (ed.), *Philosophy of Education 1968*, Proceedings of the Twenty-fourth Annual Meeting of the Philosophy of Education Society, Edwardsville, Ill.: Philosophy of Education Society, 1968, pp.94–105; reply by R.D. Heslep, pp.109–13.

L. Stenhouse, 'Open-Minded Teaching', *New Society*, XIV (24 July), 1969, 126–28; also 'Controversial Value Issues in the Classroom', in W.G. Carr (ed.), *Values and the Curriculum*, A Report of the Fourth International Curriculum Conference, Washington, D.C.: National Educational Association Center for the Study of Instruction, 1970, pp.103–15; 'The Idea of Neutrality', *Times Educational Supplement*, 2959 (4 February, 1972), 2; and 'Neutrality as a Criterion in Teaching: the Working of the Humanities Curriculum Project', in M. Taylor (ed.), *Progress and Problems in Moral Education*, Slough: National Foundation for Educational Research, 1975.

R.P. Wolff, *The Ideal of the University*, Boston: Beacon Press, 1969, pp.69–76.

J. Eckstein, 'Is it Possible for the Schools to be Neutral?' *Educational Theory*, XIX, 4 (Fall, 1969), 337–46; reply by R.H. Ennis, 347–56.

Schools Council/Nuffield Foundation, *The Humanities Project: An Introduction*, London: Heinemann, 1970, Sect. 4.

J. Elliott, 'The Concept of the Neutral Teacher', *Cambridge Journal of Education*, I, 2 (Easter, 1971), 60–67; reply by C. Bailey, 'Rationality, Democracy and the Neutral Teacher', 68–76; updated versions of these papers appear as J. Elliott, 'The Values of the Neutral Teacher' and C. Bailey, 'Neutrality and Rationality in Teaching', in D. Bridges & P. Scrimshaw (eds.), *Values and Authority in Schools*, London: Hodder & Stoughton, 1975, pp.103–19, 121–34; see also C. Bailey, 'Teaching by discussion and the Neutral Teacher', *Proceedings of the Philosophy of Education Society of Great Britain*, VII, 1 (January, 1973), 26–38; reply by J. Elliott, 'Neutrality, Rationality and the Role of the Teacher', 39–65.

'Open-ended Discussion: Procedural Neutrality', in *Religious Education in Secondary Schools*, Schools Council Working Paper 36, London: Evans/Methuen Educational, 1971, Ch.XII, pp.88–91.

W.P. Metzger, 'Institutional Neutrality: an appraisal', in F. Machlup *et al.*, *Neutrality or Partisanship: a dilemma of academic institutions*, New York: Carnegie Foundation for the Advancement of Teaching, 1971, pp.38–62.

R.L. Simon, 'The Concept of a Politically Neutral University', in V. Held, K. Nielsen & C. Parsons (eds.), *Philosophy & Political Action*, New York: O.U.P., 1972, pp.217–33.

J. Hipkin, 'Neutrality as a Form of Commitment', *Trends in Education*, 26 (April, 1972), 9–13.

I.A. Snook, 'Neutrality and the Schools', *Educational Theory*, XXII, 3 (Summer, 1972), 278–85.

B. Crittenden, *Education and Social Ideals*, Ontario: Longman Canada Ltd., 1973, Ch.IV.

R.L. Holmes, 'University Neutrality and ROTC', *Ethics*, LXXXIII, 3 (April, 1973), 177–95.

K. Strike, 'The Logic of Neutrality Discussions: Can a University be Neutral?', *Studies in Philosophy and Education*, VIII, 1 (Summer, 1973), 62–91.

M. Warnock, J. Norman & A. Montefiore, Symposium: 'The Neutral Teacher', in S.C. Brown (ed.), *Philosophers Discuss Education*, London: Macmillan, 1975, Part IV.

S.E. Nordenbo, 'Pluralism, Relativism and the Neutral Teacher', *Journal of Philosophy of Education*, XII (1978), 129–39.

M.A. Oliker, 'Neutrality and the Structure of Educational Institutions', in J.R. Coombs (ed.), *Philosophy of Education 1979*, Proceedings of the Thirty-fifth Annual Meeting of the Philosophy of Education Society, Normal, Ill.: Philosophy of Education Society, 1980, pp.252–259; reply by J. Palermo, pp.260–63.

R.F. Dearden, 'Education and Politics', *Journal of Philosophy of Education*, XIV, 2 (November, 1980), 149–56; idem, 'Controversial Issues and the Curriculum', *Journal of Curriculum Studies*, XIII, 1 (1981).

Chapter 10: *Equality, Schooling and Education*

R. Wollheim & I. Berlin, Symposium: 'Equality', *Proceedings of the Aristotelian Society*, LVI (1955–56), 281–300, 301–26.

L. Bryson et al. (eds.), *Aspects of Human Equality*, New York: Harper, 1956.

G.L. Abernethy (ed.), *The Idea of Equality*: an *Anthology*, Richmond, Va: John Knox Press, 1959.

B.P. Komisar & J.R. Coombs, 'The Concept of Equality in Education', *Studies in Philosophy and Education*, III, 3, (Fall, 1964), 223–44; reply 'Equality and Sameness', by C.J.B. Macmillan & 'Equality as Uniqueness', by P.H. Phenix, III, 4 (Winter, 1964–65), 320–32, 332–35; rejoinder, 'Too Much Equality', IV, 2 (Fall, 1969), 263–71.

J.R. Lucas, 'Against Equality', *Philosophy*, XL (October,

1965), 296-307; also 'Equality in Education', in
B.R. Wilson (ed.), *Equality, Education and Society*,
London: Allen & Unwin, 1975, and 'Against Equality
Again', *Philosophy*, LII (July, 1977), 255-80.
J. Wilson, *Equality*, London: Hutchinson, 1966.
A.F. Kleinberger, 'Reflections on Equality in Education',
Studies in Philosophy and Education, V, 3 (Summer, 1967),
293-340; reply by J.R. Perry, V, 4 (Fall, 1967), 433-45;
rejoinder by Kleinberger, VI, 2, (Spring, 1968), 209-25.
J.S. Coleman, et al., *Equality of Educational Opportunity*,
Washington: U.S. Department of Health, Education and
Welfare, 2 vols. 1968; also J.S. Coleman, 'Rawls,
Nozick and Educational Equality', *The Public Interest*, 43
(Spring, 1976), 121-28; see further F. Mosteller &
D.P. Moynihan (eds.), *On Equality of Educational
Opportunity*, New York: Random House, 1972 (reviewed by
G.E. Grant in *Harvard Educational Review*, XLII, 1
(February, 1972), 109-25).
G.W. Mortimore, 'An Ideal of Equality', *Mind*, LXXVII (April,
1968), 222-42.
Special Issue: 'Equality of Educational Opportunity',
Harvard Educational Review, XXVIII, 1 (Winter, 1968).
J. Charvet, 'The Idea of Equality as a Substantive Principle
of Society', *Political Studies*, XVII, 1 (1969), 1-13.
T.F. Green, 'Equal Educational Opportunity: the Durable
Injustice', in R.D. Heslep (ed.), *Philosophy of Education
1971*, Proceedings of the Twenty-seventh Annual Meeting of
the Philosophy of Education Society, Edwardsville, Ill.:
Philosophy of Education Society, 121-43 (reply by
M. Greene, 144-149); also 'The Dismal Future of Equal
Educational Opportunity', in T.F. Green (ed.),
Educational Planning in Perspective, Guildford, U.K.:
IPC Science and Technology Press, 1971.
H. Bedau (ed.), *Justice and Equality*, Englewood Cliffs,
N.J.: Prentice-Hall, 1971.
C. Jencks, *et al.*, *Inequality: a reassessment of the effect
of the family on schooling in America*, New York: Basic
Books, 1972; see also review issue *Harvard Educational
Review*, XLIII, 1 (February, 1973); and D.M. Levine &
M.J. Bene (eds.), *The 'Inequality' Controversy :
Schooling and Distributive Justice*, New York: Basic
Books, 1975.
Special Issue: 'Equality and Education', *Oxford Review of
Education*, I, 1 (1975); see also R.M. Hare, 'Opportunity
for What? Some Remarks on Current Disputes about
Equality in Education', III, 3 (1977), 207-16.
B. Crittenden, *Education and Social Ideals*, Ontario:
Longman Canada Limited, 1973, Ch. VI; also 'Equality
and Education', in J.V. D'Cruz & P.J. Sheehan (eds.), *The
Renewal of Australian Schools: a Changing Perspective in
Educational Planning*, Melbourne: A.C.E.R., 1978,
pp.225-41.

R.H. Ennis, 'Equality of Educational Opportunity', *Educational Theory*, XXVI, 1 (Winter, 1976), 3-18; reply by G. Harvey, XXVIII, 2 (Spring, 1978), 147-51.

J. Raz, 'Principles of Equality', *Mind*, LXXXVII (July, 1978), 321-42.

N.C. Burbules & A.L. Sherman, 'Equal Educational Opportunity: Ideal or Ideology?', in J.R. Coombs (ed.), *Philosophy of Education 1979*, Proceedings of the Thirty-fifth Annual Meeting of the Philosophy of Education Society, Normal, Ill.: Philosophy of Education Society, 1979, pp.105-14; reply by T.F. Green, pp.115-20.

Chapter 11: *Intelligence*

L. Terman & M. Merrill, *Measuring Intelligence*, London: Harrap, 1937.

A.E. Heim, *The Appraisal of Intelligence*, London: Methuen, 1954.

P.E. Vernon, *Intelligence and Attainment Tests*, University of London Press, 1960; also *Intelligence: Heredity and Environment*, San Francisco: W.H. Freeman & Co., 1979.

W. Mays, 'A Philosophical Critique of Intelligence Tests', *Educational Theory*, XVI, 4 (October, 1966), 318-32.

S. Vandenberg, 'The Nature and Nurture of Intelligence', in D.C. Glass (ed.), *Genetics*, New York: Rockefeller U.P. & Russell Sage Foundation, 1968, pp.3-58; replies by I.I. Gottesman, pp.59-68; and D. Rosenthal, pp.69-78.

R. Cancro (ed.), *Intelligence: Genetic and Environmental Influences*, New York: Grune & Stratton, 1971.

H.J. Eysenck, *Race, Intelligence & Education*, London: Temple Smith, 1971 (published in the U.S. as *The I.Q. Argument: Race, Intelligence & Education*, New York: Library Press, 1971).

K. Richardson & D. Spears (eds.), *Race, Culture and Intelligence*, Harmondsworth: Penguin, 1972.

A.R. Jensen, *Genetics and Education*, New York: Harper & Row, 1972; also *Educability and Group Differences*, New York: Harper & Row, 1973; *Educational Differences*, London: Methuen, 1973. Jensen's major paper, 'How Much Can We Boost I.Q. and Scholastic Achievement?', reprinted in *Genetics and Education*, was the subject of replies in two issues of *The Harvard Educational Review*, XXXIX, 2 & 3 (Spring & Summer, 1969).

H.J. Butcher & D.E. Lomax (eds.), *Readings in Intelligence*, London: Methuen, 1972.

R. Herrnstein, *I.Q. in the Meritocracy*, Boston: Little Brown & Co., 1973.

L. Kamin, *The Science and Politics of I.Q.*: Potomac, Md.: Erlbaum Associates, 1974.

M. Martin, 'Equal Education, Native Intelligence and

Justice', *Philosophical Forum* (Boston), VI, 1 (Fall, 1974), 29–39; and N. Daniels, 'I.Q., Intelligence and Educability', 56–69.

F.L. Jones, 'Obsession Plus Pseudo–Science Equals Fraud: Sir Cyril Burt, Intelligence, and Social Mobility', *Australian and New Zealand Journal of Sociology*, XVI, 1 (March, 1980), 48–55.

Chapter 12: *Curriculum Choice*

H. Taba, *Curriculum Development*, *Theory and Practice*, New York: Harcourt Brace & World, 1962.

P.H. Phenix, *Realms of Meaning*, New York: McGraw–Hill, 1964; for criticism, see C.E. Goss, 'A Critique of the Ethical Aspects of Phenix's Curriculum Theory', *Educational Theory*, XVII (1967), 40–47.

R.S. Peters, *Ethics and Education*, London: Allen & Unwin, 1966, Ch.V; for criticism see K. Robinson, 'Worthwhile Activities and the Curriculum', *British Journal of Educational Studies*, XXII (1974), 34–55.

H.S. Broudy, D.P. Dryer & B.S. Crittenden, 'Philosophy and the Curriculum', in B.S. Crittenden (ed.), *Philosophy and Education*, Toronto: Ontario Institute for Studies in Education, 1967, pp.59–77.

J.R. Martin (ed.), *Readings in the Philosophy of Education: A Study of Curriculum*, Boston: Allyn & Bacon, 1970; see further, Martin's paper 'Needed: A Paradigm for Liberal Education', in J.F. Soltis, *Philosophy and Education*, Eightieth Yearbook of the National Society for the Study of Education, Chicago: NSSE, 1981, Part I, pp.31–59.

M. Levit (ed.), *Curriculum*, Urbana: University of Illinois Press, 1971.

D.C. Phillips, 'The Distinguishing Features of Forms of Knowledge', *Educational Philosophy and Theory*, III, 2 (October, 1971), 27–35.

H. Sockett, 'Curriculum Aims and Objectives: Taking a Means to an End', *Proceedings of the Philosophy of Education Society of Great Britain*, VI, 1 (January, 1972); reply by M. Skilbeck, 62–72; also Sockett, *Designing the Curriculum*, London: Open Books, 1976.

J. Holt, *Freedom and Beyond*, New York: E.P. Dutton, 1972, Ch.6.

A. Truefitt & P. Newell, 'Abolishing the Curriculum and Learning Without Exams', in P. Buckman (ed.), *Education Without Schools*, London: Condor, 1973, pp.75–83.

D.R. Olson, 'What is Worth Knowing and What Can be Taught?', *School Review*, LXXXII, 1 (November, 1973), 27–43.

J.P. White & K. Thompson, *Curriculum Development: a Dialogue*, London: Pitman, 1975; for criticism of White see M. Bonnett, 'Authenticity, Autonomy and the Compulsory Curriculum', *Cambridge Journal of Education*,

VI, 3 (Michaelmas, 1976), 107-21; reply by White, 122-26.

E.W. Eisner & E. Vallance (eds.), *Conflicting Conceptions of Curriculum*, Berkeley, Calif.: McCutchan, 1974.

M.E. Downey & A.V. Kelly, *Theory and Practice of Education: An Introduction*, London: Harper & Row, 1975, Ch.6.

W. Pinar, *Curriculum Theorising*, Berkeley, Calif.: McCutchan, 1975.

R. Pring, *Knowledge and Schooling*, London: Open Books, 1976.

D.I. Lloyd (ed.), *Philosophy and the Teacher*, London: Routledge & Kegan Paul, 1976, Chs. 6, 7.

'Cognitive Structures and Forms of Knowledge', in I.S. Steinberg (ed.), *Philosophy of Education 1977*, Proceedings of the Thirty-third Annual Meeting of the Philosophy of Education Society, Urbana: Ill.: Philosophy of Education Society, 1977, pp.203-14 (reply by L. Waks, pp.215-21).

C. Jencks, 'Forms of Knowledge & Knowledge of Forms', in *Rationality, Education and the Social Organisation of Knowledge*, London: Routledge & Kegan Paul, 1977.

K. Harris, *Education and Knowledge : the Structured Misrepresentation of Reality*, London: Routledge & Kegan Paul, 1979.

M. Matthews, *Epistemology and Education*, Sussex, U.K.: Harvester, 1981.

Chapter 13: *Competition*

W.W. Willoughby, 'The Ethics of the Competitive Process', *American Journal of Sociology*, VI, 2 (September, 1900), 145-76.

J. Harvey *et al.*, *Competition: a Study in Human Motive*, London: Macmillan, 1917.

F.C. Sharp, 'Some Problems of Fair Competition', *International Journal of Ethics*, XXXI, 2 (January, 1921), 123-45.

F.H. Knight, *The Ethics of Competition*, London: Allen & Unwin, 1935, see also C.E. Ayres 'The Ethics of Competition', *International Journal of Ethics*, XLVI, 3 (April, 1936) 364-70.

M.A. May & L.W. Doob, *Competition and Co-operation: A Report*, Bulletin No. 25, New York: Social Science Research Council, 1937.

Anonymous, 'Competition', *Times Educational Supplement* (27 July, 1951), 640; replies: 10 August, 640.

C.A. Bucher, 'Must there always be a Winner?', *Education Digest*, XXI, 2 (October, 1955), 25-27.

R. Lynn, 'The Value of Unhappiness', *Times Educational Supplement* (8 February, 1957), 154; replies: 15 February, 205; 22 February, 238; and rejoinder: 8

March, 311.

M. Mead (ed.), *Co-operation and Competition among Primitive Peoples*, enlarged edn., Boston: Beacon Press, 1961.

C. Weinberg, 'The Price of Competition', *Teachers College Record*, LXVII, 2 (November, 1965), 106–14.

C. Fink, 'Some Conceptual Difficulties in the Theory of Social Conflict', *Journal of Conflict Resolution*, XII, 4 (December, 1968), 412–60.

G.B. Thompson, 'Effects of Co-operation and Competition on Pupil Learning', *Educational Research*, XV, 1 (November, 1972), 28–36.

L.R. Perry, *Competition in Education*, Montefiore Memorial Lecture, Froebel Education Institute, 16 May, 1972; also 'Competition and Co-operation', *British Journal of Educational Studies*, XXIII, 2 (June, 1975), 127–34.

W.E. Brownson, 'The Structure of Competition in the School and its Consequences', in M.J. Parsons (ed.), *Philosophy of Education 1974*, Proceedings of the Thirtieth Annual Meeting of the Philosophy of Education Society, Edwardsville, Ill.: Philosophy of Education Society, 1974, pp.227–40.

C. Bailey, 'Games, Winning and Education', *Cambridge Journal of Education*, V, 1 (Lent, 1975), 40–50; replies by D. Aspin, 51–61, K. Thompson, V, 3 (Michaelmas, 1975), 150–52, and F. Dunlop, 153–60.

F. Dunlop, 'Competition in Education', *Cambridge Journal of Education*, VI, 3 (Michaelmas, 1976), 127–34; reply by M. Fielding, 134–38.

Chapter 14: *Assessment and Grading*

D.A.T. Gasking, *Examinations and the Aims of Education*, Melbourne U.P. 1945.

B. Hoffman, *The Tyranny of Testing*, New York: Macmillan, 1962.

J. Holt, *How Children Fail*, London: Pitman, 1964; also *The Underachieving School*, New York: Pitman, 1969, pp.53–70; *What do I do Monday?*, New York: Dell, 1970, Ch.27; *Instead of Education : Ways to Help people Do Things Better*, New York: E.P. Dutton, 1976.

National Union of Students (U.K.), *Executive Report on Examinations*, submitted to November Conference, London: NUS, 1968.

B.S. Bloom, 'Some Theoretical Issues Relating to Educational Evaluation', in R.W. Tyler (ed.), *Educational Evaluation: New Roles, New Means*, Sixty-eighth Yearbook of the National Society for the Study of Education, Chicago: NSSE, 1969, Pt. II, pp.26–50;

R.L. Thorndike, s.v. 'Marks and Marking Systems!, in R.L. Ebel (ed.), *Encyclopedia of Educational Research*[4], New York: Macmillan, 1969, pp.759–66; also (ed.),

Educational Measurement [2], Washington: American Council on Education, 1971.

D. McIntyre, 'Assessment and Teaching', in D. Rubinstein &: C. Stoneman (eds.), *Education for Democracy*, Harmondsworth: Penguin, 1970.

K.R. Conklin, 'Educational Evaluation and Intuition', *Educational Forum*, XXXIV, 3 (March, 1970), 323-32; also 'Due Process in Grading: Bias and Authority', *School Review*, LXXXI, 1 (November, 1972), 85-95.

R. Cox, 'Traditional Examinations in a Changing Society', *Universities Quarterly*, XXVII, 2 (Spring 1973), 200-16.

A. Flew, 'Teaching and Testing', in B. Crittenden (ed.), *Philosophy of Education 1973*, Proceedings of the Twenty-ninth Annual Meeting of the Philosophy of Education Society, Edwardsville, Ill.: Philosophy of Education Society, 1973, pp.201-12; replies by J. Soltis, 213-16; and L.J. Waks, 217-24.

W. Guy & P. Chambers, 'Public Examinations and Pupils Rights', *Cambridge Journal of Education*, III, 2 (Easter, 1973), 83-89; reply by C. Wringe, III, 3 (Michaelmas, 1973), 169-73; rejoinder, IV, 3 (Michaelmas, 1974), 47-50.

Australian Union of Students, *Examination Papers*, Melbourne: Australian Union of Students, July 1974; also *The Student's Work Situation: Assessment*, Melbourne: Australian Union of Students, July, 1974.

C.M.L. Miller & M. Parlett, *Up to the Mark - a Study of the Examination Game*, London: Society for Research into Higher Education, 1974.

C.T. Husbands, 'Ideological Bias in the Marking of Examinations', *Research in Education*, XV (1976), 17-38.

R. Montgomery, *A New Examination of Examinations*, London: Routledge & Kegan Paul, 1978.

C.A. Wringe, 'Teaching, Monitoring and Examining', *Educational Philosophy and Theory*, XII, 2 (October, 1980).

Chapter 15: *Children and Rights*

H. Lane, *Talks to Parents and Teachers*, London: Allen & Unwin, 1928.

A.J. Kleinfeld, 'The Balance of Power Among Infants, their Parents and the State, I, II & III', *Family Law Quarterly*, IV, 3 (September, 1970), 319-50; IV, 4 (December, 1970), 409-43; and V, 1 (March, 1971), 63-107.

F. Schrag,, 'The Right to Educate', *School Review*, LXXIX (May, 1971), 359-78; also 'Rights Over Children', *Journal of Value Inquiry*, VII, 2 (Summer, 1973), 96-105; 'The Child's Status in the Democratic State', *Political Theory*, III, 4 (November, 1975), 441-57 (replies by

C. Cohen, 158–63, and E. Spitz, IV, 3 (August, 1976), 372–74); 'Justice and the Family', *Inquiry*, XIX, (1976), 193–208; and 'From Childhood to Adulthood: Assigning Rights and Responsibilities', in K.A. Strike & K. Egan (eds.), *Ethics and Educational Policy*, London: Routledge & Kegan Paul, 1978, pp.61–78.

M. Vaughan (ed.), *Rights of Children*. Report of the First National Conference on Children's Rights, 1972, London: NCCL, 1972.

J. Hall (ed.), *Children's Rights*, London: Panther/New York: Praeger, 1972.

Special Issue: 'Rights of Children: Human and Legal', *Peabody Journal of Education*, L (January, 1973), 87–141.

A.E. Wilkerson (ed.), *The Rights of Children*, Philadelphia: Temple U.P., 1973.

B. Bandman, 'Do Children have any Natural Rights? A Look at Rights and Claims in Legal, Moral and Educational Discourse', in B. Crittenden (ed.), *Philosophy of Education 1973*, Proceedings of the Twenty-ninth Annual Meeting of the Philosophy of Education Society, Edwardsville, Ill.: Philosophy of Education Society, 1973, pp.234–46.

C. Sachs, 'Children's Rights', in J.W. Bridge *et al.*, (eds.), *Fundamental Rights*, London: Sweet & Maxwell, 1973, pp.31–42.

V.L. Worsfold, 'A Philosophical Justification for Children's Rights', *Harvard Educational Review*, XLIV, 1 (February, 1974), 142–57; and idem, 'Justifying Students' Rights: John Rawls and Competing Conceptions', in J.R. Coombs (ed.), *Philosophy of Education 1979*, Proceedings of the Thirty-fifth Annual Meeting of the Philosophy of Education Society, Normal, Ill.: Philosophy of Education Society, 1979, p.323–33; reply by B. Bandman, pp.334–38.

J. Holt, *Escape from Childhood: the Needs and Rights of Children*, New York: E.P. Dutton, 1974.

H. Sockett, 'Parents' Rights', in D. Bridges & P. Scrimshaw (eds.), *Values and Authority in Schools*, London: Hodder & Stoughton, 1975, pp.38–59.

D.N. MacCormick, 'Children's Rights: A Test Case for Theories of Rights', *Archiv für Rechts- und Sozialphilosophie*, LXII, 3 (1976), 305–16.

O. O'Neill & W. Ruddick (eds.), *Having Children : Philosophical and Legal Reflections on Parenthood*, New York: O.U.P., 1979.

I.A. Snook, & C.J. Lankshear, *Education and Rights*, Melbourne U.P., 1979.

H. Cohen, *Equal Rights for Children*, Totowa, N.J.: Littlefield, Adams & Co., 1980.

L.D. Houlgate, *The Child & the State: A Normative Theory of Juvenile Rights*, Baltimore, Md.: Johns Hopkins U.P., 1980.

W. Aiken & H. LaFollette (eds.), *Whose Child? Children's*

Rights, *Parental Authority*, *and State Power*, Totowa, N.J.: Littlefield, Adams & Co., 1980.

C.A. Wringe, *Children's Rights*: *a philosophical study*, London: Routledge & Kegan Paul, 1981.

Chapter 16: *Education and Authority*

K.D. Benne, *A Conception of Authority*: *An Introductory Study*, New York: Teachers' College, Columbia University, 1943; also 'Authority in Education', *Harvard Educational Review*, XL, 3 (August, 1970), 385-410; for critiques, see M. Terris, 'On Authority and Education', in M.A. Raywid (ed.), *Philosophy of Education 1972*, Proceedings of the Twenty-eighth Annual Meeting of the Philosophy of Education Society, Edwardsville, Ill.: Philosophy of Education Society, 1972, 246-55; L.J. Hetenyi, 'On Authority: the Thoughts of Kenneth D. Benne', *Educational Theory*, XIII, 2 (Spring, 1973), 177-84.

S. de Grazia, 'The Principle of Authority in its Relation to Freedom', *Educational Forum*, XV, 2 (January, 1951), 145-55; also 'Authority and Rationality', *Philosophy*, XXVII (April, 1952), 99-109; 'What Authority is *Not*', *American Political Science Review*, LIII, 2 (June, 1959), 321-31.

F. La T. Godfreys, 'The Idea of Authority', *Hermathena*, XCI (1958), 3-19.

C.J. Friedrich (ed.), *Nomos I*: *Authority*, Cambridge, Mass.: Harvard U.P., 1958.

J. Day, 'Authority' *Political Studies*, XI (1963), 257-71.

S.I. Benn, s.v. 'Authority' in P. Edwards (ed.), *The Encyclopedia of Philosophy*, New York: Collier Macmillan, 1967, Vol. I, pp.215-18.

H. Arendt, 'What is Authority?' in *Between Past and Future* : *Eight Exercises in Political Thought*, New York: Viking Press, 1958, pp.91-141.

R.P. Wolff, *In Defence of Anarchism*, New York: Harper Torchbooks, 1970; for replies, see M.D. Bayles, 'In Defense of Authority', *Personalist*, LII, 4 (Autumn, 1971), 755-59; L.H. Perkins, 'On Reconciling Autonomy and Authority', *Ethics*, LXXXII, 2 (January, 1972), 114-23; D. Sobers, 'Wolff's Logical Anarchism', ibid., 173-76; S. Bates, 'Authority and Autonomy', *Journal of Philosophy*, LXIX, 7 (6 April, 1972) 175-79; R.F. Ladenson, 'Wolff on Legitimate Authority', *Philosophical Studies*, XXIII (1972), 376-84; J.H. Reiman, *In Defense of Political Philosophy*: *A Reply to Robert Paul Wolff 'In Defense of Anarchism'*, New York: Harper Torchbooks, 1972.

D.R. Bell, 'Authority', in G.N.A. Vesey (ed.), *The Proper Study*, Royal Institute of Philosophy Lectures, 1969-70,

London: Macmillan, 1971, pp.190–203.

J. Holt, *Freedom and Beyond*, New York: E.P. Dutton, 1972, Ch.5.

B.S. Crittenden, *Education and Social Ideals*, Ontario: Longman Canada Ltd., 1973, Ch.III.

M.E. Downey & A.V. Kelly, *Theory and Practice of Education*: *An Introduction*, London: Harper & Row, 1975, Ch.V.

R. Pring, 'In Defence of Authority – or how to keep knowledge under control' in D. Bridges and P. Scrimshaw (eds.), *Values and Authority in Schools*, London: Hodder & Stoughton, 1975, pp.20–37.

M. Coady, 'Authority – A Natural Necessity?', in D. Cave (ed.), *Problems in Education: a philosophical approach*, Australia: Cassell, 1976, 155–68.

D.N. Silk, 'Aspects of the Concept of Authority in Education' *Educational Theory*, XXVI, 3 (Summer, 1976), 271–78.

R.B. Harris (ed.), *Authority : a philosophical analysis*, Ala.: University of Alabama Press, 1976.

Chapter 17: *Schooling, Education and Discipline*

H. Lane, *Talks to Parents and Teachers*, intro. A.A. David, London: Allen & Unwin, 1928, Part 2: 'Thoughts on the Self-Determination of Small People'.

G.V. Sheviakov & F. Redl, *Discipline for Today's Children and Youth*, rev. edn., Washington. D.C.: National Education Association, Department of Supervision and Curriculum Development, 1956.

A.G. & E.H. Hughes, *Education*: *Some Fundamental Problems*, London: Longmans, 1960, Ch.8.

A.S. Neill, *Summerhill* (1960), Harmondsworth: Penguin, 1968; cf. R. Hemmings, *Fifty Years of Freedom*: *A Study of the Development of the Ideas of A.S. Neill*, London: Allen & Unwin, 1972.

W.J. Gnagey, *Controlling Classroom Misbehaviour*, Washington, D.C.: National Education Association, Association of Classroom Teachers, 1965; also *The Psychology of Discipline in the Classroom*, New York: Macmillan, 1968.

L. Stenhouse (ed.), *Discipline in Schools*: *a symposium*, Oxford: Pergamon Press, 1967.

P.H. Hirst & R.S. Peters, *The Logic of Education*, London: Routledge & Kegan Paul, 1970, pp.125–28.

P.S. Wilson, *Interest and Discipline in Education*, London: Routledge & Kegan Paul, 1971, esp. Ch.3.

J. Holt, *Freedom and Beyond*, New York: E.P. Dutton, 1972, Ch.7.

G.C. Penta, 'Discipline: a Theoretical Perspective', *Educational Theory*, XXVII, 2 (Spring, 1977), 137–40; reply by M. Smith, XV, 2 (Spring, 1978), 154–55.

Chapter 18: *Education and Punishment*

E.L. Pincoffs, *The Rationale of Legal Punishment*, New York: Humanities Press, 1966.

E.H. Madden, R. Handy & M. Farber (eds.), *Philosophical Perspectives on Punishment*, Springfield, Ill.: C.C. Thomas. 1968.

H.L.A. Hart, *Punishment and Responsibility*, London: O.U.P., 1968.

H.B. Acton (ed.), *The Philosophy of Punishment*, London: Macmillan, 1969.

J. Feinberg, *Doing and Deserving*, Princeton U.P., 1970.

H. Morris (ed.), *Guilt and Shame*, Belmont, Calif.: Wadsworth, 1971.

G. Ezorsky (ed.), *Philosophical Perspectives on Punishment*, Albany, N.Y.: State University of New York Press, 1972.

J. Gerber & P. McAnany (eds.), *Contemporary Punishment: Views, Explanations and Justifications*, South Bend: University of Notre Dame Press, 1972.

P. Moore, 'Perspectives on Punishment', *Proceedings of the Philosophy of Education Society of Great Britain*, VIII, 1 (January, 1974), 76-102; reply by P.S. Wilson,, 108-34.

M. Goldinger (ed.), *Punishment and Human Rights*, Cambridge, Mass.: Schenkman, 1974.

K. Baier, 'The Strengths and Limits of the Theory of Retributive Punishment', *Philosophic Exchange*, II, 3 (Summer, 1977), 37-53.

M. Foucault, *Discipline and Punish: The Birth of the Prison*, New York: Pantheon, 1978.

J.G. Murphy, *Retribution, Justice, and Therapy*, Dordrecht: Reidel, 1979.

Chapter 19: *Moral Education*

E. Durkheim, *Moral Education: A Study in the theory and application of the sociology of education* (1925), trans. E.K. Wilson & H. Schnurer, Glencoe, Ill.: The Free Press, 1961.

J. Piaget, *The Moral Judgment of the Child*, trans. M. Gebain, London: Routledge & Kegan Paul, 1932.

M.L. Hoffmann, 'Moral Development' in P. Mussen (ed.), *Carmichael's Manual of Child Psychology*, New York: Wiley, 1970, Vol.II, pp.261-360.

T.R. & N.F. Sizer (eds.), *Moral Education: Five Lectures*, Cambridge, Mass.: Harvard U.P., 1970.

D. Wright, *The Psychology of Moral Behaviour*, Harmondsworth: Penguin, 1971.

T. Mischel (ed.), *Cognitive Development and Epistemology*, New York: Academic Press, 1971.

J. Wilson, *Practical Methods of Moral Education*, London: Heinemann, 1972; idem, *The Assessment of Morality*,

Slough: NFER, 1973; idem, *A Teacher's Guide to Moral Education*, London: Geoffrey Chapman, 1973.

B. Chazan & J.F. Soltis (eds.), *Moral Education*, New York: Teachers College Press, 1973.

G. Langford & D.J. O'Connor (eds.), *New Essays in the Philosophy of Education*, London: Routledge & Kegan Paul, 1973.

Special Issue: 'Moral Education', *Monist*, LVIII, 4 (October, 1974).

R.S. Peters, *Psychology and Ethical Development*, London: Allen & Unwin, 1974, Part II.

P.H. Hirst, *Moral Education in a Secular Society*, London: University of London Press/National Children's Home, 1974.

Special Issue: 'Moral Education', *Phi Delta Kappan*, LVI, 10 (June, 1975).

M. Taylor (ed.), *Progress and Problems in Moral Education*, Slough: NFER, 1975.

J.E. McClellan, *Philosophy of Education*, Englewood Cliffs, N.J.: Prentice-Hall, 1976, Ch.5.

A.J. Watt, *Rational Moral Education*, Melbourne University Press, 1976.

B.S. Crittenden, *Bearings in Moral Education*, Hawthorn, Vic.: ACER, 1978.

A.V. Kelly & M. Downey, *Moral Education : Theory and Practice*, London: Harper, 1978.

D.B. Cochrane, C.M. Hamm & A.C. Kazepides (eds.), *The Domain of Moral Education*, New York: Paulist Press, 1979.

C.M. Beck, 'The Reflective Approach to Values Education', in J.F. Soltis (ed.), Eightieth Yearbook of the National Society for the Study of Education, Chicago: NSSE, 1981, pp.185–211.

Chapter 20: *Religious Education*

H. Loukes, *New Ground in Christian Education*, London: SCM, 1965.

A.G. Wedderspoon (ed.), *Religious Education 1944-1984*, London: Allen & Unwin, 1966.

C.D. Hardie, 'Religion and Education', *Educational Theory*, XVIII, 2 (July, 1968), 199–223.

The Fourth R: Report of the Commission on Religious Education in Schools 1970 (Durham Report), London: National Society/S.P.C.K.: 1970).

D.Z. Phillips, 'Philosophy and Religious Education', *British Journal of Educational Studies*, XVIII, 1 (February, 1970), 5–17, reply by P.H. Hirst, 2 (June, 1970), 213–15.

R.J. Neuhaus, 'No More Bootleg Religion in the Classroom', in R.D. Heslep (ed.), *Philosophy of Education 1971*, Proceedings of the Twenty-seventh Annual Meeting of the Philosophy of Education Society, Edwardsville, Ill.:

Philosophy of Education Society, 1971, pp.95-110; replies by P.H. Phenix, pp.111-15, and S.W. Itzkoff, pp.116-20.

Schools Council, *Religious Education in Secondary Schools* (Working Paper, No. 36), London: Evans/Methuen Educational, 1971; also *Religious Education in Primary Schools* (Working Paper, No. 44), London: Evans/Methuen Educational, 1972. See commentary in D.G. Kibble, 'Religious Studies and the Quest for Truth', *British Journal of Educational Studies*, XXIV, 2 (June, 1976), 144-54.

M.H. Stannus,'Knowledge of God: the Paradox of Christian Education', *Educational Philosophy and Theory*, IV, 1 (March, 1972), 29-46.

W.D. Hudson, 'Is Religious Education Possible?' in G. Langford & D.J. O'Connor (eds.), *New Essays in the Philosophy of Education*, London: Routledge & Kegan Paul, 1973, pp.167-96.

R. Barrow, 'Religion in Schools', *Educational Philosophy & Theory*, VI, 1 (March, 1974), 49-57.

D.J. Vold, 'A Case for Religion in the Public Schools', *Educational Theory*, XXIV, 1 (Winter, 1974), 99-109.

N. Smart & D. Harden (eds.), *New Movements in Religious Education*, London: Temple Smith, 1975.

N. Curry, 'Why Religion?' in D. Cave (ed.), *Problems in Education: A Philosophical Approach*, Victoria: Cassell Australia, 1976, Ch.11.

R. Marples, 'Is Religious Education Possible?', *Journal of Philosophy of Education*, XII (1978), 81-91; reply by D. Attfield, 93-97.

R. Holley, *Religious Education and Religious Understanding: An Introduction to the Philosophy of Religious Education*, London: Routledge & Kegan Paul, 1978.

D.C. Meakin, 'The Justification of Religious Education', *British Journal of Religious Education*, II, 2 (1979), 49-55.

P. Gardner,, 'Religious Education: in defence of non-commitment', *Journal of Philosophy of Education*, XIV, 2 (November, 1980), 157-68.

R. Jackson (ed.), *World Religions and Developing Minds*, London: John Murray, 1981.

Abernethy, G.L., 282
Acton, H.B., 292
Aiken, W., 289
Althusser, L., 280
Andris, J.F., 272
Anthony, A.S., 273
Aquinas, T., 1, 264
Arendt, H., 290
Ariès, P., 208
Aristotle, 14, 21, 33, 122
Arnold, M., 150
Arnstine, D., 272
Aspin, D., 287
Atkinson, R.F., 131
Attfield, D., 294
Austin, J., 219
Austin, J.L., 38-9
Ausubel, D.P., 229, 273, 274
Ayres, C.E., 286

Babeuf, F.-N.E., 130
Baier, K., 276, 292
Bailey, C., 281, 287
Bambrough, R., 246
Bandman, B., 271, 289
Bantock, G.H., 274
Barrow, R.St.C., 270, 277, 278, 280, 294
Bartley, III, W.W., 268
Bates, S., 290
Bayles, M.D., 290
Beck, C.M., 271, 293
Bedau, H.A., 242, 283
Beery, R.C., 229
Bell, D.R., 290
Bene, M.J. 283

Benn, S.I., 123-4, 130, 232, 277, 290
Benne, K.D., 290
Benson, T.L., 67
Bentham, J., 88
Bereiter, C., 279
Berger, P.L., 161
Berlin, I., 282
Binet, A. 132, 137-8, 143
Block, N.J., 137, 139, 140, 142, 143-4
Bloom, B.S., 146, 181, 191, 287
Bonnett, M., 70, 285
Boring, E.G., 133, 140
Bower, G.H., 272
Bowers, W., 194
Bowles, S., 144, 280
Broad, C.D., 9
Broudy, H.S., 269, 272, 285
Brown, R.R., 242
Brown, S.C., 273
Brown, S.I., 274
Browne, D.E., 130
Brownson, W.E., 287
Brubacher, J.S., 55
Bruner, J.S., 45
Bryson, L., 282
Buber, M., 271
Bucher, C.A., 286
Buckman, P., 280
Burbules, N.C., 161, 278, 284
Burch, R.W., 254
Burgess, J., 279
Burt, C., 132-3, 136, 145, 193

Butcher, H.J., 144, 284
Butterworth, B., 193

Campbell, W.J., 274
Camus, A., 262
Cancro, R., 284
Cave, D., 22
Chadwick, J., 186
Chalmers, A.F., 160, 255
Chamberlin, L.J., 228
Chambers, P., 288
Charvet, J., 242, 283
Chazan, B., 293
Clark, C., 273
Coady, M.M., 278, 291
Cochrane, D.B., 293
Cohen, C., 289
Cohen, H., 289
Cohen, M., 131
Coleman, J.S., 125, 283
Conklin, K.R., 288
Coombs, J.R., 282
Cooper, B.A., 271
Cooper, D.E., 59-61, 242
Cox, C.B., 184, 186, 188, 193
Cox, R., 189, 288
Crawford, M.P., 275
Crittenden, B.S., 131, 255,
    278, 279, 282, 283, 285,
    291, 293
Curry, N., 294
Curtis, B.L., 273

Daniels, L.B., 279
Daniels, N., 129, 285
Davey, A.G., 276
Day, J.P., 241, 290
D'Cruz, J.V., 131, 283
de Grazia, S., 290
De Nicola, D.R., 194
Dearden, R.F., 70-2, 74, 163-
    5, 173, 270, 274, 278, 282
Derham, D.P., 281
Dettman, H.W., 228
Deutscher, I., 173
Dewey, J., ix, 7-9, 275
Dietl, P., 38-9
Dobbin, J.E., 192
Doob, L.W., 286
Dorfman, D.D., 145
Downey, M.E., 286, 291, 293
Downie, R.S., 241, 271, 277,
    279

Dray, W.H., 16, 20, 21
Dryer, D.P., 285
Ducasse, C.J., 269
Dunlop, F.N., 270, 287
Dupuis, A., 9, 270
Durkheim, E., 292
Dworkin, G., 137, 139-40, 142-
    4, 277

Earwaker, J., 271
Eastwood, G.R., 270
Eckstein, J., 281
Edel, A., 270
Edison, T.A., 174
Edwards, P., 267
Eisner, E.W., 286
Elliott, E.C., 189
Elliott, J., 281
Elliott, R.K., 271, 273, 279
Ellul, J., 35, 39, 97
Ennis, R.H., 159, 280, 281,
    284
Eysenck, H.J., 137, 141, 284
Ezorsky, G., 292

Farber, M., 292
Farley, R.J., 229
Feher, F., 130
Feinberg, J., 130, 278, 292
Feinberg, W., 270, 277
Fielding, M., 162-3, 165-6,
    172, 287
Fingarette, H., 242
Fink., C., 287
Fitzgibbons, R.E., 271
Fleming, A., 241
Fleming, K.G., 273
Flew, A.G.N., 232, 241, 288
Foot, P., 255
Foster, J.K., 274, 275
Foucault, M., 292
Frankena, W.K., 270
Frankfurt, H., 75, 255
Freeman, H., 28-9, 59, 62,
    270
Freire, P., 34, 102, 270, 280
French, E.L., 281
Frey, R.G., 254
Friedlander, B.Z., 47
Friedrich, C.J., 290
Froebel, F.W., 14, 73

Gagné, R.M., 274
Gallie, W.B., 172
Galton, F., 132, 136, 143, 145
Gardner, J.W., 130
Gardner, P., 294
Gartner, A., 280
Gasking, D.A.T., 287
Gerber, J., 292
Gibbs, B., 278
Gintis, H., 96, 101, 280
Gnagey, W.J., 222, 291
Godfreys, F.LaT., 290
Goldinger, M., 292
Goldman, A.H., 131
Goodman, P., 206-7, 279
Gordon, D., 161
Goss, C.E., 285
Gottesman, I.I., 284
Grant, G.E., 283
Graubard, A., 280
Gray, J., 172
Green, A., 52, 280
Green, T.F., 272, 273, 274, 275, 283, 284
Greenberg, P., 169
Greene, M., 283
Greer, C., 280
Gribble, J., 56-8
Griffiths, A.P., 256
Grimmitt, M.H., 268
Gross, B.R., 131
Guildford, J.P., 140
Guttchen, R.S., 271
Guy, W., 288

Hall, J., 289
Hamlyn, D.W., 39, 51, 80, 272, 273
Hamm, C.M., 293
Hampshire, S., 278
Hand, H.C., 280
Handy, R., 292
Hanson, J., 272
Harden, D., 294
Hardie, C.D., 9, 188, 192-3, 293
Hare, R.M., 276, 278, 283
Harris, C.K., 39, 101, 286
Harris, J., 116
Harris, P.E., 242
Harris, R.B., 291

Hart, H.L.A., 61, 173, 203-5, 208, 230, 232, 292
Hart, W.A., 272
Hartnett, A., 172
Hartog, P., 189
Harvey, G., 283
Harvey, J., 286
Hastings, J.T., 194
Hawes, G.R., 280
Hedman, C.G., 101
Hegel, G.W.F., 236, 242
Heim, A.E., 284
Heller, A., 130
Herbart, J.F., 9
Herbst, P., 271, 279
Herrnstein, R.J., 143, 284
Heslep, R.D., 281
Hetenyi, L.J., 290
Heywood, J., 193
Hick, J., 268
Hickman, D.C., 267
Higginbotham, P.J., 279
Hilgard, E.R., 272, 275
Hipkin, J., 282
Hirsch, J., 143
Hirst, P.H., 24-6, 28, 30, 32, 39, 64, 67, 86, 96-7, 149-54, 156, 158, 160, 266, 269, 270, 271, 291, 293
Hodgson, D.H., 241
Hoffman, B., 287
Hoffman, D.C., 281
Hoffman, M.L., 292
Hogg, A.C., 227, 274, 275
Holley, R., 294
Holmes, R.L., 282
Holt, J., 39, 273, 279, 280, 285, 287, 289, 291
Hopkins, R.L., 279
Houlgate, L.D., 289
Hudson, W.D., 294
Hughes, A.G. 291
Hughes, E.H., 291
Hulme, T.E., 222
Hult, Jr., R.E., 22
Hurst, B.C., 272
Husbands, C.T., 288
Hutchings, R., 280
Huxley, A., 88
Hyman, R.T., 159-60, 272, 274

Illich, I., 93-6, 99-101, 161, 229

Jackson, R., 294
Jahoda, M., 187
James, R.L., 187
Jeanne Marie, Sr., 229
Jencks, C., 283, 286
Jensen, A.R., 141, 144-5, 284
Jones, F.L., 285
Joyner, R., 53

Kamin, L., 284
Kant, I., 69-70, 85, 235, 241, 247, 262
Karier, C.J., 143
Katz, M.S., 101
Katzner, L.I., 130
Kaufman, A.S., 270
Kazepides, A.C.(T.), 228-9, 276, 293
Keating, J.W., 172-3
Keisler, E.R., 274
Kelly, A.V., 286, 291, 293
Kibble, D.G., 294
Kidder, J., 242
Kilpatrick, W.H., 7, 278
Klein, J.T., 271
Kleinberger, A.F., 283
Kleinfeld, A.J., 288
Kleinig, J.I., 21, 89, 101, 116, 130-1, 173, 208-9, 229, 241-2, 255
Knight, F.H., 286
Kogan, N., 141
Koh, J.C.-W., 272, 273
Kohlberg, L., 250-2, 255-6
Kolakowski, L., 102
Komisar, B.P., 38, 272, 282
Kovesi, J., 10, 67, 192, 267
Krathwohl, D.R., 159
Krimerman, L.I., 278
Kuethe, J.L., 229
Kuhn, T.S., 151

La Mancusa, K.C., 228
Ladenson, R.F., 290
LaFollette, H., 289
Lane, H., 79, 288, 291
Langer, J., 39, 275
Langford, G., 269, 270, 271, 272, 293

Lankshear, C.J., 289
Lawson, M., 279
Lawson, R.M., 272
Lehman, H., 276
Levine, D.M., 283
Levit, M., 285
Lister, I., 161, 280
Lloyd, D.I., 286
Lloyd Thomas, D.A., 131
Lomax, D.E., 284
Loudfoot, E.M., 279
Loukes, H., 293
Lucas, C.J., 269
Lucas, J.R., 282
Luckman, T., 161
Luther, M., 100-1
Lynn, R., 169, 286
Lyons, D., 131, 173, 209, 241

MacCormick, D.N., 289
MacIntyre, A.C., 172
Mack, E., 116
Maclean, C., 79-80
Macmillan, C.J.B., 271, 272, 282
Madaus, G.F., 194
Madden, E.H., 292
Madsen, Jr., C.H., 229
Madsen, C.K., 229
Makarenko, A.S., 230
Malcolm, N., 267
Mann, H., 130
Marantz, H., 277
Marietta, Jr., D.E., 241
Marples, R., 294
Marquis, D.G., 275
Marshall, J.D., 31-3, 242
Martin, J.R., 39, 161, 285
Martin, M., 284
Marx, K., 1-2, 70, 119
Masia, B.B., 159
Matthews, M., 286
May, M.A., 286
Mays, W., 284
McAnany, P., 292
McCaughey, J.D., 281
McCarthy, C., 279
McClellan, J.E., 67, 270, 272, 273, 276, 277, 279, 281, 293
McHugh, W.J., 52
McIntyre, D., 288

McPeck, J.E., 161
Mead, M., 287
Meakin, D.C., 294
Mechanic, D., 193
Merrill, M., 284
Merton, R.K., 39
Metzger, W.P., 281
Meynell, H., 277
Mill, J.S., 65, 69-70, 72-3,
    75, 79, 83, 88-9, 92, 118,
    192, 195-6, 197-202, 206-9
Mischel, T., 292
Mitchell, B.G., 276
Monro, D.H., 281
Montefiore, A., 106-7, 282
Montessori, M., 225
Montgomery, R., 288
Moore, G.E., ix-x, 9
Moore, P., 292
Morris, H., 241, 292
Mortimore, G.W., 283
Mosteller, F., 283
Moynihan, D.P., 283
Murphy, J.G., 241-2, 292

Naish, M., 172
Nash, P., 229, 242
Neely, W., 70
Neill, A.S., 279, 291
Nelson, B.K., 159
Nelson, T.W., 271
Nelson, V.I., 144
Neuhaus, R.J., 293
Neurath, O., 74
Newell, P., 285
Nicholson, L.J., 270
Nordenbo, S.E., 282
Norman, J., 282
Norton, D.L., 277
Nozick, R., 219
Nyberg, D., 280
Nyquist, E.B., 280

Oakeshott, M., 91, 92
O'Connor, D.J., 8, 293
O'Hagan, T., 131
Ohliger, J., 279
Oliker, M.A., 282
Olson, D.R., 285
O'Neill, O., 289
Oppenheim, A.N., 187

Page, R.C., 277
Palermo, J., 282
Parent, W.A., 277
Paske, G., 276
Passmore, J.A., 22, 269, 272,
    274, 275, 278
Paton, K.R., 208
Pavlov, I., 50
Penta, G.C., 291
Perkins, L.H., 290
Perry, J.R., 283
Perry, L.R., 275, 287
Peters, R.S., ix, 7-10, 12-
    21, 56, 83-7, 96-7, 101,
    120-2, 130, 219, 241, 249,
    255, 269, 270, 271, 272,
    275, 278, 285, 291, 293
Petrie, H.G., 39
Phenix, P.H., 282, 285, 294
Phillips, D.C., 161, 278, 285
Phillips, D.Z., 293
Piaget, J., 21, 292
Pidgeon, D., 186
Pieron, H., 189
Pinar, W., 286
Pincoffs, E.L., 242, 276, 292
Pitcher, G.W., 255
Plato, 1-5, 14, 21, 132, 244
Pollock, L., 241
Poole, R.G., 73-5
Popper, K., 262
Postman, N., 274
Powell, A., 193
Powell, J.P., 274, 275
Prescott, A.J., 228
Price, H.H., 268
Price, K., 67, 269
Pring, R., 159, 269, 286, 291

Quine, W.V.O., 152, 160
Quinton, A.M., 219, 277

Rawls, J., 128-9, 251
Ray, W.E., 274
Raywid, M.A., 277, 281
Raz, J., 284
Redl, F., 291
Reiman, J.H., 290
Reimer, E., 91
Rescher, N., 89, 209
Rhodes, E.C., 189

Richards, C., 274
Richardson, K., 284
Richmond, W.K., 280
Riegle, R.P., 273
Riessman, F., 280
Ritchie, D.G., 173-4
Robinson, K., 21-2, 285
Rogers, C.R., 271, 272
Rose, S., 143
Rosemont, H. jr., 276
Rosenthal, D., 284
Ross, S.D., 278
Rozycki, E.G., 242
Ruddick, W., 289
Russell, B., 7
Russell, D.H., 52
Ryle, A., 190, 193
Ryle, G., 13, 21, 28, 31-4,
    134-5, 143, 254, 271, 274,
    275

Sachs, C., 289
Santayana, G., 260
Savage, C.W., 192
Schain, R.L., 227
Sheffler, I.,viii, 8-9, 35-7,
    270, 273
Sheid, D.E., 242
Schofield, H., 275
Schrag, F., 208, 288-9
Schumacher, E.F., 101
Scriven, M., 191
Sharp, F.C., 286
Sharp, R., 52, 280
Sheehan, P., 57-60, 283
Sherman, A.L., 284
Sheviakov, G.V., 291
Shockley, W., 141
Shulman, L.S., 274
Silk, D.N., 291
Simmel, G., 173
Simon, B., 144
Simon, R.L., 256, 282
Simon, T., 132
Singer, P., 245
Sizer, N.F., 292
Sizer, T.R., 292
Skilbeck, M., 285
Skinner, B.F., 50-1, 88
Smart, N., 257-8, 294
Smart, P., 276
Smith, A.Z., 192

Smith, L., 276
Smith, M., 291
Smith, M.B.E., 229
Smith, P.G., 270
Smith, W.C., 267
Snook, I.A., 60-1, 67, 276,
    282, 289
Snow, C.P., 150
Sobers, D., 290
Sockett, H., 159, 285, 289
Soltis, J.F., 269, 270, 288,
    293
Spahr, M., 208
Spearman, C., 133, 140, 143
Spears, D., 284
Spelman, E.V., 241
Spencer, H., 9, 23, 69, 173,
    201, 209
Spitz, E., 289
Spring, J., 271, 278
Stannus, M.H., 294
Starch, D., 189
Steinberg, I.S., 278, 286
Stenhouse, L., 281, 291
Stevenson, C.L., 236
Stirner, M., 23
Stocker, M.A.G., 116, 241,
    255
Stormon, E.J., 281
Strike, K., 282
Szabados, B., 254

Taba, H., 39, 285
Taylor, M., 293
Telfer, E., 241, 271, 277,
    278, 279
Terman, L., 284
Terris, M., 290
Thatcher, A., 271
Thompson, G.B., 287
Thompson, K., 269, 285, 287
Thorndike, R.L., 287
Troost, C.J., 280
Truefitt, A., 285
Tunnell, D.R., 242
Turnbull, C.M., 89, 208
Tyler, R., 39

Urmson, J.O., 192, 254

Vallance, E., 286
Vandenberg, D., 272

Vandenberg, S., 284
Vaughan, M., 289
Vernon, P.E., 284
Vesey, G.N.A., 275
Vold, D.J., 294
von Wright, G.H., 192, 241
Vredevoe, L.E., 221, 227-8

Waks, L., 286, 288
Wallach, M.A., 141
Walton, J., 229
Wardle, D., 198
Warnock, M., 131, 282
Washburne, C., 276
Watson, A.J., 51
Watson, G., 80
Watt, A.J., 160, 256, 279, 293
Weber, M., 213, 219
Webster, S.W., 224-5
Wedderspoon, A.G., 293
Weinberg, C., 287
Weingartner, C., 274
Weinstein, W.L., 277
Wertheimer, A., 10
White, J.P., 143, 154-8, 161, 269, 273, 279, 285, 286

White, M., 267
White, P.A., 279
Whitehead, A.N., 7
Wilkerson, A.E., 289
Willoughby, W.W., 286
Wilson, J., 88, 159, 222, 227, 255, 267, 271, 276, 278, 283, 292
Wilson, J.R.S., 241
Wilson, P.S., 240, 278, 291, 292
Wittgenstein, L., ix-x, 1, 5, 9-10, 151, 219, 258
Wolff, R.P., 175-6, 281, 290
Wollheim, R., 282
Woods, J., 20
Woods, R.G., 40, 276, 277
Worsfold, V.L., 289
Wright, D., 242, 292
Wringe, C.A., 288, 290

Yates, A., 186
Young, G., 219
Young, M., 130

Zingg, R.M., 79

agency, 26, 65, 69-70, 81, 87
assessment, 46, 94, 175-94
    appraisal and, 175-6,
      191-2
    continuous, 181, 185,
      190-1
    criticism and, 175-6,
      191
    defined, 176
    evaluation and, 175-6
    grading and, 94, 97,
      175, 177, 180, 185-
      8, 191-2
    importance of, 179
    marking and, 175, 177-
      8, 185-6, 188
    measurement and, 175,
      178, 192
    ordering and, 175-7
    scoring and, 175, 177-8
    sorting and, 175-7
    summative and formative,
      191
    see also examinations
authoritarianism, 18, 23-4,
  58, 94, 96, 170, 210, 217-
  18, 222
    personal and structu-
      ral, 218
authority, 24, 34, 48, 52, 66,
  96, 115, 152, 158, 210-19,
  221-2, 231, 253, 262
    autonomy and, 216-17,
      219
    de facto, 115, 211, 213,
      216-17

    de jure, 152, 211-18
    epistemic, 66, 152,
      211-18
    institutionalisation
      of, 214-15
    power and, 211, 215,
      218
    see also punishment
autonomy, 15, 18-19, 44, 47-
  9, 51, 65, 69-79, 82-3,
  88-9, 118-19, 146-8, 170-
  2, 178, 180, 197, 201,
  206, 210, 224-5, 235, 244,
  250-1, 261, 267
    authenticity and, 76,
      80-1
    community and, 76-8,
      249-50
    heteronomy and, 72-3,
      75-6
    rationality and, 70-1
    self-determination and,
      70-1, 196, 200-2,
      206
    self-examination and,
      74-6
    self-origination and,
      70, 73-4
    value of, 88-9
    see also authority

behaviourism, 35-7, 39, 147-8

care, 16, 22, 250, 252-3
childhood, concepts of,
  196-202

children
    feral, 13, 75
    see also childhood, concepts of; rights.
coercion, 23, 93-5
    compulsion and, 94-5; see also competition; curriculum; schooling
community, 4, 76-8, 82; see also autonomy
competition, 10, 17-18, 46-7, 60, 94, 97, 127-8, 162-73, 179-80, 184-5, 253
    conflict and, 164
    co-operation and, 77, 164, 168, 170, 172, 180
    defined, 163-6
    emulation and, 163
    essential contestability of, 162-3, 165-6, 172
    optional and compulsory, 165, 167
    rivalry and, 60, 163-4
    socialist, 165-6
    structural and motivational, 164-7
    with oneself, 163
conditioning, 41-2, 48, 50-51
    classical (respondent), 50-1, 54
    operant (instrumental), 50-1
co-operation, 46-7, 227, 254
    see also competition
curriculum, 19, 39, 69, 85, 94, 97, 110-12, 115, 118-19, 146-61, 175, 191, 194, 226, 253-4, 257
    compulsory, 154-5, 157-8, 184; see also schooling, compulsory
    content of, 10, 15-16, 18, 86, 118-19, 148-59
    defined, 146, 159
    hidden, 24, 34, 66, 94, 115, 158, 161
    integrated, 150
    lesson and, 146
    objectives of, 146-8, 159-60

syllabus and, 97, 146
    see also moral education; religious education.

discipline, 185, 220-9, 238
    as chastisement, 223-4, 238
    as control, 220-1, 223-5
    as self-discipline, 224-6
    concepts of, 221-4
    learning and, 226
    punishment and, 223
    techniques of, 222-3
    see also moral education
discovery methods; see learning
doctrines; see indoctrination, content-criterion of
drilling, 23, 41, 47-9, 58; see also education

education, 1, 6, 9-20, 23, 31, 42, 44, 52, 54-5, 78, 81-90, 92, 96-7, 115, 146-8, 175, 178-9, 182-3, 185-6, 257
    as initiation, 17, 19, 91
    concepts of, 11-15, 180
    content- v. child-centred, 12, 148
    discriminatory v. non-discriminatory concepts of, 11-14
    drilling and, 47-8, 52-3
    erudition and, 15
    instruction and, 44
    instrumental v. non-instrumental accounts of, 12-14, 16, 84-6, 90
    justification of, 16, 81-9
    liberal, 149
    personal development and, 14-15, 18-19, 69-70, 87-8, 93, 97,

146, 202
task *v.* achievement
  accounts of, 13, 29
teaching and, 24
training and, 48-50
see also agency; know-
  ledge; punishment;
  schooling, education
  and
equality, 100, 111, 117-29
compensatory justice
  and, 127-8
formal, 119-22
mathematical, 117-18
of consideration, 123-4
of humanity, 122-3
of opportunity, 124-8,
  170
presumptive, 120-2
procedural justice and,
  128-9
quality and, 124
examinations, 50, 175, 178,
  181-91
reliability of, 148,
  179, 181, 188-90
tests and, 105, 175,
  178
validity of, 148, 179,
  181-8, 190
see also assessment

happiness, 51, 88-9

ideology, 14, 17, 21, 37-8,
  66, 71, 78-9, 94-5, 97-8,
  102, 110, 112, 114, 129,
  164, 170, 188, 197, 215,
  217-18
individualism, 4, 70, 73,
  166, 170-1, 180, 216
indoctrination, 23, 29, 41,
  42-4, 48, 54-67, 94, 185,
  202, 210, 224-5, 254
brainwashing and, 57-8,
  105
censorship and, 58
conditioning and, 54
content-criterion of,
  55-8, 65-6
education and, 54, 65-6
intentions-criterion

of, 55, 60-2, 64, 66
methods-criterion of,
  55, 57-61, 66
neutrality and, 110,
  114
normativeness of, 54-5,
  61, 64-7
outcomes-criterion of,
  55, 59-60, 62-5
propagandising and, 58
responsibility for,
  60-2, 64-5
teaching and, 60, 62-5
see also religious edu-
  cation
institutions; *see* schooling
instruction, 23, 41-8, 52, 57
intelligence, 132-45
concepts related to,
  133-5
creativity and, 141
fixed *v.* flexible, 132-
  3, 136, 138-9, 141-3
general, 133, 140
measurement of, 132-41
occupational status and,
  138, 139
race and, 132, 135, 141-
  2
scholastic success and,
  138
validation of, 136-7
theory of, 136-8
intentions; *see* teaching; indoctrination
interests, 4-5, 82, 118, 122-
  4, 154, 161, 205, 250
conceptualisation, 2-6,
  26, 232

knowledge, 46, 48-9, 84, 86-
  7, 150-2, 180, 216
education and, 15-16,
  18-19, 84-5
forms of, 50, 86, 149-
  55, 158
social determination of,
  3-4, 15-17, 43-4, 66,
  71-2, 150-2, 154,
  180, 185
see also learning

learning, 14, 23-38, 41-52,
    62, 75, 78, 82, 87, 148,
    178-9, 191, 226
        assessment of, 178; see
            also assessment
        by discovery, 41-7, 52
        dialogical, 34, 46, 52
        knowing and, 35-6
        rote-, 39, 48
        understanding and, 36-
            7, 48-50, 69, 84,
            148
        see also discipline;
            teaching
liberalism, 69, 70-6, 83,
    102, 111-12, 116, 195
love, 77, 206-7, 209, 247-8,
    250

Marxism, 69, 98, 258-9, 261,
    266, 268
mastery, 48-9, 179
moral education, 243-56
        character training and,
            149, 243-4
        discipline and, 226-7
        in schools, 248-50, 252-
            4
        moral development and,
            18, 250-2
morality,
        diversity of, 243; see
            also relativism
        emotive theory of, 244-
            5
        expertise in, 244-6
        form and content in,
            248-50
        nature of, 243-8
        virtue and, 244, 247
            250-3
        see also moral educa-
            tion; neutrality

neutrality, 99, 102-16, 154,
    180, 246, 255, 260
        bias and, 113
        desirability of, 102-3,
            109-16
        impartiality and, 102,
            107, 114, 116
        meanings of, 103-7

objectivity and, 114
of philosophy, 5
of schooling authorit-
    ies, 102, 109-12
of schools, 102, 109-12
of teachers, 102-5, 108-
    10, 113-116
prejudice and, 113
procedural, 113-15
subject of, 103, 110-11
university, 112-13

paternalism, 83, 88, 195-6,
    199-202, 206, 252
perficiences, 29, 34, 49, 59,
    62, 67; see also teaching
philosophy
        analytic, ix-x, 2-6, 9,
            18, 54
        logical positivist, 3,
            8, 56-8
        nature of, ix, 1-6
        radical, ix-x, 2, 5, 7,
            9
philosophy of education, 69
        development, viii-x
        nature of, ix-x, 1, 6-
            10
punishment, 18, 223, 231-42,
    251
        authority and, 233, 237,
            239
        corporal, 231, 234, 240
        consequentialism and,
            234-5
        defined, 223, 231-4
        discrimination and, 233
        education and, 231, 238-
            40
        in schools, 238-40
        justification of, 234-8
        penalisation and, 223,
            233
        persecution and, 233
        retributive, 223, 234-6,
            240
        revenge and, 233
        therapy and, 234, 239
        vengeance and, 233-4
        victimisation and, 233,
            236
        see also discipline

reason, 5, 18, 58-9, 62-3, 70-2, 265
    faith and, 262-5
relativism, 107-8, 243, 245-6, 252
religion, 243, 257-60
    evidence for, 153, 257, 262-5
    metaphysics and, 259
    nature of, 149, 153, 257-60, 261
    see also reason
religious education, 104-5, 149, 155-6, 243, 257-67
    in schools, 265-7
    indoctrination and, 62, 66, 257
    kinds of, 260
    philosophical education and, 261
    possibility of, 260-2
    religious instruction and, 253
respect for persons, 118-19, 123, 241
results and consequences, 61
rights, 197, 203-7
    love and, 206-7
    of children, 195-206
    of parents, 202
    to liberty, 200-2

schooling, 10, 14, 17, 19, 24, 38, 41, 44, 46-8, 52, 66, 78-9, 91-102, 110-11, 117-19, 123, 125, 129, 132, 150, 156-9, 162, 166-7, 171, 175, 191, 197, 213, 217, 227, 231, 248, 266-7
    addictiveness of, 93-4
    alternatives to, 99-100
    coerciveness of, 93-5
    compulsory, 10, 91, 94, 100, 118, 123, 154-5, 157-8, 191, 195, 206, 215, 222, 257, 266; see also coercion
    counterproductivity of, 93, 217
    defined, 91-2, 96, 227
    divisiveness of, 93, 95

education and, 6, 9, 13-16, 18, 44, 92-100, 158
    purposes of, 7, 16, 18, 79, 91-2, 95-8, 111, 148-9, 156, 175, 179-80, 190, 226, 238, 265
    see also moral education; neutrality; religious education
selfishness, self-interestedness, and self-regard, 166-7
self-realisation, 12, 14, 19, 72-3, 75, 78, 99, 225
socialisation, 11, 12, 74, 76, 81, 168-9, 223

task v. achievement, 13, 27-34, 59, 63-4
teaching, 14, 23-38, 41-52, 60, 62-5, 210
    as a perficienary transaction, 29-34
    as an activity, 24-8
    as intended, 24-8, 31
    as polymorphous, 23-4, 94
    indicativeness of, 30, 67
    learning and, 24-38, 41-2; see also learning
    methods of, 10, 23-5, 34-5, 38, 41-4, 48, 51, 118, 175
    responsibility in, 26-7, 29-31, 34, 36, 38
    senses of, 27-8
    teachers and, 27, 34, 38, 41-2, 45, 60, 64
    see also training; indoctrination
training, 11, 13-15, 41-2, 48-50, 52, 54
transcendental arguments, 85-7, 121-2

vocational training, 12, 16, 92, 96-8, 146-59

worthwhile activities, 15, 16, 83-4, 86; see also education